Terror Tracks

Genre, Music and Sound

Series editor: Mark Evans, Macquarie University, Sydney

Over the last decade screen soundtrack studies has emerged as a lively area of research and analysis mediating between the fields of cinema studies, musicology and cultural studies. It has deployed a variety of cross-disciplinary approaches to illuminate an area of film's audio-visual operation that was neglected for much of the late twentieth century. This new series extends the field by addressing the development of various popular international film genres in the post-war era (1945–present), analysing the variety and shared patterns of music and sound use that characterize each genre.

Forthcoming titles

Drawn to Sound: Music, Sound and Animation Cinema, edited by Rebecca Coyle

Sexuality, Sound and Cinema, edited by Bruce Johnson

Terror Tracks
Music, Sound and Horror Cinema

Edited by
Philip Hayward

LONDON OAKVILLE

First published in 2009 by

UK: Equinox Publishing Ltd, Unit 6, The Village, 101 Amies Street,
London, SW1 1 2JW
USA: DBBC, 28 Main Street, Oakville, CT 06779

www.equinoxpub.com

British Library Cataloguing-in-Publication Data

A catalogue record for this book is available from the British Library.

ISBN   978 1 84553 202 4   (paperback)

Library of Congress Cataloging-in-Publication Data
Terror tracks : music, sound and horror cinema / edited by Philip Hayward.
      p. cm. — (Genre, music and sound)
  Includes bibliographical references (p.   ) and index.
  ISBN 978-1-84553-202-4 (pb)
1. Motion picture music—History and criticism. 2. Horror films—History and
criticism. I. Hayward, Philip. ML2075.T47 2009
781.5'42—dc22
                              2007030272

Typeset by S.J.I. Services
Printed and bound in Great Britain by Athenaeum Press Limited, Gateshead, U.K.

Contents

Acknowledgements — vii

About the Authors — ix

Introduction: Scoring the Edge — 1
Philip Hayward

1 *Psycho*-Analysis: Form and Function in Bernard Herrmann's Music for Hitchcock's Masterpiece — 14
James Wierzbicki

2 An Audiovisual Foreshadowing in *Psycho* — 47
Scott Murphy

3 Sound and Music in Hammer's Vampire Films — 60
Michael Hannan

4 Creative Soundtrack Expression: Tôru Takemitsu's Score for *Kwaidan* — 75
Kyoko Koizumi

5 Prog Rock, the Horror Film and Sonic Excess: Dario Argento, Morricone and Goblin — 88
Tony Mitchell

6 Inflamed: Synthetic Folk Music and Paganism in the Island World of *The Wicker Man* — 101
Jon Fitzgerald and Philip Hayward

7 Rhythms of Evil: Exorcizing Sound from *The Exorcist* — 112
Mark Evans

8 Texas Chainsaws: Audio Effect and Iconicity — 125
Rebecca Coyle and Philip Hayward

9 Incorporating Monsters: Music as Context, Character and Construction in Kubrick's *The Shining* — 137
Jeremy Barham

10 Music of the Night: Scoring the Vampire in Contemporary Film — 171
Janet K. Halfyard

11 Scary Movies, Scary Music: Uses and Unities of Heavy Metal in the
    Contemporary Horror Film   186
    Lee Barron and Ian Inglis

12 "Like Razors through Flesh": *Hellraiser*'s Sound Design and Music   198
    Karen Collins

13 Spooked by Sound: *The Blair Witch Project*   213
    Rebecca Coyle

14 Popular Songs and Ordinary Violence: Exposing Basic Human Brutality
    in the Films of Rob Zombie   229
    Laura Wiebe Taylor

15 Terror in the Outback: *Wolf Creek* and Australian Horror Cinema   238
    Philip Hayward and Harry Minassian

16 The Ghostly Noise of J-Horror: Roots and Ramifications   249
    James Wierzbicki

    Index   269

Acknowledgements

One of the more curious aspects about being an academic working in interdisciplinary studies is that your activities and schedules are not easily compartmentalized. The nature of deadlines means that you are often working on one project in the margins of another. This was the case for this book. Much of the editing of the anthology and co-authoring of my chapters occurred in the somewhat unlikely environs of Port Vila (Vanuatu) and Nadi and Suva (Fiji) while researching an ARC-funded project on the Melanesian music industry. The bright sunshine, warmth and verdancy of these locations provided an unlikely counterpart to the chilling DVD films I examined on my laptop and the dark scenarios and soundtracks that I analysed. Unlike my colleague Paul Théberge, who became so preoccupied with the scores of David Cronenberg films while writing a chapter on the topic for my previous anthology on science-fiction soundtracks (*Off the Planet*, 2004) that they began to invade his dreams, my Pacific locations ensured that I slept soundly during the production of this book.

My thanks to my colleague Mark Evans for both providing me with the opportunity to initiate the Equinox series of soundtrack studies and coping with yet another of my absences from our home institution, Sydney's Macquarie University. Also – as always – thanks to my family for their similar tolerance of my regular absences and, particularly, to my daughters Amelia and Rosa, for enduring the regular stream of chainsaw noises, screams and atonalities that emanated from the domestic DVD player during much of 2005 to 2007.

In its initial stages this anthology was developed as a jointly edited project with Rebecca Leydon, and several of the chapters were commissioned from authors she identified and approached. My thanks for her early input and, more generally, for her inspirational soundtrack scholarship. Rebecca Coyle also merits acknowledgement for providing a series of insights and critical feedback on individual chapters and the overall project of this anthology. Final thanks to Sandra Margolies for her careful copy-editing.

About the Authors

Jeremy Barham is a lecturer in Music at the University of Surrey, where he teaches courses in screen music studies. His research focuses on the use of pre-existent music, science fiction and horror-film scoring, music in experimental and avant-garde film, and musical temporality in film. He is currently working on a monograph for Cambridge University Press entitled *Music, Time and the Moving Image*.

Lee Barron is a senior lecturer in Media and Communication at Northumbria University. His main research and teaching interests are in the areas of cultural theory, media and popular culture. His writings have appeared in journals such as *Fashion Theory*, *The Journal of Popular Culture* and *International Review of the Aesthetics and Sociology of Music*.

Karen Collins is Canada Research Chair in Technology and Communication at the University of Waterloo, where she teaches game development and sound design and is developing software for interactive audio applications. She has published two books and numerous articles on audio for film and games.

Rebecca Coyle is a senior lecturer at Southern Cross University, Lismore, who has edited two anthologies on Australian cinema soundtracks, *Screen Scores* (1998) and *Reel Tracks* (2005). She is currently researching the Australian film music production sector and editing a volume on animation film sound and music (for publication in this series).

Mark Evans is the head of Media, Music and Cultural Studies at Macquarie University, Sydney. He is the author of *Open up the Doors: Music in the Modern Church* (2006) and editor of the *Encyclopedia of Film Music and Sound* (Equinox, forthcoming).

Jon Fitzgerald is an associate professor at Southern Cross University, Lismore, and a practising guitarist and composer. He has previously written on a variety of musical topics and is author of *Popular Music: Theory and Musicianship* (1999).

Janet K. Halfyard is a senior lecturer at Birmingham Conservatoire. Her publications include *Danny Elfman's Batman: A Film Score Guide* (2004) and an edited volume on Luciano Berio's *Sequenzas* (2007).

Michael Hannan is a professor at Southern Cross University, Lismore, and a practising composer. His publications include *The Australian Guide to Careers in Music* (2003) and he is currently researching the Australian film music production sector.

Philip Hayward is Director of Research Training at Southern Cross University and an adjunct professor in the Department of Media, Music and Cultural Studies at Macquarie University, Sydney. His previous books include *Off the Planet: Music, Sound and Science Fiction Cinema* (2005).

Ian Inglis is a reader in Popular Music Studies, and Research Director in Media and Communication, in the School of Arts & Social Sciences at the University of Northumbria. He has edited three books: *The Beatles, Popular Music and Society: A Thousand Voices* (2000); *Popular Music and Film* (2003); and *Performance and Popular Music: History, Place and Time* (2006).

Kyoko Koizumi is an associate professor of music at Otsuma Women's University, Tokyo, Japan. She received her PhD from the University of London Institute of Education. Her research interests include youth studies of popular music and film music studies.

Harry Minassian is a multi-instrumentalist, composer and arranger with a degree in Creative Arts from Macquarie University, Sydney. His recent projects include event management for Ara Gevorgian's 2006 Sydney concert.

Tony Mitchell is a senior lecturer in Cultural Studies at the University of Technology, Sydney. He is the author of *Popular Music and Local Identity: Rock, Pop and Rap in Europe and Oceania* (1996) and editor of *Global Noise: Rap and Hip Hop Outside the USA* (2001).

Scott Murphy is an associate professor of music theory at the University of Kansas. His publications include articles on Brahms, Ives, Bartók, Penderecki, and on music in science-fiction films.

Laura Wiebe Taylor is a PhD candidate in the Department of English and Cultural Studies at McMaster University, Hamilton, Canada, where she is examining boundary issues in speculative fictions and theory. Her publications include articles on the relationships between science fiction, dystopia and metal music.

James Wierzbicki is a musicologist who teaches at the University of Michigan and serves as executive editor of the MUSA (Music of the United States of America) series of scholarly editions.

Dedicated to Clive Barker for inspiring my interest in
Horror and for writing *Sacrament* and *Weaveworld*

Introduction
Scoring the Edge

Philip Hayward

In commercial terms, John Carpenter's *Halloween* (1978) is probably the most success-ful horror film of all time. Made on a budget of under $500,000, it went on to take over $47 million in the United States alone. In genre terms it also spawned a whole series of so-called 'slasher' films that scared audiences for much of the following two decades. The film's success can be attributed to various factors, including its updating of elements from Alfred Hitchcock's earlier *Psycho* (1960) for a contemporary audi-ence. *Halloween* had its origins in producer Irwin Yablans's idea of attempting to emulate the major box-office success of the supernatural horror film *The Exorcist* (William Friedkin, 1973), in a more everyday scenario that would resonate with the youth audience that was identified as cinema's principal demographic. To this end, Carpenter and his co-writer Debra Hill developed a narrative and script that featured a killer who preyed on babysitters. Yablans added a further refinement by requesting that it take place at Halloween. By tying in the folkloric (Halloween and its rituals of trick-or-treating, illuminated pumpkins, etc.), everyday contemporary realism (adoles-cents smoking marijuana and making out) and the shock impact of a masked, knife-wielding killer with preternatural abilities, the film activated a bank of proven themes from popular cultural history (as discussed below).

Along with its scenario, script and performances, the film's visual composition (and especially its use of light and shadow) was particularly effective. Carpenter skilfully engineered sudden intrusions of the killer (and his knife) onto the screen, thus scaring audiences through surprise more than by displays of on-screen gore (which are minimal). The film also benefited from its use of (then new) steadicam technology to take the viewer smoothly through its dark suburban houses and streets, alternating the killer's point of view and that of the female protagonist who survives the ordeal (the quintes-sential 'final girl' of Clover's 1992 characterization of contemporary horror cinema). Despite all these elements, Carpenter (1983) has recalled that an initial presentation of the film was far from impressive:

> *I screened the final cut minus sound effects and music, for a young executive*
> *from 20th Century-Fox (I was interviewing for another possible directing*

> *job). She wasn't scared at all. I then became determined to "save it with the music"… Halloween was dubbed in late July and I finally saw the picture with an audience in the fall. My plan… seemed to work. About six months later I ran into the same young executive… Now she too loved the movie and all I had done was add music. But she really was quite justified in her initial reaction.*

While music routinely accents and amplifies aspects of various film texts and genres in the manner described – this, after all, being its very *raison d'être* – its capacity to create tension and shock *supplementary* to narrative and visual design is a key element in the horror genre and its omission from early cuts of *Halloween* would undoubtedly have diluted its impact.

Like many other aspects of the film, *Halloween*'s 'saving' music drew on a series of cinema traditions. As Carpenter has identified, Bernard Herrmann's score for *Psycho* was an influence in terms of its "ability to create an imposing, powerful score with limited orchestra means, using the basic sound of a particular instrument, high strings or low bass" (*ibid.*). Constrained by budget, Carpenter collaborated with Dan Wyman to produce a rhythmic, synthesizer-based score which made frequent use of abrupt 'stingers'. Commenting on the director's work, composer Allan Howarth (who worked on subsequent films in the *Halloween* series) characterized stingers as "the ultimate horror sound" and identified them as standard musical effects:

> *Carpenter's famous for that kind of stuff, in fact a lot of times we'll score the show and then I'll make him what's called a grab bag of stingers, just all these horrible sounds with sharp attacks, that go "eeaaahhhh", and then he can go and cut those in just in the moments he needs to sweeten the score. Things like that are usually layers of sound. I'll certainly always put some sound effects in that, I have some wonderful sound effects I made with dry ice and metal pans, and then I have some other scraping things, and sort of bending metal and then all the fantasy sounds you can generate with the synthesizers themselves, and then usually there's some bass drum or snare right on the attack to give it the extra smack to make it jump.* (quoted in Larson, 1989)

Along with its use of short impact sequences, *Halloween* also drew inspiration from *The Exorcist*'s score and, in particular, its use of the opening theme from Mike Oldfield's 1973 album *Tubular Bells*. This sequence inspired Carpenter to write the unsettling 5/4 keyboard motif that became the film's – and its sequels' – signature music. To further inscribe *Halloween* within the popular cultural context (and lexicon) of its target audience, Carpenter also made use of pre-recorded music with clear thematic allusions to the film's genre, featuring tracks such as Blue Oyster Cult's 'Don't Fear The Reaper' (1976).

As this brief description of the film and the inspiration and generic context of its text emphasizes, *Halloween* utilized, inflected and – perhaps most significantly –

refreshed a set of pre-existent traditions and referents. While neither the film nor its score can be considered as particularly original, its efficient activation and reinvigoration of genre traditions identify the variety and potency of the genre. The conventions and history that engendered *Halloween* and the films that followed it are the subjects of this volume.

Genre origins

Horror cinema, like all other film genres, is a medium-specific crystallization of narratives, themes and conventions that have been circulated in previous cultural media. Stories of ghosts and spirits occur across the planet, as do macabre fascinations with terror, injury and death affected by human (or other) protagonists. Archaeologists of the violent and uncanny have easy pickings in rich traditions of folklore from countries of the developed and developing world alike. In terms of its accretion as a western film genre, its main progenitor was a series of fresh interpretations of folkloric themes that developed in Europe in the late eighteenth century.[1] The modern origins of horror fiction are commonly traced to a group of novels that included Horace Walpole's influential *The Castle of Otranto* (1795). Staples of modern horror cinema such as the vampire (discussed in two chapters of this volume) became popular with the publication of John Polidori's *The Vampyre* in 1819 and the English-language translation from German of Johann Tieck's earlier *Wake Not the Dead* in 1823. Mary Shelley's *Frankenstein* (1818) created another enduring icon.

Theatre also embraced the power of these dark tales, with productions such as *The Vampire* and *Presumption: or The Fate of Frankenstein*[2] attracting sizeable audiences in London in 1819 and 1823 respectively. A series of similar productions enjoyed a popularity until the mid-1820s. This vogue also manifested itself in music, with a number of composers writing instrumental pieces or songs that represented supernatural and/or horrific themes. One of the best known of these was Franz Schubert's setting of Goethe's 1782 poem, 'Der Erlkönig' [The Elf King], a narrative about a child's death through enchantment. Schubert's song for piano and voice was highly popular as a concert and parlour piece following its premiere in 1820. Combining rapid, rhythmic chords (to signify galloping horses) and expressive chromaticism, the piece was so successful that it set a stylistic model for musical combinations of dramatic action and supernatural themes in the theatre (and, later, cinema).

Horrific fiction continued in various forms throughout the 1800s, most notably in cheap mass-circulation publications (termed 'Penny Dreadfuls' in the UK) that often included tales of violence and terror. In 1847 the London stage was enlivened by the production of a drama about a murderous barber named Sweeney Todd (based on a story that had originally appeared in *The People's Periodical* in 1846 under the title 'The String of Pearls').[3] Shocking as its spectacle may have been, the horror ante was upped considerably with the opening in 1897 of a new theatre in Paris entitled Le Grand

Guignol. This small playhouse specialized in short dramas designed to shock its audiences, often using a combination of stage illusion, offal and blood to add impact.

Other notable additions to the canon of horrific fiction included Robert Louis Stevenson's *The Strange Case of Dr Jekyll and Mr Hyde* (1886) and further embellishments of vampire fiction in J. Sheridan Le Fanu's *Carmilla* (1872) and Bram Stoker's *Dracula* (1897). While nowhere as visceral as the Parisian Grand Guignol performances, stage adaptations of recent horror fiction became popular in North America from the late 1800s. A production of *Dr Jekyll and Mr Hyde* was particularly successful, touring from 1897 to 1908 (with director William Selig filming a 16-minute-long condensed version in 1907). Further film versions occurred in 1912, 1920 and 1931 and through into the synch-sound era. Early cinema also mirrored the 'Penny Dreadfuls' by initiating another cycle of films that has continued to the present with a series of lurid murder dramas. The British period piece *Maria Marten*, for example, proved so popular with audiences that it was shot in five (increasingly longer) versions (in 1902, 1908, 1913, 1928 and 1935).

The development of early cinema scholarship, restoration and aesthetic appreciation over the last thirty years has led to an understanding that – in its major production/exhibition forms (at least) – pre-synch-sound cinema can be understood as a coherent audio-visual medium in its own right (rather than an incomplete, unsatisfactory predecessor to synch-sound film). While much is correct in that evaluation it should also be said (although it rarely is) that, with particular regard to early cinema's adoption and continuation of specific theatrical genres and texts (such as those we now regard as precursors of the horror genre), cinema was a somewhat *deprived* genre. Major theatrical venues of the nineteenth and early twentieth century were noisy and often spectacular places. In addition to the various gas-lighting, projection, smoke and flash effects that graced supernatural melodramas, theatres often used a combination of music, sound effects and off-stage vocalizations to accentuate climactic moments of dramas. These required careful co-ordination of individual elements to avoid simple cacophony and to allow actors to pitch their voices and use timing in such a manner as to complement and exploit what was, effectively, a live sound-mix. In a similar manner to the problems that Carpenter identified with the lack of impact of an early version of *Halloween*, early cinema had to compensate for the absence of a battery of sonic techniques through inventive visual composition and (as the period progressed) musical cues and (in some venues) sound effects. It is a tribute to the ingenuity of directors, cinematographers, designers and editors (*et al.*) that many works of the period achieved impact in this new medium with their versions of established theatrical genre forms.

As the popularity of Stevenson's *Dr Jekyll and Mr Hyde* with film-makers illustrates, the rich repertoire of horror narratives gave them a ready resource to draw upon. Indeed, this was almost instantly accessed in Georges Méliès's two-minute gothic cameo *Le Manoir du diable* (1896), often regarded as the first vampire-themed film. A number of vampire productions followed in the 1910s and 1920s,[4] including

European films such as Károly Lajthay's Hungarian *Drakula Halála* (1921).[5] Frankenstein was also an early cinematic presence, inspiring a number of early short films, such as Thomas Edison's *Frankenstein* (1910), and being adapted in Italy by Eugenio Testa as *Il Mostro di Frankenstein* (1921). The Judaic myth of the Golem inspired several German productions, Paul Wegener directing three versions (1914, 1917 and 1920), the last of which is best known to contemporary audiences. Two of the most notable horror films of the pre-synch-sound era were also German, Robert Wiene's famous exercise in Expressionist horror *Das Kabinett des Doktor Caligari* (1919) and F. W. Murnau's thinly disguised adaptation of Dracula, *Nosferatu, eine Symphonie des Grauens* (1922) (starring Max Schreck as the brooding vampire).

For the purposes of this anthology, *Nosferatu* is notable for both the musical allusion of its subtitle ('a symphony of Horror') and the music composed for it by Hans Erdmann (under the title 'Fantastich-Romantische Suite'). The score takes the form of ten cues (with descriptive titles that translate as 'Ghostly', 'Strange', 'Grotesque', etc.) that were available with the film in small and full orchestral arrangements (with the latter being reconstructed in 1995[6]). These cues suggest that Erdmann's approach to scoring drew on the standard conventions of musical manuals of the pre-synch-sound period. From the inception of cinema through to the synch-sound era, film screenings were accompanied by either solo accompanists (usually pianists but, later, organists at major cinema theatres) or ensembles of various kinds. The music performed by these musicians, in the main, comprised combinations, embellishments and/or improvisations around a number of short, stock musical motifs. These were (initially) informally codified, then printed in trade magazines and later collated and published as compendia of musical motifs and styles. The best-known early publication of this kind was J. S. Zamecnik's *Sam Fox Moving Picture Music* (1913). While this did not feature any specified 'horror' cues, it offered a combination of themes for topics such as 'Death Scene', 'Mysterious-Burglar Music', 'Storm Music', 'Fairy Music' and various types of 'Hurry Music' that could be deployed to accompany early (proto-) horror films. Zamecnik's prior training with Dvorák in Prague educated him in European art music traditions and he held up Wagner, Tchaikovsky and Berlioz as models for film music composers.[7] While the use of prominent tremolo chords in the 'Storm Music' cue (an established device for conveying tension) might be seen to reflect this background, cues such as 'Mysterious-Burglar' embody the overtly mannered sequences commonly associated with 'silent' cinema accompaniment and also hark back to earlier theatrical music traditions.[8] J. Bodewalt Lampe's 1914 *Remick Folio of Moving Picture Music* also featured similar cues (with titles such as 'Misterioso of Foreboding [Grotesque]' and 'Misterioso Pizzicato'), along with various 'Hurry' and battle-music sequences. These volumes, and later seminal works such as those of Lang and West (1920) and Rapée (1925), established a musical template for aspects of the emergent genre during the pre-synch-sound era.

Genre in the initial synch-sound period

In addition to musical scoring (discussed below), the advent of synchronized sound film allowed for dialogue (and dialogue-based character interactions) to become key elements of screen dramas. The medium also supported a range of human non-verbal vocalizations and other recorded and modified sounds. In the case of the former, horror's dramatic scenarios were open for dramatic acting and voice performances and allowed the (previously silent) representation of the scream to be accompanied by its dramatic voice – creating an enduring feature of horror-film soundtracks.[9] Along with this came a set of sound effects already established in theatrical performance, many of which – mysterious bird and animal noises, creaks, thunder and lightning, etc. – are now easily recognizable genre clichés. With the employment of sound crews at major studios, a number of technicians became adept in the generation of sounds to accompany onscreen action.[10] The introduction of sound dubbing in 1929 allowed for sound to be added subsequent to shooting. The importance of this aspect of soundtrack production was quickly realized, with the creation of an Academy Award for Sound Mixing in 1930.

The growth of the Hollywood studio system in the late 1920s and 1930s provided major opportunities for composers. An increasing proportion of feature films featured original scores, and the major studios set up highly organized music divisions to create and manage their production. Caryl Flinn has argued that this resulted in a situation (in the United States, at least) whereby

> film music was assigned a remarkably stable set of functions. It was repeatedly and systematically used to enhance emotional moments in the story line, to establish moods and maintain continuity between scenes. (1992: 12)

While this statement refers to a wide range of film genres, it offers a succinct characterization of the role of music (and sound) in horror cinema, the "emotional moments" and "moods" in question usually being ones of tension, action and shock (and/or the alternation or resolution of these by calmer passages). As Flinn also identifies, stating the crux of her book's thesis:

> A similar uniformity was suggested by its style as well, since most scores were composed in a manner deeply influenced by late romantic composers like Richard Wagner and Richard Strauss... this period of overall stability is usually identified as the 'golden age' of Hollywood composition, a period that started in the mid-1930s and endured until the studio system began to draw to a close in the early 1950s... Not surprisingly, critics have noted how Hollywood scoring techniques became routinized and standardized at about the same time that the style of the classical film was itself established and secured. (ibid.)

The score for James Whale's *Bride of Frankenstein* (1935) exemplifies Flinn's characterization as it applies to the horror genre. The film was made for Universal

Pictures as a follow-up to the director's earlier box-office hit *Frankenstein* (1931). Based on Shelley's original novel, Whale's first film was striking for its Expressionist-influenced visual design. Since it was made in the early synch-sound period, music was a minor element[11] and there was little, if any, 'atmos' sound behind many dialogue passages. The film's most prominent sound sequence accompanied the scene of the monster's (re-)animation, with thunder and lightning and the crackling and whirring of electrical devices creating a dramatic cacophony. In his sequel, which provided Frankenstein's monster with a reluctant female partner, music played a far more prominent role. The film's score was provided by Franz Waxman, a German émigré who had studied at the Dresden Music Academy and Berlin Conservatorium in the 1920s and contributed to the score of von Sternberg's *Der blaue Engel* (1930) before moving to Hollywood in 1934. Along with Max Steiner's music for RKO's *King Kong* (Merian Cooper and Ernest Schoedsack, 1933), Waxman's score for *Bride of Frankenstein* established the tradition of leitmotifs (short signifying themes for particular characters) that came to typify much Hollywood music over the next two decades and pioneered the use of stingers.[12] Steiner's *King Kong* score also popularized another technique, complementing on-screen action with analogous music (often called 'mickey-mousing' in reference to its use in 1930s Disney animation films). One of the most effective examples in *King Kong* is the sequence where Kong climbs the Empire State Building, with the music rising as the giant ape moves upwards.

The scores for *Bride of Frankenstein* and *King Kong* established many of the conventions that came to typify horror-film music in the late 1930s and 1940s. Working in a high-turnover industrial environment, subsequent composers employed by Universal on horror-film scoring variously imitated and took inspiration from Waxman's example. The most accomplished exponents of this emergent tradition were Hans Salter and Frank Skinner, who wrote their own distinctive scores, collaborated on orchestrations and, in Salter's case, reinterpreted Skinner's dramatic score for *Son of Frankenstein* (Roland Lee, 1939) in his music for *Frankenstein Meets the Wolf Man* (Roy William Neill, 1943). Although Steiner left RKO shortly after completing *King Kong*, his influence on that studio's music division was a lasting one. Roy Webb – Steiner's collaborator on earlier scores for films such as *Side Street* (Malcolm St Clair, 1929) and *The Delightful Rogue* (Leslie Pearce and Lyn Shores, 1929)[13] – used similar techniques with smaller orchestral ensembles in a series of low-budget thrillers made by producer Val Lewton's designated horror unit. In his scores for films such as *Cat People* (Jacques Tourneur, 1942) and *The Body Snatcher* (Robert Wise, 1945), Webb combined the scoring techniques pioneered by Waxman and Steiner with a distinctive use of songs woven into the narratives and incorporated into the score.

In addition to Waxman's music, *King Kong* had another element that was to assume considerable importance in the latter twentieth century, the design of sound effects used in conjunction with score and dialogue. The pioneer of this approach in US cinema was director Rouben Mamoulian. After exploring the use of multiple microphone recording and sound editing as early as 1929 in his debut feature *Applause*, Mamoulian pre-empted the post-war development of *musique concrète* in Europe in the 1940s by manipulating and re-editing a collage of sounds to accompany scenes of physical trans-formation in his version of *Dr. Jekyll and Mr. Hyde* (1931). The arrival of multi-track recording in the same year allowed Hollywood to expand such sonic creativity, and sound technician Murray Spivak created a number of dramatic filmic voices using tape collage and sound reversal for the giant ape and other monsters featured in *King Kong*'s Skull Island sequence.[14] While *King Kong*'s integration of score and sound design was somewhat exceptional in the 1930s, it showed the ingredients and imagination of later horror cinema to have been firmly in place in the pre-war era, available to be activated when budgets and genre dynamics allowed.

Genre and project

Before proceeding further it is pertinent to examine the nature of the (post-war) film genre this book addresses. Like many genres, horror often overlaps with others (such as comedy in the *Scary Movie* series, science fiction in the *Alien* films or the musical in *The Rocky Horror Picture Show* [Jim Sharman, 1975]). Discussing horror cinema, Jancovich emphasized the fluid boundaries of genres as they develop historically and called for an examination of "the historically specific contexts of production, mediation or consumption through which texts are generically categorized or recategorized" (2002: 2) as the basis for precise delineations of the horror-film genre. Useful as such an examination might be to determine the porous limits of the form, the working definition used to assemble this anthology is the aggregate of film texts that feature supernatural malevolence and/or extreme, 'irrational' human violence as a dominant aspect of the narrative (and/or the depiction of psychological states of terror and instability linked to these). Similarly succinctly, Philip Brophy has characterized the genre's operation and appeal in the following terms:

> Contemporary Horror film is based upon tension, fear, anxiety, sadism and masochism... The pleasure of the text is, in fact, getting the shit scared out of you – and loving it: an exchange mediated by adrenalin. (1986: 5)[15]

There are a number of elaborate ways of dressing this up in terms of its relation to various psychological states and psychoanalytic formations but this core of the genre remains. As subsequent chapters analyse, film composers and sound designers have worked within this parameter in different ways, attempting to emphasize and/or elaborate the dynamics of the genre in individual texts. While this might suggest an overly functionalist constraint, the contributors to this volume document and analyse the manner in which the prescribed parameters engender a range of articulations and nuances.

This anthology, like previous studies of music and sound in particular film genres (such as Hayward, 2004), comprises a series of in-depth analyses of widely recognized seminal film texts, film series and/or notable composer–director collaborations, together with studies of less prominent works that argue a particular significance for them in the history of the genre. While Jancovich (2002) cautions against the former aspect of this approach, as reinforcing somewhat arbitrary canons, certain texts and teams were automatic choices for inclusion – such as Bernard Herrmann's work with Alfred Hitchcock (discussed in Chapters 1 and 2), Italian director Dario Argento's oeuvre (Chapter 5) and Tôru Takemitsu's soundscore for Masaki Kobayshi's 1964 film *Kwaidan* (Chapter 4). Other chapters analyse significant film series and subgenres (Chapters 3, 10, 12 and 16) or else provide case studies of the operation of music and/or sound in individual films. As the contents pages of the volume reveal, the films discussed are exclusively western (Australian, British, Italian and American) or Japanese. Given the global prominence of the genre, the characterizations of film music and sound in this Introduction reflect the volume's concentration on these national sources. Further research needs to be pursued on aspects of other European traditions, such as that of France – from George Franju's *Les Yeux sans visage* (1959) through to Jean Rollin's vampire series;[16] or the work of other Italian directors aside from Argento. Similarly, the horror traditions of Mexican and South American cinema appear to have been minimally researched (in English-language studies, at least), affording little insight into the musical and sonic aspects of that area, and local versions of horror cinema in South East Asia also merit further study. While some mapping of contemporary Hong Kong horror films has been achieved in O'Brien (2003) – a volume that includes some mention of film music – this is another area in which more work could be usefully accomplished. These qualifications to the volume's international project underline the manner in which a single anthology can neither exhaust (nor even comprehensively represent) such a prolific international genre as horror cinema. There is extensive further work to be undertaken on its history and unfolding present.

Scopes and ambits

The discussions and analyses offered by the contributors to the volume are intended to provide models for future work on both specific texts and the operation of the genre as a whole. The chapters take one (or sometimes more) of four approaches to their topics:

1. detailed analyses of the relationship between image, sound and music in specific films and/or film sequences (Chapters 1, 2, 4, 6, 7, 8, 9 and 15);
2. studies of particular composers' and/or directors' oeuvres (Chapters 5 and 14);
3. analyses of musical approaches used in particular subgenres or film series (Chapters 3, 10, 11 and 12);
4. an analysis of the use and affectivity of sound in the (primarily) non-musical soundtrack to a single film, *The Blair Witch Project* (Chapter 13).

Drawing on the diverse set of approaches individual authors bring to bear, their analytical intersections with the post-war genre allow for the following characterization:

1. The genre continues to draw on, and expand, an established tradition of musical devices developed and exemplified by composers such as Bernard Herrmann (who, in turn, drew on aspects of pre-war practice). This tradition aims to unnerve and shock the audience through use of atonalities, glissandi, ostinati and various musical and/or sonic rumbles and booms (present in the form of either developed passages or short stingers) and, frequently, to create identification and engagement through use of leitmotifs. Similarly, there is a range of standard and thereby commonly (if subliminally) perceived sound effects used to signify threat and incite terror.[17]

    While these characterizations will hardly come as a surprise to any regular horror-film viewer or soundtrack aficionado, the analysis of their operation and extension in various chapters allows for a greater understanding of the devices' application in particular film texts and series.

2. Allied to the above, the genre has facilitated a substantial vein of musical modernism, manifest in the work of early post-war composers such as Herrmann through to contemporary composers such as François Tétaz.

    Along with science-fiction film scores, horror-film music is one of the prime genres for the exploration of (what was once characterized as) musical avant-gardism and (what now) increasingly appears to be an established sonic practice with an extensive genre history. Indeed, in this volume, inspired by his detailed discussion of *The Shining* (Stanley Kubrick, 1980), Jeremy Barham argues that:

    > [The] *entrenched traditions of cinematic and mass media 'association'
    > modify, perhaps permanently, the reception history of a musical modern-
    > ism and post-war avant-garde that may themselves be complicit in their
    > own cultural downfall.* (p. 157)

3. Despite the obvious potential for non-musical sound effects to be developed into more complex sound compositions – paralleling several decades of development of audio art – non-musical sonic scoring is rarely used in feature film production.

    While the sound score of such a highly individual film as *The Blair Witch Project* can be explained by its narrative premise (i.e., that its audio-visual text has been assembled from unprocessed *vérité* footage), it is surprising that more experimentation in this area, including the compositional manipulation of found sounds as foreground audio text (as in sequences from *Kwaidan*) has not occurred. One explanation, suggested by characterizations 1 and 2 above, is that the orchestral horror tradition pioneered by Herrmann (and also developed in more contemporary instrumentation) seems so ingrained, and so continually effective, that it is a standard industrial 'default' option, with the result that alternative approaches primarily occur at the edges of the genre.

4a. Pre-recorded – and/or original – popular music has been commonly used since the 1980s either to unsettle audiences through its (apparent) disjuncture from anticipated horror-film moods and atmospheres or else to provide a sense of realist banality to representations of extreme violence or malevolence (making them seem more of this world and less fictionally fantastic).

4b. Use of rock music, and particularly hard rock, has become a significant aspect of 1990s and 2000s horror cinema, linking the genre with aspects of rock and associated subcultures.

Uses of popular music in horror are hardly surprising since forms of popular music are now commonly used in a variety of film genres, with pre-recorded music providing ready associations for score compilers and audiences. The use of hard rock appears particularly prevalent in the horror genre, reflecting the convergence of aspects of iconography and rock music – associated subcultures (such as, most obviously, Goths). As Barron and Inglis identify in their chapter in this volume, the traffic between the two media has created a thriving interface of imagery, association and musical style.

There has also been significant interchange between horror cinema and the 'survival horror' genre of videogames. Just as the content, themes (and names) of early games derived from popular films (such as *'Halloween'* [1983] and *'Friday the 13th'* [1985]), games products such as the seminal *'Resident Evil'* (1996) and *'Silent Hill'* (1999) have been adapted into films. The extent to which the sonic conventions of gaming might be influencing cinema merits analysis in its own right. Given the range of sonic and musical tools available to production personnel – and the emergence of computer games as a mature medium – a substantial chapter of creative achievement may still be written. Similarly, considering that cyber-horror has been slow to develop, outside of early experiments such as *The Lawnmower Man* (Brett Leonard, 1992), this area may yet provide film-makers (and games-makers) with appropriate themes and milieux to develop new veins of sonic experimentation akin to those that Evans (2004) identified as operating in *The Matrix* (Wachowski Brothers, 1999). However, to link accomplishment with innovation provides only one aspect of the picture. The strengths of horror scoring and sound design are more often infra- (rather than extra-)generic (as befits such a well-established medium as cinema). In this regard it seems apparent that so long as horror cinema continues to enjoy its extended commercial prime it is likely that invention and innovation will continue to occur within the parameters sketched in this volume.

Acknowledgement

Thanks to the authors of individual chapters in this volume and to James Wierzbicki and John Whiteoak for their advice on earlier drafts of this introduction.

Notes

1. Although, of course, these in turn revised and re-inflected previous traditions.
2. As James Wierzbicki has observed, the melodrama is "fairly loaded with indications for music, not just songs and choruses but lots of 'incidental music' that depict[s] such creepy things as storms, the creation of the monster, etc." (personal communication to the author, November 2006). The music for the first production seems to have been provided by a Mr Watson (*ibid.*).
3. Famously adapted into a musical by Steven Sondheim and Hugh Wheeler and made into a compellingly dark feature film by Tim Burton in 2007.
4. See http://www.wsu.edu/~delahoyd/vampirefilms.html, accessed September 2006.
5. See http://www.carpathiafilm.com/en/drakula.html (accessed September 2006) for an account of the rediscovery of the film.
6. A sample of which is available online (http://www.salzburg.com/phoenix/cd_titel.html, accessed September 2006).
7. See the composer's statement on his inspirations archived online (http://www.mont-alto.com/photoplaymusic/aboutmusic.html, accessed September 2006).
8. As Michael Hannan has identified:

   The first 'Mysterious-Burglar' music cue through its detached series of melodic notes (in octaves) perhaps suggests (in a comical way) the careful and stealthy steps of the burglar, In bar 4 there is an accented diminished chord perhaps indicating uncertainty, danger, freezing of action. Diminished chords are typically used to indicate danger in melodrama. The same techniques are used in the second 'Mysterious-Burglar' music cue. This time the first two bars suggest the tentative step of the burglar while the next two suggest more of a skipping motion, as if to gather pace to find a hiding place. As in the first cue the accented chord (this time a major chord) in bar 4 suggests something dramatic. The second half could be an attempt to represent stopping and starting movements. (personal communication to the author, October 2006)

9. See Brophy (1999).
10. One, Jack Foley, became so well known for his production of noises in synch with screen actions that 'foley artist' is now the usual appellation for such a worker.
11. In the form of a title theme by Bernhard Kaun and a short sequence of diegetic fiddle music.
12. For instance, in sequences such as that in which Frankenstein's intended bride's eyes are revealed.
13. The duo provided the scores for foreign-release, non-dialogue versions of these films.
14. For further discussion, see Tom Huntingdon 'How the greatest special-effects movie was made with the simplest technology' (http://www.americanheritage.com/entertainment/articles/web/20051214-king-kong-monster-special-effects-movie-fay-wray.shtml, accessed September 2006).

15. I should like to acknowledge my engagement with Brophy's article (as a member of the *Screen* editorial board in 1985) as the beginning of my interest in critical analysis of the genre.
16. Commencing with *Le Viol du vampire* (1968) and continuing into the twenty-first century with *La Fiancée de Dracula* (2002).
17. While this area has often been overlooked by critics – perhaps due to this factor – it is beginning to achieve recognition in a broader context (composer Brian Carpenter providing a most useful overview in the second, third and fourth programmes of his 2003 WZBC (Boston) radio mini-series *The Sound of Horror*).

References

Bodewalt Lampe, J. (1914), *Remick Folio of Moving Picture Music*, New York: Remick.

Brophy, P. (1986), 'Horrality – the Textuality of Contemporary Horror Films', *Screen* 27(1), 2–13.

Brophy, P. (1999), 'I Scream in Silence: Death and the Sound of Women Dying', in P. Brophy (ed.), *Cinesonic: The World of Sound in Film*, Sydney: Australian Film, Television and Radio School, pp. 51–78.

Carpenter, J. (1983), 'Soundtrack Halloween' (archived at his official website: http://www.theofficialjohncarpenter.com/pages/themovies/hw/hwstrk.html, accessed September 2006).

Clover, C. (1992), *Men, Women and Chain Saws: Gender in the Modern Horror Film*, Princeton: Princeton University Press.

Evans, M. (2004), 'Mapping *The Matrix*: Virtual Spatiality and the Realm of the Perceptual', in P. Hayward (ed.), *Off the Planet: Music, Sound and Science Fiction Cinema*, Eastleigh, Hampshire: John Libbey Publishing, pp. 188–98.

Flinn, C. (1992), *Strains of Utopia: Gender, Nostalgia and Hollywood Film Music*, Princeton: Princeton University Press.

Hayward, P. (ed.) (2004), *Off the Planet: Music, Sound and Science Fiction Cinema*, Eastleigh, Hampshire: John Libbey Publishing.

Jancovich, M. (ed.) (2002), *Horror: The Film Reader*, London: Routledge.

Lang, E., and West, G. (1920), *Musical Accompaniment of Moving Pictures: A Practical Manual for Pianists and Organists and an Exposition of the Principles Underlying the Musical Interpretation of Moving Pictures*, New York: The Boston Music Company.

Larson, R. D. (1989), 'Hyper-reality: Alan Howarth's synthesized scores and specialized sound effects' (transcript of 1989 interview published online: http://www.alanhowarth.com/press-articles.html).

O'Brien, D. (2003), *Spooky Encounters: A Gwailo's Guide to Hong Kong Horror*, Manchester: Headpress/Critical Vision.

Rapée, Erno (1925), *Encyclopaedia of Music for Pictures*, New York: Baldwin.

Zamecnik, J. S. (1913), *Sam Fox Moving Picture Music*, New York: Fox.

1 PSYCHO-ANALYSIS

Form and Function in Bernard Herrmann's Music for Hitchcock's Masterpiece

James Wierzbicki

Alfred Hitchcock insisted that he never intended it to be "an important movie" (quoted in Truffaut, 1984: 283). Nevertheless, *Psycho* (1960) has generated more discussion of an 'important' nature than any other of his films has. Indeed, *Psycho* is probably the most closely and most seriously scrutinized film ever made.

Much-studied masterpiece though it is, *Psycho* at first got something of a brush-off. In a pithy summary of the film's early career, Robert E. Kapsis notes that:

> *Many newspaper and magazine reviewers, especially those catering to the more educated and sophisticated filmgoer, agreed that this time around [in his efforts to keep audience members on the edge of their seats] Hitchcock had simply gone too far.* (1992: 62)

Moreover, some reviewers simply found *Psycho* boring. The critic for *Newsweek* wrote, "[It is] plainly a gimmick movie, whose suspense depends on a single, specific twist [and whose] climactic scenes are rather standardly spooky and contrived." According to the reviewer for *Time*, "Hitchcock bears down too heavily in this one, and the delicate illusion of reality necessary for a creak-and-shriek movie becomes, instead, a spectacle of stomach-churning horror." For the *Esquire* critic, *Psycho* came across as:

> [Merely] *one of those television shows padded out to two hours by adding pointless subplots and realistic details… a reflection of a most unpleasant mind, a mean, sly, sadistic little mind.*[1]

Psycho was released in June 1960; five months later, by which time the relatively low-budget film had scored extraordinary success at the box office,[2] at least a few critics were suggesting that there was more to *Psycho* than thrills and chills. *Psycho* historian Stephen Rebello notes that the *New York Times*'s influential Bosley Crowther, whose first reaction was to dismiss *Psycho* as a slow-paced collection of melodramatic clichés and a blot on Hitchcock's otherwise distinguished career, by Christmas-time "led a contingent of critics who would later revise their opinions" (1990: 165).[3] But Crowther was not the first to suggest that *Psycho* was somehow 'special'. As early as August

1960 Andrew Sarris in the *Village Voice* was advising that connoisseurs of film needed to confront *Psycho* at least three times:

> The first time for the sheer terror of the experience… the second time for the macabre comedy inherent in the conception of the film; and the third for all the hidden meanings and symbols lurking beneath the surface.[4]

It is these sub-surface symbols and meanings that, over the years, have garnered for *Psycho* the most attention. The late Raymond Durgnat figured that "the interpretations of *Psycho*… must by now be well into three figures" (2002: 3). The first crop of these sprang up in the mid-1960s and, inspired by the post-war fashion for Freudian thinking, tended to offer psychoanalytic readings of the plot in general and, in particular, of the character of Norman Bates.[5] In the 1970s, after the first waves of self-consciously postmodern thinking gave rise to so-called Film Theory,[6] readings of *Psycho* began to focus less on the film's action and more on its visual/verbal imagery. Following the lead of the psychiatrist who in the penultimate scene attempts to explain the curious events that transpired at the Bates residence, the earlier takes on *Psycho* explore the rather obvious lines of misogyny, multiple personality and the Oedipus complex; later interpretations spin variations on these Bates-specific themes, but they prefer to concentrate on subtler threads represented by details of *Psycho*'s screenplay and its various *mises en scène*. Apparently less intrigued by the film's characters than by the perspectives of audience members,[7] critics in recent decades have wrung significance from *Psycho*'s wet mops and rain-soaked clothes, reflected upon its mirrors and eyeballs, probed the semiotic content of toilets and brassieres; they have gone over the film's roads, staircases, corpses, tools, cages, beds, money, birds, food, teeth, bathrooms, knives, etc., and discovered their relevance to such states of mind as sibling rivalry, fear of the sexual 'Other,' fetishism, scopophilia, infantile regression, anal retentiveness, and castration anxiety.

Doubtless *Psycho* contains much that has yet to be 'de-coded', and doubtless – as new ideologies replace those current – the stream of 'deep readings' will continue to flow. But already the *Psycho* literature seems as fecund as it is huge; indeed, so rich is it in hermeneutics that one cannot help but notice how relatively poor it is in Herrmann-eutics.

To be sure, Bernard Herrmann's score for *Psycho* has attracted attention from writers who specialize in film music. The commentary most readily available is Royal S. Brown's 'Herrmann, Hitchcock, and the Music of the Irrational', which first appeared in *Cinema Journal* in 1982 and was later reprinted, with only slight revisions, both in Brown's *Overtones and Undertones: Reading Film Music* (1994) and in Robert Kolker's anthology *Alfred Hitchcock's Psycho: A Casebook* (2004). As its title suggests, Brown's essay deals in general with the Herrmann–Hitchcock relationship,[8] but several pages deal exclusively with the score for *Psycho*.[9] Less accessible but more sharply focused studies – featuring cue-by-cue analyses and a bounty of musical examples – are the chapter on

Psycho in Graham Bruce's *Bernard Herrmann: Film Music and Narrative* (1985)[10] and Fred Steiner's (1974–75) 'Herrmann's "Black and White" Music for Hitchcock's *Psycho*'.[11] Roy Prendergast in his *Film Music: A Neglected Art* (1992) offers a thorough summary of Steiner's paper, including musical examples. Surveys of film music by Christopher Palmer (1990), Irwin Bazelon and George Burt feature at least a few pages devoted to Herrmann's *Psycho* score. In addition, Jack Sullivan's new book on music in the entirety of Hitchcock's oeuvre (2006) of course includes a chapter on *Psycho*.[12]

However much attention musicologists have paid to the score, it seems that the film studies community in general have long found Herrmann's contribution to *Psycho* to be elusive. Wood observed that for the car-driving segments Hitchcock used every means at his disposal, including music, to enforce the audience's identification with the female protagonist (1965: 144–5). Naremore acknowledged that the force of the first murder scene depends on a rhythm generated by the length of the shots, by the actors' movements, and ultimately by the music (1973: 57). Rothman similarly granted that "much of the shattering impact" of the very start of the murder scene derives from the "sudden high-pitched shriek of violins" (1982: 298), and he noted as well that the poignancy of the film's opening scene, in the hotel room, is expressed not so much by the female character's face as by Herrmann's music (*ibid.*: 256). Beyond those scattered credits, in the voluminous interpretive literature *Psycho*'s score gets barely a mention. Durgnat admits that his monograph on the film, "deplorably, no doubt," has little to say about the music; the excuse he offers is that while "every spectator is shaken by [the music]… its very 'language,' and its relation to emotional dynamics, is difficult to discuss" (2002: 3). And with that, perhaps, Durgnat speaks for the great majority of his colleagues.

The 'startle' reflex

It is not as though the *Psycho* music goes unrecognized. Surely one of the most clichéd gestures in all of film music involves screeching, repetitive dissonances of the sort that Herrmann concocted for the incident that takes place in a shower at the Bates Motel (Figure 1.1). Rip-offs are heard in the soundtracks of countless 'slasher' movies, and to a certain extent they lack an element of mystery that must have figured into *Psycho*'s first screenings. Because they are derivative of such a well-known model, they convey the entirety of their message with their first instant of sound; there is no suspense in them, no room for the audience to wonder about what might ensue, just the announcement that a brutal murder – no matter how long it takes to enact – is in effect a *fait accompli*. But even the most tawdry of imitations can be potent. So long as the music begins abruptly and loudly, as Herrmann's does, almost invariably it triggers what psychologists and physiologists call the 'startle' reflex.[13]

Figure 1.1 Psycho, 'The Murder', bb. 1–8[14]

Indeed, this clichéd musical gesture and the predictable 'startle' reflex are now so closely linked that the combination has migrated to the field of comedy. On the big screen, parodies of *Psycho*'s shower scene add to the levity, for example, of Mel Brooks's *High Anxiety* (1976), Harold Ramis's (*National Lampoon's*) *Vacation* (1983), Wes Craven's *Scream* (1996), and Joe Dante's *Looney Tunes: Back in Action* (2003). On television, the shower scene has been jocularly referenced by *Mr. Bean* (in the final sequence of a 1990 episode titled 'The Curse of Mr. Bean'), by *The Simpsons* (in 'Itchy and Scratchy and Marge', from December 1990, and in 'The Springfield Files', from January 1997), and by *That '70s Show* (in 'Too Old to Trick or Treat, Too Young to Die', from October 2000). Not surprisingly, the original material has lately been spoofed on the internet, perhaps most outrageously in a *Turtles TV* video aptly titled 'The One with the Shower Scene'.[15] Probably no other genuinely horrific film music, with or without its concomitant imagery, has so often been played for laughs.

Of course, the brief cue titled 'The Murder' is not the only music in Bernard Herrmann's *Psycho* score. Nor is the shower scene all there is to the film, although nowadays it might be difficult to argue that point to the general public.

When *Psycho* was first released it was hardly a secret that the narrative included a female character who comes to a bad end while taking a shower. Hitchcock freely admitted this in a 1959 newspaper interview that quoted him as saying "Men do kill nude women, you know",[16] and a tongue-in-cheek trailer for *Psycho* ended with the director pulling aside a shower curtain to reveal an apparently startled actress. But the actress whose face is momentarily shown in the trailer was the film's female co-star, Vera Miles, not the top-billed Janet Leigh. Along with the identity of the fictional killer, Hitchcock painstakingly kept under wraps the information that it was Leigh's character who would be murdered and that the murder would occur relatively early in the film.[17] Apropos of this, *Psycho*'s original lobby posters deliberately misled the prospective audience by emphasizing a 'MacGuffin' that had little to do with the film's basic plot;[18] the posters are dominated by a monochrome photograph of Leigh, sitting on a bed, clad in half-slip and bra, and wearing on her face an expression not of terror but of arguably erotic wistfulness.[19] In contrast, the 1999 'Collector's Edition' DVD of *Psycho* features on its cover a colourized headshot of Leigh, wet-haired and screaming.[20]

From the point of view of a modern advertiser, the idea of Marion Crane (Leigh) as victim is apparently far more marketable than the idea of Marion as participant in an affair. It seems that almost everyone, including persons who have never experienced *Psycho* in its entirety, know very well what transpires in the film's shower scene. The image of Marion's reaction to her surprise visitor has evolved into *Psycho*'s trademark,[21] and Herrmann's scream-like motif is surely its aural equivalent. For film-literate persons, the dramatic content of the shower scene and its supporting music are all but inseparable.

Shower music

In curious fact, Hitchcock at first wanted the shower scene not to be accompanied by music. Aware that since early in his career Hitchcock had paid very close attention to the sonic elements in his films,[22] writer Joseph Stefano in his 1 December 1959 'final revised' draft of the screenplay described the scene thus:

> [Marion] *turns in response to the feel and SOUND of the shower curtain being torn aside. A look of pure horror erupts in her face. A low terrible groan begins to rise up out of her throat. A hand comes into the shot. The hand holds an enormous bread knife. The flint of the blade shatters the screen to an almost total, silver blankness.*
> THE SLASHING
> *An impression of a knife slashing, as if tearing at the very screen, ripping the film. Over it the brief gulps of screaming. And then silence. And then the dreadful thump as [Marion's] body falls in the tub.*
> REVERSE ANGLE
> *The blank whiteness, the blur of the shower water, the hand pulling the shower curtain back. We catch one flicker of a glimpse of the murderer. A woman, her face contorted with madness, her head wild with hair, as if she were wearing a fright-wig. And then we see only the curtain, closed across the tub, and hear the rush of the shower water. Above the shower-bar we see the bathroom door open again and after a moment we HEAR the SOUND of the front door slamming.* (*Psycho* screenplay)

Rebello reports that test footage for the shower scene, based on storyboard draw-ings by art director Saul Bass, was shot on 10 December 1959, and that photography involving both Janet Leigh and a nude stand-in took place between 18 and 23 Decem-ber. The filming of *Psycho*'s second murder scene – the one featuring detective Milton Arbogast (Martin Balsam), who visits the Bates Motel in search of Marion – occupied the middle of January 1960; principal photography was completed on 1 February, and supplementary footage (devoted primarily to cityscapes of Phoenix, the detective's entrance into the Bates house, and the discovery of Mrs Bates's corpse) was shot both on location in Phoenix and on the Universal lot during the last week of February. The first 'rough cut' – lacking not only music and special sound effects but also the close-up images of Norman Bates's stuffed birds – was screened on 26 April 1960 (Rebello, 1990: 104–36).

These dates conflict with the account given by Smith (2002), but not with the idea that Hitchcock originally wanted the shower scene to be devoid of music. Relying almost entirely on a statement by Herrmann that appeared in Evan Cameron's *Sound and the Cinema; The Coming of Sound to American Film* (1980),[23] Smith writes that a 'final cut' of *Psycho* was ready as early as mid-December 1959. As Herrmann told the story:

> When I was first shown this film, Hitchcock was depressed about it. He felt it didn't come off. He wanted to cut it down to an hour television show and get rid of it. I had an idea of what one could do with this film, so I said, 'Why don't you go away for your Christmas holidays, and when you come back we'll record the score and see what you think'... 'Well,' he said, 'do what you like, but only one thing I ask of you: please write nothing for the murder in the shower. That must be without music.' (Cameron, 1980: 132; Smith, 1991: 237)

In a reminiscence not pinned down to a date and attributed to a conversation with director Brian De Palma, for whom he scored the films *Sisters* (1972) and *Obsession* (1975), Herrmann supposedly said:

> I remember sitting in a screening room after seeing the rough cut of Psycho. Hitch was nervously pacing back and forth, saying it was awful and that he was going to cut it down for his television show. He was crazy. He didn't know what he had. 'Wait a minute,' I said. 'I have some ideas. How about a score completely for strings? I used to be a violin player, you know'... Hitch was crazy then. You know, he made Psycho with his own money and he was afraid it was going to be a flop. He didn't even want any music in the shower scene. Can you imagine that? (quoted in Rebello, 1990: 138)

However vague (and arguably self-serving) Herrmann's recollections may be, they are consistent in their claim that Hitchcock intended the shower scene to be audibly embellished only by more or less naturalistic sounds. In this they are supported by documentary evidence. A memorandum titled 'Mr. Hitchcock's Suggestions for Place-ment of Music', dated 8 January 1960 and sent to Herrmann as well as to the sound technicians, is quite explicit:

> Start music the moment Marion drives away from the Highway Patrolman and continue when she arrives at the used car lot. Music all through the Used Car Lot continuing until she arrives at the Motel. Stop music when she blows her horn. There should be no music at all through the next sequence (the first Motel sequence). Start music in the Hardware store.[24]

As for the shower scene *per se*, in his 'Suggestions' Hitchcock specified only that:

> Throughout the killing, there should be the shower noise and the blows of the knife. We should hear the water gurgling down the drain of the bathtub,

> *especially when we go close on it... During the murder, the sound of the shower should be continuous and monotonous, only broken by the screams of Marion. (ibid.)*

A few days later (12 January) Hitchcock in his music notes was emphasizing the importance of music to indicate Marion's troubled state of mind, not only as she leaves the patrolman but also as she catches a glimpse, on the streets of Phoenix, of the boss from whom she has stolen $40,000. And in a memo dated 25 January he reneges on his earlier pronouncement and suggests that the first motel sequence indeed include some music, but only in the scene during which the guilt-laden Marion unpacks her bags.[25]

In preparation for his new book on music in all the Hitchcock films, Jack Sullivan not only scoured the archives but elicited interviews from screenwriter Stefano and other surviving members of the *Psycho* crew. He concludes that what happened next, *vis-à-vis* music for the murder scene, is not at all clear. "Some say Hitchcock himself finally asked Herrmann for a shower cue," Sullivan writes, and "others [say] that Herrmann made the proposal" (2006: 248).

On this, the literature is indeed confusing. On the one hand, we have a statement from film-music historian George Burt, who writes authoritatively (albeit without citing a source) that:

> [Because of] *the intensity and chilling starkness of the scene... coupled with a relentless pacing in the editing... Hitchcock was convinced that the scene should be handled without music. After numerous viewings of the completed film, Hitchcock was forced to admit his error. Though Bernard Herrmann had already completed and recorded the rest of the score, Hitchcock recalled him to create music solely for this scene. (1994: 212)*

On the other hand, we have Herrmann's recollection:

> *When Hitchcock returned* [from vacation] *we played the score for him in the mixing and dubbing studio (not at a recording session). We dubbed the composite without any musical effects behind the murder scene, and let him watch it. Then I said, 'I really do have something composed for it, and now that you've seen it your way, let's try mine.' We played him my version with the music. He said, 'Of course, that's the one we'll use.' I said, 'But you requested that we not add any music.' 'Improper suggestion, improper suggestion,' he replied. (quoted in Cameron, 1980: 133; and Smith, 1991: 239–40)*

Since the 'stabbing' motif is reprised several times, it seems incredible that Herrmann composed all the score before concocting this crucial element. Yet Herrmann's account, at the very least because its chronology is verifiably off the mark, needs to be taken with a grain of salt.

It is a matter of record that Herrmann's manuscript of the complete *Psycho* score bears the inscription 'Jan–Feb 12/60' and that the recording sessions – under Herrmann's baton – took place at the Paramount studio on 9 and 10 March 1960. In the long run, precisely how and when Hitchcock second-guessed himself and decided to use music for the shower scene is less important than the fact that the decision was made. The decision is certainly an historic one, and after almost a half-century its results have achieved the status of the iconic. Today it is difficult even to imagine the shower scene without Herrmann's music.[26] As noted earlier, for most film-literate persons the shower scene's action and music are inseparable. Indeed, for film-lovers whose experience is shallow or still limited, perhaps the shower scene is what *Psycho* is all about.

But the famous shower scene is just a portion of *Psycho*. Undeniably shocking and memorable, the montage with its 56-second musical accompaniment occurs less than halfway through a 108-minute film.[27] It is a peak moment, to be sure, but in terms of the narrative as a whole it represents not so much a climax as a turning point. What of the rest of *Psycho*? More importantly, what of the rest of the music?

Music beyond the shower

The official *Psycho* cue sheet lists 60 musical items, but some of these in essence are fragments that function as components of larger, titled sequences.[28] Fred Steiner – who analysed the *Psycho* score for the purposes of a 1973 University of Southern California research project – is correct when he writes that the film music is divided into 40 separate cues.[29] The titles of these cues are shown in Table 1.1, along with their start times in the film and their durations both in the film's soundtrack and in the recording of the *Psycho* music that Herrmann made with London's National Philharmonic Orchestra (an orchestra that existed purely for recording purposes) in 1975.[30]

Figure 1.2 shows the distribution of these cues over the entire length of the film, with cues that underscore dialogue or monologue indicated by grey markings and cues mixed only with naturalistic sound effects indicated by black markings.

The duration of *Psycho*, beginning with the first chord of the 'Prelude' music and ending with the fade-to-black after the final scene, is 1 hour, 48 minutes and 12 seconds. In total, Herrmann's music lasts 46 minutes and 20 seconds, which represents

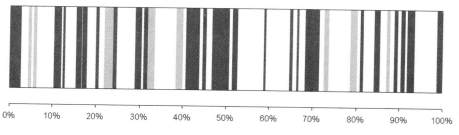

Figure 1.2 Distribution of music in Psycho

Table 1.1   Musical cues in *Psycho*

1.	Prelude	0:00:00	1:50	2:07
2.	The City	0:01:50	1:02	1:25
3.	Marion *	0:04:31	0:49	1:27
4.	Marion and Sam *	0:05:55	0:40	1:48
5.	Temptation	0:10:50	1:45	3:12
6.	Flight	0:12:56	0:41	1:08
7.	Patrol Car	0:16:13	1:20	1:09
8.	The Car Lot	0:17:43	1:14	1:40
9.	The Package	0:20:57	0:55	1:33
10.	The Rainstorm *	0:23:09	3:03	3:19
11.	Hotel Room	0:30:35	1:28	1:36
12.	The Window	0:32:46	0:55	1:00
13.	The Parlor *	0:33:54	1:32	1:32
14.	The Madhouse *	0:40:30	1:45	2:18
15.	The Peephole	0:43:06	2:24	3:15
16.	The Bathroom	0:45:30	0:45	0:45
17.	The Murder	0:47:10	0:56	0:53
18.	The Body	0:49:34	0:09	0:32
19.	The Office	0:50:21	1:13	1:27
20.	The Curtain	0:51:34	1:06	1:10
21.	The Water	0:52:48	1:20	1:14
22.	The Car	0:54:08	0:48	0:43
23.	The Swamp	0:55:41	1:24	2:11
24.	The Search (A)	1:03:25	0:37	0:46
25.	The Shadow	1:09:44	0:45	0:48
26.	Phone Booth	1:11:26	0:48	0:53
27.	The Porch	1:13:38	0:58	1:06
28.	The Stairs	1:14:36	2:17	3:02
29.	The Knife	1:16:53	0:14	0:29
30.	The Search (B) *	1:18:12	1:12	1:25
31.	The First Floor *	1:24:29	1:51	2:31
32.	Cabin 10	1:28:00	0:53	1:04
33.	Cabin 1	1:31:30	1:26	1:11
34.	The Hill	1:34:33	0:52	1:36
35.	The Bedroom	1:36:14	1:03	1:01
36.	The Toys	1:37:58	1:00	1:06
37.	The Cellar	1:39:34	1:12	1:24
38.	The Murder	1:40:46	0:24	—
39.	Discovery	1:41:10	0:10	0:20
40.	Finale *	1:46:54	1:16	1:48

Note: Cues that run together without interruption are boxed; cues that underscore dialogue or monologue are marked with asterisks.[31]

42.5 percent of the film's length. Although there has yet to be a formal study on the proportional relationships between scored and non-scored segments of Hollywood films from the 1940s and 1950s, this percentage seems easily within the norm. What is strikingly abnormal about *Psycho* is the relatively large amount of music – 32.1 percent, almost a third of the film's duration – that accompanies segments that for all intents and purposes are presented in pantomime.

To be sure, screams resound during the cues titled 'The Murder' and 'The Knife', there is a potent gasp during 'The Bedroom', and the very end of 'The Cellar' features the inquisitive pronouncement by Lila Crane (Miles) of the name of the woman she sees sitting in the rocking-chair. But these vocalizations hardly count as plot-furthering language. And there is something unusual about the vocalizations heard in certain of the cues that do feature language. The dramatically significant words that figure in the first two-thirds of 'The Rainstorm', for example, come from voices that the guilt-plagued Marion only imagines; the conversation that transpires during 'The First Floor', although unsuspecting audience members might not realize it, involves Norman Bates speaking alternately for himself and for his long-dead mother, and the verbal overlay of 'Finale' is clearly a 'silent' monologue emanating from the deep recesses of Norman's troubled mind.[32] Aside from the repeated shouting of Arbogast's name by Marion's boyfriend Sam (John Gavin), the cue titled 'The Search (B)' supports dialogue – between Sam and Lila – only in its final moments. Beyond that, the only segments of *Psycho* that mix music with dialogue in a more or less conventional manner are the two romantically flavoured bits that embellish the opening scene in the hotel room ('Marion' and 'Marion and Sam') and the two dark-coloured cues ('The Parlor' and 'The Madhouse') that accompany Marion's exploratory conversations with Norman.

Musical relationships

The traditional reading of *Psycho* holds that the film is divided into two parts, one in which the main character is clearly Marion and another in which the centre of attention, just as clearly, is Norman Bates.[33] Rooted in Freudian psychoanalysis, this line of thinking regards Marion and Norman as sharing certain traits, among them repressed sexuality and nagging guilt over their more or less dark secrets. The essence of *Psycho* in this view is not the murderer's and victim's polarity but, rather, their linkage. Norman's and Marion's bond is verbalized at the end of their conversation in the motel's parlour, when Norman, in discussing his mother, says, "She just goes a little mad sometimes. We all go a little mad sometimes. Haven't you?" Marion, reflecting on the impulsive theft that has made her a fugitive, responds, "Yes. Sometimes just one time can be enough." The narrative's bifurcation then occurs with the shower scene, at which moment the woman who had been the protagonist suddenly becomes a non-entity and the audience's focus perforce shifts – through a process of transference – to the young man who hitherto had been portrayed as troubled yet sympathetic.

The studies of the *Psycho* score by Steiner, Bruce, and Brown support such a reading. Primarily through close analysis of cues associated specifically with Marion and Norman, they show how music that on first acquaintance might seem quite different in fact has much in common. For example, the violent music that illustrates Norman's unbridled psychosis (in 'The Knife' and the two cues titled 'The Murder'[34]) is in subtle ways anticipated by the merely agitated music that illustrates Marion's anxiety (in 'Flight', 'Patrol Car', and 'The Rainstorm'). Similarly, cues that describe Marion's relationship with Sam (in 'Marion' and 'Marion and Sam') are echoed by cues that limn Norman's devotion to his mother (in 'The Bedroom' and 'The Toys'). And the moto perpetuo figures that power the in-car sequences and bother the otherwise contemplative music identified with the stolen money ('Temptation', 'The Package' and 'Hotel Room') are built of intervals comparable to those in the grim three-note motif that seems to represent Norman's psychosis (especially prominent in 'The Madhouse', 'The Swamp' and 'The Shadow', and at the very end of 'Finale').

There is no disputing these purely musical connections between the Marion- and Norman-oriented components of the *Psycho* score, and only a curmudgeon would suggest that the cues' obvious shared elements result from nothing more than efforts by a skilled composer, in producing a score for a particular film, to be stylistically consistent. As for the structure of the narrative, however, there is still room for debate. The standard interpretation has it that *Psycho* is split, by a sharp knife's brutal violation of a patently vulnerable naked woman — into two distinct parts,[35] but *Psycho* might also be regarded as falling into not two parts but three.

A tripartite view of *Psycho* breaks the film into sections whose main characters are not Marion and Norman but, rather, Marion, Arbogast and Lila, each of whom comes to the Bates Motel with some sort of problem to solve and each of whom, as a result of earnest efforts to solve their problems, dramatically encounters 'Mother.' An encounter-based reading of the narrative is suggested by the filmic editing; after all, the only extended fades to black in *Psycho* follow the killing of Arbogast and, earlier, the denouement during which Norman dutifully cleans up after Marion's murder. More to the point of this structure-based analysis, a triple division of the narrative is strongly indicated by the film's placement of music.

A tripartite division

Figure 1.3 shows the narrative of *Psycho* framed by prologue and epilogue but otherwise divided according to the three characters who in one way or another make the acquaintance of 'Mother'. Whereas the black and grey shadings of Figure 1.2 indicate placement of dialogue-free or dialogue-accompanied music, the vertical lines here indicate only changes of scene.

In the case of the relatively large section of the film that focuses on Marion, the narrative can be subdivided into a trio of portions that represent, in turn, Marion's affairs in Phoenix, her adventures as she embarks on her journey, and her activities — dead or

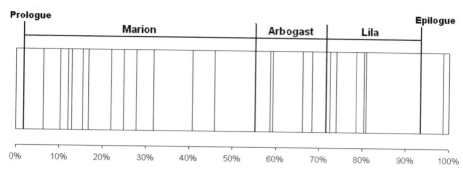

Figure 1.3 A tripartite division of the *Psycho* narrative

alive — at the Bates Motel. Similarly, the sections that focus on Arbogast and Lila can be subdivided into portions that contain these characters' activities before and after their visits to the motel. These subdivisions, which will prove to be significant when regarded in light of specific musical cues, are shown in Figure 1.4.

Specifically, in the 'Marion' section of Figure 1.4 the vertical lines in the portion labelled 'Phoenix' represent the scene in the hotel room with Sam, the scene in the real estate office where Marion is employed, the scene in Marion's apartment, and the scene during which she drives her car through the streets of the city; the subdivisions of the portion labelled 'journey' represent Marion's roadside encounter with the highway patrolman, the sequence during which she gets back on the road and fears she is being pursued, her visit to the used-car lot, and the sequence that has her again on the road and arriving at the motel;[36] the five subdivisions of the 'motel' portion represent, in turn, Marion's initial meeting with Norman Bates, her retreat into her own room, her conversation with Bates in the parlour behind the motel's office, her second retreat and her subsequent murder, and, finally, Norman's 'clean-up' activities. As marked by the vertical lines in the preceding figure, the narrative's 'Arbogast' section consists of the

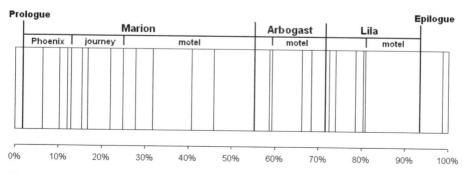

Figure 1.4 An encounter-based division of the *Psycho* narrative, subdivided by locale

scene in the hardware store during which the detective makes the acquaintance of Sam and Lila, the brief montage sequence that depicts Arbogast's visits to various motels, Arbogast's arrival at the Bates Motel and the triggering of his suspicions, his telephone conversation with Lila, and, finally, his ill-fated intrusion into the Bates house. The six portions of the 'Lila' section in turn represent the conversation between Lila and Sam at the hardware store, Sam's unproductive first visit to the motel, Sam and Lila's informative meeting with the sheriff, Norman's conversation with 'Mother' after the sheriff's telephone query, the hurried formulation (at the church and then on the road) of Sam and Lila's plan to search the motel, and Lila's arrival at the motel and her sustained exploration of the house's bedrooms and cellar.

Figure 1.5 shows the narrative, divided and subdivided as described above, combined with the film's distribution of dialogue-free and dialogue-accompanied music. Immediately apparent from the figure is the absence of music at the beginnings not only of the narrative's three main sections (and of the epilogue) but also at the onsets of the three subdivisions of the 'Marion' section.

As presented thus far, the first portion of the narrative's 'Marion' section indeed begins with music, but in this case the music – the cue titled 'The City' that accompanies the camera's sweep across the cityscape and eventual zoom through the window of the hotel room – segues directly from the preceding 'Prelude' music. It could easily be argued, however, that the film's 'Marion' section begins not with the ambiguous cityscape but with the intimate scene in the hotel room. If the graph is adjusted accordingly – that is, if the line separating the prologue from the 'Phoenix' subdivision is shifted slightly to the right, as in Figure 1.6 – it shows that each of the non-accompanied scenes that open the three portions of the 'Marion' section is indeed preceded by music that is not overlaid with language.

Regardless of how one slices the first few minutes of the film, the illustrations make clear that the narrative's 'Arbogast' and 'Lila' sections, but not its 'Marion' section, end with language-free music. And if one accepts the premise that the 'Marion' section begins not with the cityscape but with the scene in the hotel room, it is just as clear

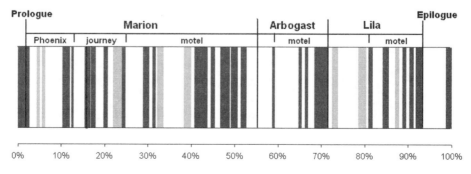

Figure 1.5 Distribution of music in *Psycho* compared with the narrative

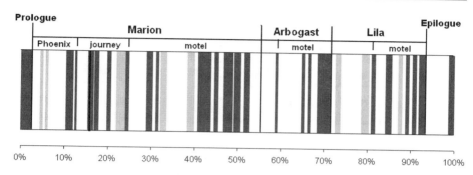

Figure 1.6 Distribution of music in *Psycho* compared with adjusted division of the narrative

that all three sections – as well as all three subdivisions of the 'Marion' section – begin with a music-free soundtrack. Simply from viewing these illustrations one might start to suspect that in *Psycho* the placement of music-free dialogue and dialogue-free music serves some sort of structural purpose. Such a suspicion is confirmed as soon as the relevant cues are considered in terms of their emotional affect.

The 'Prelude'

Assuming that the 'Phoenix' portion of the 'Marion' section indeed begins when the camera first peeps through the hotel window, the musical sequence that sets up the scene – indeed, the music that sets up the entire film – is the nervous 'Prelude', after which 'The City' can be heard to function as a relatively calm coda. On the cue sheet, the 'Prelude' in fact consists of four variants of music labelled '*Psycho* Prelude' (with durations, respectively, of 28, 22, 17, and 16 seconds) alternated with three virtually identical iterations (each 9 seconds in length) of music labelled '*Psycho* Theme'. If the composer himself picked the label for the '*Psycho* Theme' (Figure 1.7), the choice would have been ironic. Brown aptly notes that "Herrmann never had a great deal of use for themes per se" (1982: 22).[37] More intriguingly, Herrmann, long after he and Hitchcock had gone their separate ways, identified the three-note figure associated with madness as "the real *Psycho* theme".[38]

Although it is hardly a 'theme' in the conventional sense, the eight-bar passage is nevertheless, as Steiner points out, "the only motive in the entire film which might be thought of as a tune" (1974–75: 71). For Steiner, this music "imparts a brief hint of lyricism" and serves as "a strange moment of relief in the midst of all the nervous, fearful, forward motion" (*ibid.*); Bruce opts for the same descriptive term, writing that the "long-spanned legato figure" offers a "slight relief" during an otherwise tension-filled cue (1985: 185). Herrmann likely exaggerated when he claimed that "the climax of *Psycho* is given to you by the music right at the moment the film begins" (quoted

Figure 1.7 *Psycho*, 'Prelude', bb. 37–44

in Cameron, 1980: 132). But surely tension, perhaps not so much relieved as exacerbated by brief melodic respites, is the dominant affect of *Psycho*'s 'Prelude'.

Affectively complex though it is, the *Psycho* 'Prelude' suggests, in a word, anxiety. After its initial sounding in the title sequence, this musical evocation of anxiety – the rhythmically insistent materials as well as their lyric foil – recurs three times (Figure 1.8). All three recurrences happen relatively early in the section of the film in which the centre of attention is Marion. Significantly, in terms of a *Psycho*-analysis that emphasizes placement of music within the narrative structure, each of them in effect covers a transition to a locale whose qualities are established by means other than musical.

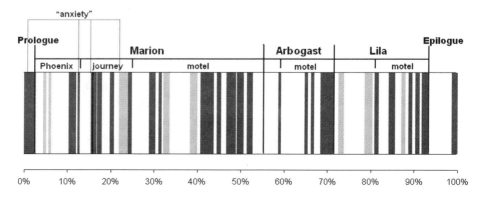

Figure 1.8 The placement in *Psycho* of 'anxiety' music

In the cue titled 'Flight', the anxiety-fraught music first heard in the 'Prelude' takes Marion from the noisy, yet relatively safe, environment of Phoenix to the quiet, yet decidedly scary, environment of the roadside. After Marion falls under the suspicion of the highway patrolman, this same music (in the guise of 'Patrol Car') transports her, nervously, to the used-car lot. Finally, in the extended cue titled 'The Rainstorm' (the first two-thirds of which are overlaid with voices emanating from a troubled conscience), the music delivers Marion to the Bates Motel. Notwithstanding whatever might be implied by Saul Bass's animations for the film's title sequence, the 'Prelude' music has no real narrative context. As reprised in the cues titled 'Flight', 'Patrol Car' and 'The Rainstorm', however, this music invariably supports images of Marion behind the wheel of one or another of her automobiles. The music illustrates driving, literally, but it also suggests the forces that with increasing intensity drive Marion toward her destiny.[39]

Clearly there are affective commonalities in the music that precedes each portion of the narrative's 'Marion' section.[40] The same can be said for the language-free music that ends the sections of the narrative marked 'Arbogast' and 'Lila'. Arbogast exits the film to the accompaniment of 'The Knife', which is a 14-second recapitulation of the screechy motif that in the shower scene heralds the surprise entrance of Marion's killer. Were it not for Sam's timely intervention Lila would likely taste the same fate, for immediately after she comes face to face with 'Mother' she is intruded upon by a knife-wielding Norman. Although this time no bloodshed transpires, the cue that marks Norman's entrance is nevertheless titled – as was the music for the shower scene – 'The Murder'. It features an almost identical iteration of the 'stabbing' chords that brought down Marion, but in this case the aftermath is not a coda that leisurely glosses a fresh-slain body but a separate cue ('Discovery') that momentarily reflects upon a desiccated corpse. In all three cases, the music is onomatopoetically depictive of knife-related violence (Figure 1.9). While in the narrative's 'Marion' section the event associated with this music is followed by a denouement,[41] in the 'Arbogast' and 'Lila' sections the music resonates with an air of finality. In the last two cases, followed as

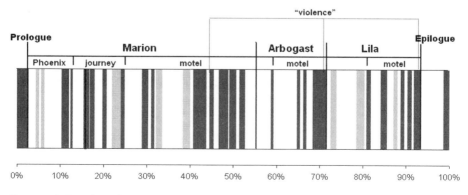

Figure 1.9 The placement in *Psycho* of 'violence' music

they are by filmic editing that indicates transitions of both time and place,[42] the music cues representative of violence emphatically serve as structural markers.

There are at least two other components of Herrmann's score that, in terms of the *Psycho* narrative, seem to serve purposes that are not merely affective but also structural. One of these is the music associated with temptation, first heard in the cue titled 'Temptation' (Figure 1.10) and reprised in 'The Package' and 'Hotel Room';[43] the other is the music that features what Herrmann called the 'real' *Psycho* theme, the three-note motif associated with madness that is introduced in the opening bars of 'The Madhouse' (Figure 1.11) and then recapitulated in 'The Swamp', 'The Shadow', 'Phone Booth', 'The Porch', 'The Stairs' and 'Finale'.

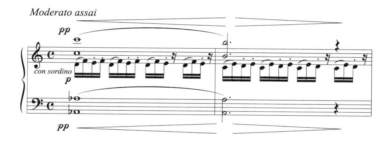

Figure 1.10   Psycho, 'Temptation', bb. 1–2

Figure 1.11   Psycho, 'The Madhouse', bb. 1–7

The 'temptation' and 'madness' music does not occur at narrative points as obviously structural as the 'anxiety' and 'violence' music. That is to say, they serve neither as vehicles that move the narrative from one locale to another (as is the case with all of the 'anxiety' music) nor as dividers that separate one narrative section from the next (as is the case with the second and third instances of the 'violence' music). The 'temptation' and 'madness' cues do, however, form patterns that interweave with those formed, respectively, by the 'anxiety' and 'violence' cues. Indeed, each of the two groups of cues might be regarded as a complex made up of music representative of cause and effect, and in both cases the cause-related music frames the effect-related music in a way that suggests – apropos of a suspense-filled Hitchcock film – a lack of resolution.

Marion's anxiety, to put it simplistically, results from the temptation aroused by the $40,000 that her employer entrusts to her. In *Psycho*'s 'Prelude' there is, of course, no context for anxiety-ridden music. The 'Flight' cue that marks Marion's departure from Phoenix is, however, preceded almost immediately by the lingering 'Temptation' (see Figure 1.12), during which Marion in her apartment weighs the consequences of theft and eventually makes a decision. Likewise, the 'Rainstorm' cue that delivers Marion to the Bates Motel is preceded, again almost immediately, by 'The Package', during which she retreats into the car lot's restroom and removes from the stolen money enough cash to close the deal on a substitute automobile. Soon afterward, during 'Hotel Room', Marion appears to be concerned only with hiding the money, and with this she falls still deeper into the trap of her own making, but in this case temptation does not result in further anxiety. Indeed, after her conversation with Norman, Marion seems to have found the conscience-clearing answer to her problem. Her entrance into the shower doubtless symbolizes her determination to wash away her sins, but ablution is cut short by the visit from 'Mother'.

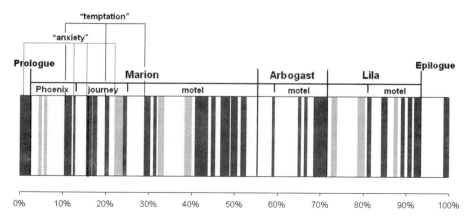

Figure 1.12 The relationship in *Psycho* of 'anxiety' music to 'temptation' music

Similarly lacking in closure is the complex formed by the 'madness' and 'violence' cues (Figure 1.13). The 'madness' motif first occurs at the start of the cue titled 'The Madhouse', darkly underscoring Norman's sudden change in demeanour after Marion suggests that his mother might be better off were she to be institutionalized. Then, after the dialogue-free 'Peephole' and 'Bathroom' cues, whose voyeuristic creepiness only confirms Norman's mental instability, violence bursts forth in 'The Murder'. This section, of course, represents not the conclusion but the climax of the 'motel' sequence. After Marion falls dead, another 9 minutes pass before the fade-to-black; during this time, as Norman cleans up and disposes of the body, no fewer than six cues are heard, but the 'madness' motif is featured only in the one titled 'The Swamp'.[44]

In the 'Arbogast' section 'madness' cues occur in quick succession: as the detective from a distance catches a glimpse of 'Mother' ('The Shadow'), as he leaves the motel to relay news of his discovery to Lila ('Phone Booth'), as he returns to the motel in order to seek out Mrs Bates ('The Porch'), as he enters the house and proceeds to the second floor ('The Stairs'). More obviously than before, madness here begets violence, which erupts conclusively (*vis-à-vis* the narrative section) in 'The Knife'.

Curiously, the film's 'Lila' section features no iterations whatsoever of the 'madness' motif. 'The First Floor', during which Norman and 'Mother' converse in the privacy of a bedroom, has both a tempo and a 'sighing' melodic figure in common with the sultry music that in the opening scene followed the camera's slow approach to the hotel room in which Marion and Sam were conducting their affair,[45] and the eerily gentle music that accompanies Lila's furtive exploration of the house ('The Bedroom' and 'The Toys') features the same insistent rhythm that earlier animated 'The Peephole'.[46] But these musical hints of perversion are all subtle, doubtless designed to lull audience members into a false sense of security. When the violence finally comes, with the reprise of 'The Murder', it seems all the more shocking.

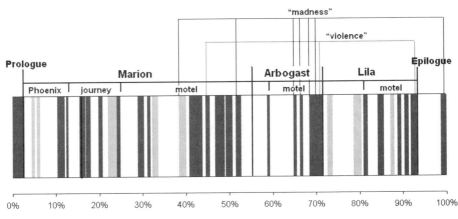

Figure 1.13   The relationship in *Psycho* of 'madness' music to 'violence' music

The psychiatrist's pedantic lecture at the start of the epilogue gives the impression that with Norman's arrest the case is closed. Closure is suggested as well by the relationship that thus far has been established between the 'madness' and 'violence' cues: musical indicators of cause have been followed by representations of the appropriate effect, and the last statement of the 'violence' music sounds especially conclusive. During the scene in the jail cell, however, the quiet 'madness' music that veils the monologue hints that 'Mother', regardless of what becomes of Norman, has a long life ahead of her. More chillingly, the bold iteration of the 'madness' motif at the very end of 'Finale' (Figure 1.14), as the camera briefly shows the recovery of Marion's car, implies that the swamp still has secrets to reveal. The otherwise neat binary pattern of antecedent and consequent musical ideas is broken; as was the case with Marion's 'temptation' music, the questions raised by Norman's 'madness' music go unanswered.

A sound appreciation

Judging from the 'final revised' screenplay, the 'suggestions for music' documents, and the various anecdotes pertaining to the shower scene, Hitchcock conceived *Psycho* as a film with relatively little music. But one thing led to another, and eventually the film was fitted with the score discussed above. "As for Bernard Herrmann's 'background' music," Raymond Durgnat asks, "would *Psycho* be itself without it?" (2002: 2). The answer is 'no', but *Psycho* would also not be 'itself' without Janet Leigh or Anthony Perkins, or without the opening series of crane shots that were originally intended to be a single helicopter zoom. Minus some of Herrmann's cues, or with music by another composer, *Psycho* would likely still be a powerful film, but it would be a film different from the one we know.

As Herrmann biographer Steven C. Smith notes, Hitchcock was unusually generous in his praise of the *Psycho* music, going so far as to grant, in a 1961 interview, that the film "depended heavily on Herrmann's music for its tension and sense of pervading doom" (2002: 237).[47] Hitchcock told the interviewer that "thirty-three percent of the effect of *Psycho* was due to the music" (quoted in *ibid.*: 241), and years later

Figure 1.14   Psycho, 'Finale', bb. 17–18

screenwriter Joseph Stefano recalled that Hitchcock "gave [Herrmann] more credit than anyone else he ever spoke of" (quoted in Rebello, 1990: 139). Indeed, Hitchcock rewarded Herrmann with not just credit but cash; after revenue from *Psycho* started to pour in, the director raised the composer's fee from the originally contracted $17,500 to $34,501.[48]

Obviously, Herrmann's music transformed the film from what it might have been into what it now is. As Hitchcock surely knew, however, to quantify the extent of this transformation is ridiculous. And even a qualitative explanation remains elusive. Nevertheless, while the precise nature of what Herrmann's music did for the film is perhaps ineffable, it is at least possible to articulate something that the music did not do. For example, it certainly seems not to be the case, as Stefano has recently suggested to Sullivan,[49] that Herrmann "[took] the picture and turned it into an opera" (2006: 255).

This was intended to be a compliment, and what Stefano probably meant is that in his view Herrmann's score made the content of *Psycho* – its characters, its locales, its action, its plot – somehow larger than life. Herrmann knew plenty about opera. For his first Hollywood project, *Citizen Kane* (Orson Welles, 1941), he produced a scene for a fictional opera in the grand nineteenth-century style, and between 1943 and 1951 he composed a four-act opera treatment of Emily Brontë's *Wuthering Heights*. Herrmann was well aware of opera's characteristic gestures, its action-stopping arias in which heightened emotion is not just expressed but explored, and its propensity to build its stories around just a handful of archetypes.[50] He was well aware, too, that any attempt to amplify elements of a film narrative by means of grafted-on music would have been grievously contrary to the Hitchcock aesthetic.

In 1936, in an essay titled 'Why I Make Melodramas', Hitchcock granted that the term 'melodrama' is generally taken to mean a "naïve type of play or story, in which every situation [is] overdrawn and every emotion underlined". Then he explained that he was nevertheless attracted to melodrama. "I use melodrama because I have a tremendous desire for understatement in film-making," he wrote. "Understatement in a dramatic situation powerful enough to be called melodramatic is, I think, the way to achieve naturalism and realism." Realism, Hitchcock noted, is his "greatest desire". But to be literally realistic on the screen would be unwise, for real life, "in all but its more exceptional aspects, such as crime", tends to be very dull. Instead of genuine realism, he sought to portray "[what] might as well be called ultra-realism" by being melodramatic albeit in an understated way.[51]

Hitchcock held to that ideal, more or less, throughout his entire career. A few of his films do indeed centre on characters that in themselves are fascinating (one thinks of the glamorous protagonist of 1955's *To Catch a Thief*, or the severely neurotic title character of 1964's *Marnie*). But the vast majority of Hitchcock films exemplify the director's adage, quoted and paraphrased so many times in the literature that it has attained the status of holy writ, that the most intriguing dramas are those that deal with ordinary persons who find themselves, by accident, in extraordinary circumstances.

Few would argue that Norman Bates is an 'ordinary' person, but he is first portrayed as ordinary enough and certainly all the other characters in *Psycho* fall into that category. To be sure, with his violence music Herrmann helps make shockingly vivid what little cinematic action there is in *Psycho*. Beyond that, the score, like the film as a whole, is remarkably understated. Most often, even in the cues that pertain to Norman, the music depicts not what the characters are actually doing but what they might be thinking or feeling. Herrmann's music, it could be argued, effectively invites the audience simply to 'get inside the heads' of the various characters. In keeping with Hitchcock's lifelong goals, the score succeeds largely because of its understatement, not because it inflates the characters or their situations to operatic proportions. While *Psycho* is certainly not an 'operatic' film, it is nonetheless interesting that screenwriter Stefano would use a musical term to describe its totality.

Near the beginning of a recent essay on the effect that horror films in general have on their audiences, Michael Grant digresses briefly on the subject of poetry. He quotes from Wasserman, who opined that since the end of the eighteenth century

> the poet has been required to conceive his own structure of order, his own more-than-linguistic syntax, and so to engage that structure the poetic act is creative both of a cosmic system and of the poems made possible by that system. (1968: 172)

Grant makes the point that, seen in this light, the essence of poetry is not poetry *per se* – that is, verbal matter, with all its concomitant meanings and resonances – but, rather, the act of designing the framework into which verbal matter somehow fits. He writes tellingly:

> One might say that, whatever else may appear to engage the poem's interest, its fundamental concern is with its own processes of coming into being. The crucial analogy is, of course, with music, a condition to which Psycho unquestionably aspires, an aspiration driven home by Herrmann's score. (2003: 120)

Grant is not the first to suggest that *Psycho*, and perhaps Hitchcock's work as a whole, is somehow 'musical' in nature. Commenting specifically on *Psycho*, Bellour wrote that the black-and-white film was issued between the "colorful symphonies" of *North by Northwest* and *The Birds* (1986: 311), that the playing out of its themes involves not just "harmony" but "counterpoint" (*ibid.*: 314–15), that the progression of its "three movements" features a "circular orchestration" (*ibid.*: 316), that the animation of the title sequence is marked by the visual equivalent of "vibrato" (*ibid.*: 325). During his interview with Hitchcock, Truffaut remarked apropos of *Psycho*:

> Even better than the killing, in the sense of its harmony, is the scene in which Perkins handles the mop and broom to clean away any traces of the crime. The whole construction of the picture suggests a sort of scale of the abnormal. First there is a scene of adultery, then a theft, then one crime

> *followed by another, and, finally, psychopathy. Each passage puts us on a*
> *higher note of the scale.* (1984: 277)

While Bellour's and Truffaut's use of musical terminology in describing Hitchcock's work might be dismissed as merely metaphorical, Brown's is substantive. Remarking on Herrmann's "anti-'tune' tendency" and characteristic "isolation of harmonic colors," Brown writes:

> *It would seem that Hitchcock provided Herrmann with the impetus to*
> *develop certain devices and to carry them further than he had previously*
> *done. One reason for this might be the* musical *nature of Hitchcock's*
> *cinematic style.* (1982: 23–4; emphasis is Brown's)

What makes Hitchcock's films 'musical' is a quality that, ironically, Brown finds absent from Herrmann's work. "The entire body of shots of a given film follows a prearranged plan," Brown writes; the result is that "[Each shot] has meaning only when considered in the context of the shots surrounding it and, more broadly, within the temporal elaboration of the entire artistic conception" (*ibid.*: 23, 24).

Had Herrmann offered Hitchcock cues that followed "Western music's natural tendency to organize itself into temporally elaborated blocks" – in other words, scores based on graspable melodies and logical chord progressions – the linearity of these cues would have either "gild[ed] the lily of Hitchcock's ingeniously organized filmic totalities or... cut into their effectiveness by setting up conflicting movements." Built as they are of fragmentary motifs and harmonies not syntactically related to whatever comes before or after, Herrmann's cues "set up a strong opposition" to the "horizontally created synchronicity" of Hitchcock's shots and sequences. Thus, Herrmann's non-conventional music is the ideal complement to Hitchcock's conventionally 'musical' style (*ibid.*).

Brown's assessment makes sense when Herrmann's music, for *Psycho* or any other Hitchcock film, is examined instant by instant *vis-à-vis* the footage it accompanies. But just as a plan governs the typical Hitchcock film, so does a plan, likely not so much prearranged as responsive, govern the typical score that Herrmann produced for Hitchcock. In the case of the *Psycho* score the plan has been somewhat revealed (it is hoped) in the foregoing analysis, but it is patently apparent when the music is removed from its filmic context.

On two occasions Herrmann decontextualized his *Psycho* music. In December 1968, shortly after he completed the score for François Truffaut's *The Bride Wore Black* (1968),[52] he extracted eleven cues from *Psycho* and arranged them, in advance of a recording session with the London Philharmonic Orchestra, into a suite titled '*Psycho*: A Narrative for Orchestra'.[53] And in October 1975, just two and a half months before his death, Herrmann led London's National Philharmonic Orchestra in a recording of what was billed as the "complete" *Psycho* score.[54] In terms of musical structure, it seems significant that Herrmann, in the first commercial recording of a score that by this time seemed likely to enter the pantheon of film music, opted to omit the brief reprise of 'The Murder' that in the soundtrack occurs just before 'Discovery' and doubtless for some audience members represents *Psycho*'s climax. Even more significant, in terms of a decontextualized film score, are the tempos Herrmann chose for the recording (see Table 1.1). For only six cues ('Patrol Car', 'The Murder', 'The Water', 'The Car', 'Cabin 1', and 'The Bedroom') does Herrmann in the NPO recording opt for a pace quicker than what is heard in the film, and in all these cases the differences of timing are only slight. For most of the cues, especially those that underscore not overt action but the quiet workings of a character's mind, Herrmann takes tempos considerably slower than those of the soundtrack.[55] Comparable alterations of tempo – specifically, an exaggerated slowing of 'interior' cues – are heard in his recording of '*Psycho*: A Narrative for Orchestra', and in a 1970 interview the composer was asked to account for the differences. Herrmann explained:

> Well, one was the tempo for the film, and the other is the tempo of a concert piece. The tempo that's used in the film is based upon visual relationships. In a straight piece of music, the relationships are musical.[56]

Because it is embedded in a film soundtrack, Herrmann's *Psycho* score is hardly a 'straight' piece of music. Nevertheless, as is pointed out by the astute analyses of Steiner and Bruce, the score features relationships that are indeed purely musical. Moreover, the score demonstrates a bounty of supportive relationships not just with the basic narrative of Hitchcock's film but also with its structure. If the flow of *Psycho*'s imagery can be construed as 'musical,' surely the same adjective applies to the totality of Herrmann's musically unconventional score. Between imagery/narrative and music there is friction aplenty, but all of it is provocative of both thought and emotion. To use the term metaphorically, harmony – unsettled, yet perfect in its way – exists between *Psycho* and its music. In the score as in the film, form follows function, and perhaps therein lies its genius.

Notes

1. These reviews, and others, are quoted in Janet Leigh's autobiographical *Psycho* (1990: 99–102).
2. Filmed at Universal Studios and distributed by Paramount, *Psycho* was produced by Hitchcock himself on a budget of only $800,000. In his 1962 interview with Truffaut, Hitchcock said that the film had grossed more than $15 million worldwide (Truffaut, 1984: 283), but clearly this was an understatement. Citing a report from *Variety*, Kapsis notes that by November 1960 the film had grossed approximately $18 million in Canada and the United States alone (1992: 258).
3. Crowther's first review of *Psycho* appeared on 17 June 1960. His revised opinion was included in a column titled 'The Year's Best Films' (25 December 1960). At least some of the early negative reviews, Rebello suggests, were prompted by the circumstances under which critics were required to experience the film. Rebello quotes from a 1973 *Observer* (London) reminiscence by Kenneth Tynan:

> *Hitchcock's major sin was to have antagonized the critics before they ever saw the picture. He had urged them by letter not to divulge the ending, and he had announced that nobody would be admitted to the cinema once the film had begun. Thus they went to the press show already huffy and affronted, and what they reviewed was not so much the film itself as the effect of its publicity on their egos.* (1990: 184)

4. Earlier in his review, Sarris concurs with critics from the Parisian journal *Cahiers du Cinéma*, who throughout the 1950s argued that Hitchcock's Hollywood films marked him as an important artist. "A close inspection of *Psycho*", he writes, "indicates not only that the French have been right all along, but that Hitchcock is the most daring avant-garde film-maker in America today." Sarris ends the review by declaring that *Psycho* is "the first American movie since [Orson Welles's 1958] *Touch of Evil* to stand in the same creative rank as the great European films."

5. The major early psychoanalytic interpretations include a chapter in Robin Wood's *Hitchcock's Films* (1965) (an expanded version of 'Psychoanalyse de *Psycho*', *Cahiers du Cinéma* 113, November 1960), Jean Douchet's *Alfred Hitchcock* (1967) (the *Psycho* material of which derives from 'Hitch et son public,' *Cahiers du Cinéma* 113, October 1960), and the chapter titled 'Inside Norman Bates' in Durgnat's own *Films and Feelings* (1967).

6. In the introduction to their anthology *Post-Theory: Reconstructing Film Studies* (1996), Bordwell and Carroll explain:

> *What we call Theory is an abstract body of thought which came into prominence in Anglo-American film studies during the 1970s. The most famous avatar of Theory was that aggregate of doctrines derived from Lacanian psychoanalysis, Structuralist semiotics, Post-Structuralist literary theory, and variants of Althusserian Marxism. Here, unabashedly, was Grand Theory — perhaps the first that cinema studies ever had. The Theory was put forth as the indispensable frame of reference for understanding all filmic phenomena: the activities of the film spectator, the construction of the film text, the social and political functions of cinema, and the development of film technology and the industry.* (xiii)

7. A seminal essay in point-of-view film criticism is by Laura Mulvey (1975). Taking a strong feminist stance, Mulvey in this essay discusses depictions of the female body in a great many Hollywood films; she examines Hitchcock's *Rear Window*, *Vertigo* and *Marnie* but, curiously, does not mention *Psycho*. Mulvey's ideas are expanded upon, and applied specifically to *Psycho*, in Raymond Bellour's 'Psychosis, Neurosis, Perversion' and Janet Bergstrom's 'Enunciation and Sexual Difference', both published in *Camera Obscura* in the summer of 1979. A thorough feminist analysis of *Psycho* is by Carol J. Clover (1987).

8. Along with the 1960 *Psycho*, Herrmann scored Hitchcock's *The Trouble with Harry* (1955), *The Man Who Knew Too Much* (1956), *The Wrong Man* (1956), *Vertigo* (1958), *North by Northwest* (1959) and *Marnie* (1964). Herrmann served as musical advisor for *The Birds* (1963), which features no conventional score but

only birdlike electronic sounds created on the trautonium by Remi Gassmann and Oskar Sala; Herrmann began work on Hitchcock's *Torn Curtain* (1966), but before the film was finished he was dismissed and his score was replaced with one by John Addison.

9. Brown's essay is perhaps best known for its coining of the term 'Hitchcock chord' to describe the inherently unstable harmony – a minor triad to which is added a major seventh – that figures horizontally in the title music of *Vertigo* and vertically in the title music of *Psycho*. The essay is also well known, unfortunately, for a rhythmically incorrect transcription of the violin triplet figure heard in the fifth bar of the *Psycho* prelude.

10. Bruce's book is a revision of a New York University Ph.D. dissertation. While Bruce covers the full range of Herrmann's music for films, the only two scores to which he devotes entire chapters are those for *Psycho* and *Vertigo*. Royal S. Brown was in contact with Bruce while the latter was writing his dissertation, and Brown's explication of Herrmann's trademark minor–major seventh chord draws heavily from Bruce's work.

11. Steiner's study was subsequently published, in instalments, in Elmer Bernstein's *Film Music Notebook*. Long out of print, Bernstein's *Film Music Notebook* has recently been made available in facsimile, through subscription, by the Los Angeles-based Film Music Society.

12. Still in the editing stages at the time of this writing, Sullivan's book is not so much a musicological study as an interpretative overview from a music-oriented perspective. I am grateful to Jack Sullivan for sharing with me not only his in-progress manuscript but also some of his research materials.

13. For a history of the 'startle' effect in cinema, see Baird (2002), and for a scientific explanation of the phenomenon, see Davis, Walker and Lee (1997).

14. This example and those that follow are © 1960 by Ensign Music Corporation and are used with permission of the publisher.

15. The URL for *Turtles TV* is http://humor.about.com/gi/dynamic/offsite.htm?zi= 1/XJ&sdn=humor&zu=http%3A%2F%2Fwww.turtletvnetwork.com.

16. James W. Merrick, 'Hitchcock Regimen for a Psycho', *New York Times*, 27 December 1959. Rebello (1990: 105) properly attributes the article to Merrick, but he says the interview appeared not in the *New York Times* but in *Variety*.

17. Just as French director Georges Clouzot did with his 1955 *Les Diaboliques*, often said to be an influence on *Psycho*, Hitchcock dramatically implored the audience not to reveal the film's ending to anyone. But whereas Clouzot's request was offered as a text message during the film's closing credits, Hitchcock's came in the form of spoken statements in featurettes screened during *Psycho*'s initial theatrical run.

18. According to Hitchcock biographer Donald Spoto, the term 'MacGuffin' was first applied to the director's misleading plot devices by Angus MacPhail (1983: 159). MacPhail had been a schoolmate of Hitchcock and in the 1930s was head of the scenario department at the Gaumont-British studios.

19. Doubtless in an attempt to emphasize *Psycho*'s erotic 'red herring,' the lobby posters also depict – in a much smaller image – actor John Gavin naked from the waist up. The posters include a small headshot of Anthony Perkins as well, but his face is simply intense, not murderous.

20. Universal 20251. More cryptically, the illustration on the covers of the VHS and DVD releases of Gus Van Sant's 1998 remake of *Psycho* (Universal 84642 and Universal 20538) depicts only a hand clawing at a bloody translucent curtain. Below the image are the film's title, in crimson, and a teasing blurb that says: "Check in. Relax. Take a shower."

21. Designers of book covers, interestingly, have generally eschewed the scream icon. James Naremore's *Filmguide to Psycho* (1973), the earliest book devoted specifically to the film, features on its cover only the imagery that at the time was standard for Indiana University Press's filmguide series. More recently, the cover of Robin Wood's *Hitchcock's Films Revisited* (1989) shows Leigh not as victim but as actress, being directed by Hitchcock. Leigh's own *Psycho: Behind the Scenes of the Classic Thriller* (1995) opts for the post-scream image of her character's dead stare. Stephen Rebello's *Alfred Hitchcock and the Making of Psycho* (1990) contains two pages of stills from the shower scene, but in a slash-like inset the cover offers only a peek at four of them, and none of them depicts the scream. Raymond Durgnat's *A Long Hard Look at 'Psycho'* (2002) has on its cover 'staring' images of the characters played by Anthony Perkins and Vera Miles; the cover of Robert Kolker's *Alfred Hitchcock's Psycho: A Casebook* (2004) shows only the knife-wielding character who provokes the scream.

22. For an insightful study of Hitchcock's use of non-musical sound, see Elisabeth Weis's *The Silent Scream: Alfred Hitchcock's Sound Track* (1982).

23. Cameron's book is based on a symposium that took place in October 1973 at the George Eastman House/International Museum of Photography in Rochester, New York. Herrmann's statement, which includes remarks on his scores for *Citizen Kane* and *Fahrenheit 451* (1966) as well as on his score for *Psycho*, is a transcript of remarks delivered orally.

24. The document titled 'Suggestions for Placement of Music', along with other production materials related to *Psycho*, is in the Hitchcock collection at the Margaret Herrick Library in Beverly Hills, California.

25. The 25 January memo calls for music to "cover the scene of Norman pushing [Marion's] car into the swamp and watching it disappear". Hitchcock's early music notes request that music accompany the detective's tentative ascent of the stairs of the interior of the Bates house, but a memo dated 2 February asks that this be cut. Whereas Hitchcock at first wanted the music to end completely after the discovery of Mrs Bates's corpse, in a memo dated 4 February he writes, "Start music on cut to Norman in Interior of Police Station jail. Continue as camera dollies in and cover last speech. Music ends on fade End title."

26. The scene without music may be difficult to imagine, but it is easy enough to experience. As a bonus feature, the 'Collector's Edition' DVD of *Psycho* offers back-to-back presentations of the shower scene with and without Herrmann's cue.

27. To be precise, *Psycho* lasts 1 hour, 48 minutes and 12 seconds. The character of Marion Crane closes the shower curtain at the film's 46:24 mark. Nine seconds later she turns on the water and at 46:58 the murderer stealthily makes his/her entrance. The actual stabbing sequence begins, simultaneous with the cue titled 'The Murder', at 47:10; after 19 seconds (and thirty-four film cuts) the murderer exits; Herrmann's cue ends at 48:06, the music broken off by the crisp noise of Marion pulling down the shower curtain.

28. The document is Paramount Cue Sheet no. 19,752, dated 1 July 1960. Items listed separately but which function as components of larger sequences are all elements of the 'Prelude' and its three recapitulations. Throughout his score, Herrmann used the term '*Psycho* Theme' to refer to the lyric music that is introduced in bar 39 of the title music; for those segments of the title music that do not feature this lyric theme, Herrmann used the term '*Psycho* Prelude', and upon their recurrences he called them 'Flight', 'Patrol Car', and 'The Rainstorm'. The cue that is titled 'Prelude' consists of four different segments labelled 'Psycho Prelude' and three basically identical segments labelled '*Psycho* Theme'. The sequence titled 'Flight' consists, on the cue sheet, of a brief 'Flight' segment and a '*Psycho* theme' segment that is almost twice the length of the same-named items heard in the title music. 'Patrol Car' consists, on the cue sheet, of two similar but not identical items labelled 'Patrol Car' and two items – one 9 seconds in length, the other 15 seconds – labelled '*Psycho* Theme'. On the cue sheet, 'The Rainstorm' consists of six items labelled 'The Rainstorm' that range from 13 to 32 seconds in length and five brief items labelled '*Psycho* Theme'.

29. An additional sequence was composed and recorded but ultimately not used in the film. The sequence is titled 'The Cleanup' and was to have occurred between 'The Car' and 'The Swamp'.

30. Recorded in Barking Assembly Hall, London, on 2 October 1975, *Psycho: Bernard Herrmann's Complete Music for Alfred Hitchcock's Classic Suspense Thriller* is available on Unicorn-Kanchana UKCD 2021. The recording, perhaps significantly, does not include the brief reprise of 'The Murder' that in the film soundtrack occurs just before 'Discovery'.

31. In the case of the cue titled 'The Rainstorm', which accompanies Marion's drive from the used-car lot to the Bates Motel, only the first 2 minutes and 10 seconds are overlaid with imagined voices.

32. For a probing analysis of the late Mrs Bates's verbal contributions to the final scenes of *Psycho*, see Chion (1999).

33. This view was first articulated by Wood in 1965, and then expanded by Naremore and Bellour in the 1970s.

34. The 'stabbing' music is alluded to, but not quoted exactly, in the brief cue titled 'The Body' that accompanies Norman's return to the motel room after apparently finding 'Mother' covered with blood.

35. Readers who subscribe to the idea that *Psycho*'s shower scene represents a bipartite narrative's moment of separation might be interested to know that in the novel on which the screenplay is based the victim is not stabbed to death but,

rather, is instantly beheaded (Bloch, 1959: 51). Bloch's novel is based, loosely, on events that occurred in rural Wisconsin in the mid-1950s. For gory details, see Gollmar (1981); Gollmar is the judge who tried the murderer's case and found him not guilty by reason of insanity.

36. A subdivision of the narrative based solely on locale might well regard Marion's activity at the used-car lot as a separate unit. As will be shown, the placement of music indeed supports such a view.

37. Brown further explains:

> In fact, what in Herrmann often strikes the listener as a particularly attractive melody actually owes most of its character to a striking harmonic progression or coloration, with instrumental hues also playing a considerable role... the core of most Herrmann themes generally consists of a motive a measure or two in length. The extension of such a motive into what resembles a theme more often than not is accomplished by the repetition of the motive, either literally or in harmonic sequence. (1994: 162)

38. In an endnote to his commentary on Herrmann's music in general, Palmer (1990: 293) suggests that the phrase originated with an inscription that Herrmann made over the final bars of Palmer's personal copy of Herrmann's score for *Taxi Driver* (Martin Scorsese, 1975). Regarding Herrmann's self-quotation at the very end of his last film project, Palmer writes:

> The unexpected reappearance of this motif at the end of Taxi Driver *may suggest that Herrmann viewed the hero, [played by Robert] de Niro, as a madman; or it may be that the motif was, for Herrmann, a musical synonym for mortality. If that is so Herrmann wrote his own musical epitaph.*

Brown, who uses the phrase but does not cite a source for it, notes that almost the same motive is used in Herrmann's 1936–38 cantata *Moby Dick* and 1950 opera *Wuthering Heights* (1982: 42–3).

39. Once Marion arrives at the Bates Motel this music is not heard again. But there are hints of the 'Prelude' music – not the lyric motif but only the rhythmic elements – in the cue titled 'The Search (A)' that accompanies the montage during which Arbogast is shown visiting various motels. Arbogast is never depicted actually behind the wheel of a car, but a car is obviously his mode of transportation from one motel to the next.

40. If one were inclined to split the narrative's 'Marion' section into not three portions but four, defined by locale, the placement of the 'Patrol Car' cue in advance of the scene at the used-car lot easily supports the idea that *each* of the 'Marion' portions is preceded by music.

41. The proportional graphs in the figures represent the entire duration of *Psycho*. If one were to create a comparable graph that contained only the 'motel' portion of the 'Marion' section, the graph would show that the cue titled 'The Murder' occurs 65 percent of the way through the entire section. More significantly, the scene during which Marion prepares for her shower, accompanied by neither

dialogue nor music, begins at the duration's 62 percent mark; 62 percent is consistent with the so-called Golden Mean, or Golden Proportion, which numerous analysts have shown to mark the climaxes of compositions by various twentieth-century composers (especially Webern and Bartók) and of compositions in general from the late eighteenth century. For more on the Golden Mean and its applications to music, see Rothstein (1995: 159–83).

42. A fade-to-black follows the murder of Arbogast. After Lila's encounter with 'Mother' there is a slow dissolve to the crowd scene outside the police station.

43. Bruce (1985: 208–9) makes a case that this music is also echoed in 'The Hill'.

44. The cue underscores, not the actual scene at the swamp, but the scene immediately preceding it, during which Norman finishes his work at the cabin. Bruce (1985: 215) notes that, in spite of its misleading title, the cue features synchronization points that suggest it was indeed intended to accompany the pre-swamp action. Among the more prominent of these, he writes (197), are the sounding of the three-note 'madness' motif just as Norman closes the door upon entering the room and its recurrence at the end of the scene when Norman, now out of the porch, is startled by the headlights of a passing car.

45. Bruce (1985: 186–93) links the content of 'The Search (B)' and 'The First Floor' with the harmonies first heard in 'The City' and then echoed in 'The Car Lot', 'The Window', 'The Parlor' and 'The Bathroom'. Following the example of Bellour and other critics who argue that certain camera angles in *Psycho* force the audience member into the role of dispassionate spy, he writes that all seven of these cues are "bound into a paradigm which explores the voyeuristic, penetrating, aggressive glance" (191).

46. The same rhythmic figure, Bruce observes, is also present in 'The Office' and 'The Curtain', and he suggests that in all cases it expresses "something of the mental state of the obsessive" (1985: 204).

47. The interview from which Smith takes the phrase was with Michael Ratcliffe. Headlined 'Composing the "Emotional Scenery" for the Screen,' it appeared in the *Sheffield Telegraph* of 25 March 1961.

48. The first figure is given by Smith (2002: 240), the second by Rebello (1990: 139).

49. Stefano's interview with Sullivan took place on 15 April 2005.

50. In the statement included in the Cameron book, Herrmann makes reference to operas by Gluck, Berg, Orff, Debussy, Massenet and Richard Strauss (1980: 117–29).

51. The essay, apparently from a newspaper or magazine, is reprinted on *The MacGuffin* website (http://www.labyrinth.net.au/%7Emuffin/melodramas_c.html). Ken Mogg, editor of *The MacGuffin*, notes that the original source of the essay is unknown. It is listed neither in Jane Sloan's *Alfred Hitchcock: A Guide to References and Resources* (1993) nor in the extensive bibliography appended to Sidney Gottlieb's *Hitchcock on Hitchcock: Selected Writings and Interviews* (1995).

52. In May and June of 1966 Herrmann composed the score for Truffaut's *Fahrenheit 451*; earlier that year he worked on music for Hitchcock's *Torn Curtain*, and

allegedly it was a dispute over the score that marked the end of his relationship with Hitchcock. Herrmann composed no film music in 1967, but he did produce a chamber music work, for clarinet and string quartet, titled *Souvenirs de voyage*.

53. As conducted by Herrmann on 12 December 1968, the eleven-movement *Psycho: A Narrative for Orchestra* (also known as *Psycho: Suite for Strings*) lasts 14 minutes and 29 seconds and consists of the cues titled 'Prelude', 'The City', 'The Rainstorm', 'The Madhouse', 'The Murder', 'The Water', 'The Swamp', 'The Stairs', 'The Knife', 'The Cellar' and 'Finale'. Perusal of currently available recordings reveals suites of shorter duration (a five-movement grouping of 'Prelude', 'The City', 'The Rainstorm', 'The Murder' and 'Finale' and a three-movement set comprising only 'Prelude', 'The Murder' and 'Finale'), but these are not of Herrmann's making.

54. A recording of the actual complete score, including the cue titled 'The Cleanup' that was composed but omitted from the film, was made in 1997 by Joel McNeely and the Royal Scottish National Orchestra.

55. The McNeely recording, noted above, likewise features tempos generally slower than those heard in the film.

56. Zador and Rose (1998: 222). The interview was conducted in September 1970 and portions of it first appeared in the *Los Angeles Free Press*.

References

Allen, R., and Gonzales, W. I. (eds) (1999), *Alfred Hitchcock: Centenary Essays*, London: British Film Institute.

Anobile, R. (1974), *Alfred Hitchcock's Psycho*, New York: Avon.

Baird, R. (2000), 'The Startle Effect: Implications for Spectator Cognition and Media Theory', *Film Quarterly*, 53(3), 12–24.

Bellour, R. (1986), 'Psychosis, Neurosis, Perversion,' in M. Dettlebaum and L. Poague (eds), *A Hitchcock Reader*, Ames: University of Iowa Press (first published in *Camera Journal*, 1979, 3/4, 311–31).

Bloch, R. (1959), *Psycho*, New York: Simon & Schuster.

Bordwell, D., and Carroll, N. (eds) (1996), *Post-Theory: Reconstructing Film Studies*, Madison: University of Wisconsin Press.

Brown, R. S. (1982), 'Herrmann, Hitchcock, and the Music of the Irrational', *Cinema Journal*, 21(2), 14–49.

Brown, R. S. (1994), *Overtones and Undertones: Reading Film Music*, Berkeley: University of California Press.

Bruce, G. (1985), *Bernard Herrmann: Film Music and Narrative*, Ann Arbor: UMI Research Press.

Burt, G. (1994), *The Art of Film Music*, Boston: Northeastern University Press.

Cameron, E. (ed.) (1980), *Sound and the Cinema: The Coming of Sound to American Film*, Pleasantville, NY: Redgrave.

Chion, M. (1999), *The Voice in Cinema*, trans. Claudia Gorbman, New York: Columbia University Press (first published in 1982, *La Voix au cinéma*, Paris: Editions de l'Etoile).

Clover, C. (1987), 'Her Body, Himself: Gender in the Slasher Film', *Representations*, 20, 187–228.

Cohen, T. (1995), 'Beyond "The Gaze": Žižek, Hitchcock, and the American Sublime', *American Literary History*, 7(2), 350–78.

Crowther, B. (1960a), Review of *Psycho*, *New York Times*, 17 June.

Crowther, B. (1960b), 'The Year's Best Films', *New York Times*, 25 December, p. X3.

Davis, M., Walker, D., and Lee, Y. (1997), 'Amygdala and Bed Nucleus of the Stria Terminalis: Differential Roles in Fear and Anxiety Measured with the Acoustic Startle Reflex', *Philosophical Transactions: Biological Sciences*, 352(1362), 1675–87.

Douchet, J. (1967), *Alfred Hitchcock*, Paris: Editions de l'Herne.

Durgnat, R. (1967), *Films and Feelings*, Boston: MIT Press.

Durgnat, R. (2002), *A Long Hard Look at 'Psycho'*, London: British Film Institute.

Gollmar, R. (1981), *Edward Gein: America's Most Bizarre Murderer*, Delevan, WI: Chas. Hallberg & Co.

Gottlieb, S. (ed.) (1995), *Hitchcock on Hitchcock: Selected Writings and Interviews*, Berkeley: University of California Press.

Gottlieb, S., and Brookhouse, C. (eds) (2002), *Framing Hitchcock: Selected Essays from the Hitchcock Annual*, Detroit: Wayne State University Press.

Grant, M. (2003), 'Philosophical (Horror) Investigations: On the Question of the Horror Film', in S. J. Schneider and D. Shaw (eds), *Dark Thoughts: Philosophic Reflections on Cinematic Horror*, Lanham, MD: Scarecrow Press, pp. 118–34.

Jameson, F. (1982), 'Reading Hitchcock', *October*, 23, 15–42.

Kapsis, R. E. (1992), *Hitchcock: The Making of a Reputation*, Chicago: University of Chicago Press.

Knight, D., and McKnight, G. (2003), '*American Psycho*: Horror, Satire, Aesthetics, and Identification,' in S. J. Schneider and D. Shaw (eds), *Dark Thoughts: Philosophic Reflections on Cinematic Horror*, Lanham, MD: Scarecrow Press, pp. 212–29.

Kolker, R. (ed.) (2004), *Alfred Hitchcock's Psycho: A Casebook*, Oxford: Oxford University Press.

Leigh, J. (with C. Nickens) (1995), *Psycho: Behind the Scenes of the Classic Thriller*, New York: Harmony Books.

Mulvey, L. (1975), 'Visual Pleasure and Narrative Cinema', *Screen*, 16(3), 6–18.

Naremore, J. (1973), *Filmguide to Psycho*, Bloomington: Indiana University Press.

Palmer, C. (1990), *The Composer in Hollywood*, London: Marion Boyars.

Palmer, R. B. (1986), 'The Metafictional Hitchcock: The Experience of Viewing and the Viewing of Experience in *Rear Window* and *Psycho*', *Cinema Journal*, 25(2), 4–19.

Prendergast, R. (1992), *Film Music: A Neglected Art*, revised edn, New York: W. W. Norton (first published 1977).

Psycho screenplay, Alfred Hitchcock Papers, Margaret Herrick Library, Beverly Hills, California.

Rebello, S. (1990), *Alfred Hitchcock and the Making of Psycho*, New York: St. Martin's Griffin.

Rothman, W. (1982), *Hitchcock: The Murderous Gaze*, Cambridge, MA: Harvard University Press.

Rothstein, E. (1995), *Emblems of Mind: The Inner Life of Music and Mathematics*, New York: Avon.

Sarris, A. (1960), Review of *Psycho*, *Village Voice*, 11 August.

Sloan, J. (1993), *Alfred Hitchcock: A Guide to References and Resources*, New York: G. K. Hall.

Smith, S. C. (2002), *A Heart at Fire's Center: The Life and Music of Bernard Herrmann*, 2nd edition, Berkeley: University of California Press (first published 1991).

Spoto, D. (1983), *The Dark Side of Genius: The Life of Alfred Hitchcock*, New York: Ballantine Books.

Steiner, F. (1974–75), 'Herrmann's "Black and White" Music for Hitchcock's *Psycho*', *Film Music Notebook*, 1, 28–36, and 2, 26–46.

Sterritt, D. (1993), *The Films of Alfred Hitchcock*, Cambridge: Cambridge University Press.

Sullivan, J. (2006), *Hitchcock's Music*, New Haven: Yale University Press.

Toles, G. (1984), '"If Thine Eye Offend Thee …": *Psycho* and the Art of Infection', *New Literary History*, 15(3), 159–74.

Truffaut, F. (1984), *Hitchcock*, New York: Simon & Schuster.

Wasserman, E. (1968), *The Subtler Language*, Baltimore: The Johns Hopkins University Press.

Weis, E. (1982), *The Silent Scream: Alfred Hitchcock's Sound Track*, Rutherford, NJ: Associated University Presses.

Wood, R. (1965), *Hitchcock's Films*, London: Tantivy Press.

Wood, R. (1989), *Hitchcock's Films Revisited*, New York: Columbia University Press.

Zador, L., and Rose, G. (1998), 'A Conversation with Bernard Herrmann,' in *Film Music I*, Los Angeles: The Film Music Society, pp. 209–53.

2   An Audiovisual Foreshadowing in *Psycho*

Scott Murphy

In June 1960, throngs of moviegoers waited in line to see Alfred Hitchcock's new film *Psycho*, the relatively low-budget 'chiller-thriller' that would steer plenty of people away from their showers and plenty of revenue into the studio's coffers. Odds are that these moviegoers saw the film from the beginning, which would have included its opening main titles. One reason for this was the stipulation that moviegoers would not be admitted to the theatre once the film had begun. Hitchcock was supposedly concerned that those who arrived fashionably late might miss Janet Leigh's screen time altogether, as her character is murdered about two-fifths into the film. Of course, this was also an effective publicity gimmick. But the film-makers had other, more aesthetic, reasons for promoting the main title as integral to the film. Saul Bass, the titles designer for *Psycho*, had already staked this claim in the mid-1950s in his work with director Otto Preminger, as Bass recounts in a documentary on his film-title work, *Bass on Titles* (1977):

> I had felt, for some time, that the audience's involvement with the film should really begin with the very first frame. But you have to remember that, until then, titles had tended to be lists of dull credits, mostly ignored or used for popcorn time. So there seemed to be a real opportunity to use titles in a new way, to actually create a climate for the story that was about to unfold.

Indeed, as late as the early 1950s, it was not uncommon to draw the curtains only after the main titles – the "lists of dull credits" – had finished and the film proper had commenced. However, this practice began to change after the premiere of Preminger's *The Man with the Golden Arm* in 1955. The film's main title pits Bass's simple yet unnerving visuals – culminating in the famous crooked-arm logo – against Elmer Bernstein's relentless big-band score, immediately setting a frenzied and dire tone that is tragically concretized as the film's story, centred on drug addiction, unfolds. It is no wonder that the film was sent to theatres with the note "Pull curtain before titles", and undoubtedly Bass's subsequent titles, including those for *Psycho*, were afforded a similar treatment.

Scholars suggest several ways in which Bass's titles for *Psycho* succeed in 'creating a climate' for the ensuing horror narrative. For Raymond Durgnat, both the fragmentation of the type, and the horizontal and vertical grey bars that frantically dart just beneath the type, invoke descriptors such as disorganization, chaos, hypnagogia ("the 'break-up' of gestalts and forms, well-known in the states between sleeping and waking"), obsession, and hysteria: "Narrative-wise, the credits of *Psycho* are entirely meaningless; yet, like an 'abstract overture', in visual kinetic, they presage its theme — disintegrating thought" (2002: 20–1). Robert Kolker (2004), along with other authors, opts for a more precise reading of the broken letters as a premonition of dismemberment and bifurcation. Bass's own interpretation taps into more of the narrative's mystery rather than its violence: "I was trying to make [the word 'PSYCHO'] more frenetic and I liked the idea of images suggesting clues coming together" (quoted in Rebello, 1990: 140).

Bernard Herrmann, the composer for *Psycho*, shared sentiments very similar to those of Bass regarding the purpose of a main title:

> *In film studios and among filmmakers, there is a convention that the main titles have to be cymbal crashes and be accompanied by a pop song – no matter what! The real function of a main title, of course, should be to set the pulse of what is going to follow. I wrote the main title music for* Psycho *before Saul Bass even did the animation. They animated to the music. The point, however, is that after the main title nothing much happens in the picture, apparently, for 20 minutes or so. Appearances, of course, are deceiving, for in fact the drama starts immediately with the titles! The* climax *of* Psycho *is given to you by the music right at the moment the film begins. I am firmly convinced, and so is Hitchcock, that after the main titles you know that something terrible must happen. The main title sequence tells you so, and that is its function: to set the drama.* [emphasis Herrmann's] (quoted in Cameron, 1980: 132).

Again, scholars hear different ways in which Herrmann's agitated title music for string orchestra sets the drama. Fred Steiner describes the *Psycho* prelude as "fast music — urgent, nervous, harshly accented", whose "constant, hard, forward driving motion… anticipates the key emotion of the first part of *Psycho*: the fear (almost panic) in Marion's mind during her long flight with the stolen money" (1974–75: 26). Royal S. Brown essentially makes this same observation two decades later:

> For while the Psycho *prelude has a much more ominous cast to it than* North by Northwest*'s, like the latter its fast-moving, frenetic pace also suggests the flight and pursuit that are what the opening of* Psycho *seems to be about.* (1994: 164)

Brown also finds correlations between dramatic aspects of the film and intrinsic features of the prelude's harmonic language. He understands the striking harmony that opens Herrmann's title music – an example of what he dubs the "Hitchcock chord" due to its marked presence in multiple Herrmann/Hitchcock films – as an intrinsic signifier of the irrational. This association requires a somewhat lengthy and technical argument, summarized in the claim that such a chord takes "the triadically oriented harmonic system familiar to listeners and… turn[s] it against itself" (*ibid*.: 174).[1] Brown applies his intrinsic hermeneutics to other harmonies in the prelude as well:

> The prelude also goes beyond any other Hitchcock music, Herrmann-scored or otherwise, in its array of jarringly dissonant chords, the bitonality of which reflects on the film's ultimate narrative theme. (*ibid*.: 161)[2]

These interpretations of both music and visuals are insightful, but they are not terribly specific to *Psycho*: themes of disorientation, mania, irrationality and duplicity could just as easily apply to other horror or suspense films, such as other Hitchcock/Herrmann collaborations. But, of course, both title music and images are quite abstract in *Psycho*, and thus perfectly qualified to set a general dramatic tone of what is to follow, while leaving specific narrative details alone. Bass's choice of the word 'climate' is thus perspicacious. Yet the quote from Herrmann takes this notion one step (if not several steps) further: "The <u>climax</u> of *Psycho* is given to you by the music right at the moment the film begins." By "climax," one can probably assume that Herrmann is referring to the scene in the fruit cellar, when the true natures of Norman and Mother are revealed, and, if this is so, this is a tall order for music to fill. In other statements, Herrmann has employed exaggeration and even a little dishonesty to cast his talent in a better light; perhaps this sentence is another example of this.[3] This essay, however naively, grants Herrmann the benefit of the doubt, and proposes a way of reading the film and analysing the structure of both the aural and visual components of the main title that supports his claim. My proposal comes in two parts: the first uncovers a structural similarity between Herrmann's music and Bass's titles, and the second relates aspects of these structures to a psychoanalytic interpretation of Norman Bates's character.

The music and the words: a correspondence

Figure 2.1 shows the first six bars of Herrmann's 'Prelude', the designation the composer chose for his main title music. Multiple aspects of the five 'hammer-blow' chords in the first three bars, the qualities of its harmonic structure aside, are pertinently expressive: for example, a volume of double forte for muted (con sordino) strings exudes repressed intensity, and the down-bow indication (indicated by ⊓ on the score) for each chord literally requires each string player to execute rapid, multiple thrusts with the right hand.[4] Intertextually, not only does this sonority invoke dark themes through its associations with previous films that Herrmann scored – such as *The Ghost and Mrs. Muir* (Joseph L. Mankiewicz, 1947), *Vertigo* (Alfred Hitchcock, 1958), and *North by Northwest* (Alfred Hitchcock, 1959) – but it also served as a signature harmony for Arnold Schoenberg's atonal expressionist music from the early twentieth century, whose extra-musical associations are rife with themes of illusion, despair and horror.[5]

Figure 2.1 Herrmann, *Psycho*, 'Prelude', bb. 1–6

The structure of the 'Hitchcock chord' itself considerably augments the unsettling quality of the prelude. The left side of Figure 2.2 represents *Psycho*'s 'Hitchcock chord' — what I will call the '*Psycho* chord' hereafter — in a manner apart from traditional musical notation. The piano keyboard shows the customary division of the pitch continuum into intervals of half-steps, or semitones, where twelve semitones span an octave (the interval at which note labels and the pattern of white and black keys are iterated). The top of the keyboard corresponds to the keyboard's rightmost part in its usual orientation, the part 'higher' in pitch.

The 'Hitchcock chord' is simply constructed by starting on any pitch — B♭ in the case of the '*Psycho* chord', E♭ in the case of the opening of *Vertigo* — and adding three more notes 3, 7 and 11 semitones above the root. First of all, the 11-semitone interval that frames the harmony (in this case, between B♭ and A) is a harsh major-seventh dissonance. Second, despite employing both major thirds (4 semitones) and minor thirds (3 semitones) between registrally adjacent pitches — a variety it shares with most tonal harmonies — this harmony cannot fit within one of the most common kind of scales: the major scale. In other words, it is impossible to play a 'Hitchcock chord' using only the white notes of the piano. Respectively, these two structural elements may be heard to embitter and estrange the harmony.

However, this study focuses less on the structure of the chord itself, and more on how this structure is manipulated. Brown astutely recognizes that "the prelude's first motif [bars 5–6 in Figure 2.1, which I will call the '*Psycho* theme' hereafter] starts off

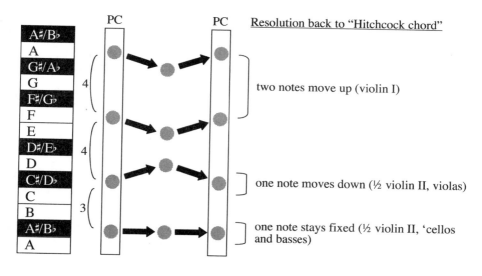

Figure 2.2 Transformations of the '*Psycho* chord' (PC) in the main title to *Psycho*

as a simple breaking up of the 'Hitchcock chord'" (1994: 161). It is not difficult to imagine Herrmann at the piano, playing first the '*Psycho* chord', then embellishing parts of the chord with notes a single semitone away, spinning melodic lines out of the raw harmonic material of the opening. First, the Db, rewritten as C♯ in the third bar, alternates with D to create a two-note ostinato in the violas. Second, beginning in the fifth bar, the first violins fashion a swirling motif from a double substitution of E for F and G♯ for A. Lastly, the Bb remains fixed in cellos and basses, although the latter indulge in octave leaps. (The second violins divide into two parts: one part plays with the violas, the other part plays with the cellos.) Therefore, as shown in Figure 2.2, the '*Psycho* chord' is 'broken' into three parts: the 'top' part comprised of two notes (F and A) moves down, then back up by semitone, the 'middle' part comprised of one note (C♯/Db) moves up, then back down by semitone, and the 'bottom' part comprised of one note (Bb) remains unmoved. Even though this 'Hitchcock chord' is itself a dissonant sonority, its conspicuous appearances at the beginning, the end, and through-out the prelude – as a kind of Doric column supporting the overall musical form – promotes it to the status of tonic harmony for the main title. As Brown puts it:

> In *Psycho*'s prelude, the '*Hitchcock chord*' is repeated so often and at such musically strong moments that it seems to be not only a point of departure, but a point of return as well. (*ibid.*)

The right-hand side of Figure 2.2 describes this 'return' or 'resolution' to the referential '*Psycho* chord' as it occurs within the '*Psycho* theme'.

Bass's manipulation of significant words in the main title bears a strong resemblance to Herrmann's musical manipulation of the '*Psycho* chord'. As Durgnat describes it:

> On the black background, the scattering of broken letters slide and snap together, spelling 'Psycho', for about two seconds, until that word, too, cracks into three strata. They slip a little notch sideways, but in opposite directions, so that each letter, vertically misaligned, seems to jerk and tug against itself. (2002: 19)[6]

Using the 'P' of 'PSYCHO', Figure 2.3 models in more detail how each of the letters of the film's title is shifted in Bass's visuals. The top stratum does not move at all, whereas the bottom two strata shift in opposite directions, as Durgnat observes. (The visual 'trifurcation motif' appeared a year earlier in Bass's output in the titles for Preminger's *Anatomy of a Murder* [1959], with more straightforward connotations: about two-thirds of the way into the titles, abstract cut-outs of a human leg and head are horizontally split into three parts.) Furthermore, closer inspection reveals that the two bottom strata are displaced unevenly. More precisely, if the line width of the type is set to one unit distance, then the middle stratum moves one unit to the left and the bottom stratum moves half a unit to the right. Thus the transformations of the '*Psycho* chord' and the transformations of the word 'Psycho' share several structural features: a trifurcation where one part remains fixed and the other two parts move in opposite directions and establish some kind of asymmetry by a ratio of 2 to 1. Lest one think that this ratio in Bass's transformation is anything but deliberate, the same proportions result when the two bottom strata reverse directions, and, more significantly, when the exact same transformation takes place at the end of the titles on the words 'ALFRED HITCHCOCK', which are set in a different font with a smaller line width.

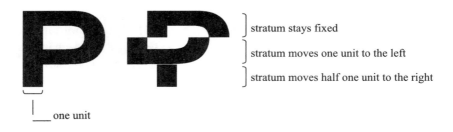

>] stratum stays fixed
>
>] stratum moves one unit to the left
>
>] stratum moves half one unit to the right

one unit

Figure 2.3   Transformations of the word 'PSYCHO' in the main title to *Psycho*

David Cooper might call this similarity between music and visuals an "isomorphism", which, in his definition:

> indicates a structural identity between different elements… [In film music], it denotes a kind of functional recoding, translation, or mapping from one of the domains of sensory data (whether visual, aural, or tactile) or from the conceptual, to music. (2001: 24–5)

Or, in this case, is it the converse: a recoding of the music to the visual domain? After all, Herrmann claimed in the quote cited earlier that "Bass animated to the titles". No other source of which I am aware either corroborates or refutes this contention, but it is possible that some aspects of *Psycho*'s title design were influenced by the music. After all, some visual shifts and choices of pacing in many of Bass's other main titles seem derived from a set musical piece: for example, the close synchronizations in the title for *Anatomy of a Murder*. Indeed, the last two of the three shifts of the word 'PSYCHO' match the beat of the music, perhaps coincidentally, perhaps not. But this does not necessarily mean that Bass's decision to trifurcate and asymmetrically shift two of the three layers was consciously or subconsciously sparked by Herrmann's music; he may well have generated these ideas beforehand.[7] Therefore, rather than explore any inference of influence, I prefer to use this isomorphism as a means to an end, supporting an interpretation that both the musical and visual contents of the titles foreshadow the climax of the film, where Norman's psychological abnormalities are revealed.

The symbolic and the real: a correspondence

In his 1998 book on Hitchcock, Robert Samuels applied the psychoanalytical theories of Jacques Lacan to a reading of, among other subjects, the character of Norman Bates in *Psycho*.[8] Lacan expanded upon and modified Sigmund Freud's psychological theories by incorporating concepts from structural and post-structural linguistics and semiotics.[9] Whereas Freud's three stages of oral, anal and phallic trace the subject's changes in sexual expression and pleasure, Lacan's three stages of the Real, Imaginary and Symbolic trace the subject's conceptualization of language. During the Real stage, symbolic language is unnecessary: just as the infant does not perceive a separation between self and the external world (particularly the mother), the infant does not perceive a need to have signifiers that stand in for signifieds. The Symbolic stage is ushered in by the introduction of the structure of language. In this stage, the child experiences loss through the absence of known objects (particularly the absence of the mother), and thus requires the representative nature of language in order not only to refer to such lost objects, but also to conceive of one's self as 'I'. (The details of the intermediary Imaginary stage are ancillary to the following argument.) Also, unlike Freud's three stages, which are strictly successive, Lacan's three stages can overlap, and are perhaps better regarded metaphorically as separate 'places' within a healthy adult human psyche.

Samuels accounts for Norman Bates's condition by the melding of two of these psychic 'places':

> [Hitchcock's] *need to represent Symbolic attributes in the Real* [in *Psycho*] *can be, in part, explained by the central focus of the film, which is Norman Bates' psychosis. As Lacan has often pointed out, one of the major defining characteristics of psychosis is that certain Symbolic relations and concepts, that are 'normally' abstract factors of structure and order, become perceived in the Real during psychotic states. In the case of* Psycho, *the subject's Symbolic desire to identify with his mother will be acted out on the level of the Real, when he actually attempts to take on his mother's voice and clothing.* (1998: 136)

Bates's character brings a horrific corporeal Reality to mental Symbols: instead of preserving the Symbolic memory of his mother, he preserves her Real corpse; instead of experiencing and then Symbolically purging guilty thoughts that stem from sexual desire, he Really murders the object of the desire. Such physical incarnations of abstract concepts take place in the main title as well. The word 'PSYCHO' is a Symbol, representing the concept of an individual with a psychological abnormality, which can further connote certain mental states or behaviours of this individual, such as fragmentation of thought and violent destruction. Bass was fully aware of the semantic import of the words in his title: "I liked giving more zip to [the word] Psycho because it was not only the name of the picture but a word that means something" (quoted in Rebello, 1990: 140). When Bass fragments and destroys the word 'PSYCHO' itself, the signifier is physically manipulated by a transformation, "acted out on the level of the Real", that reflects the abstract and Symbolic nature of the signified.[10] This violent fragmentation of the image may anticipate violent acts to come – as does the use of the same 'trifurcation motif' in Bass's titles for *Anatomy of a Murder* a year before *Psycho* – but the additional conflation of the Real and the Symbolic in the single word 'PSYCHO' anticipates Norman's particular psychosis.

I claim that the '*Psycho* chord' of Herrmann's main title also participates in a similar conflation. It was suggested earlier that the '*Psycho* chord' is the best choice for the prelude's tonic harmony, in that it begins, ends and occurs throughout the prelude as a referential and, in the case of the '*Psycho* theme', a 'prolonged' sonority. And this would be an entirely accurate interpretation of many commercial recordings of the *Psycho* prelude – usually as part of a suite, instead of the entire score – which conclude with a fortissimo *Psycho* chord suspended high in the violin and violas. However, in the original soundtrack's prelude, Herrmann follows this chord with a final low D played fortissimo and pizzicato in the cellos and basses. By virtue of being the last word, this single note brings the status of the '*Psycho* chord' into question: despite its inherent dissonance, does it still persevere as the prelude's tonic harmony due to its rhetorical posturing throughout the prelude, or does its dissonance finally discharge into a last-minute assertion of D as tonic? Brown considers the possibility of the latter:

> *This potential of* Psycho*'s particular 'Hitchcock chord' to be utilized as a rather kinky cadence chord is borne out by the end of the prelude, in which a differently voiced version of the opening chord, repeated a number of times in groups of four in the high violins, finally gives way to a single, pizzicato, unison D, thus creating something not unlike a 5–1 cadence with the fifth (A) as the top note and the D-flat/C-sharp leading tone prominent in the chordal construction.* (1994: 162)

If the four notes of the high '*Psycho* chord' were to resolve to a tonic triad in D above this final bass note – and a tonal hearing in D, like Brown's, would infer such resolutions – the motions of the four notes would most likely adopt one of the two voice-leading formations shown in Figure 2.4. Not only would the leading tone C♯ rise by a semitone to the tonic note D, but also the B♭ would drop by semitone to A, the fifth of the tonic triad, which is already fixed an octave higher. Regardless of whether one hears the mode as minor (Figure 2.4a) or major (Figure 2.4b), the collective motions of the four voices should be familiar: the chord is divided into three parts, in which one part stays fixed, and the other two parts move up and down by one semitone, respectively. Furthermore, of the twelve possible bass notes, D is the only note that could follow the '*Psycho* chord' and accomplish this. Thus, when we recall how the '*Psycho* chord' is embellished to create the '*Psycho* theme', the '*Psycho* chord'-as-consonance is physically manipulated by a transformation, 'acted out on the level of the Real', that reflects the abstract and Symbolic nature of the '*Psycho* chord'-as-dissonance. Therefore, Herrmann's manipulation and contextualization of the '*Psycho* chord' in the main title may be interpreted as a musical manifestation of Norman's psychosis, as diagnosed by Lacan-cum-Samuels.

Admittedly, the voice-leading resolutions of the Real and Symbolic are only identical (one note stays fixed, and two notes move up) when the key is D major, as annotated on the right side of Figure 2.4. However, D minor would seem to be the better tonal reading; Herrmann analyst Graham Bruce, for one, hears the end this way: "This final [bass note] D, which we presumably experience as D minor after the predominantly minor orientation of the prelude..." (1985: 185). This argument is a little weak; minor triads in general may still make a strong showing in a major-mode piece. Rather, an argument involving voice-leading economy would make more sense, since F is already consonant with D, and there is no F♯ acoustically sounding above this bass note to prod the F up a semitone. Or is there? A close listening to the pizzicato bass D that ends the prelude in the film exposes the sound of another pitch not written in the score: an A an octave and seven semitones higher. This pitch is one of the natural overtones, a by-product of a note with a rich timbre such as that of a cello or string bass. Typically, natural overtones are not heard as distinct pitches, but rather as covert contributors to the note's timbral quality. However, on the film's soundtrack, this overtone A is particularly distinct; in fact, it is the only bass note played unmuted in the prelude.

a. Resolution to D minor   b. Resolution to D major

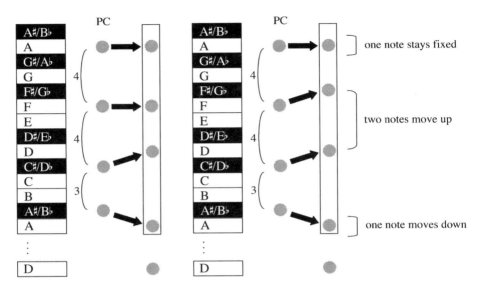

Figure 2.4   Resolutions of the 'Psycho chord' (PC) to a tonic triad in the key of D

The next higher, different, and most audible, pitch in an overtone series built on D is indeed F♯, but, unlike the overtone A, F♯ is not audible at the end of the prelude. However, as Steiner, Brown, and others have noted, the prelude music recurs during the first third of the film, accompanying Marion's flight from Phoenix after stealing the money. Brown says that the recycling of the prelude music "corresponds with the 'red herring' nature of the film's initial action" (1994: 164). Close attention to Herrmann's score suggests that this does not have to be the only interpretation. The prelude music that includes presentations of both the '*Psycho* chord' and the '*Psycho* theme' are used for three scenes of Marion in her car. The first scene begins as Marion's employer sees her headed out of town, and ends with nightfall and the cut to the following morning, revealing that Marion has spent the night in her car on the side of the road. The musical cue for this scene concludes with an abrupt '*Psycho* chord' and a middle-range F, sustained for six seconds, that fades out. The second scene begins after the police officer has warned Marion about sleeping in her car, and ends as she pulls into a used-car lot. For this second cue, the music concludes in exactly the same fashion as the first. However, the third scene is noticeably different, both musically and dramatically. It begins as Marion pulls out of the car lot with a new vehicle, and ends as she drives into a nocturnal rainstorm. The music's final measures are much more reminiscent of the prelude's final measures, with the sustained '*Psycho* chord' in high violins and violas, and the final low fortissimo D in cellos and basses. Yet this closing D is much more prominent, as it is played with the bow and sustained for at least 10 to 12 seconds before it finally dies away, and this emphasis exposes a clearly audible F♯ overtone above the bass D. Therefore, at this moment, the resolution of Figure 2.4 is given its clearest realization, and the Symbolic and Real treatments of the '*Psycho* chord' come into their closest correspondence. Immediately thereafter, through her wiper-swept windshield, Marion makes out the sign for the Bates Motel – where Norman and his psychotic blurring of the Symbolic and the Real await.[11]

Notes

1. David Cooper (2005) suggests that Brown's label misses the mark somewhat, for the "Hitchcock chord" was "an ingredient of Herrmann's harmonic repertoire for many years before his association with Hitchcock began in 1955 with *The Trouble with Harry*": in *The Ghost and Mrs. Muir*, it is found prominently toward the end of the cue 'The Sea' and in 'The Painting', "where it… is suggestive of a threatening or sinister atmosphere" (38–9).

2. By "bitonality," Brown is almost certainly referring to the dissonant but not entirely inharmonious relationship resulting from the registral juxtaposition of two contrasting tertian sonorities – perhaps better labelled 'bichordality' – rather than the juxtaposition of two established keys where the identity of each tonic can be perceptually teased apart from the other.

3. For instance, in an interview with Leslie Zador, Herrmann acerbically insists that he did not reuse portions of his opera *Wuthering Heights* for his score to *The Ghost and Mrs. Muir*, but scholars generally agree that he did. See Cooper (2005: 74–6) and Wrobel (2003).

4. Graham Bruce (1985) alludes to this observation: "The chords hurl us into the center of the film, anticipating mimetically the downward thrusts of Norman's knife" (184). An acknowledgement of bow direction makes the mimicry more physical, especially when successive down-bows are also used for the famous shower scene. However, in this case, particularly with the violins and violas, playing repeated notes on their highest string means that the right-hand motions are not only rapid and numerous, but also literally much more downward. These "hammer blows" of the 'Prelude' have another, more oblique, connection with the film: Beethoven's Third Symphony, a vinyl recording of which is stationary on a turntable in the Bates's house, begins with two such 'hammer blows' (on a more consonant major triad).

5. David Cooper (2001: 29) notes this chord's use by Béla Bartók, another important composer of early-twentieth-century atonal music. However, I claim that Schoenberg's use of the harmony is more frequent and pronounced, and Schoenberg's link with the gloomy aesthetics of abstract expressionism is more direct. For support of the former claim, see Simms (2000).

6. Rebello (1990: 140–1) recounts how Harold Adler, a movie advertising artist and title design letterer, constructed the fragmentation of the type. It should also be

mentioned that, on *Psycho*'s advertisements such as movie posters, the title word is divided into three parts, albeit in a different manner: the entire word is horizontally split in two by a jagged tear, and the top half is vertically split in two by another jagged tear.

7. Daniel Kleinman, director of numerous music videos and titles designer for the five most recent James Bond films from *Goldeneye* (1995) to *Casino Royale* (2006), describes one situation in which the conceptualization of the titles comes before the music. Music video, he says, is

> *filmmaking the wrong way around. You have a music track and you put pictures to it. In theory you should have a story and have the pictures, and then find the right music to put to it. After doing hundreds of these, I didn't want to be dictated by the music any more. The Bond sequence is similar to music video because you get the track and you have to put pictures to it. But, oddly, I've always received the track quite late, so I've had the ideas before I had the music, and just hoped that the music fits with the ideas.* (quoted in Edgar, 1998: 29)

8. See Samuels (1998), particularly the final chapter entitled 'Epilogue: *Psycho* and the Horror of the Bi-Textual Unconscious'.

9. A reliable summary of Lacan's theories can be found at http://www.colorado.edu/English/courses/ENGL2012Klages/lacan.html (accessed 4 June 2006).

10. Kyle Cooper, a movie-title designer whom many consider to be Bass's heir, has long recognized the aesthetics of blurring the line between the Symbolic and the Real:

> *Type* [font] *is like actors to me. It takes on characteristics of its own. When I was younger, I used to pick a word from the dictionary and then try to design it so that I could make the word do what it meant...* (http://www.twenty4.co.uk/on-line/issue001/project01/proj01index.htm; accessed 5 June 2006)

One only has to see his titles for *True Lies* (James Cameron, 1994) and *Twister* (Jan de Bont, 1996) to find simple examples of this, although the defacement of the film stock itself in his landmark titles for *Se7en* (David Fincher, 1994) establishes a connection with the titles to *Psycho* more relevant to this study.

11. Cohn (2004: 285–323) also provides a psychoanalytical reading of the harmonic progression in Figure 2.4b, minus the dissonant A of the '*Psycho* chord'. Cohn interprets such a progression as *unheimlich* or 'uncanny' (according to Freud, a coincidence of the alien and the familiar) because each triad is acoustically consonant and contextually dissonant simultaneously. There is a significant mutual resonance between the overtones of Cohn's article and those of the present study.

References

Bass, S. (1977), *Bass on Titles*. Pyramid Films.

Brown, R. S. (1994), *Overtones and Undertones: Reading Film Music*, Berkeley: University of California Press.

Bruce, G. (1985), *Bernard Herrmann: Film Music and Narrative*, Ann Arbor: UMI Research Press.

Cameron, E. W. (ed.) (1980), *Sound and the Cinema*, Pleasantville, NY: Redgrave Publishing.

Cohn, R. (2004), 'Uncanny Resemblances: Tonal Signification in the Freudian Age', *Journal of the American Musicological Society*, 57(2), 285–323.

Cooper, D. (2005), *The Ghost and Mrs Muir: A Film Score Guide*, Lanham, MD: Scarecrow Press.

Durgnat, R. (2002), *A Long Hard Look at* Psycho, London: British Film Institute.

Edgar, R. (1998), 'Microfilm', *World Art*, 19, 24–9.

Kolker, R. (ed.) (2004), *Alfred Hitchcock's* Psycho: *A Casebook*, Oxford: Oxford University Press.

Rebello, S. (1990), *Alfred Hitchcock and the Making of Psycho*, New York: Dembner Books.

Samuels, R. (1998), *Hitchcock's Bi-Textuality: Lacan, Feminisms, and Queer Theory*, Albany: State University of New York Press.

Simms, B. (2000), *The Atonal Music of Arnold Schoenberg*, Oxford: Oxford University Press.

Steiner, F. (1974–75), 'Herrmann's "Black and White" Music for Hitchcock's *Psycho*', *Film Music Notebook*, 1 (Fall 1974), 28–36, and (Winter 1974–75), 26–46.

Wrobel, W. (2003), 'Self-Borrowing in the Music of Bernard Herrmann', *Journal of Film Music*, 1(2/3), 249–71.

3   Sound and Music in Hammer's Vampire Films

Michael Hannan

During the 1940s and 1950s the traumas and upheavals of the war years cast a long shadow over British culture. With food rationing continuing until 1954, and with shattered cities, psyches and bodies recovering from the impact of conflict, these decades have been seen as a period of austerity, social–sexual restraint and inhibition. Aspects of this Britain can be glimpsed in films such as David Lean's *Brief Encounter* (1945) (in which, after tortured, frustrated interaction, the two protagonists decide not to consummate their attraction) or his northern, working-class drama *Hobson's Choice* (1954). But British cinema also produced a divergent strand, a series of florid (and often risqué) films that gave vent to repressed sexuality and general recklessness. The genres that spawned these productions were ones that – superficially at least – seemed anything but contemporary. The period costume dramas produced by Gainsborough Films during the 1940s and 1950s, for example, provided actress Margaret Lockwood with the opportunity to play a number of assertive, sexually charged roles, most notably that of the bold highwaywoman celebrated in the title of *The Wicked Lady* (Leslie Arliss, 1945). Period dramas also allowed dark male figures to dominate the screens, such as the fictionalized poet protagonist of *Bad Lord Byron* (David Macdonald, 1948), who preys on his female conquests in a manner that foreshadows aspects of the genre addressed in this chapter. The low-budget science fiction (henceforth SF) genre also produced such colourful oddities as the fetishistic female android movie *The Perfect Woman* (Bernard Knowles, 1949) or (the self-explanatory) *Devil Girl from Mars* (David Macdonald, 1954).

Against such a cinematic history, the emergence of Hammer's horror films can be seen as an intensification of post-war preoccupations expressed through the revival of key literary texts from a previous period (the 1800s), specifically Mary Shelley's *Frankenstein* (1818) and Bram Stoker's *Dracula* (1897). While discussion of these literary works' relation to nineteenth-century British culture is beyond the scope of this chapter, the coincidence of their emergence during another era often characterized in terms of repression is obviously significant.

While the name 'Hammer films' has become virtually synonymous with British horror cinema in general, the horror genre only accounted for a small proportion of the output of a company that began production in the 1930s. The genre's success provided Hammer with its first major box-office earners and gave it a brand identity that a series of previous (and parallel) productions had failed to do. The impetus behind Hammer's move into gothic horror was the success of their earlier diversification into another genre: SF[1] In 1955 Hammer adapted the successful BBC radio and TV series *Quatermass* into a feature film entitled *The Quatermass Xperiment* (Val Guest). Well received at the box office, its success spawned a popular sequel by the same director in *Quatermass II* (1957). The films featured dramatic narratives, blending supernatural associations and attacks by alien forces, ingenious (if low-budget) special effects and dramatic scores (for strings and percussion) provided by the young composer James Bernard.[2]

Experimenting with a further genre diversification, Hammer decided to produce a version of Shelley's *Frankenstein*, famously filmed by Universal Studios in 1931 and directed by James Whale. The distinctive production look and narrative of Hammer's film was largely due to advice from Universal that copying of any elements from their 1931 feature that were not in Shelley's original (and, by then, in the public domain) novel would result in legal action. Bernard was employed to provide a tense, jarring score similar to his previous work for SF thrillers, and the film was made and released under the title *The Curse of Frankenstein* (Terence Fisher, 1955). The significant box-office success and controversy over the film (which was characterized by many reviewers as too horrific and disturbing to be seen) convinced the studio of the mileage in the genre. Utilizing available talent, various country-house locations and a set of peculiarly British sensibilities, the blueprint for Hammer's British horror style was drawn and was executed in a series of low-budget productions that continued for nearly two decades.

Despite the company's tight budgetary policy, it recognized the value of effective scores and, as Larson (1996) documents, a significant number of high-profile composers worked for Hammer at this time. These included James Bernard (twenty-four scores), Don Banks (nine), Leonard Salzedo (seven), Harry Robinson (six), Malcolm Arnold (four), Stanley Black (four), Richard Rodney Bennett (three), Elizabeth Lutyens (two), Edwin Astley (two), Malcolm Williamson (two) and Tristram Cary (two).

Between 1957 and 1974 Hammer made forty-six horror films that featured *Frankenstein*'s monster, vampires, mummies, werewolves, gorgons, zombies, abominable snowmen, witches, devils and mad people. The studio's most enduringly popular monster was the vampire, represented in sixteen separate films, beginning with *The Curse of Frankenstein* and ending with the Hong Kong co-production *Legend of the 7 Golden Vampires* (Roy Ward Baker, 1974). This chapter focuses on the soundtracks of five of these vampire films: *Dracula* (Terence Fisher, 1958), *Brides of Dracula* (henceforth *Brides*) (Terence Fisher, 1960), *The Kiss of the Vampire* (henceforth *Kiss*) (Don Sharp, 1964), *The Satanic Rites of Dracula* (henceforth *Satanic Rites*) (Alan Gibson, 1973), and *Legend of the 7 Golden Vampires* (henceforth *Legend*). The score for *Brides* was composed by Malcolm Williamson, the score for *Satanic Rites* by John Cacavas, with Hammer's most prolific composer, James Bernard, composing the remaining three scores.

The first three of these films fit squarely in the classic vampire genre. Although Count Dracula appears only in the first, they all involve an earlier period (the late nineteenth or early twentieth century), a gothic castle in an Eastern European setting, travellers and locals (particularly young women) who fall prey to broodingly powerful vampires, a terrified local population, and a learned man who comes to the rescue and destroys the vampires. By contrast, the last two films combine vampire horror-film conventions with other genres. *Satanic Rites* is set in modern London and uses elements of the crime, spy and satanic cult film genres. *Legend* is set in China in the early twentieth century and is essentially a martial arts film, made in Hong Kong as a co-production with the Chinese production company, Shaw Brothers.[3] Unlike the three earlier films, both these 1970s films involve a more overtly sexualized representation of the female victims, some of whom are depicted with bare breasts – in line with the company's more general shift into (lesbian-inflected) horror-erotica with the 'Carmilla trilogy', initiated with *The Vampire Lovers* (Roy Ward Baker, 1970). (See the Appendix for plot summaries of the five films under discussion in this chapter.)

The production of the sound and music for Hammer films was highly organized through the use of musical directors John Hollingsworth (from 1954 to 1963) and Philip Martell (from 1965). These experienced musicians worked closely with the composers in spotting the films and also conducted their scores (although neither composed music for any Hammer films). According to James Bernard:

> An important factor in the success of a film score is the exact choice of scenes or moments where music can really speak effectively, so that it does not become a mere dim background. This was something to which both John Hollingsworth and, later, Philip Martell always gave great attention. When a film was in its almost final cut, there would be a music breakdown session. The producer, the director (if possible), the music team, the sound effects team, the editor, and the assistant editor would watch the film in minute detail, stopping after each reel to discuss exactly where music should be placed (if at all). These sessions took a whole day or more and a number of friendly arguments, and even then our decisions might well be fallible. (1996: xii)

The following section compares aspects of the films under discussion in three categories: sound effects, diegetic music and score, examining patterns of usage in order to give a sense of their combined operation in the series of film texts.

Sound effects

One distinctive feature of the soundtracks of the Hammer films examined in this chapter is the careful placement of music and sound effects. In many instances, when sound effects need to be emphasized there is care either to use no music or to make the music subservient to the sound effects. The most prominent effect in these vampire movies is the blood-curdling scream that occurs when a female character is bitten by a vampire (emphasizing gender-differentiated sexuality in the films; male bite victims don't scream). Similar screams occur when a stake is driven through a vampire's heart to kill it. To emphasize the horror of a premeditated staking and the scream that eventuates, music is sometimes omitted entirely before the event (e.g., the staking of the vampire woman and of Lucy in *Dracula*; and the staking by Professor Zimmer of his daughter in *Kiss*). Other symbolic sound effects include spooky wind (used to indicate the evil presence of the vampire in all five films except *Brides*); thunder (used for the same purpose in *Kiss*, *Brides* and *Legend*); and bat sounds, such as wing-flapping or squealing (used in *Kiss*, *Brides* and *Legend* to indicate a transformation of the vampire into a bat). Tolling bells or chimes are used to indicate impending danger or drama in *Kiss*, *Brides*, *Satanic Rites* and *Legend*; and agitated horse vocalizations are used to indicate the presence of death or danger in *Kiss*, *Brides* and *Legend*.

Other nocturnal animal calls also serve to create and enhance aural atmosphere. Wolf howls and owl cries are used in *Dracula*, *Satanic Rites* and *Legend* to create a spooky night-time ambience (suggesting that vampires are active); crow calls occur as a daytime evocation of evil in *Kiss* and *Legend*; and other diurnal bird calls are used to indicate that dawn is approaching in *Dracula* and *Brides*. Conversely, the absence of diurnal bird calls, caused by the presence of vampiric evil, is noted in Harker's voice-over in *Dracula* and in the dialogue of *Legends*. Other significant avian sound occurs in *Kiss*, with a caged bird in the Ravna castle whose calls sound electronic (and thus other-worldly) and, in the same film, when a colony of bats is summoned by Professor Zimmer's occult incantations to attack and annihilate Dr Ravna and his followers. This scene is clearly a reference to *The Birds* (Alfred Hitchcock, 1963), particularly in the way the bat noises are sound-designed: a kind of hum while they are hovering, *en masse* over the castle and an accumulation of individual screeches and wing-flapping as they attack, combined, of course, with the victims' distressed cries.

Diegetic music

With the exception of *Kiss*, diegetic music is not prominent in the vampire movies discussed in this chapter and, when it occurs, it mainly enhances contextual elements of the narrative. One particular device used in three films is the presentation of diegetic music that is interrupted to dramatic effect. Two of the films (*Dracula* and *Brides*) feature music playing in a local inn. In *Dracula* the music, issuing from a mechanical musical box, is stopped and the customers go quiet when the stranger, Dr Van Helsing, enters. In *Brides*, a dance piece played on plucked stringed instruments is heard (as if performed by live musicians somewhere off screen), which similarly cuts off, and the conversations of the customers come to a halt, when a feared thug enters the inn. In *Brides*, a student is playing a piano arrangement of Brahms's 'Lullaby' ('Wiegenlied',

Op. 49, No. 4), when Marianne, escorted by Van Helsing, arrives to take up her position at the school. The pianist stops playing and the room full of female students falls silent as they enter. As an example of an uninterrupted performance, *Legend* features a consular reception scene where a group of musicians playing mock-Chinese pentatonic music (scored for flute and gongs) are providing the entertainment.

In *Satanic Rites* solo organ music is played during the ritual scenes and seems to be diegetic because it is also heard on the video monitor in the Pelham House surveillance room. Even so, its source is never revealed, and it functions more like underscore. Indeed, in dramatic moments of the ceremonies, other instruments are added to it. In a pivotal scene of *Kiss*, Dr Ravna's son, Carl, plays one of his own extremely chromatic piano compositions, which puts Marianne into a kind of trance (see below for more discussion of the mesmerizing function of some non-diegetic music cues). This piano work, composed by James Bernard, also contains several of the main thematic ideas used throughout the film in the underscore. Prior to this performance Carl is also heard playing Chopin's Nocturne in D flat (Op. 27, No. 2) when Marianne and Gerald arrive for dinner at Castle Ravna. The idea of the 'nocturne' is perhaps emblematic of vampirism, but the selection of this particular work with its exquisite decorative right-hand figurations may also be considered to reinforce the idea, promoted in the script, that Dr Ravna and his family are highly cultured. This idea is further emphasized at their masked ball where the buffet chef is imported from Paris and the orchestra from Vienna. James Bernard also wrote the selection of diegetic pieces for dance orchestra, mostly waltzes in the style of Johann Strauss II.

Incantation of ritual texts occurs in several of the films. In *Kiss* the opening burial scene uses Latin liturgical chanting and later Professor Zimmer intones his own occult text to mobilize the colony of bats (although his vocalization is more like exaggerated Shakespearian acting than intoning); and in both *Satanic Rites* and *Legend*, the focus of the evil deeds to be overcome is on the intoned blood-taking rituals of the vampires. In *Legend* a tam tam (Chinese flat gong) is repeatedly struck by Kah/Dracula to summon the army of the undead from their graves.

Scores

Three of the scores considered in this chapter (*Kiss*, *Brides* and *Satanic Rites*) feature occasional use of a solo organ – evocative perhaps of the gothic ambience expected of vampire movies. Other individual instrumental features include certain cues in the score of *Satanic Rites*, notably chase scenes, which use a drum kit (particularly hi-hats) and passages where electric guitar, usually with heavy reverb and tremolo effects, is used sparingly. The opening and end titles for *Satanic Rites* seem influenced by John Barry's theme music and instrumental line-up for his early James Bond film scores, for example, *Goldfinger* (Guy Hamilton, 1964), a decision that may have been prompted by the cross-genre aspects of the *Satanic Rites* script. But with these exceptions, all five films are scored for full orchestra. According to James Bernard: "Hammer liked to have symphonic scores, written by classically trained composers, conducted by classically trained conductors and performed and recorded by players and sound engineers of the highest calibre" (1996: xii).

In general, the approach to scoring is a highly chromatic nineteenth-century style combined with dissonant modernist techniques. According to Neumeyer and Buhler:

> In horror films, the monster often embodies a kind of dystopian projection, a means of figuring unintended consequences in the system, which take musical shape as tonality gone awry to the point of incomprehension. (2001: 23)

This is a fair comment when applied to the scores under consideration. To some extent, however, the scores use the Wagnerian operatic (and traditional Hollywood) scoring technique of the leitmotif, where certain instrumental melodic ideas are associated with characters, objects or specific actions. For *Dracula*, Bernard wrote a very distinctive three-note leitmotif for the arch-vampire, in the form of a setting of the word, 'Dracula' (Figure 3.1). The Dracula leitmotif appears in various guises in all Bernard's scores for vampire films which involve the character Dracula, including *Legend*, where the octave interval is replaced by a tritone (augmented fourth) as well as being used in its original form. Whereas the Dracula leitmotif is used unfailingly (some might say overused) for the appearance of, or references to, the character himself, the other leitmotifs used by Bernard tend to have a more general application. In *Dracula* there is a second prominent motif that is associated with Harker, Van Helsing and the various female victims (Figures 3.2 and 3.3). Larson refers to this as the 'Good theme' and observes that it is usually

Figure 3.1 Dracula motif

Figure 3.2 Harker motif (unresolved version)

Figure 3.3 Harker motif (resolved version)

overshadowed by the more aggressive Dracula leitmotif and is harmonically resolved only twice: after Lucy is staked (and thus released from being a vampire) and when Dracula is destroyed at the end of the story (1996: 23).

As mentioned above, Bernard derives a number of motifs from the themes of Carl Ravna's piano piece in *Kiss* (Figures 3.4 and 3.5). The second of these examples is used unchanged to symbolize the evil of the Ravna family. There are a number of other motifs derived from these two motifs that exhibit various combinations of semitone, minor third and major third intervals. The rising major third followed by falling semitone seems to be associated with Marianne; the falling minor third followed by falling semitone is

Figure 3.4 Carl Ravna's piano piece (theme 1)

Figure 3.5 Carl Ravna's piano piece (theme 2)

associated with the vampire Tania; while the rising minor third followed by rising semitone is associated with Professor Zimmer's drive to destroy Ravna. For example, it underscores his ritual incantations that lead to the destruction of the Ravnas and their followers.

Malcolm Williamson was instructed by Hammer to study Bernard's scores before writing the score for *Brides* (Larson, 1996: 77). In this film he employs a dramatic three-note motif for the vampire (Figure 3.6), which is used sparingly, for example, when Professor Van Helsing discovers Baron Meinster's coffin-shaped tomb, as well as a more pervasive angular motif to signify the constant danger that Marianne is in (Figure 3.7). In addition, there is a wistful theme to represent the tender feelings that Marianne has for the Baron.

John Cacavas uses a different approach for motivic material in *Satanic Rites*. The material of its main title music is only used again for the end titles and for one bridging music cue. The most prominent motif is the four-note idea used for the organ music accompanying the satanic rites (Figure 3.8). With the exception of this piece, the approach to designation of characters or action is more textural than motivic. For example, danger is signified by a raucous jangling bell roll, and mention of Dracula is often accompanied by a dissonant arpeggiated electric harpsichord chord, which, although functioning as a signifier for Count Dracula, is not a leitmotif in the sense of being a clearly defined melodic entity. Although Bernard employs the Dracula motif and

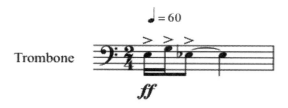

Figure 3.6   Brides vampire motif

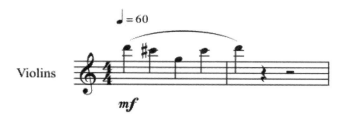

Figure 3.7   Brides danger motif

Figure 3.8   Satanic Rites organ theme

others in *Legend*, his approach to scoring in this film is also more by textural layering than in his earlier scoring. For example, the Chinese vampires and the army of the undead have their own complex music textures for the many action shots in which they appear.

There are a number of formulaic techniques used in the scoring of the Hammer vampire movies. Firstly, a build-up of dramatic tension, for example, to indicate danger or fear, is typically represented by repeating a motif or a chord at an ever-increasing level of pitch, usually by increments of a semitone. To cite three examples from each film, in *Dracula* this technique is used for the first appearance of Dracula; when Harker is walking through the castle at night searching for the vampire woman; and when Dracula is moving in to bite Lucy. In *Brides* the technique is used to support the action of the coach going faster and faster; for the organ music in the graveyard as the vampire girl escapes from her grave; and for the danger that Marianne is creating for herself by removing the rosary beads from around her neck. In *Kiss* the rising motivic technique is used for the opening vampire-slaying scene; to represent Marianne's mounting terror during the storm; and as Professor Zimmer prepares to burn his arm after being bitten by Tania. The same technique is widely used in *Legend*: in the early scene between Kah and Count Dracula; as Dracula transforms himself into Kah (and in the dramatic title music that follows); and in the many scenes where the undead leave their graves and go on their murderous rampages.

Satanic Rites does not use the rising motivic technique except for the scene where the agent Torrence is about to be assassinated, but it does feature the other most prominent formulaic tension-creating devices in these vampire movie scores, namely, the use of trilling (rapid alternation of two adjacent tones), tremolo (in stringed instruments, the reiteration of a tone created by rapid alternation of up-bow and down-bow strokes) and the drum (or other percussion) roll. Huckvale, discussing the Hammer vampire movie *Twins of Evil* (John Hough, 1971), refers to a number of standard affective devices in music:

> These concern music ideas which correlate to physiological states of emotion or adrenalin release, that is tremolo equals trembling or nervous agitation; staccato equals nervous 'jumpiness'; crescendo equals an increase in the intensity of the above mentioned symptoms. (1990: 16)

String tremolos and instrumental trills pervade all the scores under discussion, and are often used in conjunction with the increasingly ascending motif device discussed above to create the impression of heightened tension. In general, the orchestration of these scores tends to focus on high string textures, low string textures and low brass harmonies. The high strings, particularly when employed with tremolos or trills, create tension and the low strings and brass create a sense of ominousness. In highly dramatic moments such as the appearance or discovery of a vampire, louder and brighter instruments such as trumpets and cymbal and tam tam crashes and rolls are added to the orchestration. For excitement, as in action scenes, drum rolls and timpani rolls are commonly used.

In the orchestration, the woodwinds tend to be overlooked as a section in favour of strings and brass, although certain solo woodwind instruments are used for specific purposes in supporting the narrative. The bass clarinet, with its spooky low-range quality, is used as a solo instrument in *Dracula* (in the lead-up to Harker being bitten), *Brides* (when the Baroness is ascending the staircase), *Kiss* (when the coach delivers the letter of invitation for dinner at the castle), *Satanic Rites* (when the vial containing the deadly virus is brought out) and *Legend* (as Kah approaches Dracula's castle; and when Professor Van Helsing gets an intuition that the vampires know his party is approaching them). Solo flute tends to be used for gentler or sadder moments: for example, in *Kiss* (for the scene where Anna is weeping over the loss of her daughter), and in *Brides* (for the tender theme associated with Marianne's feelings for the Baron). Cor anglais is also used as a solo instrument in three of the films, in each case related in some way to the vampire narrative: in *Dracula* (as Harker realizes he will become a vampire); in *Kiss* (for Tania's graveyard scene); and in *Brides* (to underscore Greta's explanation of how she and the Baroness had kept their vampire Baron captive).

There are a number of elements of the vampire narrative that are given specific musical treatments in these films. The first is for the mesmeric state that a vampire puts his or her victims under prior to their submission to being bitten on the neck. For the seductions of Lucy and Mina in *Dracula* this is achieved through the use of a trilled, rising three-semitone motif combined with a four-tone piano ostinato (continually repeated pattern) and a pulsating vibraphone effect, all of which gradually increase in pitch. The texture is hypnotic while simultaneously providing the sense of increasing danger. In *Brides*, immediately before Gina succumbs to Baron Meinster, there is a mysterious high violin melody combined with an arpeggiated harp ostinato. In *Kiss*, when Marianne and Gerald first meet the Ravna family, the diegetic performance by Carl of his strange piano piece combines at a critical moment with non-diegetic tremolo string chords to put Marianne under a spell. The same textural combination is later used as underscore for Marianne's initiation by Dr Ravna. In *Satanic Rites*, as the agent Jane is seduced by Dracula, a spooky texture of trumpet flutter-tonguing portamento, vibraphone glissandi, wind sound effects and a sustained string chord is used; and as Chin Yang attempts to seduce Inspector Murray, a pulsating chordal texture is composed from flute flutter-tonguing, harp glissandi, bell tree strokes and a repeated descending high three-semitone motif. A variation of this texture is also used as Dracula prepares to initiate Jessica as she lies on the altar. In *Legend* there are no equivalent hypnotic music cues because the seven vampires use force rather than hypnotism.

Another formulaic musical concept that is used to mark the triumph of good over evil is the instrumental chorale, or hymn. Put simply, each melodic note in a chorale is harmonized by a different triadic chord. In *Brides* this idea is used when Van Helsing points the crucifix at Baron Meinster; when the Baroness Meinster's soul is put to rest by staking; when Van Helsing cures himself of his vampire bite using a red-hot branding iron and holy water; and when the Baron is finally destroyed by the shadow of the cross formed by the blades of the windmill against the full moon. In *Satanic Rites* the same underscoring technique is used when Inspector Murray forms a makeshift crucifix to fend off the female vampires in the cellar of Pelham House. In *Legend* the chorale idea is used to underscore the three scenes in which the Buddha's shrine appears. As the style of harmony used for the underscore in all these films tends towards chromaticism and dissonance, these chorale-style cues using block major and minor chords stand out.

Just as the repeated, continually ascending motif technique is used to create tension, a corresponding descending idea is consistently employed to represent the destruction of the vampire. In *Dracula*, a string of chromatically descending chords is used for the destruction and immediate ageing of the vampire woman; in *Kiss*, a series of descending transpositions of the Ravna leitmotif accompany Dr Ravna's demise; and in *Brides* a descending bass clarinet melodic line is used to underscore Baron Meinster's last gasp (and is followed by the chorale idea, representing the triumph of good over evil, as mentioned above). In *Satanic Rites*, a descending bass clarinet line is used to accompany the destruction of Jane, and an extended cue of descending clarinet scales which progressively gets lower by transposition is used to accompany the decay of Dracula's body; and in *Legend* the descending transposition idea is used thrice for the destruction of three of the Chinese vampires and then for the demise of Dracula. For this, the Dracula motif is repeatedly transposed down by semitones and this idea is followed by a low string unison tremolo, also transposed down by semitones as the body of Dracula decays to dust.

A common feature of these vampire movies is the 'monumentalizing' of the gothic architecture and other striking visual features of the vampire narrative. According to Huckvale:

> *Hammer, who almost always operated under small and strictly controlled budgets, was quick to realise the importance of music as a device by which frequently impoverished visual material could be 'monumentalised'. A large orchestral sound can transform a scene or an image into something more impressive (eg more spacious, more opulent), which without music would remain mundane.* (1990: 4)

Certainly there is an attempt to monumentalize by full orchestral force for the titles of *Dracula* (the exterior of the castle), for the titles of *Legend* (the stark but spacious interior of the castle), for the titles of *Kiss* (the mourners fleeing the church graveyard after the discovery of the vampire in the coffin), for the titles of *Brides* (the castle on the hill) and the end titles (the burning windmill); and for the titles of *Satanic Rites* (the official government buildings on the Thames with the shadow of Dracula super-imposed). In addition, the appearance of a vampire in action (for example, Dracula leaving his castle with cape flowing) is consistently monumentalized in *Dracula*, *Kiss*, *Brides* and *Legend*. Action music, for physical struggles between vampires and vampire-fighters, and for scenes of fleeing and chasing, also tends to be richly orchestrated, as one might expect.

Conclusion

Hammer's use of dramatic sound effects and powerful orchestrations in the vampire films discussed in this chapter dramatize a monstrous presence and threat chiefly conveyed through symbolic power and suggestion rather than graphic dismemberment and/or depictions of gore. It is no accident that the title of a CD compilation of Hammer horror music released in 2002 was *Hammer: The Studio That Dripped Blood* – whereas many later horror films spurted it. This aspect is perhaps that which renders Hammer films so quaintly dated to contemporary sensibilities. Aside from brief moments when the vampire bites (with small punctures to a proffered neck) or, as the narrative climaxes, through stakes being driven into vampires' chests, violence – and general malevolence – is suggested by combinations of visual design, stylized acting and carefully crafted orchestral passages. While Hammer's composers were not responsible for any significant musical innovations, their development of a series of scores (managed and maintained by house music directors) created a musical reference bank for future horror-film composers. In Hammer's diegeses the world is essentially rendered: Dracula's dramatic, exciting darkness against the forces of light, reason and restraint.

Returning to the cultural frame that prefaced this chapter, it is perhaps not over-fanciful to read Hammer's post-war films – and particularly their routine victories of the forces of good over evil – as a cathartic 'replaying' and purging of the traumas of the war years. In true British fashion, class also plays a strong role here. It is no accident that it is Count Dracula who terrorizes the populace and that it is an educated, bourgeois expert who routinely prevails and restores order. At the same time as British politics, and particularly the Labour Party, were championing a new, classless meritocracy in Britain and as the first generation born in the post-war years was coming to maturity to experience (however vicariously) the 'The Swinging Sixties', Hammer's vampiric star faded. The 'baton' of dramatic horror was taken up by other directors and producers who increased the graphic content of their films, and composers who either developed further dramatic approaches to orchestral scoring (as in William Friedkin's *The Exorcist* [1973]) or else introduced new rock elements (as in Dario Argento's oeuvre).

Appendix: Plot summaries

Dracula (1958)

Jonathon Harker has obtained a post at Castle Dracula as a librarian, in a quest to destroy Count Dracula but, soon after his arrival, is bitten by a female vampire at the castle. He kills her with a stake before becoming a vampire himself. Harker's friend Dr Van Helsing investigates and finds his transformed friend lying in a tomb. He stakes him, but Dracula has escaped and bitten Harker's fiancée (Lucy) in revenge. She dies from loss of blood, becomes a vampire, and is outwitted and staked by Van Helsing. In the meantime, Dracula has got Lucy's sister-in-law (Mina) under his spell. Dracula escapes back to his castle with the fading Mina but Van Helsing pursues and destroys him. Mina recovers.

Brides of Dracula (1960)

A young woman (Marianne), travelling to take up a teaching post, is stranded in a village. The local Baroness Meinster invites her to stay the night at her castle. Marianne discovers there is a man (Baron Meinster) held captive there. The Baron is a vampire and his mother the Baroness, aided by her maid Greta, has been procuring young women as a supply of blood for him. Unaware of this, Marianne releases the Baron, who goes on a biting rampage, killing his mother and a local girl. Frightened by the death of the Baroness and by Greta's hysteria, Marianne flees the castle and is discovered by Dr Van Helsing, who suspects that vampires are involved. Still blind to the danger, Marianne becomes engaged to the Baron. The Baron bites one of Marianne's new friends (Gina) at the school, and Gina dies and becomes a vampire. Van Helsing confronts the Baron at an old windmill and is bitten by him. The Baron leaves but Van Helsing manages to heal his bite wound using a red-hot branding iron and holy water. When the Baron returns with Marianne, Van Helsing is able to rescue her and destroy the Baron and his vampire harem.

The Kiss of the Vampire (1964)

A newly wed couple (Marianne and Gerald) are honeymooning when their car runs out of petrol near the castle of the vampire family of Dr Ravna and his children Sabena and Carl. Forced to stay at the local hotel (owned by Bruno and Anna), the couple is invited by Ravna to dinner, and then to a masked ball, where Marianne falls under Ravna's spell. Gerald is thrown out of the castle but enlists the help of Professor Zimmer (whose own daughter had been a victim of Ravna) to save Marianne and destroy Ravna, his children and their large vampire following (which includes the daughter of the owners of the local hotel). They rescue Marianne, and Zimmer invokes a ritual spell that causes a colony of bats to attack the castle and destroy all its vampire inhabitants.

The Satanic Rites of Dracula (1973)

In modern times, an undercover agent is caught and tortured during surveillance of a satanic cult at Pelham House in which several high-profile British men are involved. The police inspector (Murray) brought in to investigate enlists the help of Larimer Van Helsing and his granddaughter assistant (Jessica). Murray, Jessica and an agent (Torrence) visit Pelham House and discover a cellar full of chained-up female vampires. Meanwhile Van Helsing discovers that one of the prominent men (Professor Keeley) has manufactured a virus that would wipe out humanity if released. Van Helsing suspects that Count Dracula is behind the conspiracy. Murray and Jessica are captured and taken to Pelham House. Van Helsing finds Dracula, attempts to destroy him, but is also captured and taken to Pelham House. Dracula reveals his plan is to initiate Jessica as his consort and destroy all other humans with the virus. A fire breaks out and Van Helsing escapes, pursued by Dracula. Van Helsing then lures Dracula into a patch of hawthorn, where he is able to stake him.

The Legend of the 7 Golden Vampires (1974)

Inhabiting the body of a Chinese man (Kah), Count Dracula transforms himself into a Chinese vampire and with six other Chinese vampires establishes a base in a temple near a remote Chinese village. They prey on the young women of the village. Professor Van Helsing is visiting China to investigate the truth of the Chinese vampire legend. He is laughed at by the Chung King academic establishment but is persuaded by a young Chinese man (Hsi Ching) to go on a mission with his six brothers and one sister (all skilled in martial arts) to save the village of Ping Quei. Apart from love interests developing between the sister (Mai Kwei) and Van Helsing's son (Leyland) and between Hsi Ching and their Swedish sponsor (Vanessa), the narrative centres on fight scenes between Van Helsing's party and the horse-riding vampires, assisted by their army of the undead. At the end Van Helsing realizes that one of the Chinese vampires is Dracula in disguise. Dracula transforms himself back into his Eastern European image but is destroyed by Van Helsing.

Notes

1. For a discussion of British science fiction in the 1940s and 1950s, see Hunter (1990).
2. A Royal College of Music graduate who came to Hammer's attention after providing dramatic music for a BBC radio adaptation of John Webster's *The Duchess of Malfi* earlier in 1955.
3. See O'Brien (2003: 913) for a discussion of the production of the film.

References

Bernard, J. (1996), 'Introduction', in R. D. Larson (ed.), *Music from the House of Hammer: Music in the Hammer Horror Films 1950–1980*. London: The Scarecrow Press, pp. xi–xiv.

Huckvale, D. (1990), 'Twins of Evil: An Investigation into the Aesthetics of Film Music', *Popular Music*, 9(1), 1–35.

Hunter, I. Q. (ed.) (1999), *British Science Fiction Cinema*, London: Routledge.

Larson, R. D. (1996), *Music from the House of Hammer: Music in the Hammer Horror Films 1950–1980*, London: The Scarecrow Press.

Neumeyer, D., and Buhler, J. (2001), 'Analytical and Interpretive Approaches to Film Music (I): Analysing the Music', in K. Donnelly (ed.), *Film Music: Critical Approaches*, Edinburgh: Edinburgh University Press, pp. 16–38.

O'Brien, D. (2003), *Spooky Encounters: A Gwailo's Guide to Hong Kong Horror*, Manchester: Headpress/Critical Vision.

4 Creative Soundtrack Expression

Tôru Takemitsu's Score for Kwaidan

Kyoko Koizumi

Kwaidan [Japanese Ghost Stories], directed by Masaki Kobayashi in 1964, is regarded as a seminal film not only for its magnificent *mise-en-scène* but also for its experimental soundtrack, created by the Japanese composer, Tôru Takemitsu (1930–96). Although well known internationally as a concert composer, Takemitsu's work in film was not merely supplementary to his more 'serious' endeavours; it was a major aspect of his oeuvre. In writing music for over 100 films, Takemitsu avoided standard industrial approaches to composition and created a series of highly distinctive scores. Within this notable body of work, *Kwaidan* stands out – above all others – as the film that allowed him free rein to create a range of unusual and inventive sound compositions.[1]

To the extent that Western listeners know Takemitsu's concert music, it is through his use of Eastern concepts such as *ma* [emptiness] or *oto-no-kawa* [a stream of sound] and for his inclusion of Japanese traditional instruments in his orchestrations. Yet while works such as *Eclipse* (1966) or *November Steps* (1967) – commissioned by the New York Philharmonic Orchestra – are known for their innovations,[2] these two distinctive aspects of Takemitsu's oeuvre had been previously developed in his score for *Kwaidan*, where he employed (expanded) notions of *musique concrète* together with traditional Japanese instruments. Using these two approaches, he transcended conventional distinctions between underscore and sound effects in an attempt to produce tone colours appropriate for *Kwaidan*'s eerie scenes. In his score for Kobayashi's film, thematic musical leitmotifs are scarcely heard. Instead, the audience hears electronically modified sounds of musical instruments, chants or natural sounds that are radically transformed from their sources. Takemitsu's inventive sound design is the first and foremost characteristic of *Kwaidan*'s soundtrack and by analysing his work on the film, this chapter provides a case study of an approach to horror-film scoring that is indigenous to Japan.

The innovative nature of Takemitsu's film music

While Takemitsu's first concert piece was composed in 1950, it was not until 1956 that he started composing music for commercial films. Instead of studying at a conservatory, Takemitsu had become a disciple of Yasuji Kiyose in 1948. Kiyose was a key member of *Shin Sakkyokuka Kyōkai* [the New Academy of Composers], an organization of composers who wished to move beyond the conservative mainstream approaches to art music and which included the *Godzilla* film-music composer Akira Ifukube[3] and Fumio Hayasaka (1914–55). The encounter with Hayasaka, in particular, proved a turning point for Takemitsu. When Kiyose introduced them in 1948, Hayasaka was already known as a composer who had closely collaborated with the film director Akira Kurosawa (1910–98). Although Hayasaka died prematurely, at forty-one, he composed music for nearly 100 films, including Kurosawa's films *Drunken Angel* (1948), *Rashōmon* (1950) and *Seven Samurai* (1954). Hayasaka welcomed the input of young composers, and Takemitsu worked alongside another young talent, Masaru Satô (1928–99), assisting Hayasaka with his film-score composition. These two young film-music composers responded to Hayasaka's influence and musical instruction in different ways. Satô took over from Hayasaka as Kurosawa's collaborator while Takemitsu went on to develop ideas for innovative soundtracks drawing on the example of Hayasaka's underscores.

Takashi Tachibana, a Japanese journalist who conducted in-depth interviews with Takemitsu and his colleagues, revealed that Takemitsu did not initially intend to become a film-music composer and originally intended to compose 'pure' concert music. By contrast, Satô became a disciple of Hayasaka specifically in order to start his career as a full-time film-music composer. Takemitsu and his lifelong comrade Kuniharu Akiyama (1929–96), a music critic, were members of *Jikken Kôbô* [The Experimental Workshop],[4] and had a considerable awareness of European and North American avant-garde music. As a teacher, Hayasaka liked the dialogue between these younger, experimentally inclined colleagues and his own more experienced perceptions of film music. Takemitsu studied orchestration by assisting with Hayasaka's works on film. When Hayasaka died in 1955, he was so shocked that he could not finish the orchestration for the Kurosawa film they were working on, *Record of a Living Being*, and Satô finally completed it (Tachibana, 1992). Later, Takemitsu composed a tribute to Hayasaka titled *Requiem for String Orchestra* (1957), which was praised by Stravinsky and was instrumental in establishing Takemitsu as a well-regarded serious music composer.

Aside from a few trial pieces for experimental films, Takemitsu's first score was for *Crazed Fruit* (Kô Nakahira, 1956). The score was a collaboration between Satô and Takemitsu, with the former being responsible for the theme song and the latter for the underscore. In this film, Takemitsu used Hawaiian guitar and a jazz band – styles of popular music that were still rarely heard in Japanese films at that time (Akiyama, 1972: 124). After *Crazed Fruit* Takemitsu composed underscores for several films but became increasingly frustrated by the conventions of the established Japanese studio system,

which he felt restricted his creative ideas. One outlet that afforded him more opportunity to experiment was his 1950s radiophonic work. Through his works for radio he
was able to use those *musique concrète* techniques that he later employed in his 1960s
film scores.

Musique concrète began in Paris in the late 1940s. Experimental composers
collected 'concrete' sound sources, recorded them on tape and modified them electronically through tape editing and manipulation. Pierre Schaeffer's *musique concrète*
was produced and premiered in 1948. Toshirô Mayuzumi introduced *musique concrète*
to Japan in the early 1950s and composed a piece of *musique concrète* in 1953, shortly
after studying in Paris. Two years after Mayuzumi's innovation Takemitsu was commissioned by Japanese radio to create broadcast radiophonic pieces such as *Oto no Shiki*
[Symphonic Poem for Concrete Sound Objects and Music] and *Honô* [The Flame] using
musique concrète techniques. As its Japanese title suggests, *Oto no Shiki* uses a
montage of actual source sounds related to the four seasons. *Honô* featured intensive
use of *musique concrète*, with Takemitsu modifying the original sound sources (such as
wind or human voices) so as to make them unidentifiable by changing the tape playback
speeds or playing them backwards to produce reverse echoes (Tachibana, 1993a: 281).[5]
These 1950s radio experiments developed the original sound palette that Takemitsu
used in his 1960s film scores.

One result of the period of modernization that commenced in the Meiji Era (1868–
1912) was a marked westernization of Japanese music culture, and music and sound in
cinema followed this tendency. In the 1950s and 1960s, except for a few innovative
soundtracks by composers such as Hayasaka that used Japanese traditional instruments,
most domestic films (even Japanese samurai warrior films [*jidai-geki*]) were saturated
with western music similar to that used in classic Hollywood cinema. For this reason,
Takemitsu's 1960s innovations in film music were revolutionary. Takemitsu expanded the
creative dimension of his soundtracks in collaboration with directors such as Hiroshi
Teshigawara, Masaki Kobayashi and Masahiro Shinoda. In Teshigawara's *Otoshiana* [The
Pitfall] (1962), for example, Takemitsu effectively used prepared piano[6] to create an
impression of fear. After this film, the sounds of prepared piano were heard in various
contexts in Takemitsu's film scores. In *Suna-no-onna* [Woman in the Dunes], directed
by Teshigawara in 1964, he added emphatic harp sounds to a string orchestra in order
to express the fantastic world of the dunes. In addition, he used musical instruments
(including traditional Japanese ones) in unexpected ways. As Takemitsu assisted
Hayasaka's film compositions in his youth, he came to understand the sound and music
of film through actually experiencing sounds themselves (rather than writing orchestrations based on book-derived knowledge). Without standardized academic induction,
Takemitsu was free to create sounds and music appropriate to each film and scene.

It is no exaggeration to state that Takemitsu originated new conventions for the
relationship of sound and image that were an alternative to the classical Hollywood film
score (or its Japanese imitation), which itself was substantially derived from Wagnerian

concepts. Howard Shore, a film-music composer whose collaboration with David Cronenberg is well known, admits Takemitsu's influence on his score for films such as *Crash* (Cronenberg, 1996):

> *I was certainly aware of the composer Tôru Takemitsu who did a lot of work with sound and electronics as well as composed music. That influenced me a lot in the sixties when I started listening, on one hand to rock 'n' roll and on the other to a lot of avant garde material, so a bit by accident I started listening to electronic music. He [Takemitsu] might have had an influence on me to write something like Crash because he was doing it many years ago.* (quoted in Brophy, 1999: 2)[7]

Kwaidan and Japanese Ghost Stories

Kwaidan's title derives from the Japanese term *kaidan* [horror/ghost story]. The film comprises four narrative sequences – *Black Hair, The Snow Woman, Hôichi the Earless*, and *In a Cup of Tea* – based on original works by the Irish writer Lafcadio Hearn (1850–1904) that were, in turn, derived from Japanese stories. Hearn's interest in Japanese ghost stories derived from his long-term residence in Japan, where he became naturalized, adopting the name Yakumo Koizumi. Hearn identified the traditional Japanese cosmology behind Japanese ghost stories and interpreted this in English-language versions of the tales.

In contrast to many recent Japanese cult horror movies, *Kwaidan* emphasizes an animistic aspect of the phantom world specific to traditional Japanese culture. Jay McRoy categorizes Japanese horror films into the following six subgenres: the *kaidan* [avenging spirit's film], the *daikaiju eiga* [the giant monster film], the apocalyptic film, the techno/body-horror film, the torture film and the serial killer film (McRoy, 2005). Although each subgenre requires explanation, for the purpose of this chapter it is sufficient to state that Kobayashi's *Kwaidan* can be categorized as a Japanese *kaidan* that:

> draw[s] on a multiplicity of religious traditions... as well as the plot devices from traditional literature and theatre (including Noh theatre's shunen- [revenge-] and shura-mono [ghost-plays], and Kabuki theatre's tales of the supernatural. (ibid.: 3)

In accordance with Hearn's original ghost stories, the film is not primarily focused on horrifying spectral manifestations but rather on the wandering nature of human souls and of spirits coming and going between life and death.

Hearn believed in the reincarnation of human spirits. The following excerpt from a lecture he gave in Japan, titled 'The Value of the Supernatural in Fiction', shows why he was motivated to collect traditional Japanese ghost stories:

> *If we do not believe in old-fashioned stories and theories about ghosts, we are nevertheless obliged to recognize today that we are ghosts of ourselves – and utterly incomprehensible. The mystery of the universe is now*

weighing upon us, becoming heavier and heavier, more and more awful, as our knowledge expands, and it is especially a ghostly mystery. All great art reminds us in some way of this universal riddle; that is why I say that all great art has something ghostly in it. (Quoted in Cott, 1991: 346)

Hearn adds:

Dreams certainly furnish us with the most penetrating and beautiful qualities of ghostly tenderness that literature contains. For the dead people that we loved all come back to us occasionally in dreams, and look and talk as if they were actually alive, and become to us everything that we could have wished them to be... From the most ancient times such visions of the dead have furnished literature with the most touching and the most exquisite passages of unselfish affection. (Quoted in *ibid.*: 353)

As this passage suggests, Hearn preferred the irrational values of supernatural cosmology to the rational modernist views dominant in western countries.

The relevant point for this discussion of *Kwaidan*'s soundtrack is the manner in which Takemitsu interprets Hearn's ghostly world and embodies it in sounds. Hearn's perceived animistic view of the world informs Takemitsu's soundtrack to the film. Takemitsu has emphasized that when he creates a soundtrack, he first watches the rushes of a film and thinks about how to 'prune' sounds from the image:

Sometimes when I watch 'dumb' rushes, I get sounds and music coming from the screen; I didn't think it was a good idea to plaster music like thick make-up onto an image that was already laden with hidden meanings that would powerfully stimulate the viewer's imagination. I only add music to give the audience a little help hearing the pure music that is already there in the images – in other words, that it is much more important to prune away the sound than to add more music. (Takemitsu, 1996: 33)[8]

In a documentary about Takemitsu's film music, *Music for the Movies* (Charlotte Zwerin, 1994), the composer talks about non-synchronism in the 'Black Hair' sequence from *Kwaidan* (discussed further below):

Timing is the most crucial element in film music. Where to put the music? Where to end it? How forcefully? In Kwaidan, I wanted to create an atmosphere of terror. But if the music is constantly saying, "Watch out! Be scared!" then all the tension is lost. It's like sneaking up behind someone to scare them. First, you have to be silent. Even a single sound can be film music. Here, I wanted all sounds to have the quality of wood. We used real wood for effects. I'd ask for a "cra-a-ck" sound, and they'd split a plank of wood, or rip it apart, or rend it with a knife. Using all these wood sounds, I assembled the track. Sometimes, I'd want to cut the sound just a bit, even a foot, to heighten the tension. I'd ask Kobayashi, the director. Then we'd try it, and he'd agree.

In order to create a direct relationship between sound and image, Takemitsu matches appropriate sounds to each scene. After removing what he deems to be inappropriate sounds, *ma* [emptiness, space] occurs. *Ma* is close to John Cage's concept of 'silence', but means 'between two sounds'. As befits its derivation from a Zen Buddhist concept, *ma* is not simply the replacement of sound by silence – it has a positive sense of lingering sound. In 'Black Hair', non-synchronism is effective because Takemitsu passes over just one *ma* and then brings in the sound (instead of putting sound where it would be expected). The sounds of shakuhachi (a bamboo flute) in 'The Snow Woman' and the sounds of biwa (a Japanese lute) in 'Hôichi the Earless', for instance, also emphasize this *ma* quality during the soundtrack of the film. With this respect for *ma*, Takemitsu came to appreciate the importance of everyday sounds. He treats concrete sounds as equal to instrumental sounds. He writes, "Composing is giving meaning to that stream of sounds that penetrates the world we live in" (Takemitsu, 1995: 79). He desires to "search out that single sound which is in itself so strong that it can confront silence" (*ibid.*: 52).

Sound and music in *Kwaidan*

Takemitsu wrote the scores for ten of Kobayashi's films during his career. *Kwaidan* was their third collaboration and the composer's unique use of electronically modulated natural sounds in combination with Japanese traditional music contributed to the film's success at the 1965 Cannes International Film Festival (where it gained the Special Jurists' Prize). This success was the fruit of a series of experiments that immediately preceded the film. In 1962, for instance, Takemitsu had explored the use of Japanese traditional instruments in a TV programme entitled *Nihon no Mon'yô* [Japanese Crests]. *Seppuku* [Harakiri], directed by Kobayashi in the same year, was the first film in which Takemitsu used a Japanese traditional instrument, the biwa. Following that, in 1964, he used the shakuhachi in Shinoda's film *Ansatsu* [The Assassin]. *Kwaidan*'s successful use of traditional Japanese instruments was, in part, due to the skills of biwa player Kinshi Tsurura and shakuhachi player Katsuya Yokoyama. For Takemitsu, the players' idiosyncratic sounds were much more important than conventional rules of playing traditional instruments and, as a result of Takemitsu's exploration of tone colours, we can hear surprisingly varied biwa and shakuhachi sounds in Kwaidan's score.[9]

According to Takemitsu, before composing the sounds and music of *Kwaidan*, he first decided on a basic tone colour for each episode (Akiyama, 1998: 206). It is worth emphasizing that he uses recorded sounds such as stones, bamboo or ice together with biwa and shakuhachi as the basic tone colours of the film. Table 4.1 shows how normal sound effects (real sounds which are not modified) and electronically modified sounds created by Takemitsu are used in each scene of *Kwaidan*'s four episodes.

The first episode of the film is titled *Kurokami* [Black Hair].[10] In ancient Kyoto, a samurai warrior has left his wife and home to marry the daughter of a rich family in order to increase his prospects of promotion. Despite his new life, he cannot forget his first wife and her kindness and eventually returns to his old home in Kyoto in the hope of seeing her. When he arrives at his home, which has already decayed, he sees the ghost of his previous wife. The black hair from her remains attacks him and he flees across rotten planks and goes insane. In this episode the kokyū (a bowed lute) is used as the signature sound for the animated hair (and, thus, the dead first wife). In contrast to the passionate sounds of kokyū, the dry sounds of a prepared piano evoke his second wife. At the climax of *Kurokami* the synchronous enunciation of sound and image is broken as Takemitsu deliberately positions the sound effects one or two seconds later than the appearance of the image that is its apparent source. As the samurai husband falls in slow motion, the impact of his crash is not heard; instead we hear electronically modified noises of cracking wood and the peculiar sound of ice breaking known in Japan as *kami-watari* [God walking] (famously heard at Suwa Lake in Nagano Prefecture) rising weirdly on the soundtrack.[11] This non-synchronical employment of sound effects gives an uncanny sense of time and space to the film. While synchronism and diachrony are products of modernism, the chasm between temporality and spatiality has been suggested as "spectral time" (Lim, 2001). Using the asymmetrical liaison between frame and soundtrack to create an uncanny and horrifying displacement, Takemitsu succeeded in evoking the phantom world in this haunting sequence.

The second episode is *Yuki-Onna* [The Snow Woman], based on a well-known Japanese legend. One night during a snowstorm, a young woodcutter named Minokichi meets a beautiful snow woman but is forbidden to say anything about his encounter. Later he meets a girl named Oyuki; they marry and have lovely children. On the night of another snowstorm, some years later, Minokichi breaks his vow and tells his wife about the woman he met on the snowy night. His wife reveals that she is the snow woman he once encountered — and then promptly disappears. In order to create a sonic impression of a snowstorm, Takemitsu avoided using actual wind sounds and instead electronically manipulated various shakuhachi sounds played by Yokoyama. These sounds are so modulated in the final film that it is difficult to identify their source. In addition, Takemitsu used a tapped sanukite (a stone from the Sanuki area of western Japan), to express the snow woman's icy power.

The third episode is *The Story of Mimi-nashi-Hôichi* [Hôichi the Earless] and concerns a young, blind biwa player named Hôichi who is haunted by Heike ghosts (spirits of a clan that fell in the Dan-no-ura battle of 1185). A Buddhist priest and other young monks write sutras on Hôichi's body to save him from ghostly harm but forget to write sutras on his ears, leaving them the only visible part of his body. As a result, the Heike ghosts wrench his ears off. Here Tsuruta's biwa is played diegetically (on screen) but in such an original and imaginative manner that Takemitsu does not have to modify the sounds to suit the scene. While Tsuruta's biwa and the monks' chants accompany the main narrative, Takemitsu also provides another element, modifying the sound of *noh* chanting[12] to suggest the waves of the sea haunted by the Heike clans.

Table 4.1 Normal sound effects and electronically modified sounds in *Kwaidan*

Episode	Scene	Normal sound effects (real sounds)	Electronically modified sounds
'Black Hair'	Departure of the samurai		Bamboo, prepared piano
	Wedding ceremony with the second wife	Rustle of kimono, water, birds	Bamboo, prepared piano
	Regret and remorse	Weaving sounds	Bamboo, prepared piano
	Archery on horseback	Gallop, arrow, cracked target	Prepared piano
	The samurai's decision	Falling fan	Bamboo, prepared piano, ice breaking
	Meeting again with the first wife	Door, water jar, spinning	Bamboo
	In a bedroom		Bamboo
	In the morning sunshine		Kokyū (a bowed lute), wood cracking, ice breaking
'Snow woman'	Wandering Mosaku and Minokichi		Sanukite, shakuhachi
	A red stop flag for the boat service		Sanukite, shakuhachi
	A pledge to the snow woman	Squeal of door	Sanukite, shakuhachi
	Minokichi on his sickbed		Sanukite, harp with bell
	Encounter with Oyuki	Door	Sanukite, harp with bell, birds' chirping
	Inviting Oyuki to Minokichi's home		Harp with bell
	Gossiping neighbours	Birds, serving soup	
	Modest happiness	Children's song, birds, washing	
	Breaking a taboo	Straw, rustle of kimono	Shakuhachi
	Oyuki's true colours		Shakuhachi
	Farewell straw sandals		Shakuhachi

'Hōichi'		
The spring sea		Biwa
The war of Dan-no-ura	Biwa, singing	Biwa, *noh* singing
Hōichi at the Amida-ji temple	Water, crow	
Spiritual atmosphere	Door, biwa (real sound)	
Invitation by an armoured warrior	Sea	*Noh* singing
Hōichi's return in the morning	Bell, crow, well	
Promised time	Sea	*Noh* singing
Searching inquiry by a Buddhist priest	Birds, serving tea	
A stormy night	Rain, wind, knocking, thunder	
Biwa songs to the ghosts of Heike clan	Biwa, singing	*Noh* singing
Hōichi and will-o'-the-wisps	Biwa, singing	Biwa, *noh* singing
Transcription of sutras	Cicadas, bell	Biwa, *noh* singing
Wrenched ears		Biwa
Hōichi the earless	Biwa (real sound), biwa singing, *noh* singing (real sound)	Biwa, whistling arrow, *noh* singing
'In a Cup of Tea'		
A story without an end	Battledore	
A New Year's Day, the fourth year of the Tenwa Era		
A face in a cup of tea	Walking, drinking	String (perhaps, futozao)
At Nakagawa Sadomori's house		Clock sound (sound source unknown)
Shikibu Heinai	Torch	Clock sound (sound source unknown)
Visitors in the night	Fan, sliding door	
Three vassals	Sword	
Disappeared author	Woman walking	Futozao, Gidayū reciter's voice
Beckoning from a well	Running away, falling teapot	Futozao

The last episode is *Chawan-no-naka* [In a Cup of Tea]. A samurai is disturbed by the appearance of a younger samurai's face in a cup of tea and shortly after kills a phantom of the young samurai. Later the young samurai's vassals visit to take revenge for their master's murder. The highlight of this episode is a sword fight. This scene is dramatized by the non-diegetic music of a futozao shamisen (Japanese three-string fretless lute with broad neck) and a gidayû reciter's voice. These sounds are much more stylized than the actors' movements on screen. During this sequence sound effects such as clock sounds are also used by Takemitsu to enhance the audience's psychological tension.

Peter Burt, a scholar of Takemitsu's music, concisely summarizes the soundtrack in *Kwaidan* as follows:

> *Here Takemitsu goes so far as to blur the traditional distinctions between 'sound effects' and 'incidental music'... For example, sounds usually categorized as 'effects', such as the splitting of wood and creaking of doors, are electronically treated and artfully arranged into a 'musical' composition. Conversely, sounds that the listener interprets in an illustrative fashion, such as the howling of a snowstorm or the roar of the ocean, turn out to be electronic metamorphoses of 'musical' sounds of a shakuhachi or slowed-down nô chanting: transformed so as to be no longer recognisable as such, yet at the same time no longer 'realistic' and imparting to these ghost stories an eerie, dream-like quality.* (Burt, 2001: 45–6)

While it is obvious that Takemitsu drew on his prior knowledge of *musique concrète* composition for *Kwaidan*'s soundtrack, the inspiration for his use of natural sounds compatible with those of Japanese traditional instruments in the film is less clear in this account. For Burt, Takemitsu worked in an intuitive fashion with source sounds, considering their qualitative aspect (*ibid.*: 43). Noriko Ohtake, another Takemitsu scholar, also emphasizes the influence on Takemitsu's concept of composition exerted by Cage. According to Ohtake, the encounter with Cage's music and thought allowed Takemitsu to understand the importance of silence, the lives of each sound and the power of listening (Ohtake, 1993). Indeed, the extent of Takemitsu's sound exploration in *Kwaidan* cannot be fully grasped without an understanding of these broader concepts of sound.

Conclusion

In *Kwaidan* Takemitsu's concept of *ma* and the importance of each single sound is admirably executed through the technical devices analysed in this chapter. Supporting Brophy's observation that "Japanese culture supports the animist notion of spiritual energy contained within the apparently 'inanimate'" (Brophy, 2005: 155), Takemitsu has an animistic view of natural sounds when using the sounds of stone, ice or bamboo in *Kwaidan*. Takemitsu's mission in the film is to give a strong life to each natural and instrumental sound to the extent that it can confront *ma*. By bestowing equal value to each sound, regardless of its origin, his work in *Kwaidan* transcends conventional distinctions between underscore and sound effects. The uniqueness of Takemitsu's soundtrack to *Kwaidan* is three-fold. The first aspect is the effective use of *musique concrète* through modulating concrete sounds and juxtaposing them with Japanese traditional instruments. The second is non-synchronism, used in order to instil feelings of horror in the audience. The third is the emphasis on *ma* to give the in-between moments a positive meaning. Given these three distinguishing characteristics, it is possible to identify *Kwaidan* as marking a peak in the aesthetics of horror-film scores to date. As these three features were subsequently heard in Takemitsu's later work and in film scores by other composers, the extent to which *Kwaidan* exerted a strong and enduring impact on horror-film scoring merits further analysis.

Acknowledgements

Research for this paper was funded by the Japanese Ministry of Education, Culture, Sports, Science and Technology (the Grant-in-aid for Young Scientists (B), No. 15720023).

Notes

1. Takemitsu himself believed *Kwaidan* to be one of his most innovative and creative scores for film (Takemitsu, 1980: 163). *Kwaidan* was also chosen as the best of his film scores on a questionnaire survey sent out by Tokyo Opera City Cultural Foundation before Takemitsu Golden Cinema Week, held from 29 April to 7 May 2006 at Tokyo Opera City Art Gallery.
2. Musicologist Hugh de Ferranti has identified how expert biwa and shakuhachi players were able to offer their idiosyncratic interpretation of Japanese traditional instruments for Takemitsu's compositional innovation (de Ferranti, 2002).
3. Akira Ifukube's underscores for films are worth mentioning from the viewpoint of film-music history in Japan; however, as Takemitsu has been less influenced by Ifukube than by Hayasaka, in this paper Ifukube's works are not mentioned. See Hosokawa (2004) for a discussion of Ifukube's music and sounds in *Godzilla*.
4. Jikken Kôbô was an avant-garde group of multimedia young artists founded in 1951. The experimental spirits of the members were encouraged by Shûzô Takiguchi, the leading poet and art critic of the time. Its contribution to the development of the art history of post-war Japan was re-evaluated after the death of Takemitsu.
5. The soundtrack of *Honô* was re-edited by Takemitsu himself to be a tape piece, *Relief statique* (1955).
6. Prepared piano, an innovation of John Cage's, involves placing rubbers, nails or coins between the strings of the piano.
7. It is notable that Takemitsu's experimental film scores in the 1960s have an impact on the atonal scores of Cronenberg's psychological horror films. After Takemitsu's innovative compositions for films, later film-music composers began to use harps, guitars or prepared piano in order to produce psychological tension on the screen. Although analysing Takemitsu's influence on younger film-music composers is

beyond the range of this paper, a study of how Takemitsu's idioms are integrated into contemporary horror-film scores would be a valuable research project.

8. This and all subsequent translations are by the present author.

9. There are two cinematic versions of *Kwaidan*; one is the original 182-minute version and the other is a shortened 161-minute version, specially edited for a competition in Cannes. As the original version was reproduced as a DVD (Tôhô, TDV2721D) in 2003, I will use this longer version for my analysis in this paper. As original concrete and instrumental sounds are electronically modified, some sounds are beyond my ability to identify them. Therefore, I refer to Akiyama (1973) and Tachibana (1993b, 1995a, 1995b, 1995c, 1995d), in which Akiyama and a sound engineer, Jyûnosuke Okuyama, recall how Takemitsu created the soundtrack for *Kwaidan* with them in the studio. In addition to them, it is helpful that the shakuhachi player, Yokoyama, and the biwa player, Tsuruta, recollected their collaboration with Takemitsu in Tachibana's reports.

10. The original title of Hearn's story was 'The Reconciliation'.

11. Working before the invention of stereo recording, the sound engineer, Okuyama, devised a method of passing these sounds over the heads of the audience by using the Doppler effect.

12. *Noh* is one of the forms of traditional Japanese theatre and its chant has idiosyncratic reverberation.

References

Akiyama, K. (1972), 'People in the History of Japanese Film Music, Takemitsu Tôru', *Kinema Junpô*, 589, 123–8. [In Japanese]

Akiyama, K. (1973), 'Takemitsu Tôru: Centered on Film Music of *Kwaidan*,' in K. Akiyama (ed.), *How to Listen to Contemporary Music*, Tokyo: Ongaku-no-tomo-sha, pp. 160–76. [in Japanese]

Akiyama, K. (1998), *Lectures on Cine-music: Hearing the Centennial History of Film Music*, Tokyo: Film Art-sha. [in Japanese]

Brophy, P. (1999), *Cinesonic: The World of Sound in Film*, Sydney: Australian Film, Television, and Radio School.

Brophy, P. (2005), 'Arashi ga oka (Onimaru): The Sound of the World Turned Inside Out', in J. McRoy (ed.), *Japanese Horror Cinema*, Honolulu: University of Hawaii Press, pp. 150–60.

Burt, P. (2001), *The Music of Tôru Takemitsu*, Cambridge: Cambridge University Press.

Cott, J. (1991), *Wandering Ghost: The Odyssey of Lafcadio Hearn*, New York: Knopf.

de Ferranti, H. (2002), 'Takemitsu's Biwa', in H. de Ferranti and Y. Narazaki (eds), *A Way a Lone: Writings on Tôru Takemitsu*, Tokyo: Academia Music, pp. 43–71.

Funayama, T. (1998), *Tôru Takemitsu: Towards the Sea of Sound*, Tokyo: Ongaku-no-tomo-sha. [in Japanese]

Hosokawa, S. (2004), 'Atomic Overtones and Primitive Undertones: Akira Ifukube's Sound Design for *Godzilla*', in P. Hayward (ed.), *Off the Planet: Music, Sound and Science Fiction Cinema*, Eastleigh, Hampshire: John Libbey Publishing, pp. 42–60.

Lim, B. C. (2001), 'Spectral Times: The Ghost Film as Historical Allegory', *Positions*, 9(2), 287–329.

McRoy, J. (ed.) (2005), *Japanese Horror Cinema*, Honolulu: University of Hawaii Press.

Ohtake, N. (1993), *Creative Sources for the Music of Tôru Takemitsu*, Aldershot: Ashgate.

Tachibana, T. (1992), 'Takemitsu Tôru: A Journey to Musical Creation, No. 4', *Bungaku-kai*, 46(9), 234–49. [in Japanese]

Tachibana, T. (1993a), 'Takemitsu Tôru, No. 14', *Bungaku-kai*, 47(8), 268–81. [in Japanese]

Tachibana, T. (1993b), 'Takemitsu Tôru, No. 16', *Bungaku-kai*, 47(10), 218–32. [in Japanese]

Tachibana, T. (1995a), 'Takemitsu Tôru, No. 32', *Bungaku-kai*, 49(6), 202–13. [in Japanese]

Tachibana, T. (1995b), 'Takemitsu Tôru, No. 33', *Bungaku-kai*, 49(7), 234–45. [in Japanese]

Tachibana, T. (1995c), 'Takemitsu Tôru, No. 34', *Bungaku-kai*, 49(8), 235–44. [in Japanese]

Tachibana, T. (1995d), 'Takemitsu Tôru, No. 35', *Bungaku-kai*, 49(9), 234–45. [in Japanese]

Takemitsu, T. (1980), *Ongaku no Yohaku kara* [From the Space Left in Music], Tokyo: Shinchôsha. [in Japanese]

Takemitsu, T. (1995), *Confronting Silence: Selected Writings* (Y. Kakudo and G. Glasow, trans. and eds), Berkeley: Fallen Leaf Press.

Takemitsu, T. (1996), *Toki no Entei* [The Gardener of Time], Tokyo: Shinchôsha. [in Japanese]

5 Prog Rock, the Horror Film and Sonic Excess
Dario Argento, Morricone and Goblin

Tony Mitchell

Introduction: Argento and Morricone

Italian cult horror director Dario Argento is well known for the distinctively skewed, offbeat and often jarringly dominant role which music plays in his films, which have attracted both extravagantly positive and violently negative critical responses in the past four decades. Since he is known for trying to scare his actors into their roles by playing the already composed music of Italian prog rock group Goblin to them during the shooting of *Suspiria* (1976), and for wanting to introduce extra speakers into cinemas where the film was showing for maximum sonic effect, the musical dimension of his films is uniquely eccentric (McDonagh, 1991: 146). He also arguably extended the boundaries of thriller and horror-film music in the 1970s by introducing jazz and keyboard-based prog rock as a sonic ingredient (prog rock being a term – derived from the word 'progressive' – applied to a genre of 1970s rock music typified by the work of British acts such as Yes and Emerson, Lake and Palmer). A further trademark was his incorporation of chants, percussive effects, nursery rhymes and other vocal effects influenced by *The Exorcist* (William Friedkin, 1973). Argento's films of the 1970s remain an important, if often kitsch or even camp, corpus of work whose music was enormously distinctive.

Argento's early collaborations with Ennio Morricone in his 'animal trilogy' of *gialli* [thrillers] – *L'uccello dalle piume di cristallo* [The Bird with Crystal Plumage; hereafter *Bird*] (1970), *Il gatto a nove code* [The Cat O'Nine Tails; hereafter *Cat*] (1971) and *Quattro mosche di velluto grigio* [Four Flies on Grey Velvet; hereafter *Four Flies*] (1972) – are quite eccentric in the range of music they employ. Excerpts from Morricone's scores for these films were included on the recent Morricone compilation CD *Crime And Dissonance* (2005), compiled by Mike Patton of Fantômas and other avant-garde projects, evidence of their recuperation into a contemporary canon of 'cool' film music. Morricone's use of a classically oriented palette of often dissonant and jarring avant-garde horror-film music in the Argento trilogy can be related to the music by British composers such as Richard Rodney Bennett and Elizabeth Lutyens in the Hammer horror films of the 1960s, as well as Morricone's own, more experimental, work with the improvising chamber music group Nuova Consonanza, formed in 1965 by Franco Evangelisti and lasting for almost twenty years. Morricone's work on the Argento trilogy involved using standard horror-film music effects along with blander but also experimental orchestral music. The rather anodyne, melodic orchestral music for *Bird*, some of which verges on the banality of muzak, was Morricone's first venture into *giallo* film music, but according to Didier C. Deutsch, "it set the tone for the classy 'erotic thriller' that pervaded the Italian production in the 1970s" (1995). In her authoritative monograph on Argento, *Broken Mirrors/Broken Minds*, Maitland McDonagh argues that *Bird*'s "lilting Ennio Morricone score provides a none-too-subtle counterpoint to its lurid story" (1991: 31), which is, to some extent, true in that the music was often contrapuntal to the images rather than merely underscoring them. Deutsch suggests more convincingly that *Bird* also provided Morricone with "a new voice, different from the spaghetti westerns he had been so closely identified [with] until then" (1995).

Morricone's eclectic range of compositions extend from mainstream pop songs such as Mina's top-40 hit '*Se Telefonando*' (1966), which was later recorded in French by Françoise Hardy, to the free improvisations of Nuova Consonanza, his concertos and string quartets and chamber music, a piece he wrote to commemorate September 11 in 2002 called *Voci dal silenzio* [Voices from the Silence], which was conducted by Riccardo Muti, and his Schoenbergian piano music for Pier Paolo Pasolini's lurid exposé of fascist perversion, *Salò* (1974). He is something of a musical chameleon, having composed more than 400 film soundtracks since 1961, as well as over 100 classical and pop compositions. All these works, as well as the crime and gangster film soundtracks he wrote for a number of Italian films of the 1970s, and the 'easy listening', sometimes bossa nova-flavoured, music he composed for the singer Edda Dell'orso and the Cantori Moderni di Alessandrini for a number of minor cult Italian films in the late 1960s and early 1970s, illustrate his impressive versatility as a composer. His music has also been remixed by European, North American and Japanese electronica artists such as Crazy Baldheads, Fussible (of the Mexican Nortec Collective), Haroumi Hosono and Yukihiro Fukutomi.[1]

Morricone's work with Argento, which combined classical, jazz and rock elements, embodied a level of experimentation and sometimes frenetic abandon which he never quite managed to reproduce in his subsequent, rather prolific work for *gialli* by other 'lesser' directors such as Lucio Fulci, Damiano Damiani and Alberto De Martini. In his florid liner notes for the Classic Italian Soundtracks compilation, *Morricone: The Thriller Collection* (1992), John Bender has said of Morricone's music for *Il gatto a nove code*:

> Morricone... pushed an urban jazz foundation into the realm of semi-abstract contemporanea. His score for Cat O' Nine Tails is metaphorical of the evil mind of an insane genius. As you listen to... 'Passeggiata Notturna' [Night Walk], imagine that each note represents a synaptic firing, every chord struck

is a neuron relaying its fraction of a malignant thought through the wormy pathways of a brain. The music advances to a sinister pattern, and describes a cold, potentially virulent purpose.

Gary Needham has noted that:

The most ingenious aspect of the film is its displacement of the agency and potency of the eye for that of the ear. The enigma is an aural clue picked up by the blind crossword-maker, Franco Arno. (2002: 1)

This throws particular emphasis on the film's music as complementary to its line of aural detection. On the other hand, McDonagh is far more sanguine about the score for *Cat*, regarding it as clichéd 'suspense music':

It actually does sound like a Morricone Western soundtrack, with its reedy accompaniment to female voices crooning an incongruous lullaby. Though not actively deleterious to the film, Cat's score is not its strongest point, and often lapses into painfully conventional 'suspense music'. (1991: 93)

The truth no doubt lies somewhere in between these two views, but when listened to independently of the film, Morricone's music for *Cat* and the other two Argento films certainly succeeds in sustaining much more surprise and interest than his sometimes rather routine spaghetti Western soundtracks such as *The Good, the Bad and the Ugly* (Sergio Leone, 1966). That is where, of course, Argento first encountered Morricone, having served his apprenticeship as a screenwriter with Bernardo Bertolucci on Sergio Leone's *Once upon a Time in the West* (1969), which contains one of Morricone's more distinctive, motivic and varied scores. Philip Brophy, who has mobilized a concept of film music he refers to as 'cinesonics', is eloquent about Morricone's often diegetic harmonica theme music for this film (which even has a character called Harmonica, played by Charles Bronson):

Many instances of musical grandeur and thematic orchestration dance across the opulent soundtrack to Once upon a Time in the West: *the warm waltz and its cascading arrangement which choreograph Jill's (Cardinale) reveries, the 'clip clop' banjo pluck which hiccups along to loveably amoral Cheyenne's (Robards) numerous double-crosses, the dark fuzz guitar riff which vibrates down the inhuman backbone of Frank. Yet they all whirl around the harmonica's morbid leitmotiv. It lives as aberrant aural sign and composed musical device. Its three-note refrain atomizes both the high pitched train whistle… and the score's central cycling motif played by mournful horns… Harmonica thus becomes his harmonica, wearing it around his neck like a dead albatross.* (2004: 170–1)

Scoring thrillers offered a new challenge after this suturing of classic Western themes into character and action, but Morricone managed to relate some of his music in similar ways to characters in Argento's films. In '*Silenzio nell caos*' in *Bird*, he combines a woman's heartbeat with her heavy breathing as she is pursued by a killer. Another element he provided was a lullaby theme sung by a child, which in Argento's words "became part of our characters' life, coming through a window, a courtyard, from a close house or a meadow", and the film remains a favourite of Argento's, "strange, sweeping and also a little frightening... because made with a total unconsciousness" (quoted in Deutsch, 1995). Bender goes so far as to say that scoring *gialli* offered Morricone a new palette which extended his range into more experimental and expressionistic musical areas:

> The genre's extreme stylisation and exploitative bravura are indicative of an expressionistic allegorical milieu. Nothing could be better suited to the incendiary imagination of Ennio Morricone, the giallos [sic] provided him with an enhanced psychosexual canvas upon which he could paint some of the boldest aural concepts of his career. (1992)

Morricone's music for *Four Flies* is the most varied, mixed and experimental of his three Argento scores – as befits the film's protagonist being a rock drummer. Morricone even provides the organ-driven Brian Auger-styled Hammond organ funk music for the band's rehearsal in the opening scene, which shifts between diegetic and non-diegetic and includes a point-of-view shot from inside a guitar and an image of a fly being crushed between two cymbals.[2] Needham has noted: "the sounds bridging the spatial and temporal discontinuities turn an otherwise simple opening into a tour de force" (2002: 2). Morricone's remarkable 20-minute suite for the film ranges from rock to jazz to vocal, classical, Stravinskyesque, and avant-garde (with some Ligeti-like organ, percussion and piano effects), a harp and even a calliope, as well as circus-like dynamics. Deutsch describes this music plausibly as "a score which teemed with weird sonorities, chilling arpeggios, and ominous drumbeats to help reinforce the action on screen" (1995). Needham comments that the film's final sequence, in which the assassin meets a tragic fate, "is simply breathtaking. Poetic in its beauty and emotive quality, and similar in its appeal to Morricone's childhood rhyme 'Ninna nanna in blu'" (2002: 2). McDonagh, however, is again disparaging, pointing out that Argento had originally wanted British heavy metal band Deep Purple to do the music for the film, and claimed:

> The result, though again not truly damaging, wasn't precisely inspired. Morricone took a cue from Roberto's profession and added some jarring rock to his usual formula; this wasn't a particular asset because it is very bad rock indeed. It is, however, an integral part of the film's grossly amusing credits sequence... and shots of Roberto rehearsing amidst a virtual cacophony of screeching guitars and jangling drums. With the conspicuous exception of this witty montage... Morricone's score for the film is simply not very interesting. This undistinguished aural element ended with Four Flies. (1991: 94)

While McDonagh is convincing in her analyses of the visual and psychological elements of Argento's films, she is clearly deaf to Morricone's 1970s music, which since the rehabilitation of prog rock and easy listening in the 1990s has become newly appreciated. From the perspective of 2007, it is fortunate that Morricone's music for the 'animal trilogy' has been preserved, as it is in fact among the most varied and interesting film music he has composed.

Morricone worked again with Argento only once, on the 1995 film *Il sindroma di Stendhal* [The Stendhal Syndrome], about a policewoman who suffers from the eponymous psychosomatic illness, which produces a state of confusion, hallucination and mental overload as a result of looking at Renaissance paintings. The protagonist, who is tracking a serial rapist and killer in the Uffizi Gallery in Florence, is subsequently raped by him and develops a sex addiction for her attacker. The film is based on a fascinating idea but the fact that the main role is played by Argento's daughter Asia and the explicitly violent scenes of a sexual nature make it rather disturbing. Nonetheless some of Morricone's music is intriguing; as he states in the liner notes to the soundtrack recording (1999):

> I embarked on a style of composition in line with contemporary canons, as in the School of Vienna post-deterministic abstract. My score is characterised, for the first time in a film soundtrack, by the use of a passacaglia, an unusual expressive form which I don't think any other musician has used integrally in the cinema… In the trilogy the idea of music-noise, in which harsh sounds melded with traditional strings, worked very well, but in the new story there were paintings, classical material. So I had a natural impulse to write some music that would create a certain classical atmosphere.

The *passacaglia* (literally 'walking the street' in Italian, derived from strolling musicians) is a slow dance in triple time; Morricone develops a repeated four-note theme that appears in seemingly endless arrangements and variations throughout the film to the point of overkill. While some of the incidental orchestral music is effective, especially the spooky string effects, he returns to the main theme far too often – a defect in some of his other film scores as well. He also apparently takes a note from Goblin's book and incorporates a babble of voices and moans into some of the tracks, especially one entitled 'From Caravaggio To Canaletto', as well as his trademark children's chants and lullabies, percussion, piano runs and some very lush orchestration. Frequently, the effects are overstated and lack the variety of the trilogy. His music for the film seems indicative of the artistic decline into which Argento had slumped.

Argento, Hitchcock and Goblin

The strikingly innovative and dramatic effects of the collaboration between the progressive rock group Goblin and Argento are especially evident in what are considered Argento's masterpieces of film *d'orrore: Profondo Rosso* [Deep Red] (1975) and

Suspiria (1977), the latter of which has been described by Linda Schulte-Sasse as "the 'mother' of all horror movies" (2002: 1). Influenced by Bernard Herrmann's vibrantly scary music for strings in Hitchcock's *Psycho* (1960), Goblin's quest for a pulsating, hyper-narrative musical fabric bathes these films in sheets of throbbingly visceral sonic affect. Brophy has described the music for *Suspiria* as "audiovisual saturation... an hysterical unleashing of noise in libidinal, psychological and overall mind-bending modes... typically relentless, scathing and excessive" (2004: 227). McDonagh is reasonably accurate in her delineation of the differences between Morricone's and Goblin's scores for Argento's films:

> Unlike Morricone's score for the first three films, which are designed to act as straightforward (if ironic) counterpoint to the images, Goblin's composi-tions are an integral part of the unpredictable diegesis, as inherently contradictory as the deceptive imagery. (1991: 32)

Argento and Goblin pursued a frenzied aesthetic of image-matching sonic mayhem, which arguably provides one of the main ingredients of terror in *Profondo Rosso* and *Suspiria*, establishing them as historic pinnacles in horror-film music. Aaron Smuts has commented that the music in *Profondo Rosso* matches the visual excess of the images and is unprecedented in the history of film music for its power as a:

> transition device, serving to cue the entrance for often gruesome acts of bodily violence. This music... is radically out of synch with the calm Hopperesque settings and has seemingly few filmic precedents. However, Goblin's accompaniment adds distinctness to the violence numbers by serv-ing as a transitioning device into the horrific excess characteristic of Argento's films. (2002: 2)

Schulte-Sasse has noted that the score to *Suspiria* succeeds in blurring the bound-aries between diegetic and non-diegetic music, as well as often incorporating off-screen sound effects which throw the viewer off balance, producing a compulsive, even obses-sive, sonic motor to the film:

> The soundtrack... effects a sensuous immersion, a sense of compulsion as opposed to control, drive as opposed to desire... [it] renders unstable the boundary between conventional, non-diegetic 'mood' music and diegetic sound. (2002: 1)

It is something of a truism that it is often the soundtrack of horror films and psychological thrillers that scares us more than the images, and the role of film music in suturing together the three-dimensional experience that is cinema is at a premium in both genres. Atonal, discordant or jarring music in a minor key often generates suspense or provides an essential complement to the dramatic tension generated by a particular scene. An obvious example is the shower scene from Hitchcock's *Psycho*, where Bernard Herrmann's shrieking violin glissandi almost literally recreate the stabbing of

Janet Leigh's character Marion in the spectator's consciousness. They also, of course, evoke the bird cries which link the scene associatively to the stuffed birds that Norman Bates has displayed on his wall. Herrmann's music for Hitchcock, with its avoidance of melodies and motifs, represents something of a template for horror-film music and has been much imitated.

Whereas the deliberately restricted palette of Herrmann's music for *Psycho* matches sonically the film's use of black-and-white cinematography, and succeeds in bringing to the surface "the subliminal pulse of violence which in 1960 still lay beneath the rational facades of American society" (Brown, 1994: 174), Morricone's and Goblin's scores are arguably far less subtle than Herrmann's more unobtrusive music, although clearly influenced by it. Argento and Goblin reach in more obvious ways for a violent, irrational pulse more in keeping with the director's extravagant use of colour and murder set pieces in his films.

Argento is often compared to Hitchcock in his use of set pieces involving particularly lurid and gory knife murders, and his use of music often generates a sense of sonic excess which goes beyond Hermann's underscoring into a realm verging on aural hysteria that almost overwhelms the filmic images. In a 1988 interview Argento indicated this difference, as well as a distinction between the "refined" nature of Hitchcock's film and his own more blatantly commercial choices:

> Hitchcock... is... more refined. Too refined... I'm not stingy with effects, whereas he's lean and rigorous. With music, for example, he uses it as a background, almost like a chamber music concert, which at a certain point comes to the fore, whereas I use it in a much more robust way. (Ghezzi and Giusti, 1981: 91)

Argento uses the Italian word *massiccio*, which means 'massive' rather than 'robust', and this certainly conveys the effect of Goblin's music in *Suspiria*. Herrmann justly claimed that his music accounted for 40 percent of the psychological impact of some scenes in Hitchcock's films (quoted in Brown, 1994: 14). Massimo Morante of Goblin has claimed, rather exaggeratedly, that in the case of *Profondo Rosso*, Goblin's theme music (which went to number one in the pop charts in Italy and stayed in the top 40 for a year, selling more than three million copies) "takes 75% of the whole credit of the movie".[3] Although he is actually referring to the space taken up by a reference to Goblin on the advertising poster of the second edition of *Profondo Rosso*, and the commercial impact of the film and its music, the figure of 75 percent has an approximate correspondence to the degree of excess and overload that Goblin's music achieves in some scenes of *Profondo Rosso*, but even more so in what has become one of the most memorable opening sequences in horror-film history, the first 20 minutes of *Suspiria*.

Much of the impact of this opening sequence is due to the sonic onslaught of its visceral score. The opening credits are visually unprepossessing – in English and even in the Italian version of the film – and mistakenly refer to Goblin as 'The Goblins'.[4] There is also an extremely clumsy insertion of a redundant voiceover, which sets the narrative context of the opening sequence (according to Neil Young, delivered by Argento himself in the Italian version), but right from the beginning theme on celeste, the music takes control of the film's narrative drive. The sharply brittle and laceratingly metallic percussive effects by Agostino Marangolo and the sliding boom of Fabio Pignatelli's bass establishes a frenetic emotional pitch which the rest of the film never quite manages to equal. Claudio Simonetti's armoury of keyboards – credited on the soundtrack album as string mellotron, church organ and choruses, Elka organ, Logan violins, celeste, electric and acoustic piano, minimoog and moog system 55 – clearly also contributes a great deal to the music, along with Morante's guitars. But, as Morante has conceded, "Agostino allowed us to explore new musical ground... His percussive style added a lot of creepiness to our music."[5] The special effects of voices whispering 'witch', other sundry voices and the sound effects of a thunderstorm also embellish a soundscape which merges the diegetic and the non-diegetic in a way that brings added meaning to Claudia Gorbman's description of film music as providing a "psychic payoff" and a "bath of affect" for the viewer (Gorbman, 1987: 6). According to Dale Pierce:

> [The melody that opens the film is] *a twisted version of the old children's church song 'Jesus loves me, this I know. For the bible tells me so'... creating subliminal messages within the brains of the viewers and making them all the more aware of 'something evil' in the dancehall, even before the killings and satanic rituals start... The tone of this powerful main theme, one of Goblin's most popular creations, completely overshadowed all other lesser pieces of music in the film.*[6]

Goblin's music for this opening sequence literally overwhelms the images; Brophy has described it as: "audiovisual saturation... an hysterical unleashing of noise in libidinal, psychological and overall mind-bending modes... typically relentless, scathing and excessive" (2004: 227).

But, responding to the film's rather crassly generic commercial production values, which were ably contextualized by Kim Newman (1988), some critics at the time of its release tended to be rather scathing about both the film and the music. McDonagh quotes Russell Davies's dismissal of the music in the London *Observer* as "relentless and obvious" (1991: 146), while Mick Garris, described as "a free-lance music and film journalist, and lead vocalist for Horsefeathers, a Hollywood-based cinematic rock band", offers the following highly derogatory verdict in a review in *Cinefantastique* entitled 'Hackneyed in concept, but experimental in form':

> *Another good idea killed by over-exertion is the use of Goblin, a sort of pasta-fed Tangerine Dream, who provided the film's original score. Goblin, veterans of film, provide repetitive electronic motifs, complemented by heavy breathing, screams and moans which, by the time the director (who is credited as assisting with the musical composition) is through with it, sounds like the Disney 'Chilling Thrilling Sounds of the Haunted House' Halloween*

album. The film's sound is greatly enhanced by the use of stereo, and Goblin's music is capable, if a bit derivative of Tangerine Dream and Michael [Mike] Oldfield's Tubular Bells. (1977: 21)

Given that Disney's *Snow White and the Seven Dwarfs* (1937) was an influence on the colour composition in *Suspiria* (McDonagh, 1991: 129) and that Simonetti's Profondo Rosso Project later recorded a short version of *Tubular Bells* (an obvious influence on Goblin due to its highly effective use in Friedkin's *The Exorcist*), Garris is reasonably close to the mark in some respects.[7] But Goblin's music is arguably far more 'robust' and dramatic than the slur of "a pasta-fed Tangerine Dream", a group whose blandly ambient mellotron-driven soundscapes and film scores are far less dramatic and bombastic.

The most florid description I have encountered of the music in *Suspiria*'s opening sequence is by Daniel Schweiger,[8] who successfully manages to narrate the process through which the music sutures into the film's images:

Goblin hyped their orchestrations and child-like vocals into frenzied audio violence. A harsh lullaby starts the film, interrupted by shrieking violins and choruses of 'Witch!' Goblin's crashing rhythms and howls then turn a thunderstorm ride into a trip down the River Styx. Young Suzy is taxied to a dance academy that also serves as a coven.

Spastic drums and chanting ring out. A distraught student runs past Suzy. The music changes to whispers. The woman enters her friend's apartment. Speed guitars immediately take over when a window blows open. Overlapping vocals and strings generate terror when all she's doing is standing about. A hand smashes her face into the glass. Dozens of themes and instruments go off, mirroring her struggle and pain. Synths rapidly drown the victim's screaming, becoming unbearably shrill as she's forced to the roof. Drums beat relentlessly while her heart is stabbed, the electronics squealing off as her body plummets down, echoing synth vocals revealing that the debris has impaled her friend below.

For all of Suspiria's stylised shocks, it's Goblin's over-the-top music that gives the film real terror, successively flooding each scene. It's ugly enough when maggots crawl over spoiled meat, but it's crashing cymbals and tubular bells that sink in our nausea... Most murder scenes steadily pick up their themes, but Suspiria's score usually goes at full blast. Only Argento, a filmmaker totally in control of his work, would dare to pump the volume without having his ghastly images choked off with music.

Comparing Argento with his mentor, the horror director Mario Bava, Kim Newman describes Argento's approach to set pieces as "often bringing the music to the fore" in an "operatic approach [which] strains the notionally rational frame of the giallo" (1986: 23). This characterizes the sonic excess of Goblin in a way which is also evoked by McDonagh: "the curious disjunction between soundtrack and image (principally a matter of music so far out of line with the imagery as to be bizarre)" (1991: 25). After *Suspiria*, Goblin were offered work on a number of horror films, including the Italian versions of George Romero's *Dawn of the Dead* (1978) and the Australian film *Patrick* (Richard Franklin, 1977), and a string of other B-grade movies in both Italy and the USA. They also released a rock album in 1976, *Roller*, with Tartini's devil emblazoned on the front and back of the gatefold cover, and a very filmic 11-minute instrumental entitled 'Goblin'. Their psychedelic rock opera based on an LSD trip, with lyrics sung by Morante, *Il fantastico viaggio del 'bagarozzo' Mark* [The Fantastic Voyage Of Mark The Beetle] (1978), contained tracks entitled '*Terra di Goblin*' [Goblin Land] and '*Un ragazzo d'argento*' [A Silver Boy], and sounded like an imaginary soundtrack *ante litteram*. It included some impressive funk-oriented Hammond organ by Simonetti and guitar by Morante, and was reissued in 2001 by Cinevox as *Music To A Film That Doesn't Exist*. It holds its own with English-language rock operas composed around this time, and the slower tracks are reminiscent of Genesis. Tracks from both of these albums were reportedly used for B-grade movie film scores without the group's permission. For contractual reasons they could not use the group's name when they composed music for Argento's 1982 film *Tenebre*, which was credited to Simonetti–Pignatelli–Morante, while the title track for Argento's 1985 insect film *Phenomena* [Creepers] was credited to Simonetti, although three tracks were by Goblin, along with a pot-pourri of tracks by Bill Wyman, Motörhead, Iron Maiden and Andi Sex Gang. None of this music managed to achieve the sonic heights of *Suspiria* or *Profondo Rosso*. As Morante has stated:

> *Tenebre* is a cold, hi-tech electronic score... The idea was to create a disturbing wall of sound... *Tenebre* gives you an idea of how the Goblin sound was changing. If we were to score horror film now, you probably wouldn't recognise the band.[9]

This was certainly true. The theme music for *Tenebre* is turgid and bombastic pomp rock, with Simonetti's organ effects dominating, while the other tracks provide inconsequential atmospheric effects. Goblin, forced to become too prolific in their film music, had clearly lost their touch.

Almost two decades after the baroque peak of Argento's career, he attempted to rescale his mid-1970s heights in a reunion with Goblin in *Nonhosonno* [Sleepless] (2000), but to far less memorable effect than in the 1970s. In the interim, Argento had worked with British prog rocker Keith Emerson in *Inferno* (1980). He had also made an unsuccessful attempt to reunite Goblin for his 1992 film *Trauma*, which ended up being scored by the prolific composer Pino Donaggio, still best known for writing the Italian song on which the 1966 Dusty Springfield hit 'You Don't Have To Say You Love Me' was based. At the time Massimo Morante's rather wistful statement summed up why Goblin, and arguably Argento also, had become a spent force:

> *Whatever happens in the future, we'll have to deal with being best-known for our old work, because everyone will remember us for the Argento soundtracks; they're not easy to top. Look what happened to Tangerine Dream… Goblin is different; we have a legacy with horror fans, and I know that our names will never be forgotten.*[10]

As Aaron Smuts has pointed out, Argento's *Profondo Rosso* above all emphasizes "the contiguity of music and violence" and "to many, the visual/aural discord resulting from Argento's frequent collaborations with Goblin is the defining aspect of his films" (2002: 1, 4). This is certainly true of *Suspiria* and *Profondo Rosso*, but arguably could also be applied retrospectively, and perhaps in more subtle ways, to Morricone's music in the animal trilogy.

Notes

1. See *Mondo Morricone: Mindblowing Film Themes By Ennio Morricone From Italian Cult Movies (1968–1972)* (1996), *Ennio Morricone, Chamber Music* (1988) and *Ennio Morricone Remixes, Volumes 1 and 2* (2003).
2. In the Italian novelization of *Four Flies*, included in a compilation entitled *Profondo Thrilling* (which contains prose versions of *Bird*, *Cat*, *Four Flies*, *Profondo Rosso* and *Tenebre*, but surprisingly not *Suspiria*), Brian Auger is mentioned during the opening band rehearsal scene, and may have been used as a model for Roberto's band (Argento, 1994: 143).
3. 'Goblin: Massimo Morante interview' (http://www.voicenet.com/~goblin/morante_int.html, accessed 23 May 1998).
4. The symbol of the goblin-like red devil with bat's wings playing the violin which became synonymous with Goblin and was used as a logo on most of their recordings was, according to Fabio Pignatelli (see 'Fabio Pignatelli interview', in the website given in note 3), suggested by their editor Carlo Bixio, a prolific composer and arranger on the Italian music scene. It derives from a painting of the devil appearing in a dream to the eighteenth-century Italian baroque composer and violinist Giuseppe Tartini (1692–1770), and from the latter's 1713 sonata in B flat for piano and violin known as 'Il trillo del diavolo' [The Devil's Trill]. Tartini dreamt he had made a Faustian compact with the devil and lent him his violin, on which the devil played a trill of such taste and beauty that it was superior to anything he had ever heard. The composer attempted to reproduce what the devil had played, but the result was so inferior to what he had heard in his dream that he declared he should have broken his instrument and abandoned music forever (see http://vanessamae.com/devils-trill.shtml). *The Devil's Trill* is, however, considered to be Tartini's best composition, and this anecdote is possibly the source of the violin becoming known as 'the devil's instrument' in works such as Stravinsky's *The Soldier's Tale*. It is certainly an appropriate source for Goblin's horror-film music. Goblin began as a prog rock group called Cherry Ripe, who performed songs in English and whose first album was influenced by Genesis, King Crimson, Yes and Keith Emerson. After Argento had a falling-out with jazz pianist Giorgio

Gaslini on *Profondo Rosso*, he engaged the group through their label Cinevox to provide the score, some of which used Gaslini's compositions as a basis. The group, who had never written film music before, decided they needed a new name to suit the darker music of the film. They provided the opening 20 minutes of the film's music. As keyboard player Claudio Simonetti has said:

> There were radical differences between our score and Gaslini's... Dario loves rock music and Goblin was essentially a rock band, and I've always felt he wanted Deep Red to be sort of a primordial video clip. (quoted in Curci, 1998)

5. Interview cited in note 3 above.
6. Dale Pierce, 'Music to bleed by' (http://www.voicenet.com/~goblin/deepart.html, accessed 16 May 1998).
7. Simonetti has released a number of post-Goblin versions of Argento film music: *Profondo Rosso Project* (undated) includes prog rock versions of the themes from the John Carpenter films *Halloween* (1978) and *Escape from New York* (1981), as well as *Tubular Bells*; the Simonetti Project's *Mystery, Magic And Madness* has 'Albinoni In Rock' and 'Carmina Burana's Theme' [sic], as well as a mixture of Argento and non-Argento themes. Neither succeeds in achieving anything approaching the aural excitement of Goblin's original scores. Simonetti's *Music From Dario Argento's Horror Movies* (Rome: viviMusica soundtracks, 1993), is a re-recording of main themes from films such as *Profondo Rosso*, *Suspiria*, *Tenebre* and *Phenomena*, with non-Goblin rock musicians, a huge array of different keyboards – no fewer than twenty-one are mentioned in the liner notes – and even a US rapper and a scratch DJ on *Profondo Rosso*. It is mostly thudding techno re-versionings with banal sound effects and even some additional English lyrics. The paradoxically titled *Goblin: The Original Remixes–Vol.1*, in which Simonetti appears not to have been involved, contains pumping house music and bland ambient remixes (constructed at 'Underwater Studio') of themes from many of Argento's films, along with non-Argento Goblin tracks.
8. Daniel Schweiger, 'Goblin and the vicious smashing of horror's music boundaries' (http://www.voicenet.com/~goblin/toxicart.html, accessed 16 May 1998).
9. L. Curci, 'To score the gore' (http://www.voicenet.com/~goblin/fangoart.html, accessed 16 May 1998).
10. *Ibid.*

References

Argento, D. (1994), *Profondo Thrilling*, Roma: Grandi Tascabili Economici Newton.
Bender, J. (1992), *Ennio Morricone: The Thriller Collection*, liner notes, New York: DRG Records.
Brophy, P. (2004), *100 Modern Soundtracks*, London: BFI Publishing.
Brown, R. S. (1994), *Overtones and Undertones: Reading Film Music*, Berkeley: University of California Press.

Deutsch, D. C. (1995), *An Ennio Morricone–Dario Argento Trilogy*, liner notes, New York: DRG Records.

Garris, M. (1977), 'Suspiria: Hackneyed in Concept, But Experimental in Form', *Cinefantastique*, 6(3) (winter), 21.

Ghezzi, E., and Giusti, M. (1981), 'Dario Argento: La paura la music il cinema', *Filmcritica*, 32(312), 89–95.

Gorbman, C. (1987), *Unheard Melodies: Narrative Film Music*, Bloomington: Indiana University Press.

McDonagh, M. (1991), *Broken Mirrors/Broken Minds: The Dark Dreams of Dario Argento*, London: Sun Tavenfields.

Needham, G. (2006), 'From Punctum to Pentazet, and Everything in Between: Dario Argento's *Il gatto a nove code* and *Quattro mosche di velluto grigio*', *Kinoeye*, 2(11), 00–00 (http://www.kinoeye.org/02/11/needham11 no2.php, accessed 7 February 2006).

Newman, K. (1986), 'Thirty Years in Another Town: The History of Italian Exploitation', *Monthly Film Bulletin*, January, February and March, 20–4, 51–5, 88–91.

Schulte-Sasse, L. (1992), 'The "mother" of all horror movies: Dario Argento's *Suspiria*', *Kinoeye*, 2(11), 00–00 (http://www.kinoeye.org/02/11/schultesasse11.php, accessed 7 February 2006).

Smuts, A. (2002), 'The principles of association: Dario Argento's *Profondo Rosso*', *Kinoeye*, 2(11), 00–00 (http://www.kinoeye.org/02/11/smuts11.php, accessed 7 February 2006).

Discography

Ennio Morricone	*An Ennio Morricone–Dario Argento Trilogy*	DRG Records, 1995
Ennio Morricone	*The Stendhal Syndrome*	DRG Records, 1999
Goblin	*Il fantastico viaggio del 'bagarozzo' Mark*	Cinevox, 1992
Goblin	'Profondo Rosso/Death Dies'	Cinevox, 1975
Goblin	*Suspiria – Colonna Sonora originale*	Cinevox, 1987
Goblin	*The Goblin Collection 1975–1989*	DRG Records, 1995
Goblin	*Roller*	Cinevox, 1976
Goblin	*Volume II 1975–1980*	DRG Records, 1998
Goblin	*Volume III 1978–1984*	DRG Records, 1998
Goblin	*Zombi/Tenebre*	Cinevox, 1990
Assorted	*Phenomena*	Roadrunner, 1985

6 Inflamed

Synthetic Folk Music and Paganism in the Island World of The Wicker Man

Jon Fitzgerald and Philip Hayward

The 1973 British cult horror film *The Wicker Man* ends with the arresting image of a huge wicker effigy ablaze on an island clifftop. Inside the burning structure is a male police officer, restrained and consumed by fire as a sacrifice to pagan gods in an attempt to ensure the return of bountiful harvests. The horror of the film's final image and sound-scene are the climax of an audio-visual narrative in which image and sound conspire to delude and destabilize the protagonist, ultimately rendering him powerless to do more than await the resurrection he so fervently believes in. Overwhelmed with dread at the certainty of his imminent death, the entrapped policeman affirms his Christian beliefs by singing 'The Lord's my shepherd' and reciting prayers until his agonies overtake him. Meanwhile the pagan islanders look on raptly, happily singing a version of the old English song 'Sumer is i-cumen in'.

These two songs symbolize the clash of cultures and sensibilities at the core of the film's narrative. The lyrical, musical and performance contrasts are striking. The islanders' song is a version of a mid-thirteenth-century secular motet in praise of the arrival of spring. Musically, 'Sumer is i-cumen in' involves extensive repetition of a simple major key melody to create a musical round (an open-ended musical form that continues indefinitely until there is mutual agreement to end), where several parts sing the same melody, with staggered entries leading to the creation of vocal harmonies. The islanders' rendition of the song in a contrapuntal arrangement[1] to an up-tempo, bouncy 6/8 dance rhythm (a common feature of English jigs), accompanied by drums, tuba and clarinet, conveys a sense of jolly communal conviviality, all the more marked given the sacrifice unfolding before them, as they proclaim:

> Summer is i-cumen in
> Loudly sing 'Cuckoo'
> Groweth seed and bloweth mead
> And springs the wood anew.

It is hard to imagine a more contrasting musical offering than the policeman's attempt to sing 'The Lord's my shepherd'. This enduringly popular devotional hymn is an adaptation of the 23rd Psalm, originally published in the *Scottish Psalter* (hymnbook) in 1650. It employs a triple metre with a well-structured, arch-contoured melody (rising to a high note in the second phrase before falling to the tonic note to end the melody). It has a closed form (where the melody has a clear beginning and end). The tempo is slow, and there is no focus on rhythmic elements. With flames rising around him, the Scottish police officer's defiant attempt to render the opening lines serves to focus attention on the lyrics – which attest to the comfort that the Christian God offers to believers:

> *The Lord's my shepherd,*
> *I'll not want;*
> *He makes me down to lie*
> *In pastures green...*

As the fire advances, crackling and roaring in the sound mix, the sacrificial victim's screams and declarations ultimately subside, while the islanders' motet continues unchallenged, victorious over the individual Christian voice, and adding a broader symbolic level to the film's narrative closure.

The prominent role of music during the film's climax is consistent with its role within the film as a whole, where it is used continually to mark boundaries between the islanders and the policeman (isolating the officer both literally and symbolically). In key scenes this approach is often enhanced through switches in 'points of audition' and complexity for the soundtrack as a whole, blending music, dialogue, atmospheres and effects to edge the film's naturalistic scenario into sequences of more allusive, paganish 'magical realism'.

History and context

The Wicker Man was inspired by David Pinner's 1967 novel *Ritual*, which concerned the occult-associated murder of a child in a remote, pagan-tinged Cornish community. Its situation of a supernatural/horror scenario in a British regional location conformed to a tendency in British horror fiction of this period to shift from the archetypal Transylvania and Middle Europe of much of Hammer film and literary fiction to a more local/regional context. In this regard, both Pinner's *Ritual* and *The Wicker Man* were significantly prefigured by John Gilling's 1966 feature film *A Plague of Zombies*, also set in Cornwall, in which a maniacal aristocrat subjected the local population to his deranged will. The focus on local paganism in British culture in the 1960s was inspired by a revival of interest in the work of the Scottish cultural anthropologist James Frazer, occasioned, at least in part, by the publication of an abridged and annotated version of his seminal study *The Golden Bough* in 1958. With the growth of 1960s counter-culture and interest in various alternative and esoteric practices, paganism and psychedelia crossed paths. One striking manifestation of this was the rise of interest in (and theorization about) the significance of the Stonehenge circle in Wiltshire and

Druidism in general, resulting, amongst other things, in the first annual Summer Solstice 'Free Festival' at Stonehenge in 1974, when 500 young people scaled its fences and held impromptu musical performances and dances. This wave of interest in British paganism and folklore was also represented in music through the work of groups such as Scottish ensemble the Incredible String Band, which achieved commercial success in 1967–72 with subtle, theatrical songs of magic, mystery and romance performed in experimental folk-rock style (on albums such as *5,000 Spirits* [1967] and *The Hangman's Beautiful Daughter* [1968]).

Influenced by this cultural backdrop, the playwright Anthony Shaffer purchased the rights to adapt Pinner's novel for film and formed a consortium with actor Christopher Lee and film producer Peter Snell to develop the project. After consulting Frazer's *The Golden Bough* and conducting further research on British pagan rituals and folklore, Shaffer extensively revised the narrative in consultation with director Robin Hardy and produced a new outline. In the revised scenario, the principal action took place in the (fictional) Scottish community of Summerisle, whose inhabitants lure a pious off-islander, in the form of an upright, Christian Scottish police sergeant, into its web and, finally, into the sacrificial pyre.

The film was shot on location in Scotland in the autumn of 1972, with a cast including Edward Woodward as the sacrificial victim (Sergeant Howie), Christopher Lee as the local laird (Lord Summerisle), Britt Ekland as a local sex 'priestess' and Ingrid Pitt as a schoolteacher. Due to a series of industrial factors coinciding with its first release, the film received limited exposure in the United Kingdom and the USA and rapidly faded from public attention. However, it began to attract a fan following and gained a cult status in the 1980s and 1990s that produced aficionado websites,[2] dedicated documentaries,[3] a DVD double-pack release of the original film print plus a 'director's cut' in 2003,[4] a 'making of' book (Brown, 2000) and a remastered CD release of its music tracks (2002).

The release of the repackaged soundtrack CD resulted in critical attention to its music and continuing fan approbation and discussion.[5] The film has also been the subject of further musical engagements. Momus and Anne Laplantine released their 'electronic folk' *Summerisle* album in 2004,[6] British heavy metal band Iron Maiden penned a tribute track on their 2000 album *Brave New World*, and a midsummer music event, named 'The Wickerman Festival', has been held in Dundrennan, Scotland, since 2002, and culminates in a thirty-foot-high wicker man being set alight.[7]

Musical introduction

The score was envisaged early in the production process as a key element in creating the pagan themes and colourations of the film and, to this end, it combined musical elements drawn from British folk traditions with styles and arrangements characteristic of late 1960s and early 1970s folk and progressive rock. Somewhat surprisingly, for such a British-orientated production, the US actor, playwright and composer Paul

Giovanni was chosen to score the project. He employed a recent Royal College of Music (London) composition graduate Gary Carpenter as associate musical director and Carpenter, in turn, recruited two fellow graduates (multi-instrumentalists Peter Brewis and Michael Cole) and three members of Hocket, a London-based folk rock band he performed with (guitarist Andrew Tompkins, violinist Ian Cutler and drummer Bernard Murray).[8] Together these musicians provided a score that mixes traditional folk melodies with orchestral and 'progressive' folk-pop material to create a musical fantasia for the island that emphasizes its exotic difference from mainland Scotland and the modern western world in general.

The film opens with a staggered credit sequence and prelude to the main body of action on Summerisle. The first section introduces us to the main character and (a particular representation of) Scotland via images and sounds of a single-engined seaplane coming in to land at a small port (under the main titles), accompanied by a musical passage that evokes a sense of traditional stoic 'Celticness' through drone-style fifths and a triple metre. The credit sequence pauses as the police sergeant pilot emerges, is picked up by a constable, engages in verbal banter and is driven away. Overlapping the end of this sequence, the first lines of 'The Lord's my shepherd' are heard before the visual scene cuts to the interior of a church where the congregation – and, most prominently, the sergeant – are shown earnestly singing the hymn. The folk song/hymn contrast highlighted in the film's finale is thereby gently prefigured at the very beginning of the narrative, with its emphasis on the sergeant's sincere devotion.

Following another short narrative sequence, where the sergeant receives an anonymous letter telling of the disappearance of a female child (named Rowan Morrison) from Summerisle, the credit sequence recommences as the sergeant pilots his seaplane over starkly dramatic Scottish landscapes. The first part of this sequence is accompanied by drone sounds (this time a fourth interval) before morphing into a folk-styled female vocal performance of a setting of Robert Burns's ballad 'The Highland Widow's Lament'. This English-language verse, inspired by the massacre of Glencoe (1691), is punctuated (in its opening verses) with the lament "Ochon, ochon, ochrie" (further signalling its Celtic associations). In combination with the initial sequence that emphasizes Scottish puritan religiosity, this invocation of the Highlands' history of oppression and defeat by the English (over stark landscape images) serves to characterize the Scotland to which Summerisle is deeply and implacably 'other'.

The island of songs

From the establishing sounds and images detailed above, the narrative and sound world rapidly shifts. As the plane flies over the island the viewer encounters unexpectedly lush springtime fields and orchards. Burns's song fades away, replaced by a new composition ('Annie's Song') that imbues a folk melody with some of the pop sensibilities of composer Paul Giovanni. The result is a striking musical hybrid that could have been created by an early-1970s progressive rock band[9] whereby Chet Atkins-style picked acoustic guitar and recorders provide a gentle accompaniment to a standard melody that begins in Mixolydian mode (major with flat 7) with a typical Mixolydian harmonic progression (C, B♭, C).[10] The second half of the tune is somewhat adventurous harmonically – moving away from a simple folk progression to add the minor V and ♭III chords, plus chord colours, such as the added ninth and suspended fourth. Along with its melodic richness, its romantically erotic lyrics also offer a marked contrast to the preceding verses of 'The Lord's my shepherd' and the 'Highland Widow's Lament', as the vocal protagonist recalls kissing his beloved "among the leaves of barley". After this introduction, the song is repeated on a number of occasions in the film, linking abundant crops and sensuality as motifs of island life.

From the moment that Howie's plane crosses into the island's airspace, the film's music communicates a distinct character for the island and its community. While it is located with geographic coherence and contiguity as a community offshore from the mainland, the vegetation, climate and culture mark it as 'other' to the landscape and society sketched in the film's opening. As a warm, abundant agricultural isle, the location is an embellishment of those western Scottish islands touched by the last tendrils of the Gulf Stream and granted micro-climates that enable more fertile farming than in neighbouring locations. In its mixture of mysticism and agricultural success, the location suggests inspiration from the Findhorn community (on the Moray Firth coast), with its celebrated cultivation of large vegetables attributed to the syncretic mysticism of its quiet cult community (founded in the mid-1960s by Peter and Eileen Caddy and Dorothy Maclean).[11]

But the film takes otherness further and represents Summerisle as a place that houses a synthetic pagan culture and religion, one drawn from various British elements, in many cases identifiably English ones. As such, Summerisle presents itself as something of a fantasia on themes and texts derived from various regional traditions. The island 'anthem', 'Sumer is i-cumen in', is a well-known old English tune. Likewise, the horse-headed figure which features in the parade that leads to the narrative climax is clearly derived from rituals such as the Padstow Mayday 'Obby 'Oss. However, such a combination of elements is not inappropriate to its setting. Far from being represented as some remote pagan corner of the British Isles that time somehow 'forgot', the narrative expressly explains Summerisle's culture and religion as the invention of the current laird's ancestor, a Victorian agricultural experimenter, who brought agricultural prosperity to the island along with a new religion (and an approach to sexuality that has clear affinities to 1960s/1970s views on 'free love'). Representing this synthetic community and ethos, the film's island music sequences are suitably synthetic and musically exoticist (within a folk-music framework). They eschew any referential authenticity in favour of a dreamily romanticist faux paganism that takes the Victorian era reworking and representation of traditional music (memorably described by Dave Harker [1985] as "fakesong") to a further level of inauthenticity appropriate to the invented folklore and religion of the community.

Communal music-making is posed as central to island life and, in the interactions between Sergeant Howie and the islanders, is used to isolate him, both literally and symbolically. The music and the performances invariably have overt sexual connotations and are deliberately designed to tease and torment the officer, testing his distance from the events and people he encounters. While much of the music is diegetic in origin, the lines between diegetic and non-diegetic music are often unclear, with ostensibly live on-screen performances being augmented by additional unseen performers, sounds and studio enhancement.

The crucial sequence for establishing this exclusion begins when Howie enters the local pub (the Green Man Inn), triggering a brief cessation of the music being performed there and thus confirming his status as an outsider. After the landlord introduces his beautiful daughter Willow to the sergeant, the pub patrons (as if on cue) begin to sing the highly suggestive song 'The Landlord's Daughter', alternating solo passages with communal choruses. Several customers provide accompaniment on accordion, recorder, guitar, fiddle and tambourine and Willow dances provocatively with customers during an extended instrumental break. The song is intentionally sexual in nature, and the crowd boldly mocks the police officer until he stops the music abruptly by banging on the bar and raises the matter of Rowan Morrison's disappearance.

Following a meal, he goes for a walk, during which he is shocked to witness a couple making love outdoors and a naked woman crying in a graveyard – these glimpsed scenes being accompanied by a simple flute and recorder melody. On returning to the pub, the distressed police officer retires to his room, where he becomes the focus and centre of a complex scene. Visually based around (spatially logical) intercuts between the interior of his room, Willow's adjacent room, the downstairs pub lounge, the exterior of the pub and the courtyard below, the sound composition privileges Sergeant Howie's narrative centrality through mixing all external sounds prominently and clearly and by representing him reacting to these, battling sonic suggestion and temptation, and seeking strength in Christian belief to avoid falling into a pagan place of passion and emotion.

The first element in the sonic enchantment which he battles against is provided by a singer and a guitarist downstairs performing a variation of the previously heard flute and recorder melody, (Giovanni's) overtly sexual composition 'Gently Johnny':

> *I put my hand on her thigh*
> *And she said 'Do you want to try?'*
> *I put my hand on her belly*
> *And she said 'Do you want to fill me?'*

While this drifts upstairs, Howie's position close to an open window allows him to overhear the (as yet unmet) Lord Summerisle calling up to Willow to introduce an adolescent boy, whom she invites to her room in an enticing manner. Peering out of his window, Howie witnesses the Laird's dialogue with Willow (in which he calls her

'Aphrodite' – "the goddess of love in human form"), and hears the following day referred to as "the day of death". After the boy goes up to Willow's room, the musicians downstairs recommence 'Gently Johnny', which develops into a communal performance whose vocal richness and intricacy add to the erotic textures of the scene,[12] with sounds of Willow 'entertaining' her visitor at the back of the mix. Outside, Lord Summerisle conducts a monologue, apparently to himself but implicitly to the eavesdropping sergeant, commenting about those "who lie awake in the dark thinking of their sins" as the image cuts to Howie at prayer in his room, listening to the sounds of lovemaking through the wall. The patrons continue to sing, gazing raptly at the ceiling, above which are both Howie's and Willow's rooms, and the image cuts to Howie in torment.

Through the careful privileged orchestration of event and sound around the protagonist, this and subsequent scenes represent Howie as entrapped in a world where reality and illusion blur, stretching sanity. The enigmatic Lord Summerisle looms here as a puppet-master, or as the director of an extended, island-wide pageant through which Howie is carefully guided.

The unsettling paganism of the island is signified again the next day, when Howie resumes his search and visits the local school to find the boys enthusiastically dancing round the maypole to a lively song accompanied by jew's harp (and unseen, implicitly extra-diegetic) guitar and fiddle. Entering the schoolroom, he finds the female students singing along, conducted by the female teacher, adding (diegetic) percussion by hitting their desks with rulers to create a communal rhythm. Continual cutting between the group of schoolchildren and the police officer accentuates the latter's isolation, and his disapproving reactions contrast with the uninhibited joy of the children. Once again, the sexual nature of the communal celebration is overt, to the extent that the teacher explains to the class (in the officer's presence and much to his disgust) that the maypole "is the image of the penis, which is venerated in religions such as ours, symbolizing the generative forces of nature".

Fresh shocks follow as he witnesses a coven-like fertility ritual performed by minimally clad women singing and dancing within a stone circle. The music accompanying this begins with a simple melodic counterpoint before moving to an uptempo 6/8 tune in E minor. Once again, the camera cuts between the group and the police officer, highlighting his shock and disgust at what he is forced to witness. Howie then visits Lord Summerisle, who continues the blurring of the diegetic and non-diegetic by playing the fertility dance motif on the piano before launching into another raunchy ballad, joined by the schoolteacher.

By now, the audience has been exposed to a diverse collection of musical styles and hybrids (from folk tunes and folk-rock hybrids to classical counterpoint). In addition, the instrumental line-up is unusual, to say the least, incorporating sounds such as rock guitar, bass, drums, piano, recorders, jew's harp, harmonica, concertina, bassoon, fife, ocarina, Nordic lyre and brass instruments. All of these elements give the music an 'oddness' that has been noted by various observers and helps create the disturbing atmosphere of the film. In Lindsay's words, the music is "like the strange island in the film: serene and acquiescent, but also suspicious at the same time".[13]

The culmination of the technique of using sexualized music to torment the police officer occurs on his second night on the island. After pausing before his door, Willow retires to her room, with scenes and sounds intercut from the adjacent bedrooms and the downstairs bar. Willow drives the officer into a frenzy of sexual frustration. First, lying naked on her bed, she begins to bang on the adjoining bedroom wall in time to the instrumental music downstairs, then begins to sing an explicit invitation to her unseen neighbour, eventually dancing naked against the wall, slapping its surface and her thighs in building excitement (as tom-tom drums enter the mix). Lured by the sound and his imagination, Howie prowls his room, pressing against the wall, sweating, near-crazed and despondent with lust.

In sublime contrast, Howie starts the next day in the local library, reading about May Day rituals in *The Golden Bough* and learning of the virgin sacrifice he believes is about to unfold. Unable to return to the mainland for reinforcements due to sabotage of his plane, he returns, first to chase the elusive figure of a May Day 'Obby 'Oss through backstreets, then to conduct a last desperate search for Rowan. For these sequences, again, musical sources and referents are mixed, Carpenter explaining that:

> [They use] *largely traditional Scottish folk music, particularly the Strathspey 'Robertson's Rant', although we use the Irish variant of the reel 'Drowsy Maggie'. In fact a lot of the background scoring is Irish rather than Scottish-derived and a lot of that is cannibalised from old 'Hocket' arrangements.*
> (2000)

The final, climactic sequence commences with the islanders marching slowly towards the coastal hillside in festival costume, Howie disguised and capering along in the costume of the ritual 'Fool', accompanied by slow, brass-band marching music. Once again the diegetic music is unrealistically portrayed – a small group of visible instrumentalists is unconvincingly assumed to be creating a full band sound. En route they pause to perform a game in which each islander places his or her head inside a group of crossed swords. The idea of the game is that the person whose head is within the crossed swords when the music stops will have it chopped off. The childlike chant used for this scene effectively heightens the tension – yet again the seemingly innocent play of the islanders appears to be associated with potentially sinister intent.

Reaching the clifftop, Howie sees Rowan tied, as if prepared for sacrifice, and rushes to release her, heading off with her through an opening in the cliff in an attempt to escape the massed paraders. Accompanied by an incongruous passage of rock music (with distorted guitars and blues-style riffing), Howie frantically dashes through the beach caves, only to realize the deception as Rowan delivers him to Lord Summerisle once more. Before the dramatic sighting of the huge wicker effigy, we hear a musical reprise of the descending line and humming voices used in the earlier graveyard scene, symbolizing the police officer's inevitable and terrible fate. The long-suspected sinister intent of the islanders is now finally revealed in its full horror, and their happy rendition of 'Sumer is i-cumen in' emphasizes their inhuman disregard for their hapless human sacrifice. The police officer's isolation is complete, as he stands trapped in the wicker cage, along with a pig, poultry and a calf, awaiting his agonizing sacrificial death.

The game's over

The Wicker Man is distinct within both British horror cinema and, indeed, British cinema more generally, for the manner in which its music and sound design enhance and colour the mythical–magical scenarios it represents. More than this, its soundtrack operates to represent – and thereby offer clues as to – the particular manipulations of social mores, spirituality and customs it offers. With its theme of a remote, mystical (and mystifying) island explored by a male outsider, the film bears more than a passing resemblance to John Fowles's 1965 novel *The Magus* (adapted to film in 1968 by Guy Green) – a tale of a young Englishman on a Greek island, seduced, confused and destabilized by erotic games of illusion orchestrated by a mysterious millionaire. But, unlike Fowles's novel, *The Wicker Man* provides a grisly closure, condemning its protagonist to the flames. As Lord Summerisle explains to Sergeant Howie before his immolation:

> *Welcome fool, you have come of your own free will to the appointed place. The game's over… It is we who found you and brought you here and controlled your every thought and action since you arrived.*

This summary also serves to describe the manner in which the music and overall sound composition of the film serve to position the viewer/auditor to follow and experience the narrative's duping of the protagonist. In its unsettling use of point of audition and musical styles, *The Wicker Man* offers a subtly horrific scenario of destabilization and entrapment. Melodies unsettle and delude, lyrics convey double meanings and then the game's over…

Notes

1. Carpenter describes the music as a "contrapuntal feat" that sets the melody of 'Sumer is i-cumen in' to the waltz music, based on a Scottish folk tune, which was used in the preceding 'Procession' sequence. See G. Carpenter, 'The Wicker Man – settling the score' (http://www.garycarpenter.net/archive/wicker.htm).
2. Such as the 'Nuada – *The Wicker Man* journal' (http://www.nuada98.fsnet.co.uk/nuada%203) and '*The Wicker Man* journey' (http://www.sandrew.demon.co.uk/wickerman).
3. Such as two British TV documentaries *Ex-S: The Wicker Man* (1998) and *Burnt Offering – the Cult of the Wicker Man* (2001).

4. The film text discussed in the sections below is that of the 2003 'director's cut' version.
5. For examples of both, see the BBC review website entry (http://www.bbc.co.uk/music/easy/reviews/paulgiovanni_wicker.shtml).
6. Momus — otherwise known as Stephen Malmus — also wrote an essay on the original film, entitled 'Wicker meets man', which is archived online (http://www.imomus.com/wickermeetsman.html).
7. See the Wickerman Festival website (http://www.thewickermanfestival.co.uk/). While not inspired by the film (see 'Media Myth #4', http://www.burningman.com/press/myths.html#wicker), the Burning Man Festival in the USA, which started in California in 1986 as a small-scale event on a beach, has now developed into a major cultural festival held in the Black Rock Desert of Nevada that attracts over 25,000 people annually. See http://www.burningman.com for history and details.
8. Collectively referred to in the credits for the first film as 'Lodestone' but later renamed 'Magnet', to avoid clashes with another band with the former name. Hocket, which also included bassist and vocalist Ray Worman, was influenced by artists such as British folk-rock pioneers Steeleye Span, Breton harpist Alan Stivell and progressive rock band Yes, and recorded a session for DJ John Peel's evening show on BBC Radio One circa 1973 (Ian Cutler, personal communication to the authors, 2006).
9. Such as Pink Floyd, on their more acoustic compositions, e.g., 'Grantchester Meadows' on their 1969 album *Ummagumma*.
10. The guitar is actually tuned low and plays the D and C chord shapes that are common within this style.
11. It mixes Christianity with a belief in *devas* (plant spirits); see Caddy (1967).
12. Associate musical director Gary Carpenter's account on his website (see note 1 above) of the production of this sequence offers insight into the collaborative process involved in creating the music:

> *Paul would use his guitar to demonstrate what he was after to Andy Tompkins, our guitarist, who would then 'personalise' it a bit and that was the guitar 'riff' — which requires a fist of iron to maintain, by the way. I came up with little 'counter-melody' ideas which would be yes-ed or no-ed. Paul would, democratically, do likewise. In the end, it's hard to tell who inputted what, particularly as the players themselves also contributed ideas throughout the entire process. The descending violin phrase was probably Paul's invention; the oscillating tenor recorder motif was my main contribution. What was absolutely Paul was the extraordinary vocal texture at the song's climax [which was] achieved by layering. One or two parts [the women's voices in particular] were fixed in advance — the rest were put down by ear with Paul singing to each singer what was required. The result was pure magic, in my opinion, with some truly extraordinary resultant harmonies which, as no one actually seemed to be singing them, are a continuing source of wonder.*

13. C. Lindsay, The Wicker Man CD review, *Stylus Magazine* online (http://www. stylusmagazine.com/review.php?ID=1156).

References

Bartholomew, D. (1977), 'The Wicker Man', *Cinefantastique*, 6(3), 4–18.

Brown, A. (2000), *Inside 'The Wicker Man'*, London: Sidgwick & Jackson.

Caddy, E. (1967), *God Spoke to Me*, Findhorn (Scotland): Findhorn Press.

Harker, D. (1985), *Fakesong: The Manufacture of British 'Folksong' 1700 to the Present Day*, Milton Keynes: Open University Press.

Fowles, J. (1965), *The Magus*, London: Jonathan Cape.

Frazer, J. (1890), *The Golden Bough: A Study in Magic and Religion*, London: Macmillan.

Pinner, D. (1967), *Ritual*, London: Hutchison/Arrow.

7 Rhythms of Evil
Exorcizing Sound from The Exorcist

Mark Evans

> The credits give way to an image of a huge ochre sun, burning over the ruins
> of Nineveh. A young boy is seen leaping across the gullies of a vast
> archaeological dig, the rapid motion of his legs criss-crossing the screen
> which itself seems to shimmer with an almost stroboscopic pulse. All around
> the dig, picks are driven into the dirt-belching earth, creating a dysrhythmic
> throb which will be re-established a few minutes later by workmen clanging
> hammers on an anvil in a hellishly sweaty forge. (Kermode, 1998: 24)

Mark Kermode's poetic description of the opening scenes in *The Exorcist* (William
Friedkin, 1973) reveals, yet also belies, the central sonic juxtaposition of the film. What
Kermode hears as dysrhythmic is actually the complex polyrhythm of the natural order.
The opening Iraq scenes of *The Exorcist* are carefully constructed visually (note the
hyperbolized swinging action of the workers) and aurally (the sound of axes clanging
against rock in regular, discernible patterns) to establish the rhythmic vitality of the
setting. The viewer/listener is drawn further into this through the updated sound design
of the 1998 re-release of the film.[1] Now, in 5.1 surround-sound configuration,[2] the
viewer–listener is more quickly and thoroughly drawn into the world of the film –
especially the disruption of the natural order. As pickaxes in close-up smash into rock,
we hear those fragmented rocks shatter and spray outside the purview of the screen,
moving past the audience to the rear speakers. The audience has become a worker,
positioned as one holding the pick, and thus subsumed into the rhythmic throb of life.

Not only their physical work is rhythmically determined, but so are their vocal
interjections, akin to the work songs of the Bosavi people recorded by Steven Feld in
Papua New Guinea,[3] or those discussed by Ted Gioia (2006). This working environment
is a rich texture of melodic and rhythmic interplay. Yet even the vocal interjections take
their place rhythmically rather than melodically, highlighting the intrinsic beat of human
existence. Nowhere is this more evident than in the scene of the blacksmiths working
in the "hellishly sweaty forge", who choreograph their work into a physically demanding
triplet polyrhythm, which transforms immediately to a duple feel as one of the workers
extracts himself from the ensemble.

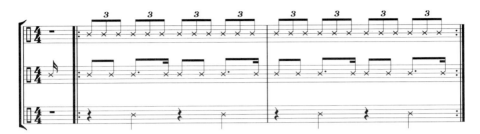

Figure 7.1 Blacksmith scene (4:28–5:34 mins)

Figure 7.1 above is a notated version[4] of the blacksmith scene, occurring between 4.28 and 5.34 mins.[5] (with the blacksmiths operating as off-screen sound until 5.22 mins). Note that, while polyrhythmic, the section is underscored by a strong quadruple pulse. The top stave represents the metallic hammering of the blacksmiths, banging out their choreographed triplets; the middle stave a hand-drum ensemble that had been introduced earlier in the market scene but which continues until we see the blacksmiths at work; and the bottom stave representing the basslike thud from the hand drums that falls on beats two and four. This strong pulse, this constancy, as in the dig proper, is the sound of the natural order – the rhythm of life. Having been established visually, this polyrhythmic constancy is now free to continue off-screen, safely demarcated as natural sound the audience can synchronize with, identify with, and therefore, ultimately, become more vulnerable through. Figure 7.2 illustrates the continuation of this rhythmic certainty, this time through a swung eighth pattern from 5.34 to 5.44 mins, once again off-screen. The audience is thus led to believe the hammering producing the rhythm is from the same blacksmith section of the marketplace. The shift to eighths produces an urgency within the rhythm, reflecting the impending peril for the natural order as the powers of evil are unleashed. Figure 7.2 shows two timbres, with the higher notes representing a high-pitched ring. This ring appears to be rather random and unintentional, and may be the result of the hammer(s) hitting the metal at a specific point of its surface area.

Yet even before the busyness of the blacksmiths, the audience has been introduced to various eighth rhythms, supposedly located in the general ambience of the marketplace. Replete with the hurried comings and goings of Middle Eastern trade, the market

Figure 7.2 Eighth pattern of blacksmiths

features an unseen, yet diegetically important, musical ensemble, performing on Arabian hand drums.[6] What is particularly striking about the rhythmic figures of the group is that they move from groupings of five to groupings of four. Obviously this prepares the audience for the more stable quadruple rhythms about to follow in the blacksmith scene, yet it also acts as a further normalizing of rhythmic pulses. The hand drums first enter at 4:08 mins, with the time change occurring at 4:25 mins. Figure 7.3 documents the change in time signatures; notice how the first measure of 4/4 is actually the original 5/8 pattern, albeit elongated at the end.

Earlier critiques of *The Exorcist* have tended to correlate the opening sonic events with the exorcism itself. The opening musical events, particularly, have been seen as purely preparatory and often disparaged. Bowles is typical: having mentioned the "irritating music" (1976: 202) of the prelude – which he never describes or delineates – he goes on, "The unnaturally loud and grating background sounds that accompany the dig prologue in the film prepare us for the similar sounds during the possession sequences" (*ibid.*). The above analysis, however, argues that there is far more at stake in these opening sequences than audience preparation. Rather than accustomizing the audience to any later sonic clatter, the film is introducing key thematic concerns that will become integral to the production of horror itself.[7]

Much has been made of the battle between good and evil in *The Exorcist* – and for good reason – yet the battle between rhythm and dysrhythm, between the naturally balanced and the demonically interrupted, is also prominently established in the film. This chapter aims to isolate the key rhythmic elements of the film music and discuss how their manipulation provides the unsettling effects so often associated with the film.

Stopping time: the demon Pazuzu

The most obvious announcement of the film's intention to explore the rhythmic dimension of the natural order is proclaimed in the prologue. As Father Merrin examines the recently discovered amulet of the demon Pazuzu[8] in the curator's office, the grandfather clock – visible in the framing of the scene (from 6.20 mins) – abruptly stops ticking (6.23 mins). As if this is too subtle a message, Father Merrin moves over to examine it briefly, before resigning himself to his chair, and the knowledge that the natural order has been displaced. Musicologist Jerome Madulid sees this as part of a

Figure 7.3 Hand drum ensemble

larger tapestry, one that the listener has been immersed in throughout the preceding scenes:

> The rhythms found in the marketplace are loud and syncopated. This rhythmic activity becomes slightly 'subdued' in the following workshop scene. The rhythms in the workshop decrease in both syncopation and texture (i.e. the ensemble performing the rhythmic pattern becomes smaller). The rhythm finally becomes stagnant with the grandfather clock, highlighting the end of this rhythmic progression between the scenes. (personal communication with the author, 7 February 2007)

Kermode, too, places much weight on the cessation of rhythm: "The suggestion is that time has stopped, that the normal flow of the present has been interrupted by a force from the past" (1998: 25). And certainly the movies that followed *The Exorcist*, and their directors, drew upon the same important sonic message. In *The Exorcist III* (William Peter Blatty, 1990) there is repetitive use of grandfather clocks, and once again a pronounced cessation of action as Detective Kinderman talks with the senior priest about the original exorcism. Even the prequel, *Exorcist: The Beginning* (Renny Harlin), released in 2004 by Warner Bros, utilizes the same trusted theme. This time, situated in a young Father Merrin's room as he flashes back to Nazi atrocities from World War II, the grandfather clock in his room stops. Here the disruption to normal rhythmic process is accompanied by Father Merrin's realization that evil is indeed afoot in the village. Despite his stated apostasy, Father Merrin is convinced of demonic forces via these interruptions to expected rhythmic nuances. Reading this later film back into the first makes sense of the protracted and disturbed attention Father Merrin grants the clock when it stops in the original film.

While it is a pointed reference to the sonic theme of *The Exorcist*, the announcement heralded by the clock stopping has been made earlier. During the preceding dig scenes, as Father Merrin reaches for the Pazuzu amulet, we are alerted to upcoming disruptions. Aurally, there is the combined sound of wind, chant and drone – as if the entire sonic landscape had been compressed into a single sound – as the artefact is discovered. This aural compression metaphorically represents the culmination of the evils of history buried in that location, specifically, in the ruins of Nineveh. Nineveh was made the capital of the Assyrian empire around 700 BC. The Assyrians were known for their cruelty and brutality,

> their kings often being depicted as gloating over the gruesome punishments inflicted on conquered peoples. They conducted their wars with shocking ferocity... The leaders of conquered cities were tortured and horribly mutilated before being executed. (Livingston and Barker, 1985: 1380)

Director William Friedkin was aware of this important historical context to the area, even if his knowledge wasn't exactly 'precise':

> [we hear] *the overall sound of the* [marketplace next to the dig]... *directly across from the actual tomb of King Nebuchadnezzar which is built on top of the tomb of the prophet* [sic] *David ... and is right alongside the walls of Nineveh ... and it was Joshua who fought the battle of Nineveh, and brought the walls down.*[9] (DVD commentary)

This is the evil being exposed in the opening scenes, centuries of human darkness and wickedness encapsulated in a single idol. Sonically we are led to believe that this single idol might even be the source. As Merrin chips away the dirt from the amulet, the crescendoing sound of compressed history is abruptly cut as Merrin realizes the nature of the find. As Stephen Bowles notes, the sound accompaniment "signals the unnaturalness of the discovery" (1976: 202). In Merrin's face we see what the aural landscape is emphasizing, that this discovery, and this idol, will spell major calamity for the natural order. Indeed, as Merrin well knows, "evil comes to him who searches for it" (Proverbs 11:27).

Background

The Exorcist, released in 1973, was a screenplay adapted from the novel of the same name by William Peter Blatty that had appeared two years earlier.[10] The success of Blatty's novel no doubt contributed to the success and media frenzy that surrounded the film's release. But some commentators feel it was the climate into which Blatty's novel was released, along with its graphic portrayal of evil and the inability of human frailty to deal with it, that led to its dramatic success:

> The Exorcist [novel] *first appeared in 1971. Against a backdrop of positivistic values, America experienced a particularly disorientating series of tremors and jolts. From assassinations, to the outrage and horror of an apparently senseless war, to the moral license of pornography, to the political sacrilege of executive corruption – each secular evil received its share of public attention.* (Frentz and Farrell, 1975: 42)

What Frentz and Farrell describe here as "tremors and jolts" are, at one level, disruptions to the natural order. The capacity for disorientating (dysrhythmic) evil to be visited upon the innocent underlies the terror of the novel, and the film. In a modern time when the USA again finds itself in a 'questionable' war, suffering from questionable political decisions, and enduring a spate of senseless school and university shootings, the horror of the "tremors and jolts" is all too real. *The Exorcist* remains a classic of horror film-making, yet by tapping into the subconscious terror of rhythmic disruption it hit upon a 'timelessness' that will continue to disturb. "The tensions that [the film] portrayed were recognizable and credible, even to those who despised the movie" (Kermode, 1998: 9), as they remain today. When conservatism is unable to insulate itself against the inevitable tensions and catastrophes of the modern world, then the isolation felt becomes deafening. As Frentz and Farrell noted in relation to the USA back in 1975: "America's repeated failure to master its own social environment... has generated a national consciousness that mirrors the helplessness, depression, and alienation felt by every socially conscious individual" (*ibid.*).

With the advertising slogan of the 'scariest movie ever made', *The Exorcist* pushed the boundaries of horror, and representations of evil in general. The film's often grotesque visualizations and extreme language, along with its deep religious themes, polarized public opinion about its place in the public domain.[11] It was praised for its profound spirituality by the *Catholic News*, branded satanic by leading evangelist Billy Graham, picketed on release by conservative groups, banned on video in the UK, and championed by many around the world (Kermode, 1998: 10). Most newspaper reportage of the time, apart from that surrounding protest, was devoted to audience response. Schuetz recorded that "most theatres showing the film can give illustrations of persons leaving, fainting, or becoming physically ill from the movie" (1975: 100). Such strong reactions confirm the film's attack on physiological processes, on natural functions that keep the body and mind balanced.

Musically, *The Exorcist* was dominated by discussions about the non-diegetic use of a section of Mike Oldfield's *Tubular Bells* (1973). Lalo Schifrin was originally contracted to write the music for the film, but after hearing portions of his composition, Friedkin was so unimpressed (colourfully so in many accounts) that he fired Schifrin and brought in Jack Nitzsche and his friend Ron Nagle to redo the music of the film. Despite many engaging uses of sound, original score and effects, it was the use of *Tubular Bells* that was to have lasting historical significance. Oldfield's music, a deliberate attempt to blend minimalist ideas with baroque counterpoint, went on to win a Grammy award for 'Best Instrumental Composition' in 1975. Yet, to the chagrin of Oldfield (Callard, 2001), the song would ever be synonymous with *The Exorcist*. Indeed, Ennio Morricone would use *Tubular Bells* as the basis for his theme to the ill-fated *Exorcist* sequel.

Treating disorder

The inability of humans to deal with the disruptive forces of evil is most clearly heard in the fearful medical procedures that Regan undergoes. During these repeated medical scenes the audience is subjected to a barrage of non-human, non-rhythmic intrusions that dominate the soundscape more than most other features of the entire movie's soundtrack. The hospital scenes feature overly loud machines, frightening to even the sanest viewer, none more so than the fearful arteriograph machine. Indeed, Harlin nominates the combined noises of the arteriogram (51:00 mins) as the "most disturbing soundtrack in the film" (DVD commentary). A feature of the arteriograph and the other machines used to 'treat' Regan are the various staccato accents produced, none of which develops in any rhythmic pattern. Given that these are machines, controlled not by haphazard decisions but via programmed sequences, their aural contribution to the film is most unsettling. Regan and her mother have come to the medical profession seeking comfort, seeking a restoration of the natural order. Instead they have been exposed to violently spasmodic rhythmic events, which often occur at frightening volumes and dangerous proximity. What we hear is the failure of human-built and controlled technology to cope with Regan's 'disorder', a disorder that doctors attempt to treat through the exposure to even more pronounced acts of disorder.

Kermode takes this critique of the film even further, discussing the film's "pornographic depiction of modern medicine" (1998: 43). He claims that the depiction of medical treatments inflicted on Regan resemble "an Inquisitional torture, perverse in its precision and horribly sexual in its execution" (*ibid.*). This 'pornographic sexuality' remains up for debate, but what is clear is the dominant intrusion of machine sounds involved in Regan's treatment. Her powerlessness at the hands of these unnatural sounds resounds with the sonic themes of the movie. Once again Bowles views the bellicose nature of these scenes as preparatory:

> The sharp metallic noise of the medical equipment... registering reactions with the sterile objectivity of controlled technology prepares us for the equally harsh and abrasive noises of Regan/demon during the possession. (1976: 202)

Yet the technology is far from controlled. Rather, the sonic presentation of it is out of control. There is no constancy of sound, no safe repetition. Each sonic thrust is random and violent. In this way it *does* echo the dire soundtrack of the exorcism itself. There too, control is lost, order is lost, and Regan is subjected to the whims of another. Following this argument, Bowles's notion that Blatty's original novel represented a "dialectic on the nature of good and evil combined with an evident distrust of medical and psychiatric science" (*ibid.*: 208) holds sway for the film version as well. For, in the soundtrack, the medical procedures of man reflect the demonic bidding of Satan.

Notably, after Regan's final treatment at the hospital she is brought home presumably heavily sedated, or else unconscious. Here a long drone sounds beneath the vision. There is no dysrhythm, yet no rhythm either. We enter a form of respite, the sedated 'spirit' for now allowing pause from the rhythmic disruptions. The drone allows the listener to take stock, to enjoy an intermission, and prepare for the onslaught that lies ahead.

Two other sound devices are utilized regularly in the film to highlight demonic interference in the everyday. The first is the use of various animal sounds to heighten the sensation of evil and/or horror. For example, the sound of dogs fighting in the prelude gives the listener a foretaste of the violence that will be unleashed through Regan. Likewise, various sounds of animals creep into the mix of the film throughout, often where they clearly do not belong diegetically – for example, in the MacNeil house. A similar technique is used in the Australian film *Romper Stomper* (Geoffrey Wright, 1992) to intensify the violence of the Nazi gang members (Miller, 1998). Both films place fierce animal sounds where they do not belong, to unsettle the audience and emphasize the horror of the events occurring. The sound engineer on *The Exorcist*, Ken Nagle, recorded many unusual animal sounds, such as fighting dogs, 'angry' bees and slaughtered pigs (Marriott, 2004: 134), in order to achieve this effect. Often these sounds were mixed together in such a way as to disguise their original source, yet retain the emotion and stimulus of the contexts from which they were taken. This type of sonic "schizophonia" (Feld and Keil, 1994) actually serves to intensify the basic sound source, dislocating it from its original context so it is free to signify whatever purpose its designator has for it.

The second sound device used throughout the film is setting the sounds of evil against the backdrop of everyday life. What is important to the horror of the film is that the evil visited upon the MacNeil family, and the Georgetown campus generally, is not exclusive. Apart from Regan's dalliance with the illusionary Captain Howdy, there is nothing to suggest she has brought such evil infestation upon herself at all. Such an intrusion of the evil upon the ordinary, the innocent, is heard sonically throughout. One example is when Father Karras and Detective Kinderman are first talking on the sports field of the university. As Friedkin noted, what was important was that they "talk against a background of life and activity" (DVD commentary). Thus various sporting and leisure activities occur around them, seen through the fence against which they lean. As they speak about goings on at the campus (63:00 mins), specifically director Burke Dennings's death, a deep bass throb begins to emanate from the soundtrack. What is most noticeable is that the conversation has been continuing for some time before this drone starts. Prior to the drone the dominant sounds are the conversation and the carefree activities of the students in the background. The natural order of things is in play. It is essential to the horror of the film that these rhythms of life, and the soundscape they produce, be interrupted by evil. In this case it is when the conversation turns to Burke's death that the soundtrack of everyday life is disrupted. More particularly, it is when Kinderman speaks of Burke's head being turned around 180 degrees on his body – clearly an act involving evil, supernatural forces. Now, the deep bass, throbbing almost imperceptibly, rises in intensity as Kinderman describes Burke's injuries. Up to this point the conversation has been innocuous, genial almost, but as evil is described the demonic forces interrupt normal human sensations, overpower the frivolity of the background scenes and consume the listener.

Demonic vocality

"Out of the overflow of the heart the mouth speaks" (Matthew 12:34), that is, unless, of course, your heart is being held captive by a demon. Then the natural order, whereby vocality matches the character and physiology of the person, is totally annihilated. The unfolding demonic vocality of Regan is often remembered as the most frightening, unsettling and haunting feature of *The Exorcist*. And it might well be, yet there are several aspects to her vocality, as well as that of others, that contribute to the overall terror of dialogue in the film.

Linda Blair was initially hailed for her vocal performance in the film, yet there were two other women who substituted for her whenever a scene involved the possessed girl barking obscenities. Their identities were originally concealed in order to disguise the effects process (Kermode, 1998) and to create more horror in offering Blair as the sole source. The woman mainly responsible for the abject vocalizations of the Pazuzu-possessed Regan was Mercedes McCambridge. McCambridge went through various physical manipulations in order to 'summon' the demonic voice. As Friedkin explained:

> She was chain-smoking; swallowing raw eggs; getting me to tie her to a chair; all these things just to produce the sound of that demon in torment... And as she did it the most curious things would happen in her throat. Double and triple sounds would emerge at once, wheezing sounds, very much akin to what you can imagine a person inhabited by various demons would sound like... and you would hear these things multiplied in her throat; these strange counterpoint noises; little skittering whistles and strange creaking rattles.[12]

Complementing McCambridge's skills in vocal manipulation are various animal noises mixed into the overall vocality. The first example occurs during Regan's first 'attack' at the hands of Pazuzu (51:00 mins). Here the non-defined animal sounds infuse into the mix, becoming one with Regan's voice. Once again the natural order is banished. As Brophy notes: "the voice of female pubescence is rendered by a hellish chorus of effects and transmogrifications... it is here that the soundtrack becomes aberrant and vilifying" (2004: 101). Yet the upheaval comes not only from the timbre of the voice,[13] but also from the perverted number of languages and personalities the voice can produce, many of which we have already been introduced to in the film. Being both alien and familiar, the voice is made more horrific.

Many different voices come out of Regan simultaneously and Father Karras is the one charged with deciphering them, as well as enduring them. The sheer babble of voices emanating from Regan point not only to the supernatural forces that have overtaken her, but also to the magnitude of their presence. Father Karras hears the voice of the homeless man who had begged from him on the subway, and later during the exorcism itself hears the demon speaking in his dead mother's voice. The importance of this dialogical duplicity is accentuated by Karras's need to record and decipher it,[14] in the same way that the dialogue recorded in *The Conversation* (Francis Ford Coppola, 1974) is crucial to understanding the identity and motivations of the main protagonists. Karras's recording of the demonic voice is made more prominent through the total absence of sound as he listens back to the recording. We strain with him to get to the heart of the vocality, to the identity of Regan's ailment. When Karras finally thinks to play the recording backwards, "he hears various demons within Regan fighting with her" (Friedkin, DVD commentary). While this casts doubts over the sole possession from Pazuzu, it produces a far more sinister notion for the audience. That notion being that, when the natural order is reversed, in this case the linear speech of different dialects, then evil is manifested. By implication then, this evil is always present under the surface.

The Regan/Pazuzu vocalizations may be the most abhorrent aspect of the soundtrack, but it is another that lays claim to the most powerful vocal delivery. "The power of Christ compels you!", repeated and returned to time and time again by Merrin and Karras, becomes the phrase that will defeat the demon; it is "the power of that phrase [that will] battle against evil" (Friedkin, DVD commentary). The phrase is rhythmic and repetitious, the sound of the natural order fighting back against the forces of darkness, discord and dysrhythm. The rhythmic nature of the phrase (106:00 mins) is emphasized at each use. It falls mostly in four beat patterns, with strong beat accents on "power", "Christ" and "compels". The rhythm is assured and strong, even as voices crescendo to overpower the desperate demon. Marriott claims that "the chanting of the priests sounds increasingly desperate after each repetition" (2004: 134). In fact, as the tempo of the repeated phrase increases, drawing further attention to the dominance of the rhythm and its centrality in the fight against evil, the rhythmic insistence builds relief that evil will, and can, be defeated. Further servicing this rhythmic attack is the call-and-response catechism of the exorcism ritual itself. The rhythmic flow of this liturgy is crucial to its success, with Merrin commending its importance to Karras prior to commencing. Victory will come through maintaining the integrity of the call and response. When Father Karras becomes distracted from his role during the exorcism and fails to answer Merrin, the moment of concern becomes palpable. Only through united rhythmic unity will the demon forces be cast out and order restored.

Conclusion

Previous accounts of sound in *The Exorcist* have tended to focus on the non-diegetic musical segments of the film (Bazelon, 1975; Brophy, 2001), or else the haunting lack of music in totality (Marriott, 2004). Most have discussed the manipulation of Regan's voice as she becomes increasingly controlled by the demon Pazuzu. Even more have paid great attention to the role of Oldfield's *Tubular Bells* (e.g., Marriott, 2004; Brophy, 2001). Missing from these accounts has been any discussion on how the soundtrack synthesizes key themes of the film. Most pointedly, it is argued here, the soundtrack achieves this via the manipulation of rhythmic elements. While the previous lack of focus on rhythm does not render previous work on the film redundant, it does, however, point to a larger void within film-sound studies. While there has been (too) much attention given to the dominance of the visual over the sonic in film analysis, what has developed more recently, I would argue, is a predilection for the melodic over the rhythmic. Certainly, the very core of leitmotif analysis often pursues this end, as do expositions of dominant theme music. A restoration of rhythm's importance to film-sound studies, especially given the required melding of a linear visual track with a linear soundtrack in the very process of producing film, would seem apt. And there are surely few better genres with which to begin this re-conceptualization than horror. For it is the acceleration towards horror, the deceleration during it and the constant uncertainty of knowing when the horror will strike that give the genre its power.

The above analysis highlights this feature, specifically noting how, over and above any good versus evil polemic, the soundtrack of *The Exorcist* re-enforces the battle between the natural (safe) rhythms of everyday life and the disruptive dysrhythm of evil. This function is set up from the beginning of the film, as we are initially drawn into the everyday cacophony of archaeological digs and Middle Eastern markets. This leads directly into the seemingly safe world of the MacNeil house and the Georgetown campus. As its director Friedkin noted, *The Exorcist*: "had to be a totally realistic view of inexplicable events. It had to be absolutely flawless in its presentation of real people against real backgrounds" (quoted in Travers and Reiff, 1974: 199). For the power of evil to be felt most shockingly it was essential that it was unleashed under the most unsuspecting and innocuous circumstances. By first establishing the natural order, with its safe and predictable rhythmic structure, the film was then able to shatter all illusions about the positive, balanced world in which we live. Attacking the very rhythm that underlies our existence, *The Exorcist* taught us to be apprehensive and suspicious of anything that halts our progress.

Notes

1. Another version of the film, with the description *The Version You've Never Seen*, was released in 2000. This features slightly updated visual and aural rendering. The analysis presented in this chapter, however, pertains to the 1998 re-release.

2. In 1998 *The Exorcist* was remastered to include a 5.1 surround sound mix. The remixing was performed by Steve Boeddeker of Skywalker Sound, who focused his mix on highlighting the prominent themes of the film, "good versus evil, light versus dark, intense sound versus silences" (P. Stack, 'Recut *Exorcist* out for another spin', *San Francisco Chronicle* (online at http://www.sfgate.com/cgi-bin/article.cgi?f=/c/a/2000/09/22/DD25486.DTL, accessed 11 November 2006).

3. See liner notes to *Bosavi: Rainforest Music From Papua New Guinea* (2001) for further information.

4. Many thanks to Jerome Madulid for notating the musical transcriptions of the market scenes.

5. All timings listed are taken from the 1998 DVD release of the film, which commences timing from the opening Warner Bros slide.

6. Subtitles to the DVD release describe this as "rhythmic Arabic music"; the delineation of "rhythmic" here is a curious addition to the present argument.

7. It is noteworthy that Renny Harlin, director of *Exorcist: The Beginning* (2004), saw the marketplace/blacksmith scene of the original film as something to be reproduced in his prequel. Speaking more from a textural point of view, he "wanted something in the opening scene that would feel familiar without being the same" (Harlin, DVD commentary). The importance of familiarity can again be seen to

reside in the establishment of the natural order and its natural rhythms, which is crucial to the horror that awaits their disruption later in the film.

8. Pazuzu was a common demonic deity of Assyrian and Babylonian times. He was often depicted in amulets and figurines as having a rectangular head, with:

> canine jaws [and] *teeth and tongue shown; and large, round, deep-set eyes under thick eyebrows. Animal horns, a horizontally cut human beard, human ears, round bulges on his head, and a throat marked by horizontal lines are further characteristic features of this demon. An elongated, small, canine body with the ribs clearly visible, human shoulders and arms ending in the claws of a predator, and human or animal thighs which turn into bird's talons form the body. Two pairs of bird's wings on his back, a penis erectus ending in a snake's head, and the tail of a scorpion complete Pazuzu's hybrid iconography.* (Heebel, 2002)

This is exactly the amulet uncovered by Father Merrin during the archaeological dig. It is also the representation of Pazuzu that abounds in *Exorcist: The Beginning*. Although there are competing, diametrically opposed, views on the role of the demon Pazuzu – some viewing his contribution as a positive one against disease (*ibid.*) – more often Pazuzu represented a ferocious wind that brought destruction to land and people (a destruction visually apparent in *Exorcist: The Beginning*).

9. Joshua is actually credited with bringing down the walls of Jericho (Joshua 6:1–21). While Jericho, near the Jordan river, is a long way south of Nineveh (on the banks of the Tigris), Friedkin may simply have been drawing the connection between the cities, given both were utterly destroyed for their wickedness. Nineveh was sacked in 612 BC, up to fifty years after the prophet Nahum announced its impending fate. It was never rebuilt and within a few centuries had been covered in desert sand. The opening archaeological dig scenes of *The Exorcist* were shot at the actual 1970s dig in modern Iraq that was uncovering the ruins of Nineveh. The history of Nineveh makes its ruins the ideal place for the discovery of the Pazuzu amulet, and the evil it releases.

10. Blatty's novel first appeared in May 1971, and reached *Publishers Weekly*'s bestseller list on 28 July. It remained on the list until 3 July 1972. As a result, there was huge public interest (and outrage) about the film, even before it began production. For a full account of the circumstances surrounding Blatty's novel, see Travers and Reiff (1974), and on its adaptation for screen, see Kermode (1998).

11. For a list of articles written in response to the film from various perspectives, including theological, psychiatric and filmic, see Bowles (1976).

12. Unattributed (no date), 'The sound of silence', online at http://theexorcist. warnerbros.com/cmp/silencebottom.html, accessed 6 November 2006.

13. For more on the timbral effects of Regan's voice and their symbolic/metaphorical connotations, see Brophy (1999).

14. Part of Karras's quest is to ascertain whether the 'voice' speaks Latin, a language totally unfamiliar to Regan and thus proof of possession. Although omitted from

the film, we learn from Blatty's original novel that the demon cannot speak Latin but merely reads the priest's thoughts as Karras asks questions in Latin and formulates answers to them in his own mind: "Do you see what I'm driving at, Karras? I cannot speak Latin at all. I read your mind. I merely plucked the responses from your head" (1971: 317). Given the film's quest to authenticate the demonic voice, such a revelation would have caused considerable narrative difficulties.

References

Bazelon, I. (1975), *Knowing the Score*, New York: Arco Publishing.

Blatty, W. (1971), *The Exorcist*, New York: Harper and Row.

Bowles, S. (1976), 'The Exorcist and Jaws: Techniques of the New Suspense Film', *Literature/Film Quarterly*, 4(3), 196–214.

Brophy, P. (1999), 'I Scream in Silence: Cinema, Sex and the Sound of Women Dying', in P. Brophy (ed.), *Cinesonic: The World of Sound in Film*, Sydney: Australian Film, Television and Radio School, pp. 51–78.

Brophy, P. (2001), 'Revolutionising the Cinema: Or, How I Put Rock n' Roll in the Movies', in P. Brophy (ed.), *Cinesonic: Sciencing the Soundtrack*, Sydney: Australian Film, Television and Radio School, pp. 1–18.

Brophy, P. (2004), *100 Modern Soundtracks*, London: British Film Institute.

Callard, P. (2001), 'Mike Oldfield – Tubular Bells', *Total Guitar*, May, 22–3.

Feld, S., and Keil, C. (1994), *Music Grooves: Essays and Dialogues*, Chicago: University of Chicago Press.

Frentz, T., and Farrell, T. (1975), 'Conversion of America's Consciousness: The Rhetoric of *The Exorcist*', *Quarterly Journal of Speech*, 61, 40–7.

Gioia, T., (2006), *Work Songs*, Durham, NC: Duke University Press.

Heebel, N. (2002), 'Pazuzu', in T. Abusch and A. Guinan (eds), *Ancient Magic and Divination IV*, Leiden: Brill Styx, pp. 1–22.

Kermode, M. (1998), *The Exorcist*, 2nd edition, London: British Film Institute.

Livingston, J., and E. Barker (eds) (1985), 'Nahum', *The New International Version Study Bible*, Grand Rapids, MI: Zondervan Bible Publishers.

Marriott, J. (2004), *Horror Films*, London: Virgin Books.

Miller, T. (1998), 'The Violence of Sound: *Romper Stomper*', in R. Coyle (ed.), *Screen Scores: Studies in Contemporary Australian Film Music*, Sydney: Australian Film, Television and Radio School, pp. 29–38.

Schuetz, J. (1975), '"The Exorcist": Images of Good and Evil', *Western Speech Communication*, 39(2), 92–101.

Travers, P., and Reiff, S. (1974), *The Story Behind* The Exorcist, New York: Crown Publishers.

8   Texas Chainsaws
Audio Effect and Iconicity

Rebecca Coyle and Philip Hayward

Tobe Hooper's *Texas Chain Saw Massacre*,[1] shot in 1973 on a budget of $US40,000 and estimated to have grossed over $US30 million at US cinemas, has been voted the greatest horror film of all time[2] and has received elite institutional recognition by being purchased for the Museum of Modern Art's film collection. Prominent in both the title and the marketing of the film, the chainsaw, once simply a durable, motorized wood-cutting device with a poor safety record, has now become a sonic and visual icon of its genre. In this manner it invites comparison to similarly iconic weapons, such as the light sabre of the *Star Wars* series. But the chainsaw is all the more effective since it represents an actual technology of dismemberment rather than an invented one. This realist element has translated directly into the canon of sonic horror effects since the mere sound of its motor starting up – let alone the increase in its pitch and rhythm as it is revved in preparation for action – now foreshadows danger in as immediate a manner as any other sound in the genre's lexicon.

Following its deployment in Hooper's original film, the device has graced a series of spin-offs including *The Texas Chainsaw Massacre Part 2* (Tobe Hooper, 1986), *Leatherface: Texas Chainsaw Massacre III* (Jeff Burr, 1990) and *Texas Chainsaw Massacre: The Next Generation* (Kim Henkel, 1994) and, more recently, an eponymous remake (Marcus Nispel, 2003) and a remake prequel (*The Texas Chainsaw Massacre: The Beginning* [Jonathan Liebesman, 2006]).[3] It has also become an icon in popular culture more generally. Its popularity as a Halloween 'toy' is emphasized in this lead item from *Halloween Online Magazine*:

> *Let's face it, whether its* [sic] *Leatherface from the movie "Texas Chainsaw Massacre", Jason Voorhees from the "Friday the Thirteenth" movies, or some other psychopath, there are few things scarier than some crazed homicidal maniac chasing you with a roaring chainsaw, particularly on Halloween night... For the home haunter, adding a scareactor with a menacing mask, costume and armed with a running chainsaw can really put the fear into your visitors. For those not wanting to use a modified, real chainsaw, there are several fake chainsaw's* [sic] *available, all with built-in sound effects.*[4]

The website then lists three plastic models available for purchase, including the top-of-the-range item, the 'Leatherface Chainsaw', which features "sawing and screaming sound effects" and "even has fake blood splattered on the blade". Other models identified are the (slightly cheaper) 'Classic Horror' and 'Bloody Black' models. The site also goes on to list 'The Real Thing' as a Halloween option, stating that:

> Commercial haunted attractions have been using modified chainsaw's [sic] to terrorize their patrons for years. They take several steps to make the effect as safe as possible, including the removal of the chain from the chainsaw and replacing the metal blade (guide) with a wooden or plastic one. (ibid.)

As the above copy suggests, the chainsaw has also become adopted as a weapon in other horror films, such as the *Friday the 13th* series. Perhaps the most curious spin-off to date is the limited-edition, promotional control interface for the '*Resident Evil 4*' game (the latest product in the 'Resident Evil' franchise at time of writing). Designed by games manufacturer Nubyetech, it comes with a chainsaw-style controller (complete with blood-splatter colouration) suitable for deploying the chainsaw featured prominently in the game, with a built-in speaker providing appropriate chainsaw sound effects when the (on-screen) device is deployed.

A brief history of chainsaws

Precursors of the contemporary chainsaw have been around since the 1800s in the form of large, fixed, chain-operated saws that used various power sources. In 1929 a German inventor and manufacturer, Andreas Stihl (born 1896), whose company remains the leading international manufacturer of the device, developed the first portable, hand-held, petrol-powered chainsaw. Prior to his invention, similar chain-operated saw devices had been so cumbersome that their mobility was severely limited. Stihl's technology was developed during the 1930s but did not emerge in an internationally popular form until after the company's reconstruction and re-equipment after World War II. In 1964 the company established a manufacturing plant whose product proved so successful in the domestic and export market that by 1969 it had manufactured over one million chainsaws, many being exported to the USA. In 1974 – in a move (presumably) unrelated to *The Texas Chain Saw Massacre*'s release – Stihl's US operation became incorporated and went on to establish manufacturing plants in the USA.

Although chainsaw technology was a rapid success in terms of its efficiency in cutting timber, the lack of safety guards on early models – and the slow adoption of protective headgear and leggings – meant that the device acquired a reputation as dangerous to handle, graphically illustrated by numerous bloody accidents. Along with this safety factor, engine noise volume has been a recurring health and safety issue with the device.[5] An (undated) analysis by the (Western Australian Government) Safety Line Institute, for instance, identified a typical chainsaw as providing a sound pressure level of 110 decibels, only exceeded by the noise of a jet engine taking off 30 metres from the auditor. Muffling headsets are now a routine safety device.[6] The increase in pitch and motor rhythm caused by revving a two-stroke engine – together with the whining sound of the chainsaw in contact with timber – provides the tool's distinct sound signature.

The chainsaw in *The Texas Chain Saw Massacre*

Hooper's decision to feature the chainsaw in his "satire on Texas hospitality"[7] was an attempt to show the process of death on film in a more graphic way than simple gunshots, and he has related that his specific inspiration derived from an incident that occurred while Christmas shopping. Trapped by the crowd in the hardware department of a store, Hooper was accidentally pushed against a rack of chainsaws and fantasized about using one of them to clear his way out of the shop:

> The focus just racked from my eyeball to the people to the saws – and the idea popped. I said, 'Ooh, I know how I could get out of this place fast – if I just start one of these things up and make that sound.'[8]

Despite Stihl's prominence in the global market, the model of chainsaw used in Hooper's 1974 film was an all-American Poulan 306A (with the brand name taped over, presumably to avoid any action by the company for detrimental marketing associations)[9] – a medium-sized saw with a 16-inch bar (in contrast to the far larger models used in the 1986 sequel and the 2003 remake). A chainsaw user (and aficionado), contributing to the Arborist website (www.arboristsite.com) discussion list, identified the representation of the chainsaw in the initial film as the most successful of the series in terms of its realism:

> This saw [the Poulan] has a really distinct sound to it compared to other saws. You may have wondered why it sounded so good in this movie compared to the somewhat lame saw dubs in the other films. They obviously used the real saw for the sound mixing... I also feel the saw work was the best in this film. No closeups of non running saws while we hear the motor going or see no chain on it etc. I assume most of the time a chain which had the teeth cut/filed off was used. If this saw hit someone or somthine [sic] it could still cut just like a fake knife might accidentily [sic] stab but it would not be as serious as the real thing. In some scenes like the door scene the real chain and setup was there just like when you cut a tree down.[10]

His characterization accords with accounts of the actual film-making process and em-phasizes the active presence of the (operational) chainsaw during the production.

The Texas Chain Saw Massacre's plot is fairly straightforward. A group of five young people (Kirk, Pam, Jerry, Sally and her wheelchair-bound brother Franklin) are driving through Texas. Along the way they pick up a hitchhiker who behaves so bizarrely that they have to eject him from the vehicle. After stopping at a gas station that is temporarily out of fuel they decide to visit Sally and Franklin's deceased grandfather's old home. Parking close to the house, Kirk and Pam hear a generator working at a nearby residence and go to ask the occupants for petrol. Unfortunately for them, the occupants are a homicidal family, the most active of whom is a masked psychopath (known as Leatherface), who proceeds to murder them all, with the exception of Sally, who escapes, severely traumatized.

The chainsaw makes its appearance at around 39 minutes into the narrative. It is first applied to Kirk's corpse shortly after he is killed by Leatherface with a hammer in the farmhouse where most of the film's action takes place. This scene unfolds in a butchering room with the action witnessed by Pam as she dangles from a meat hook on the wall, awaiting her fate. The shock here is visceral and highly symbolic: human flesh is rendered as a carcass that is butchered in a far cruder way than even the abattoir cattle evoked by the Hitchhiker in his graphic description of slaughterhouse killing techniques earlier in the film. Despite the film's title – with the term 'massacre' suggesting plural murders with the aforementioned implement – the chainsaw only features in three scenes, two of which involve the chainsaw being applied to live human flesh. Nevertheless, these scenes are pivotal to the narrative and horror effect, much of which is carried by the sound and music design.

The first scene where the chainsaw engages with live flesh is when Sally and Franklin negotiate dense undergrowth in search of Pam and Kirk, only to have their progress halted when Leatherface dismembers Franklin in his wheelchair. The scene's impact is heightened by a lengthy lead-in, showing Sally's efforts to push Franklin in dimly lit, blue-tinged sequences randomly revealed by the flashlight that Franklin shines on his surroundings. Here the narrative flow is directed by the dialogue as they comment, "There's a light", "It looks like a house" and "I can't see very well". On the audio track, the pair call to Jerry, Franklin complains and Sally grunts, and we hear the clanking of the wheelchair. Immediately after Franklin exclaims, "Sally, I hear something – stop, stop," the light reveals Leatherface and the chainsaw starts with a low-frequency revving mixed with a deep drone that starts to pulse. As the chainsaw is lifted, the sound moves into the higher-pitched whine associated with action, Leatherface attacks Franklin, and Sally screams. At this point the sound design increases in density and complexity, as the chainsaw snarls are combined with sounds like broken glass, rattling chains, processed voices, percussion and Sally's screams as she pushes through the undergrowth to the farmhouse. When her hair becomes caught in the lower tree branches, tinkly percussion sounds are added to the snarl of the saw as Leatherface saws through the branches to get to her. At the back door of the farmhouse, she yells for help but, unable to gain entrance, runs around to the front. She enters, locks the door, then runs upstairs only to find Grandpa and the corpses of an old woman and a dog. Sally's cries for help are answered only by the processed sound of creaking that rhythmically matches the rocking of Grandpa's chair. In panic, she runs downstairs to find that Leatherface has sawn the front door open. He chases her upstairs, where she jumps out of the window and runs down the road to the gas station. Throughout this scene, the point of view in terms of camera and sound focuses mainly on Sally, with cutaways to Leatherface (and the chainsaw sound is orchestrated in pitch and perspective to reinforce this). When Sally reaches the gas station, falls into the doorway and is picked up by a man (whom she later discovers to be her pursuer's father), the sound of the chainsaw abruptly stops. Her previous continuous screaming gives way to a hysterical explanation of events and then to heavy breathing. The welcome break from these sounds of terror is underscored by the comforting country-rock music playing on the radio inside the building,[11] as the father goes out to get the truck, apparently to transport her out of her nightmarish experience. Sally's relief soon dissipates. The radio's music gives way to a news report and the identity of her apparent rescuer dawns on her as she stares at the displayed barbecue meat, hears reports of recent graveyard desecrations and makes the connection between them.

The chainsaw's final short but significant outing is in the film's conclusion. When Sally escapes the crazed family's house for a second time and runs off through dense scrubland, the Hitchhiker trails her closely, slashing at her and mocking her as Leatherface follows behind, his chainsaw trailing blue smoke. As they reach the road, a petrol truck appears suddenly, sounding its horn. Unable to react in time, the Hitchhiker is struck and killed. The truck driver pulls over and Sally scrambles into the cabin but Leatherface arrives and starts chainsawing the door – prompting the driver and Sally to exit the cabin on the other side. Pursued by Leatherface, the driver flings a wrench back that hits Leatherface in the head, causing him to fall and lose control of the chainsaw, which cuts into his leg.[12] Meanwhile a passing pick-up vehicle has screeched to a halt as Sally frantically signals for help. The driver tries to fire the motor while Sally struggles to climb into the back and Leatherface limps towards her. The engine finally starts and Sally's escape is signalled by her screams giving way to hysterical laughter.

The film ends on a singularly disturbing image, that of Leatherface performing a crazed dance with the chainsaw in the road, revelling unrepentantly in his savagery and expressing his frustration at his victim's escape. The chainsaw sound rises and falls as the implement is swung around and alternates in volume with Sally's screams and hysterical laughter. As the volume fades, the density of this sound mix gives way to a few seconds of quiet before the final credits commence with the closing music composition. Employing a disquieting mix of percussion, heavy reverberation, processed pulses and beats, the sound retains a memory of the horror even after the blood-besmirched images of these final scenes give way to white-on-black credits.

In the above scenes the chainsaw and its distinctive sounds do not so much provide the film's core horror moments as complement and crystallize a broader set of audio-visual impressions that engender it. In particular, the film's suspense and shock sequences are graphically rendered through a series of intense and sonically inventive sound sequences that draw on pre-recorded music, score, human vocalization and skilfully blended sound effects.

Sound sequences

There are several ways in which sound carries significant content in *The Texas Chain Saw Massacre*, although this has been largely overlooked in the range of reviews and critical writing on the film. Indeed, reviewers frequently mistake the sound occurring in pivotal moments. For example, Richard Schieb argues that the Franklin murder scene leading into the extended Sally and Leatherface chase sequence "consists of nothing on the soundtrack bar screams and the buzz of a chainsaw".[13] As the description above shows, while these are the predominant sounds, they are by no means the only ones featured. Schieb also argues that there are "no edgy strings underscoring as the characters enter the farmhouse"[14] but this comment reflects more about the expectations of horror-genre music than the audio track itself. In the scene in which Pam and Kirk approach the farmhouse, the audio track features sparsely occurring sounds as they proceed to the residence, including the sound of a generator, the clanking of metal tins and other items hanging from the branches of the tree, the squeak of the swing as Pam waits for Kirk, and the noisy creak of the wooden stairs and the front door as events unfold. The bird tweets as the pair near the house signal that an unpleasant disruption to this rural idyll is about to occur. As Kirk opens the door, a low ambient rumble can be heard and pig squeals and other animal noises suggest the activities behind the red door decorated with animal skulls. When Leatherface attacks Kirk, his twitching body is accompanied by the rapid beats of his legs on the floor, and ominous rumbles, rattles and screeches emphasize the shock of this attack. The horrific activities occurring in these rooms are emphasized again as Pam enters the house, and falls into the plucking room filled with feathers. Her disgust and nauseated reaction is highlighted with a music cue derived from a low drone, percussion, seed-shakers, metal sheets and chicken clucks and screeches.

In a later scene in which Jerry approaches the house, a music cue features gong, cymbals and other bowed and struck percussion sounds that variously resonate and are clipped, then give way to the faint sound of screams, rattles and a low-pitched drone. Jerry reaches the front door and knocks. As he peers through the screen door, the sound of strange calls, laughter and rattling chains is heard, leading into the highlighted screech of the screen door as Jerry opens it. His footsteps are accompanied by metallic percussion sounds fading up in volume. Finding the slaughter room, Jerry hears scratching from the freezer. His shock upon finding Pam inside it is emphasized by cries and loud beats as Leatherface attacks him and throws him into the freezer. This scene gives way to shots that seem to represent Leatherface's incomprehension about just where all these people are coming from, with a close-up of his face mask of human skin, jagged teeth and misshapen and swollen lips, which he licks. A music cue assists the representation of this emotion with a mix of echoic metallic percussion, chicken clucks and squawks, and various clangs, rattles and rhythmic beats in a dense texture.

It is precisely the unusual approach to sound design that contributes to the extreme horror impact of *The Texas Chain Saw Massacre*. The importance of the sound for the film is underlined by Hooper's involvement in its production. The post-production of the film occurred in Hooper's home, with editing in one room and scoring in another. Hooper has identified how his fascination with creating sounds preceded his musical training:

> *I love music and I enjoy creating sounds. I got into making music when I was a child, starting with the spoons and the koto before moving onto the piano. I also spent around 2 weeks playing the tenor sax in a high school band.*[15]

This experimentalism was expressed in the film through the use of various musical 'toys' together with a library of source sounds, an oscillator, a parametric equalizer and post-production effects. Co-composer Wayne Bell has reported that for some scenes, Hooper was attempting to create the noises audible to creatures in a slaughterhouse. Other scenes had more general aims:

> *Often times it'd be, like, let's just do a rumble, let's just do seething. These calls came from Tobe, you know, let's just do ice… By using the unconventional, that opened up the possibilities – I mean, you're not doing a fugue, you're doing bones.*[16]

For the distinctive grating, ringing and rattling sounds, Hooper used an African metal instrument[17] and hanging items like tambourines, bowing the instrument and causing the other items to rattle. In addition, a sound heard at several critical moments was created by dragging a pitchfork across a table, making a high-pitched and grittily textured timbre that scrapes upwards in pitch towards an unpredictable crescendo. This sound is first heard in the opening sequence, then frequently associated with either Leatherface or Hitchhiker, and is the last sound heard as the film's end credits conclude. As such, it emblematizes the dysfunctionality of these two characters and the family itself.

The emphasis on sound is introduced from the film's outset as the extended opening and credit sequence commences with sound accompanying a black screen randomly lit to reveal the first images. Opening with a white-on-black date (August 18, 1973), the establishing story about the "account of the tragedy"[18] is accompanied by a newsreader-style voice (which Hooper wanted to sound like the voice of Orson Welles – in a possible connection of the film's conceit that this was a true story with that of Welles's 1938 radio adaptation of H. G. Wells's *War of the Worlds*).[19] At one minute in, barely distinguishable sounds of digging and puffing are heard, together with the pitchfork scrape that we will hear again. Glimpses of a dismembered corpse lit by flashlight become lengthier and the audio mix develops with the addition of gong, cymbals and drone. This leads into a news announcer's voice (compressed in the manner of a radio broadcast) describing graveyard robberies that are being investigated by police. As the camera pans out, the sun rises and the graveyard installation (the "grisly work of art") is revealed and the radio announcer's voice becomes embedded in industrial-sounding drones and clashes. The graveyard scene gives way to the red-and-black image of sunspots, and the film title and credits sequence commences as the radio news continues and improvised guitar sounds are heard. Accompanying images of the sun and a dead armadillo, and as we are introduced to the five travellers, the radio news transitions into diegetic sound from the van.

The effect of the opening music cues is enhanced by their contrast with the pre-recorded music tracks (all by Texan artists) that run under all of the early post-credit scenes.[20] The most clearly audible track occurs during the sequence in which the travellers pick up the Hitchhiker. After describing how cows used to be slaughtered, he cuts his palm with a knife, starts a fire in the van and then slashes Franklin's arm before being ejected from the vehicle. During this unsettling sequence, the van's radio plays Roger Bartlett and Friends' 'Fool For A Blonde'.[21] According to *Texas Chain Saw Massacre* music aficionado Tim Harden, Hooper chose this song for the sequence "because he imagined the Hitchhiker being a fool for [blond-haired] Sally".[22] With its upbeat, honky-tonk styled accompaniment, relaxed vocal style and cheerful "do do do dah" backing female vocals, the song creates an appropriate disjunctive backdrop for the irrational creepiness of the Hitchhiker.

The comfortable musical background that accompanies the travellers in their van is left behind when they arrive at the deserted family house formerly owned by Sally and Franklin's grandparents. Ominous rumbles replace the radio music as the two couples explore the house. Meanwhile downstairs, wheelchair-bound Franklin whines about being abandoned. While close-up images of spiders, a bone mobile and a nest of feathers are matched by percussive beats and seed-pod rattles, the most disturbing sounds are provided by Franklin. As Sally's paraplegic brother, Franklin (played by Paul Partain) whines and whinges through the first half of the film. His voice is pitched as a squeaky tenor and he alternates between complaints and squabbling, with childish vocal utterances of frustration and satirical mimicking. In the additional audio commentary on the film provided on the 2000 DVD release,[23] Hooper observes that much of the interaction with Sally and the other travellers was improvised and that Partain (Franklin) stayed in his character role for the duration of the production (much to the annoyance of his co-actors). Just as Franklin's voice marks him out as the outsider of his group, so Leatherface's inarticulacy marks him out from the crazed family.

Hooper conceived Leatherface as mentally underdeveloped and speech-impeded and wrote a script for actor Gunnar Hansen that comprised gibberish words with explanatory side notes to suggest the meaning. Hansen was left to devise a 'voice' for the character, which he did through grunts and limited vocality. Faced with these communication disadvantages, the chainsaw becomes the character's confident exterior 'voice', sounding out his anger and frustration – and its danger – loud and clear.

The most graphically – and gratingly – effective sound elements in the final quarter of the film are provided by actress Marilyn Burns (Sally). Her screams are both a sonic feature themselves as well as a central element in sound compositions that combine with and accompany them. Indeed so constant are Sally's screams in scenes following Franklin's slaughter that any momentary lapses are a relief. The main scream sequences take place in a dining room elaborately fitted with bone and skin decorations. Tied to a chair, Sally is initially gagged while her hand is cut to allow the decrepit grandfather to suck her blood. Later, after she passes out and then comes to, her renewed screams are satirized by the family members sitting around the table, who howl, mock and laugh in a vocal cacophony accompanied by processed and echoed sounds. The aurality here is excessive, the shock effect of individual screams being shifted into an aural onslaught as intense and disturbing as the film's passages of chainsaw noise. As the intensity of the scene mounts, this continuing soundscape is accompanied by dramatic images as the camera zooms in (in stages, intercut with images of the family looking on) to an ultra-close-up of the bloodshot white of Sally's eye (and, shortly after, her open mouth). Here the screams become more heavily processed still. Released from her confines, Sally is led to the grandfather, who tries to kill her with a hammer that drops from his hand repeatedly, clanging into a metal bucket, alternating with Sally's hoarse screams. This sound-scene is broken when Sally escapes and crashes out through a windowpane, to be pursued by the chainsaw-wielding Leatherface.

Conclusion

Following his (previously discussed) characterization of chainsaw use in Hooper's 1974 film, arborist 'hk33ka1' made a significant comment about the differences between the original and its 1984 sequel, identifying that in order to "give those critics what they accused the original of being about", the sequel "had to go crazie [sic] with a large bar and tons of gore".[24] This perceptive description points to the manner in which the small, domestic chainsaw was replaced by far larger-bladed models (in both the 1984 sequel and the 2003 remake) — amplifying the iconicity of the implement celebrated in the films' titles — and more frequent scenes of gory dismemberment to deliver the titles' promised "massacre[s]". As these two factors suggest, the impact of the original was delivered without these inflations of visual–narrative effect.

While much of *The Texas Chain Saw Massacre*'s notoriety stemmed from its (pre-textual) narrative premise and (post-textual) marketing and critical furore, these two elements were necessarily linked and activated by the focal filmic text. As this chapter has detailed, a primary level of effect and signification of horror in the film was sonic — enacted through the selection of sounds and types of sound in addition to their association with visual representations of horror. In this the chainsaw is not simply a featured weapon but an implement whose sound assumes a symbolic role, communicating an unhinged (and unforgiving) technologically enhanced menace that triggers and interweaves with a range of extreme human vocalizations and is embedded with a wider sound world of abrasive and unsettling textures and tonalities. In its imagination and accomplishment Hooper's soundtrack suggests a dialogue with musical avant-gardism that (apparently) was not present. Similarly, substantial elements of his film soundtrack prefigure elements of the 'industrial' music genre that developed in the 1980s (although there is little evidence of any causal connection). The film's avoidance of stock horror-music techniques, particularly orchestral ones of the kind introduced by Herrmann and Hitchcock in *Psycho* in the previous decade, can be regarded as a significant aspect of what many appear to have regarded as its realism. By virtue of its originality, the soundtrack did not – and, arguably, still does not – communicate easily recognizable genre cues to consumers. In this manner, despite its previous critical neglect, *The Texas Chain Saw Massacre*'s soundtrack deserves as significant a rating in the history of horror cinema sound and music as the film itself has attained.

Acknowledgement

Thanks to Tim Hardin for research assistance on the source music for the film and to Laura Wiebe Taylor for her comments on an earlier draft.

Notes

1. While subsequent films in the series have included the compound word 'Chainsaw' in their titles, the original splits the term.
2. In surveys such as *Total Film*'s 2005 poll. The full top ten listings were:
   1. *Texas Chain Saw Massacre* (1974)
   2. *Halloween* (1978)
   3. *Suspiria* (1977)
   4. *Dawn of the Dead* (1978)
   5. *The Shining* (1980)
   6. *Psycho* (1960)
   7. *The Wicker Man* (1973)
   8. *Rosemary's Baby* (1968)
   9. *Don't Look Now* (1973)
   10. *Cannibal Holocaust* (1980)
3. Not to mention parodic versions such as *Hollywood Chainsaw Hookers* (Fred Olen Ray, 1988).
4. *Halloween Online Magazine* (http://www.halloweenonlinemagazine. com/sfx/ halloween-chainsaw_1.html, accessed 22 August 2006).
5. A factor which has resulted in the production of a number of safety training videos, including the Mississippi Farm Bureau Federation's well-circulated 28-minute-long *Chainsaw Safety* (made some time in the 1980s).
6. See Safety Line Institute: 'Typical sound pressure levels' (http://www. safetyline.wa.gov.au/institute/level2/course18/lecture54/l54_03.asp).
7. To quote an aphorism often attributed to Hooper.
8. M. Baumgarten, 'Tobe Hooper remembers *The Texas Chainsaw Massacre*' (http: //www.austinchronicle.com/issues/dispatch/2000-10-27/scree). Hooper goes on to argue that after leaving the store he then wrote the film story while listening to

a popular song (although in this interview he cannot recall which song). In his commentary on the DVD special-release version of the film, Hooper argues that another influence on his idea for the film was the song 'Dead Dog In The Middle Of The Road' (probably a reference to Loudon Wainwright III's popular 1972 song 'Dead Skunk', with its chorus of "You got your dead skunk in the middle of the road/Stinkin' to high Heaven!"). For a different version of the chainsaw store story, see Scheib (2003).

9. The company commenced manufacturing in 1944 and by the early 1970s had a significant market presence with its low-medium-price range models.

10. Username 'hk33ka1', http://www.arboristsite.com/showthread.php?t=11681&page=2, accessed 10 September 2006.

11. A track by Arkey Blue, somewhat appropriately entitled 'Daddy's Sick Again'.

12. Actor Gunnar Hansen's leg was strapped with a metal plate under a wad of animal meat and a blood bag for this scene.

13. R. Scheib, 'The Texas Chainsaw Massacre' (http://www.moira.co.nz/horror/texas.htm, accessed 4 September 2006).

14. *Ibid.*

15. Cited in *The Film Asylum*, 'Tobe Hooper Sitges 2003 interview' (http://www.thefilmasylum.com/features/interviews/sitges03/tobe). See also http://www.brainyquote.com/quotes/t/tobehooper312425.html.

16. Cited in David Gregory's documentary, *The Texas Chain Saw Massacre – the Shocking Truth* (2001).

17. Hooper's description (in Gregory, 2001) – precise instrument unknown.

18. The opening crawl and announcement is:

> The film which you are about to see is an account of the tragedy which befell a group of five youths, in particular Sally Hardesty and her invalid brother Franklin. It is all the more tragic in that they were young. But, had they lived very, very long lives, they could not have expected nor would they have wished to see as much of the mad and macabre as they were to see that day. For them, an idyllic summer afternoon drive became a nightmare. The events of that day were to lead to the discovery of one of the most bizarre crimes in the annals of American history, The Texas Chain Saw Massacre.

19. Indeed, the film was loosely inspired by the activities of 1950s Wisconsin murderer Ed Gein, who also wore a mask of human skin.

20. Seven pre-recorded songs were used in the film: Roger Bartlett and Friends' 'Fool For A Blond'; Timberline Rose's 'Waco' and 'Glad Hand'; Arkey Blue's 'Daddy's Sick Again' and 'Misty Hours Of Daylight'; Los Cyclones' 'Feria De Los Flores' (Parade Of Flowers); and 'Poco A Poco No' (Not Little By Little).

21. Sometimes referred to by fans as 'Sidewalk café' due to its repeated line "spend most every day in the sidewalk café".

22. Hooper apparently paid a flat fee of $US50 for the use of this song.

23. *Tobe Hooper's Original Uncut* [Special Edition] *The Texas Chainsaw Massacre* – (2000) Force Video (with accompanying disc of the documentary *The Texas Chain Saw Massacre – the Shocking Truth*).
24. See note 10 above.

9 Incorporating Monsters
Music as Context, Character and Construction in Kubrick's *The Shining*

Jeremy Barham

The films of Stanley Kubrick, particularly from *2001: A Space Odyssey* (1968) on, were characterized by their innovative approaches to the use of music. Even by Kubrick's standards, however, *The Shining* (1980) exemplifies a level of both sophisticated inter-action of music and moving image, and general reliance on music for contextual, characterization and narrative purposes, rarely equalled in his output. The film's almost exclusive use of pre-existent music not only sets it apart from many other contempor-aneous and subsequent works in the horror genre but also raises important questions surrounding Kubrick's conceptual and constructive film aesthetic, and his crucial col-laboration with music editor Gordon Stainforth, hitherto rarely acknowledged in the published literature. With the support of material supplied to the author by Stainforth, this chapter will reinvestigate the historical context, methodology and aesthetic and structural consequences of Kubrick's use of the modernist and avant-garde music of Bartók, Ligeti and Penderecki in the film – a stylistic repertoire, which he first explored in *2001* and admired in Friedkin's *The Exorcist* (1973).[1] It will examine ways in which the music is employed to project climates of primarily psychological (rather than physi-cal) horror and to embody the omnipresent but unseen malevolence of the alien 'other', whether through propelling the narrative in visually static scenes or underpinning pas-sages of vivid action and subverting dialogue in precisely matched scenes of varying length.

A new approach to sound

Theodor Adorno and Hans Eisler would probably never have expected that, together with science fiction, the horror-film genre would arguably come closest of all film genres to responding imaginatively to their celebrated attack in 1947 against the commercial standardization of Hollywood film music (1994: 3–19; 114–33). After all, their call for a 'progressive' film-music practice, whose atonal scores would create tension with the image and expose its mediated nature rather than preserve illusions of reality and immediacy through cliché, was hardly calculated to appeal to studio bosses: it was in fact largely ignored at the time in mainstream contexts. Nevertheless, cognizant or otherwise of the Adorno–Eisler aesthetic challenge, the later composers of scores for the psychologically, technologically or sociologically dystopian visions of the following films – to varying degrees products of the early Cold War years and the socio-political unrest and gloom of the late 1960s and early 1970s – demonstrated viable new alternatives to prevailing neo-romantic scoring practices, whether through the use of pre-existent music or not:

- Fred M. Wilcox's *Forbidden Planet* (1956) – pre-synthesizer 'electronic tonalities' by Louis and Bebe Barron;[2]
- Alfred Hitchcock's *Psycho* (1960) – Bernard Herrmann's minimalist dissonant strings with which *The Shining*'s score has much in common;
- Alain Resnais's elusive *Je t'aime, je t'aime* (1968) – Penderecki's evidently alien-sounding vocal writing;
- Franklin Schaffner's *Planet of the Apes* (1968) – percussive, Varèse-like modernity from Jerry Goldsmith, who was reputedly influenced by Penderecki;
- George Lucas's *THX 1138* (1970) – grating avant-garde electronic tone clusters by Schifrin;
- Andrei Tarkovski's *Solaris* (1972) – Eduard Artemiev's harsh or brooding electronic sonorities and his similar treatments of Bach;
- The aforementioned *The Exorcist*.

It is true that Kubrick employs similar, dense vocal clusters of Ligeti's *Requiem* to accompany both the potentially threatening discovery and examination of the black monolith and the astronaut's final transcendent journey towards rebirth in *2001* – revitalizing the spirit of Francis Bacon's seventeenth-century utopian projection of microtonal musical "sound-houses" and their "harmonies… of quarter-sounds and lesser slides of sounds" ([1627] 1999: 182). But more broadly, the use of Bach, for example, (for which read functional tonal harmony) as a universal signifier of humanity in films such as *THX* and *Solaris*,[3] alongside atonal clusters as some kind of dehumanized inverse involving technological oppression or psychological disturbance, initiated an approach that has since attained the status of reactionary cliché. This is a cliché that may be traced back in cinema history (at least conceptually) to Newman's 1955 film *This Island Earth*, in which a plan for alien invasion of this planet is foiled by one of their number who learns to love the music of Mozart.

In *Forbidden Planet*, during the final attack of the monster created from Dr Morbius's Id, Commander Adams's cry "That thing out there is you!" is indicative of the closeness that has often existed between science-fiction and horror genres. Whether a monster from within or without, whether a physical or imagined threatening alien presence, the confronting of fear of the unknown, of 'otherness' as a discontinuity from ordinary reality, and of the bases of similarity and difference – the "deep and fearful concern with the foundations of the self" (Kracauer, 2004: 30) – has suggested great potential for a crossover of dramatic audio-visual cinematic techniques. Within the context of scoring films with pre-existent music, this is especially the case with Kubrick, who took one particular stylistic strand of *2001*'s eclectic musical content and developed it in startling new directions in *The Shining*. Whereas in the earlier film he deployed music to create highly original and mutually distinct aesthetic effects and audio-visual experiences that tended towards broader kinds of parallelism and instances of striking counterpoint, the later film frequently engages the musical and visual texts in micro-levels of close organic integration.

It is perhaps unsurprising that the initial, predominantly negative, critical reception of *The Shining* was mostly silent on the issue of its music. It receives no mention, for example, in Combs (1980), apart from the list of credits,[4] Hogan (1980), Jameson (1980), Macklin (1981) or Titterington (1981). Leibowitz and Jeffress merely list the stereotypical "periodic drum and rattle music" as one of the film's many Indian motifs (1981: 46), while Wells refers only to the "heavy use of non-original music to wield extra dramatic force" (Anderson and Wells, 1980: 438) and Anderson simply criticizes the scoring (illogically) as both "much too obvious" and "like padding" (*ibid*.: 438). Despite its mostly negative stance, Maslin's review describes the assembled music, without any further elaboration, as "stunningly effective" (1980), and Mayersberg briefly views the relative inaccessibility of the music in the context of his post-apocalyptic reading of the Overlook Hotel, the Ligeti "laughing at all past music and at people with notions of fixed values", and even the lyricism of the Bartók being unrecognized by "ordinary filmgoers" (1980–1: 57). These last comments obliquely raise the important issue to which I alluded previously, of *The Shining*'s collusion in, if not motivation of, the rapid appropriation in post-1960s mainstream cinema of musically avant-garde styles, pressing them into service as clichés for all manner of manifestations of the 'Other' and doing much the same for composers of this music as 1940s Hollywood had done in varied screen contexts for Wagner, Tchaikovsky, Strauss and Mahler.[5] For entirely different reasons Mayersberg and the musicologist Carl Dahlhaus consider this a situation to be lamented rather than celebrated. The latter writes of an earlier, but no less anti-populist, musical repertoire: "The discovery that audiences who detest Schönberg's music in the concert hall will accept it without a murmur as background film music is as fundamental as it is depressing" (1989: 346). With specific reference to Kubrick's film, Mayersberg goes on to say:

> The Shining *has a lot in common with post-war music. It seems technically brilliant and yet fundamentally heartless. It seems deliberately clever and yet remains enigmatic. Kubrick has tried to bridge a gap which has occurred in the language of film. How can you express dissonance and fragmentation, the essential features of our present lives, in a manner which respects traditional harmonies? Can disorder ever be expressed in an orderly way? Kubrick has reached the limits of conservative film art in* The Shining. (1980–1: 57)

In the light of these observations, *The Shining* could be said to represent something of a watershed moment in film history: both a point of departure, which signalled the imminent cementing of post-war avant-garde musical repertoire and styles as standard means of underscoring a plethora of evils in future compositional practice, and a point of closure, at which such music forever lost the opportunity of gaining wider signifying potential within public consciousness. At the centre of this crossroads stood, among others, Kubrick, an artist with exceedingly well-tuned musical sensibilities and a film-maker by no means resistant to the benefits accruing from commercial success.

Despite selective deafness to the music of *The Shining*, some of the more perceptive of its contemporary critics, like Mayersberg, discerned the significance of certain deeper shifting aesthetic processes at work in the film that have relevance to its musical dimensions. Combs (1980: 222) and Leibowitz and Jeffress (1981: 45), for example, recognized as one of its themes an economic affluence both built on past evils and potentially productive of future evils. The moral risks attached to unchecked commerce according to this view would certainly chime with the Marxist Adorno–Eisler axis of critical theory and its applications to film-music production, though this is rendered thoroughly problematic in the case of *The Shining* with Kubrick's apparent commodification of an Eastern European high-art music (written in the context of either pre-war fascist or post-war communist oppression) as an emblem of malevolence.[6] Perhaps the use of this particular nationally and politically affiliated repertoire had more to do with what Macklin identified as the film's typically Kubrickian satiric edge by which the foibles of American culture and values (represented by cartoons, space-race sweaters and chat-show shibboleths) are set against the venerable old-world values of the American Indian and 'serious' European art (1981: 93, 95).

If this is too bald an opposition, then perhaps Macklin's observation of the film's sense of abstraction through banality of dialogue and characterization (the second-level discourse others have often attributed to the film as a work of horror that is about the notion of horror or the notion of horror films) might be instructive in understanding the use of a music whose lack of many of the recognizable conventional markers of melodic and harmonic structure surely embodies a corresponding degree of technical and emotional abstraction. The trouble with this line of argument is that the modernist music of Bartók and the avant-garde music of Ligeti and Penderecki used by Kubrick do not trade on banality and cannot be said to subscribe to the self-reflexive and intertextual referencing of postmodern compositional trends. This repertoire is more firmly located in the eloquent traditions of modernist autonomy, originality and stylistic purity. In his desire to use such music, perhaps Kubrick realized that its power lay in an ability to replace what banality leaves out: meaningful levels of communication, and the reflection and counteraction of what Titterington sees as two of the film's primary metaphors of the 'coldness' (harsh, often high-pitched dissonances) and inescapable 'circularity' or perhaps labyrinthine nature (enclosed, non-progressive harmonic idioms) of contemporary existence, the latter visually and thematically symbolized by the hotel's maze (1981: 119, 120). In this way, the music participates in the film's subordination of language and "our conscious critical awareness" (*ibid.*: 121), in favour of image structures and forms of audio-visual concatenation that became part of Kubrick's development of a more intuitive and subliminal cinematic language after *2001*. For Mayersberg this renders *The Shining* "nothing more or less than a metaphor for the cinema itself" (1980–1: 57).

In what remains the most revealing interview given by the director, Ciment manages to extract from Kubrick discussion of some key aspects of his creative aesthetic in relation to *The Shining*. "I wanted to make a film constructed in the way that silent films used to be," says Kubrick:

> *I wanted very much to make a film in which the story is told in ways different from those to which the sound film has accustomed us (in other words a series of scenes which could just as well be performed in the theatre). Dialogue tends to be employed as the principal means of communication, but I believe that without doubt there is a more cinematic manner of communicating, closer to silent film.* (quoted in Ciment, 1987: 187)

Later, in response to questions about the film's supernatural and psychological elements, Kubrick finds refuge in notions of the irrationality of artistic (primarily musical) expression:

> *I do not want to give any rationalizing explanation of this story. I prefer to use musical terms and speak of motives, variations and resonances. With this kind of narrative, when one tries to offer an explicit analysis, one tends to reduce it to a point of ultra-transparent absurdity. From this point on the musical or poetic utilization of the material is that which is most appropriate... With this kind of story one is apparently in a region not only where intellectual exploration ceases but also where no-one is able to tell whether what happens is true... I like those realms of narrative where reason is of little help. Rationality takes you to the frontiers of these regions and then it remains for you to explore the poetic or musical level.* (ibid.: 192–3, 196)

It seems from this that Kubrick and *The Shining* offered as much a backward glance as they did a programme for the future. Indeed, these impulses are quite possibly mutually dependent: responding to Eisler and Adorno in providing music which is more than a "secondary piece of decoration" and which has "its own logic and integrity" (Donnelly, 2005: 45) but going far beyond this to ground aspects of the film-making process in the exploratory, instinctive world of musico-poetic expression. This may go some way towards explaining Kubrick's unusually protracted shooting schedules and his heuristic approach to filming multiple takes of identical scenes, searching for nuances and combinations of performances that cannot be obtained merely through conventional methods of directorial verbal explication. But Kubrick's aesthetic goes even further back than this to the world of pre-sound cinema, a period during which traditions of musical accompaniment shifted from an initial musical dominance, which precluded any interference with the organic integrity of musical works in screen contexts, towards a commercially driven reversal of this practice whereby the bowdlerizing of the classics became the norm. As Altman suggests, "in order to assure its film future, music had to abandon its first principles" (2004: 243). In *The Shining* Kubrick seems to toy with both aesthetic inclinations: filming extended sequences which would allow long sections of musical works (notably the Bartók) to be retained intact; and exploiting other musical material through encouraging combination, abridgement and electronic enhancement, to which it may in fact be structurally and stylistically amenable, for shorter-term ends. More than this, however, silent cinema was of necessity an art of vivid, even exaggerated, visual and physical gesture. In the search for first principles and a screen medium not reliant on the verbal, Kubrick's incitement of his actors towards extremes in the portrayal of the effects of transcendent forces (particularly Jack Nicholson whose 'mugging' in the film has often been the subject of harsh criticism) formed part of the aesthetic network of screen media functions which, together with music, *mise en-scène* and revolutionary steadicam camerawork, both paid homage to and far exceeded the magical plasticity of the conventions witnessed at the birth of cinematic storytelling, the subsequent submerging of which in widespread verbal–literary narrative procedures Kubrick appears to lament.

Musical intentions

While the musical score of *The Shining* has been given some attention in more recent generalized literature on the director and the film (for example, Hummel, 1984; Kagan, 1991; Bingham, 1996; Baxter, 1997; LoBrutto, 1997; García Mainar, 1999; Howard, 1999; Kolker, 2000; Nelson, 2000; Falsetto, 2001; Rasmussen, 2001; Phillips and Hill, 2002), it took the birth of the internet and the enthusiasm of a dedicated fan base to begin probing more deeply and seriously into its structural and aesthetic complexities.[7] The last three years (more than two decades after the film's release) have seen the appearance of a doctoral thesis (Lionnet, 2003), a research paper (Barham, 2003) and a book chapter in addition to this one (Donnelly, 2005), either wholly or partially dedicated to the film's scoring.[8] This is a reflection both of recent reorientations in musicological disciplines and institutions towards the greater scholarly appreciation of film music in general, and of renewed interest in Kubrick as an artist following his death in 1999. Table 9.1 provides Stainforth's list of all the music utilized in the film.

It is important at this stage to dispel certain myths that have developed and still exist concerning the process of the score's production and resultant levels of audio-visual interaction.[9] In the first place, Kubrick did not carry out any cutting of the film prior to the conclusion of the whole shooting process. Secondly, all the laying of the music tracks was undertaken after the final cut of the film was established. Thirdly, therefore, "none of the scenes were choreographed to the music – it was all done completely the other way round" (Stainforth, 2006: personal communication with the author). The understandable and persuasive idea that the reverse was the case persists to this day. For example, according to Donnelly, "the film is at least partly cut to music... The fact that the music existed before the film means that large sections of the film are cut to

Table 9.1 The music employed in *The Shining*

Music	Location within film
'The Shining' (main title) by Wendy Carlos and Rachel Elkind. Based on the 'Dies Irae' from Berlioz's *Symphonie Fantastique*. Carlos plays synthesizer while Elkind supplies vocal effects.	Opening sequence
'Rocky Mountains' by Wendy Carlos and Rachel Elkind	As the family is driving to the Overlook.
Lontano by György Ligeti, 1967. Sinfonie-Orchester des Sudwestfunks, conducted by Ernest Bour.	When Danny first sees the twins in the games room; Wendy and Danny in snow, Jack watching; and when Wendy first discovers that the Overlook's telephone lines are down.
Music for Strings, Percussion and Celeste (3rd movement) by Béla Bartók, 1936. Berlin Philharmonic, conducted by Herbert von Karajan (Deutsche Grammophon).	Wendy and Danny in the maze early in the film (as Jack throws the ball against the Overlook's walls and looks down upon the model of the maze). When Danny first discovers Room 237, and attempts to open the locked door, then sees the twins; carries on right through to the end of Jack typing and pulling paper out of a typewriter. Danny and Jack in the bedroom: "I'll never hurt you."
The Awakening of Jacob by Krzysztof Penderecki, 1974. Polish Radio National Symphony Orchestra, conducted by Penderecki.	Used (appropriately!) as Jack awakens from his bad dream while at his desk – starting with Wendy checking the boilers (a favourite cue of mine); and when Jack enters Room 237.
Utrenja [Morning Prayer] by Krzysztof Penderecki, 1960/70. Symphony Orchestra of the National Philharmonic, Warsaw, conducted by Andrzej Markowski, (Polski).	This excerpt of *Utrenja* is used several times. First, when Jack axes Halloran. Then it punctuates Wendy's scream as she sees 'Redrum' written in the mirror, and later her shock as she sees Halloran's lifeless body. It was also used in the original 144-minute version of the film as she witnesses the various ghosts of the Overlook coming to life. Finally, it is layered with *Polymorphia* as Jack chases Danny through the maze.
'Kanon Paschy' from *Utrenja*	When Wendy hits Jack with the baseball bat, when Jack exclaims "Here's Johnny!"; when Wendy witnesses the blood flowing from the elevator; and in many other places in reels 14 and 15 (see Appendix 9.1).

Table 9.1 – continued

Music	Location within film
'De Natura Sonoris No.1' by Krzysztof Penderecki, 1966 (Probably from a Phillips label recording).	Plays as Danny rides his tricycle, turns the hall corner and sees the twins. Also plays when Wendy discovers that Jack has sabotaged the Snowcat.
'De Natura Sonoris No. 2' by Krzysztof Penderecki, 1971. Polish Radio National Symphony Orchestra, conducted by Krzysztof Penderecki.	As Jack approaches and enters the ballroom for the first time; as Danny writes 'Redrum' in lipstick on the mirror; and as Halloran drives the Snowcat to the Overlook.
Polymorphia by Krzysztof Penderecki, 1961 (Probably from a Phillips label recording).	As Wendy discovers Jack's 'All Work and No Play Makes Jack a Dull Boy' writings; when Wendy drags Jack into the larder; and it embellishes Jack chasing Danny in the maze.
'Masquerade' by Jack Hylton and His Orchestra. Probably straight off a (cassette of a) 78-rpm record obtained by *The Shining*'s 1930s music researcher.	Plays faintly in background as Jack storms out of the kitchen service corridor and sees the balloons outside the Gold Ballroom.
'Midnight, The Stars And You' by Ray Noble and His Orchestra, Al Bowlly vocal, 1932.	Plays during the ballroom scene, and over the closing credits.
'It's All Forgotten Now' by Ray Noble and His Orchestra, Al Bowlly vocal, 1932.	As Jack talks with Grady in the red bathroom.
'Home' by Henry Hall and the Gleneagles Hotel Band, late 1920s.	As Jack talks with Grady in the red bathroom.

the music" (2005: 43, 45). Similarly, "Kubrick frequently liked having formal music pieces dictate the shape of certain scenes and sequences, so he would edit his film to match the music" (Carlos and Coppel, 2005: 37). Even Lionnet comes perilously close to suggesting this:

> The music... effectively leads the performance... it controls the picture... the music is controlling the action of the picture... individual questions and answers [are] controlled by the musical effects in the score. (2003: 41, 93, 97)

That this often appears to be the case is testament to the efforts of the film's music editor, Gordon Stainforth. However, these comments do conceal, and are perhaps confused by, the fact that on set during shooting Kubrick sometimes did play music (entirely different from that which formed the eventual score) in order to create an appropriate performance atmosphere and space for the actors.[10]

The degree and nature of Kubrick's involvement in the music editing requires clarification. At least by the beginning of the scoring process, and probably earlier, Kubrick knew he wanted to use the music of Penderecki, Bartók and Ligeti (particularly the first two) and gave Stainforth large amounts of recorded examples to sift through. He considered that Penderecki's music in particular "was most suitable for the film" (Stainforth, 2006: personal communication with the author) and was keen to use the Bartók piece (the third movement of *Music for Strings, Percussion and Celeste*), which he especially liked. Apart from this, however, what appeared to concern Kubrick more was the general mood and character of the repertoire rather than a determination to use specific pieces at chosen moments in the film. In accordance with the aesthetics of excess with which Kubrick wished to imbue the film as a whole, Stainforth recognized that "the music had to be 'over the top'... Anything less would not have been true to the underlying manic quality of the movie as the madness unfolds towards the end" (*ibid.*). On a practical level, the editor was given a precise list of the places where Kubrick wanted music cues in the film, along with broad indications of the type of music he required.[11] At no stage did the director engage in critical or analytical discussion of the repertoire in question, but rather made his intentions known in very clear and functional ways, confident that "the resonances of the music were just right for the film" (*ibid.*). Kubrick would watch scenes with alternative scoring laid by Stainforth and select the versions he preferred. Stainforth reported that more often than not their judgements coincided and that Kubrick was "by and large... very pleased with the particular pieces I selected" (*ibid.*).

The only music that Kubrick had specifically decided on before Stainforth embarked on the music-editing process was Wendy Carlos's synthesized 'Dies Irae', which accompanies the tracking shots of the Rocky Mountains at the beginning of the film.[12] He was also instrumental in the idea of layering more than one of the Penderecki tracks simultaneously in order to 'beef up' the climactic final maze scene, and, since he was seated next to the dubbing editor and faders throughout the mixing process, he almost certainly had input into elements of this final part of post-production. Nevertheless, in comparison with most other aspects of the film-making process over which he exerted considerable authorial control, Kubrick seems to have been less closely involved in the precise selection, editing and laying of the music, although of course no part of the scoring progressed beyond the music editor's cutting room without his final approval. In effect, Stainforth's role and achievements as music editor were to realize Kubrick's broad artistic intentions on a detailed practical and creative level. Stainforth's condensed versions of the film's music charts are given in Appendix 9.1, at the end of the chapter, and the more detailed dubbing charts of the final two reels of the film (from Danny writing 'REDRUM' on the mirror onwards), containing Kubrick's own handwritten instructions, are given in Figures 9.1 and 9.2.[13]

This clarification of the working process serves in no way to diminish the sense of Kubrick's authorship or artistic ownership and vision of the film, but certainly gives the lie to any belief that he operated hermetically and self-obsessively, with disregard for others. Film-making has always been one of the most collaborative of activities and

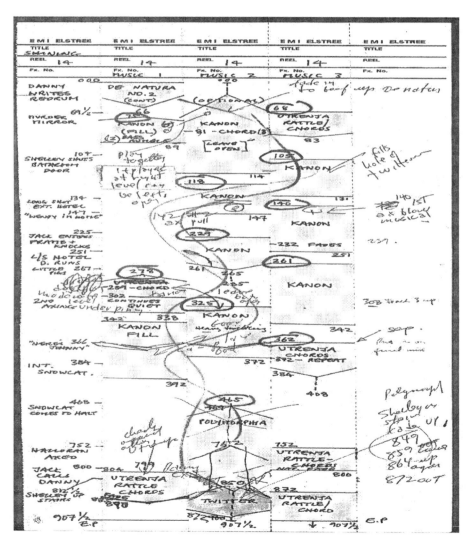

Figure 9.1   Stainforth's rough music chart to reel 14

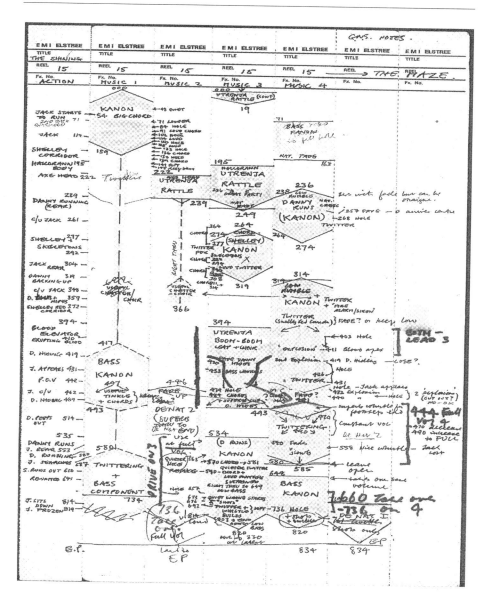

Figure 9.2 Stainforth's rough music chart to reel 15

Kubrick was able, at least in this case, to balance profound individual creative insight and determination with an understanding of how sharing and developing that insight with gifted artistic and technical partners could accomplish far-from-ordinary results. Furthermore, the issue of the aesthetic and creative hierarchy of music and image raised above in the context of the remarkable nature of much of the film's audio-visual interaction, should be qualified by recognizing that even if scenes were not cut wholesale to fit pre-existing musical structures, Kubrick's methods of shooting and editing the visual text (areas over which he exerted immediate and total control) may well have reflected, at however subliminal, recondite or marginal a level, something of his prevailing artistic preoccupation with the musical repertoire he envisaged for the film. In other words, these procedures of creating and manipulating the image may have allowed for, or lent themselves to, particular types of structural, expressive and interactive musical treatment. This may explain how, in an exhaustive process of trial and error, fine judgement and partial good fortune akin to Kubrick's own creative practice, Stainforth was able on so many occasions to distil from the material such trenchant combined configurations of scenic and aural structural dynamic. Table 9.2 outlines some of the numerous small adjustments Stainforth made to picture cuts and/or music tracks in the process of music editing.

Table 9.2 Selected details of the music-editing process

Scene	Adjustments/points of synchronization	Stainforth's comments
Jack bouncing the ball before looking at the maze model	Conventional synchronization of the music to the action	The whole thing was in fact synched from the bouncing ball and the swing of Jack's arm. I just inched it this way and that way until it felt just right, and I remember being almost beside myself with excitement when I first got it to work. Such was the nature and quality of the music that I couldn't cut it (I may have tightened it by a few frames) but we definitely had to lengthen the shot of Jack looking down at the maze to make the music fit the rest of the scene.
Danny trying the doorknob to Room 237 and then getting back on his tricycle	Conventional synchronization of the music to the action	I synched the music exactly with his head movements.
Jack and Danny in the bedroom	Some picture cuts changed by a few frames	I managed to persuade Ray [Lovejoy, the film's editor] to change some picture cuts... to make the music work exactly right.
Captions such as 'Tuesday' and 'Saturday'	Synchronized with accented chords in the music	I remember being slightly embarrassed initially by the big chords on some of the captions (where [Kubrick] had not wanted any music), but I argued that that was how the music went and that it would be much better to go along with it rather than fading out; and when he saw the alternative version(s) I'd laid up he agreed... I think he just accepted that there was no other way of doing it because that was how the music went.

Scene	Adjustments/points of synchronization	Stainforth's comments
Barroom scene	'Choreographing' the music with the action and the dialogue	I spent hours 'choreographing' the music with the action and the dialogue, e.g. "Anything you say, Lloyd, anything you say": I hit the beat when he picks up the glass, and made the phrasing of the music work with the rhythm of the dialogue.
Wendy's discovery of 'All Work and No Play' manuscript	Shifting the music in very small increments	I must have moved/relaid the music here thirty or forty times. The timing of "How do you like it?" was critical, in the end, to within about half a frame (two sprockets) i.e. about a 48th of a second. "OK, let's talk!" says Jack, and boomp – boomp goes the music: 1–2; and I make him put his fist on the table on the second beat, not the first. So much more powerful than the first, much more obvious, way that I tried it. I made a lot of tricksy music cuts and crossfades in that scene.
Jack locked in the food storeroom	Synchronization of music to action	I managed to synch up the manic music leading up to "You've got a big surprise coming to you ... go check it out! Check it out!" with Jack drumming his fingers on the door. That took an awful lot of finding, but I felt it could almost have been written for the scene.
Wendy running through the snow to the Snowcat in the garage	Synchronizing Penderecki to delayed reaction of actor	That chord when she picks up the distributor cap; I remember continually moving 'De Natura Sonoris No. 1' back and back, frame by frame, so that there was a definite time delay of nearly a second as the full import of the detached distributor cap sinks in.

In the final part of this study I will examine more closely two of the most outstanding examples of audio-visual concatenation in the film, one employing music by Penderecki (Danny's encounter with the Grady twins, DVD opening of chapter 12 [34.48–36.04 mins] and the other using Bartók (Jack and Danny in the bedroom, DVD chapter 13 [36.45–40.57 mins]). First, a brief synopsis of the film's plot: frustrated writer and former teacher Jack (Jack Nicholson) takes his wife Wendy (Shelley Duvall) and eight-year-old son Danny (Danny Lloyd), who has psychic abilities, to a remote and empty Colorado hotel to act as caretaker over the winter. Gradually Jack's mental equilibrium disintegrates as he appears to take on the characteristics of a previous tenant named Charles or Delbert Grady, who brutally murdered his wife and two daughters with an axe some years before. After many tense episodes, some involving psychic visions and threatened or actual physical violence, and a climactic outdoor chase scene, Wendy and

Danny manage to escape the hotel in a snowmobile, leaving Jack to freeze to death in the hotel's hedge maze.

In the first scene to be discussed, Danny rides along the seemingly endless hotel corridors on his small tricycle (an allusion, perhaps, to Damien's activities in similar devastating scenes of Donner's *The Omen*, 1976), captured from behind with the pioneering smooth, low flight of Garret Brown's recently invented steadicam. Rounding a particular corner he halts, confronted with a vision of what we assume to be the two previously murdered Grady sisters. As shown in Table 9.3 and Appendix 9.2, this scene uses a section from near the beginning of Penderecki's 'De Natura Sonoris No. 1' of 1966, a work which, in terms of the composer's historical and technical development, combined the techniques of aural 'saturation' through dense pitch clusters characteristic of earlier pieces such as *Polymorphia* (1961, also used in the film), *Fluoresences* (1961) and *Threnody for the Victims of Hiroshima* (1959–61) with a renewed interest in clear formal demarcations, which in the event are helpful in its application in this case to the cut of cinematic images.[14] The analysis shows that the scene is constructed in an arch, with longer shots at the beginning and end and a series of rapid shots in the middle (for example, shots 7 to 15 which occur within the space of 11 seconds), to a degree matching the changing textural activity in the score. The music (together with the unnaturally low angle and persistently lethargic camera movement) appears immediately to set up a connotative space at odds with the innocuousness of the activity visually portrayed. Thereafter various key moments in the scene such as short passages of dialogue and rapid cut-aways to an image of bloodied corpses interleave and sometimes synchronize with Penderecki's series of ready-made 'stingers' (either single percussive attacks or brief scalic passages). In order to make this work to such a high level of accuracy and refinement, and with such palpable impact, a cut of approximately four bars is made in the music from Fig. 5^{+2} to Fig. 5^{+6}, omitting the series of cello and double-bass ff attacks marked 'au talon' (with the heel of the bow) and resuming just before the first of the rising woodwind scalic figures. Particularly notable effects, some of which accrue from this, are the direct image-to-music matches at cut-away shots 7, 12 and 14 of the slaughtered girls (percussion and piano attack followed by rising scalic figures); the kinetic parallel at shot 15 where Danny raises his hands to cover his face at the end of the penultimate rising scale (Fig. 6); the first glimpse of his eyes gingerly peeping through his fingers towards the end of shot 15 synchronized with the cessation of the sustained woodwind, brass and string high cluster at one bar before Fig. 7; and the 'interpolation' of brief components of dialogue during moments of reduced volume and periods of reverberation between various musical climaxes (shots 4, 5, 6, 8, 11 and 13). Stainforth comments on the results as follows:

> What I did, I hope, throughout the scenes with Danny on the bike was something more visceral and rhythmic. Trying to make this feel more like a direct experience, like you are really experiencing it now... There was also the enormous practical problem of making a whole piece of pre-composed

Table 9.3 The Shining: analysis of 34.48–36.04 mins. Danny's encounter with the Grady sisters

Time	Shot details	Image/action/dialogue	Music (Penderecki, 'De Natura Sonoris No. 1')
34:48	Shot 1. Moving steadicam from behind and from distance	Danny cycling along corridor; disappears around corner	2 before Fig. 2 → Fig. 3 (wind and string clusters, gradual crescendo)
35:04	Shot 2. Close-up from behind	Danny cycling along narrower corridor. Turns corner, sees girls, stops.	Fig. 3 → Fig. 3 (+5) (harmonium and strings)
	Close-up from behind with medium view beyond	View over Danny's head down corridor to two girls	Fig. 3 (+4) (percussion and brass 'stinger')
35:13	Shot 3. Close-up	Danny's face	Fig. 3 (+5) → Fig. 3 (+7) (tam tam and brass → brass, string and woodwind 'stinger')
35:16	Shot 4. As end of Shot 2	View over Danny's head down corridor to girls; "Hello Danny."	Fig. 3 (+7) → Fig. 4 (+1) (woodwind crescendo)
35:22	Shot 5. As Shot 3	Danny's face. "Come and play with us."	Fig. 4 (+1) → Fig. 4 (+6) Contrabassoon lowest note; percussion and piano 'stinger'
35:30	Shot 6. As Shot 4	View over Danny's head down corridor to girls "Come and play with us, Danny."	Fig. 4 (+6) → Fig. 4 (+9) (gong and piano 'stinger', Fig. 4 (+7))
35:36	Shot 7. Medium	Bloodied corpses	Fig. 4 (+9) → Fig. 4 (+10) (percussion and piano 'stinger')
35:37	Shot 8. Medium	The girls standing. "For ever."	Fig. 4 (+10) → Fig. 5 (reverberation of percussion and piano 'stinger')
35:39	Shot 9. As Shot 7	Bloodied corpses	Fig. 5 (reverberation of percussion and piano 'stinger')
35:39	Shot 10. Close-up	Danny's face reeling	Fig. 5 (reverberation of percussion and piano 'stinger')
35:40	Shot 11. Close-up	The girls standing. "And ever."	Fig. 5 (reverberation of percussion and piano 'stinger')
35:42	Shot 12. As Shot 7	Bloodied corpses	Cut to Fig. 5 (+6) (rising chromatic woodwind 'stinger')

Table 9.3 – continued

Time	Shot details	Image/action/dialogue	Music (Penderecki, 'De Natura Sonoris No. 1')
35:43	Shot 13. Extreme close-up	Girls standing. "And ever."	Fig. 5 (+7–8) (end of rising chromatic woodwind 'stinger')
35:45	Shot 14. As Shot 7	Bloodied corpses	Fig. 5 (+9) → Fig. 6 (rising chromatic brass 'stinger')
35:47	Shot 15. Close-up	Danny covers his face	Fig. 6 → Fig. 6 (+9) (end of rising chromatic brass 'stinger' → rising chromatic woodwind; brass 'stinger', string gliss → sustained woodwind, brass, string high notes → beginning of harmonium cluster)
35:59	Shot 16. Medium	View over Danny's head of empty corridor	Fig. 6 (+10) onwards (harmonium and viola cluster)

> *music work with the scene. My music charts show that I did actually take some liberties here, but the one thing I will never do is mess with the original 'phrasing' of the music. It has to work with the film or it'll never work. What you can never do is change the whole phrasing of the music. And here all the stuff with Danny looking through the gaps in his fingers was an integral part of the whole scene – one whole big musical/visual/emotional 'phrase'.* (Stainforth, 2006: personal communication with the author)

There is a strong sense in which both the broad dynamic sweep and the local structural elements of music and image in this scene are sustained and work together on a variety of kinetic and articulatory levels to yield a momentary *Gesamtkunstwerk* in miniature, which, if not greater than its parts, operates on a multimedia aesthetic plane entirely different from those of its respective single elements. Much of the success of the passage derives from a resistance to unimaginative and repetitive clichés of cartoon-like synchronization and the retention of a degree of mutual autonomy between music and image. Such points of concurrence that do exist combine with many other moments of asynchronicity or partially overlapping material to create a distinctly malleable and much more convincingly organic unfolding of sonic and visual events.

The predominant music–image interaction of this scene is replaced in the second scene under investigation here primarily by an intimate liaison between music and dialogue.[15] Danny enters Jack's bedroom, approaches and talks with his destabilizing father to the accompaniment of the first forty-five bars of the third movement of Bartók's *Music for Strings, Percussion and Celeste* (1936). This movement is arguably the least tonally anchored of a work which marked the composer's renewed interest in large-scale orchestral composition allied to a concern for thematic intricacy and integration, and, appropriately in this context, the projection of a strong, almost pictorial, sense of atmosphere through the manipulation of textural and timbral effects. The third movement, an example of the composer's so-called 'night music' expressive mode, has frequently been celebrated in musical circles for its intense, yet detached, emotive resonances. In a study written a few years prior to the making of the film, John McCabe described the music's "remote feeling" and "inhuman iciness", and the "touches of frozen humanity" offered by the viola melody in particular (1974: 49, 52). On both microcosmic and macrocosmic levels, image, music and text seem to coalesce. In broad terms, the pace, volume and relative inertness of the score's kinetic content, often underpinned by extended pedals, and later by ostinati, match the lack of movement in the image and the attenuated dialogue whose trajectory moves from seeming inanity towards the insinuation of violence, though all is delivered in a monotone. Vital shifts in emphasis such as when Danny asks, "You would never hurt Mommy and me, would you?", are aligned with changes in the music's texture, degree of linearity and intermediate moments of climax.

In detailed terms, the following should be noted with reference to the analysis offered in Figure 9.3:[16]

1. The swish-pan to Jack sitting on the bed in the first shot concurs almost precisely with the first viola demisemiquaver turn figure (bar 7).
2. The fractured dialogue is frequently heard as if inserted in brief moments of silence within the principal melodic line.
3. Upwardly and downwardly inflected questions and answers are mirrored by string glissandi articulating similarly directed motion.
4. The passage of most sustained dialogue is underpinned by the first musical passage of sustained pulse (bars 24–30).
5. The repeated questions "What do you mean?" and "Did your mother say that to you?", referring back to Danny's original, and crucial scene-altering, question "You would never hurt Mommy and me, would you?" are all aligned with piano and celeste chords at the beginnings of bars 31, 32 and 33, which interrupt the prevailing linearity of the musical activity and pulse.

Perhaps most importantly for the scene, the later section of what should ostensibly be the most reassuring text ("I love you more than anything else in the whole world and I'd never do anything to hurt you") is reinterpreted to such a degree by the passage from bar 35 of alternating 'black-note/white-note' pentatonic ostinati (rapidly covering ten of the twelve notes of the chromatic pitch spectrum) on celeste, together with piano and harp glissandi and intensifying string tremolandi, that its rational linguistic meaning is compromised, even negated, and connotative levels of musical signification begin to appropriate the diegetic space.

SHOT 1

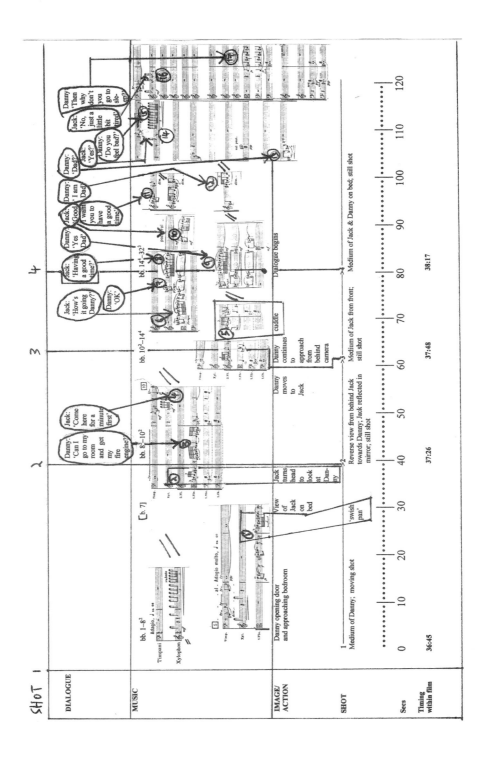

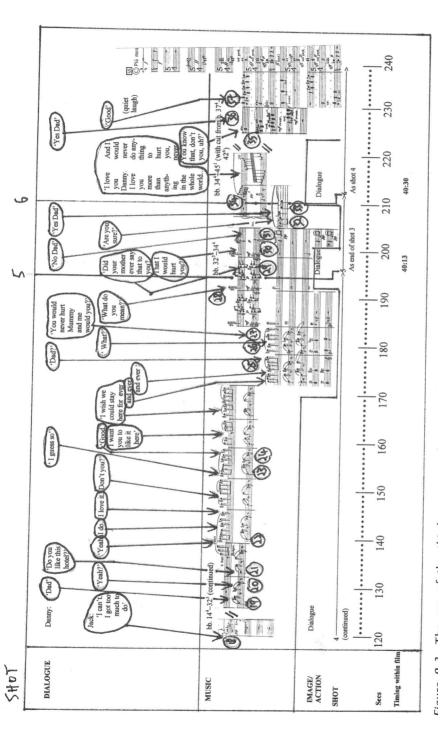

Figure 9.3 The use of the third movement from Bartók's *Music for Strings, Percussion and Celeste* in *The Shining* (36.45–40.57 mins)

Stainforth has described the painstaking editorial process thus:

> At first I cut [the music] *(simply reduced to ABA from an ABABA structure),*
> *it was still a bit too long for the scene, and it took all sorts of jiggery-pokery*
> *to make it fit really well... If my memory is correct... I had to cut out about*
> *15–20 frames of the music, maybe more, with two very subtle cuts, and then*
> *we had to lengthen at least two of the cuts of Jack and Danny, and I think*
> *the very last cut to get the final chord to come right on the title 'Wednes-*
> *day'... Fitting classical music to a scene like this always involves many*
> *compromises, but a few cues had to be absolutely right. I remember an*
> *absolutely 'key' cue was where Danny says 'You would never hurt me or*
> *Mommy would you?' and Jack says 'What do you mean?' Even then, to make*
> *it all fit, some of the picture cuts had to be changed slightly.* (Stainforth,
> 2006: personal communication with the author)

It is interesting to note that Bartók's one-time collaborator (as librettist of his opera *Duke Bluebeard's Castle* [1912]) and philosophical inspiration Béla Balázs (1884–1949) was Hungary's foremost film theorist, who supported film's anti-realist use of montage and camera angle. In his book *Der sichtbare Mensch* [The Visible Man] of 1924, one of the earliest studies of the aesthetics of silent cinema, he celebrated the kinetic and scenic attributes of the medium in terms not dissimilar from Kubrick's:

> *Film is on the point of inaugurating a new direction in our culture... We are*
> *all about to re-learn the largely forgotten language of gestural movement and*
> *facial expression. Not the replacement of words with sign language, but the*
> *visual communication of the directly embodied soul.* (2001: 17)

In the absence or diminishment of such visual elements in this particular scene, it is its music which seems to embody the very gestural, kinetic and expressive aspects of screen language which Balázs is commending for the future of the art form – sometimes to enhance and at other times to subordinate and counteract the implications of other parameters, and to incite interpretative contemplation of less obvious and explicable levels of signification. The music, like the hotel and the roving, subjective camera, partakes in the omniscience of the narrating text to provide context, psychological characterization and structural articulation for its dynamic of encroaching instabilities.

If Bartók himself moves teleologically through the successive movements of *Music for Strings, Percussion and Celeste*, from chromatic density and tonal uncertainty to diatonicism and relative stability, then it would be surprising if a cinematic appropriation of his music were to attempt to subvert this paradigm. Significantly, after the second of the scenes analysed above (about half-way through the film), the Bartók itself cedes to the more radically dissonant, non-melodic and metrically irregular avant-garde repertoire of Penderecki, and never reappears. In the face of this, we may be obliged once more to revisit Adorno's and Eisler's critique, and to conclude that the future of the music of cinematic dystopia could be a highly problematic one if it is not to escape the reification of practice into cliché: for chromaticism or dissonance read 'delusion', as Lionnet suggests (2003: 36). This is particularly the case if the so-called postmodern approach to film scoring after 1950, in which music is supposed to have become an agent of new modes of viewer cognition destructive to comfortable illusions and traditional hierarchies, is disclosed as little more than a yearning for the romanticized, populist conventions of largely nineteenth-century musical languages. Such entrenched traditions of cinematic and mass media association modify, perhaps permanently, the reception history of a musical modernism and post-war avant-garde that may themselves be complicit in their own cultural downfall.[17]

Nevertheless, in between the cracks in the commercial edifice, study of the relations between music and image may help uncover and reassess inevitable tensions in our understanding of musical value and history. Several aspects of Kubrick's practice to-gether conspire to problematize the interpretative process: his self-reflective challenges to rationality and linguistic hegemony (Jack is reduced at the end to an inarticulate, gibbering wreck); his couching of narrative uncertainty in poetic and paranormal levels of imagistic and (via Stainforth) musical manipulation; his twin commercial and artistic impulses; and his search for an elusive, cognitive dream-realm with ambiguous point of view, which transcends cause and effect and clear distinctions between the subjective and the objective, the conscious and the unconscious, and fantasy and reality, and embeds "antique metaphysics... and contemporary absurdism" (Meisel, cited in Kagan, 1991: 212) in often abstract contexts of psychological imprisonment and creative redundancy (Jack's 500 pages of 'All Work and No Play').

Does the music therefore stand for some irrevocable historical separation between nature and civilization; or for the potential of the human psyche to become an "inchoate monster of energy" (Snyder, 1982: 12)? Is its purpose to compensate for the film's flatness of dialogue and characterization or for Kubrick's ambivalence in portraying the incorporeal, his reluctance to posit unequivocally those alternative dimensions, contem-plation of which constitutes part of the traditional pleasure of the work of horror? Is it to counterbalance the strong satirical edge to some of the film's acting performances and situations, and to re-locate the film more firmly within generic traditions of con-temporary horror? Is it to legitimize, complement or temporally dramatize the often slow pacing and extended takes of the filming, as well as its occasional passages of rapid cut-aways (for example, in the corridor scene discussed above)? Is it to offer an aestheticized portrayal of the protagonist's downward psychological curve, to reflect human and social unassimilability in that of avant-garde high art within wider culture? Do we "make sense of the visuals through the structure of the music", as Donnelly suggests (2005: 48) or does its employment simply create at last a "use value for the useless" (*ibid.*: 51), the film acting as an allegory of the failure of high art and the voracious appetite of mass culture in the continual widening of its library of clichés? Does the music, as Lionnet suggests (2003: 91–7), actually invade the diegesis in the film's latter stages, propelling the narrative of violence: do the characters 'hear' it?

Part of the historical, aesthetic and technical significance of this film and its scoring lies in the sheer number of interpretative readings they generate, which is potentially as large as the number of the film's viewers. For it is very much in the nature of Kubrick's creative impulses that his works encourage self-examination and perceptual reorientation. In the case of *The Shining*, this questioning and adjustment occur in the context of the kind of dread articulated by Kierkegaard of "something unknown, something on which one dare not look, a dread of the possibilities of one's own being, a dread of oneself", and of Nietzsche's equally disturbing "paths and corridors" of the human soul which knows "secret ways towards chaos" (cited in Prawer, 1980: 122). At the centre of *The Shining*'s labyrinth lies not the minotaur but ourselves, and from this perspective of terror we are compelled to contemplate "orders of existence which cannot easily be assimilated in the categories of our waking consciousness" (*ibid.*: 281). From somewhere near the core of these orders of existence the film's musical sound world acts in many different ways as a potent aesthetic, intellectual and personal signifier of the very greatest and the very worst – the sublime, ridiculous and monstrous – of human culture and identity.

Acknowledgement

I am grateful to the School of Arts, Communication and Humanities at the University of Surrey for providing financial support to enable further work on this project to be carried out in Spring 2006, and to Gordon Stainforth for providing documentation of his work as music editor of *The Shining*.

Notes

1. Kubrick was originally offered the direction of *The Exorcist* by Warner Brothers, and later commented favourably on the film (Ciment, 1987: 196). According to Gordon Stainforth:

   Stanley had seen The Exorcist before making The Shining, and had been impressed by the music... that is definitely where he got the idea of using Penderecki from... Vivian Kubrick told me that he had been impressed by the Penderecki music in The Exorcist. (email to the author, 30 May 2006)

2. See Leydon (2004).
3. In the former, the moment of final escape from the repressive dystopian environment is accompanied by the opening chorus of the St Matthew Passion, and in the latter the organ chorale-prelude in F minor 'Ich ruf zu dir' is used as a recurring refrain.
4. Music credit listings such as this, matching the film's own, invariably cite the specific Bartók piece employed but give only the names Ligeti and Penderecki.
5. See, for instance, the tone clusters and sustained, high-pitch string sonorities employed in subsequent mainstream films dealing with the paranormal such as *The*

Sixth Sense (M. Night Shyamalan, 1999; music by James Newton Howard) and *The Others* (directed and music by Alejandro Amenábar, 2001).

6. The issue of Kubrick's ambiguous American-European orientation in relation to *The Shining* and its music is raised by Jansen (1984: 191).

7. For example, Shawn Martin's website (http://www.drummerman.net/shining).

8. Donnelly makes no reference to Lionnet's work, the most comprehensive study of the music to date, and my own work was carried out contemporaneously with, but without knowledge of, Lionnet's.

9. The following discussion is based directly on information provided to me by Gordon Stainforth, the film's music editor.

10. For example, Kubrick played Stravinsky's *The Rite of Spring* on a small portable cassette player while filming parts of the final chase in the maze (see Vivian Kubrick's documentary, 'The Making of *The Shining*', available on the commercial DVD of the film) and, according to Stainforth, Sibelius's *Valse triste* at other parts of the filming, a piece that Kubrick had intended to use as part of the eventual score of the film.

11. On occasion Stainforth laid music at places and in scenes where Kubrick had not requested it, for example, in the bedroom scene with Jack and Danny. Given the high quality of the results, Kubrick was sufficiently impressed to agree to these changes.

12. A small amount of the other music and sound effects created by Carlos and Rachel Elkind – part of a considerable quantity of music written by them that was originally intended to be the film's score before Kubrick changed his mind (most likely a few months before Stainforth's music editing began) – remained in the final edit and was used in combination with the score of pre-existent music. For further details of Carlos's involvement with the film see LoBrutto (1997: 446–8) and Carlos and Koppl (2005).

13. These charts of the last two reels are 'rough working charts' from which the final music dubbing charts were made; the latter became the property of Warner Brothers and are currently unavailable.

14. Penderecki has composed music for more than twenty films, mainly shorts and animations but significantly Resnais's previously noted *Je t'aime, je t'aime* of 1968, whose protagonist is propelled into a confusing temporal maze after an unsuccessful suicide attempt. This film was never released in the UK and has not appeared on video or DVD.

15. According to Stainforth, Kubrick had originally intended not to have any music during this scene.

16. The encircled numbers and the arrows extending to them in the figure represent, in order and as accurately as possible, the placement of either dialogue or action in relation to musical events.

17. Ironically, in Stephen King's novel, Wendy both reads gothic novels and listens to the music of Bartók.

References

Adorno, T., and Eisler, H. (1994), *Composing for the Films*, London: The Athlone Press (first published 1947).

Altman, R. (2004), *Silent Film Sound*, New York: Columbia University Press.

Anderson, P., and Wells, J. (1980), 'The Shining: Two Views', *Films in Review*, 31(7), 438–9.

Bacon, F. [1629], 'New Atlantis', in S. Bruce (ed.) (1999), *Three Early Modern Utopias: Utopia, New Atlantis, The Isle of Pines*, Oxford: Oxford University Press, pp. 149–86.

Balázs, B. (2001), *Der sichtbare Mensch oder die Kultur des Films* [Visible Man or the Culture of Film], Frankfurt: Suhrkamp (first published 1924).

Barham, J. (2003), 'Incorporating Monsters: Music of Utopia and Dystopia in Science Fiction and Horror Film Genres' (unpublished research paper given at the University of Surrey).

Baxter, J. (1997), *Stanley Kubrick – A Biography*, London: Harper Collins.

Bingham, D. (1996), 'The Displaced Auteur: A Reception History of *The Shining*', in M. Falsetto (ed.), *Perspectives on Stanley Kubrick*, New York: G. K. Hall, pp. 285–306.

Carlos, W., and Koppl, R. (2005), 'Wendy Carlos: Rediscovering Lost Scores', *Music from the Movies*, 47, 35–6.

Ciment, M. (1987), *Kubrick*, Paris: Calmann-Lévy.

Combs, R. (1980), 'Shining, The', *Monthly Film Bulletin*, 47(562), 221–2.

Dahlhaus, C. (1989), *Nineteenth-Century Music*, trans. J. Bradford Robinson, Berkeley: University of California Press.

Donnelly, K. (2005), 'The Anti-Matter of Film Music: *The Shining*', in K. Donnelly (ed.), *The Spectre of Sound: Music in Film and Television*, London: BFI Publishing, pp. 36–54.

Jansen, P. (1984), '*The Shining*. 1978–80', in C. Hummel *et al.* (eds), *Stanley Kubrick*, Munich: Carl Hanser, pp. 171–204.

Falsetto, M. (2001), *Stanley Kubrick: A Narrative and Stylistic Analysis*, Westport, CT: Praeger Publishers.

García Mainar, L. (1999), *Narrative and Stylistic Patterns in the Films of Stanley Kubrick*, Rochester, NY: Camden House.

Hogan, D. (1980), '*The Shining* – "A big-budget, elaborately shot 'Movie of the Week'"', *Cinefantastique*, 10(2), 38.

Howard, J. (1999), *Stanley Kubrick Companion*, London: B. T. Batsford.

Hummel, C., *et al.* (1984), *Stanley Kubrick*, Munich: Carl Hanser.

Jameson, R. T. (1980), 'Kubrick's *Shining*', *Film Comment*, 16(4), 28–32.

Kagan, N. (1991), *The Cinema of Stanley Kubrick*, New York: Continuum.

Kolker, R. (2000), *A Cinema of Loneliness: Penn, Stone, Kubrick, Scorsese, Spielberg, Altman*, Oxford: Oxford University Press.

Kracauer, S. (2004), *From Caligari to Hitler: A Psychological History of the German Film*, revised edition, Princeton: Princeton University Press (first published 1947).

Leibowitz, F., and Jeffress, L. (1981), '*The Shining*', *Film Quarterly*, 34(3), 45–51.

Leydon, R. (2004), '*Forbidden Planet*: Affects and Effects in the Electro Avant Garde', in P. Hayward (ed.), *Off the Planet: Music, Sound and Science Fiction Cinema*, Eastleigh, Hampshire: John Libbey Publishing, pp. 61–76.

Lionnet, L. (2003), 'Point Counter Point: Interactions between Pre-existing Music and Narrative Structure in Stanley Kubrick's *The Shining*', unpublished DMA dissertation, City University of New York.

LoBrutto, V. (1997), *Stanley Kubrick: A Biography*, New York: Donald I. Fine Books.

Macklin, A. F. (1981), 'Understanding Kubrick: *The Shining*', *Journal of Popular Film and Television*, 9(2), 93–5.

Maslin, J. (1980), '*The Shining*', *New York Times*, May 23, p. 212.

Mayersberg, P. (1980–1), 'The Overlook Hotel', *Sight & Sound*, 50(1), 54–7.

McCabe, J. (1974), *Bartók Orchestral Music*, London: British Broadcasting Corporation.

Meisel, M. (1980), 'Why *The Shining* is a Fourteenth Century Film', *Los Angeles Reader*, May 13, p. 4.

Nelson, T. (2000), *Kubrick: Inside a Film Artist's Maze*, Indianapolis: Indiana University Press.

Thomas, N. (2000), *Kubrick: Inside a Film Artist's Maze*, Bloomington: Indiana University Press.

Phillips, G., and Hill, R. (2002), *The Encyclopaedia of Stanley Kubrick*, New York: Checkmark Books.

Prawer, S. S. (1980), *Caligari's Children: The Film as Tale of Terror*, Oxford: Oxford University Press.

Rasmussen, R. (2001), *Stanley Kubrick: Seven Films Analyzed*, Jefferson, NC: McFarland.

Snyder, S. (1982), 'Family Life and Leisure Culture in *The Shining*', *Film Criticism*, 7(1), 4–13.

Titterington, P. L. (1981), 'Kubrick and "The Shining"', *Sight & Sound*, 50(2), 117–21.

Scene			No.	Notes
AERIAL SHOTS, APPROACHING OVERLOOK HOTEL	CARLOS 'DIES IRAE'		1	Main title, Wendy Carlos (Apr 30, ?1980) 'New mix of version 7' b/o 'Dies Irae', Berlioz *Symphonie Fantastique*
– The Interview –				
JACK & ULLMAN				
DANNY (TONY) & WENDY		TV cartoon music		
JACK & ULLMAN cont. Story of Mr Grady			2	Reel change during scene, just over a minute before Danny in bathroom
DANNY IN BATHROOM + WENDY KITCHEN?	PENDERECKI 'JAKOB'			Penderecki 'Jakob'
JACK ON PHONE				
DANNY IN BATHROOM (TONY)				
BLOOD ELEVATOR/DANNY CU	↓			I have no notes on this music here
– Closing Day –				
FLYING OVER ROCKIES JACK, W, D IN CAR	CARLOS 'ROCKY MOUNTAIN'		3	'Rocky Mountain' W Carlos ('Apr 19')
AERIAL > EXT OVERLOOK LS	------- ↓	'ROCKY MOUNTAIN'		
JACK + ULLMAN	↓	-------		
ULLMAN SHOWS J + W AROUND				
DANNY DARTBOARD, GRADY TWINS	LIGETI 'LONTANO'			'Lontano' (Ligeti) probably uncut
ULLMAN SHOWS J +W ROUND cont.	------- ↓			
ULLMAN SHOWS THEM				
EXT/SNOWCAT			4	
HALLORAN SHOWS THEM KITCHEN AND FREEZER				
SHOWS THEM STORE ROOM, PLUS DANNY SHINING	'LONTANO'			'Jakob' or 'Lontano'; 'Lontano' probably uncut + Carlos 'Heartbeat sandwich' as in Reel 2
HALLORAN TELLS DANNY ABOUT SHINING				
'What about Room 237?'				One or two vv low hints of 'Lontano', which was also laid here
– A Month Later –				
EXT HOTEL				

Scene	Music		No.	Notes
DANNY ON TRIKE				
WENDY WITH TROLLEY, JACK IN BED				
JACK THROWING BALL (SHORT SHOT)				
WENDY + DANNY GO INTO MAZE				
JACK WALKS TO MODEL OF MAZE W + D IN MAZE	BARTOK 'MUSIC FOR S, P AND C' → Chord		5	Bartók all laid on one track, so probably uncut. We changed picture cut to fit zoom on maze
– Tuesday –	Chord			
DUSK HOTEL				
DANNY ON TRIKE, TO 237 DOOR	BARTOK 'MUSIC FOR S, P AND C'		6	Bartók
JACK TYPING, INTERRUPTED BY W				
JACK AND WENDY 'A NEW RULE'				
W AND D IN SNOW, JACK WATCHING	LIGETI 'LONTANO'			'Lontano' on one track; I think, amazingly, uncut
– Saturday –	→			'Lontano' (Ligeti)
H/A JACK TYPING				
WENDY TRIES PHONE…				
… CALLS KDK 1 RE STORM				
DANNY ON TRIKE	PENDERECKI 'DE NATURA SONORIS NO. 1'			'De Natura Sonoris No. 1'
ENCOUNTERS GRADY TWINS	D.N.S. CHORUS	'DE NATURA SONORIS NO. 1'		
DANNY REACTION	→			
– Monday –	....		7	WHOLE SCENE CUT IN VIDEO VERSION
('MAY I GO TO GET FIRE ENGINE')		(TV cartoon music)		
DANNY GOES TO JACK'S BEDROOM	BARTOK (MFSPC)			Bartók. There is almost certainly a small cut after this line of dialogue. I also made one or two small cuts to the picture
'Why don't you go to sleep…'/ 'I'd never do anything to hurt you … Never'	→			vvv This cut/mix at the end of the scene is absolutely definite
– Wednesday –		BARTOK CHORD		
EXT HOTEL				
DANNY 'MOM ARE YOU IN THERE?'	PENDERECKI 'JAKOB'			
WENDY AT BOILERS				'Kosmogonia' mentioned in one note. I think some cuts were made in the music & poss some adjmts to picture

Appendix 9.1 – continued

Scene	Cue	Cue	Cue	Reel	Notes
JACK AWAKES FROM NIGHTMARE DANNY ENTERS	→			8	Reel change at beg. of Jack under table
DISS > JACK CORRIDOR, ENTERS GOLD ROOM	'DE NAT SON NO 2'				
JACK AND LLOYD, WENDY ENTERS 'CRAZY WOMAN'					
HALLORAN WATCHING TV WEATHER REPORT	'HEARTBEAT' →	'THOUGHT TRANSFER' →	'LOW-HIGH' →	9	3-layer 'sandwich' of Carlos' 'Heartbeat', 'Thought Transfer' & 'Low-High'
DANNY / JACK INTO 237	JAKOB (Sect 1) v cut v JAKOB (Sect 3) →	JAKOB (Sect 2) →			Jakob
JACK SEDUCED IN GREEN BATHROOM HAG CHASES JACK OUT					
HALLORAN PHONE, TROPICAL NIGHT, LINE DEAD					
W PACES BEDROOM, J ENTERS 'SAW NOTHING'					
DANNY IN BED, 'LISTENING', BLOOD ELEVATOR	HEARTBEAT S'WICH	'DANNY BELLS'		10	Heartbeat sandwich as Reel 9, now plus 'Danny Bells'
JACK EXITS APARTMENT; WENDY SOBS					
J THRU KITCHEN SCATTERING CANS, MASQUERADE	MASQUERADE				Jack Hylton
TV cartoon music CHECK THIS OUT					
JACK ENTERS BALLROOM, LLOYD, SPILLS DRINK	'Midnight, The Stars And You'				Al Bowlly/Ray Noble
RED BATHROOM WITH GRADY	'It's All Forgotten Now'				'All Forgotten Now'/'Home'
'... He is, Mr Torrance'	Home			11	For a long time I tried to make the song 'Dinner At Eight' here. Reels joined after 'Nigger Cook'.
JACK DISABLES RADIO HALLORAN IN PLANE	HEARTBEAT S'WICH →				Carlos 'Heartbeat sandwich' as per Reel 9
HALLORAN IN CAR 'YOUR HEAVY SNOW'					
[DANNY WATCHES CARTOONS; W LEAVES]		(TV cartoon music)		12	SCENE CUT FROM VIDEO VERSION. The 'Roadrunner' music mimicked the action & led v well into 'Polymorphia'
W FINDS 'ALL WORK NO PLAY'; JACK INTERVENES	'POLYMORPHIA' →				'Polymorphia' on single tk up til Danny. Prob no cuts. 'Natural fade' etc before 'what are you doing down here?'
c/a DANNY	'POLYMORPHIA'				
WENDY HITS JACK WITH BASEBALL BAT	→	'UTRENJA' CHORDS			'Kanon' (W hits J). My charts say 'Utrenja', contra Shawm (implying my 'Kanon' was not the one IN 'Utrenja')

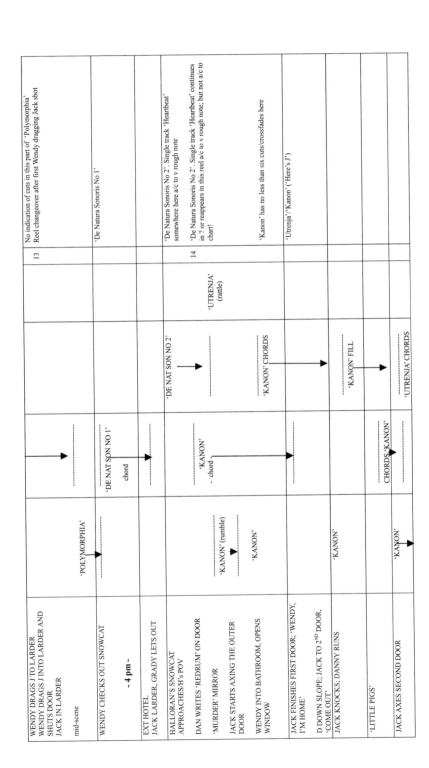

Scene				Notes
WENDY DRAGS J TO LARDER / WENDY DRAGS J INTO LARDER AND SHUTS DOOR / JACK IN LARDER / mid-scene	'POLYMORPHIA' →			**13** No indication of cuts in this part of 'Polymorphia' / Reel changeover after first Wendy dragging Jack shot
WENDY CHECKS OUT SNOWCAT		'DE NAT SON NO 1' chord →		'De Natura Sonoris No 1'
- 4 pm -				
EXT HOTEL / JACK LARDER, GRADY LETS OUT		→		
HALLORAN'S SNOWCAT APPROACHES/H's POV			'DE NAT SON NO 2'	**14** 'De Natura Sonoris No 2': Single track 'Heartbeat' somewhere here a/c to v rough note
DAN WRITES 'REDRUM' ON DOOR	'KANON' (rumble) ▶	'KANON' - chord →		'De Natura Sonoris No 2': Single track 'Heartbeat' continues in ? or reappears in this reel a/c to v rough note; but not a/c to chart!
'MURDER' MIRROR	'KANON'		'UTRENJA' (rattle) →	
JACK STARTS AXING THE OUTER DOOR				
WENDY INTO BATHROOM, OPENS WINDOW		→	'KANON' CHORDS	'Kanon' has no less than six cuts/crossfades here
JACK FINISHES FIRST DOOR; 'WENDY, I'M HOME'		→		'Utrenja'/'Kanon' ('Here's J')
D DOWN SLOPE; JACK TO 2ND DOOR, 'COME OUT'	'KANON'			
JACK KNOCKS; DANNY RUNS			'KANON' FILL →	
'LITTLE PIGS'		CHORDS 'KANON'		
JACK AXES SECOND DOOR	'KANON' ▶	→	'UTRENJA' CHORDS	

Appendix 9.1 – continued

Scene						
'HERE'S JOHNNY!'						
SNOWCAT						
WENDY BATHROOM. SOUND OF APPR OACHING SNOWCAT						
DANNY RUNS. HIDES IN CUPBOARD						
J LIMPS THRU KITCHEN. W BATHROOM. SOBS						
H ENTERS HOTEL, J LIMPS ALONG CORRIDORS						
J MURDERS H	'UTRENJA' CHORDS	'POLYMORPHIA' twitter			'Utrenja'	
W RUSHES UP STAIRS. DOGMAN		'KANON'			'Utrenja'	15
J TO SNOWY DOOR; D RUNS INTO MAZE			'KANON'			
J STARTS TO RUN	'UTRENJA' RATTLE	'KANON'				
W REACTS TO H'S CORPSE	'UTRENJA' RATTLE	'UTRENJA' RATTLE			'Utrenja'	
W REACTS TO SPLIT SKULL MAN						
DANNY CHASED BY JACK		'KANON'	'KANON'			
WENDY SEES SKELETONS						
JACK REAR; DANNY HIDES	'UTRENJA' BOOM-BOOM	'KANON'	'KANON'			
WENDY SEES BLOOD ELEVATOR	'UTRENJA' BOOM-BOOM	BASS 'KANON'			'Kanon'	
DANNY HIDING/JACK APPEARS						
JACK CU			twittering	'DE NAT SON NO 2'		
DANNY PEEPS OUT						
DANNY RUNS	'KANON'	BASS 'KANON'				
JACK SEARCHES	whine	twittering	BASS; 'KANON'			
WENDY RUNS OUT/REUNITED WITH D	whistle	+ bass				
JACK WEAKENING						
JACK SITS DOWN						
JACK FROZEN		'DE NAT SON NO 1'				
TRACK UP TO JACK PHOTO; CREDITS	MIDNIGHT STARS & YOU				16 Al Bowlly	

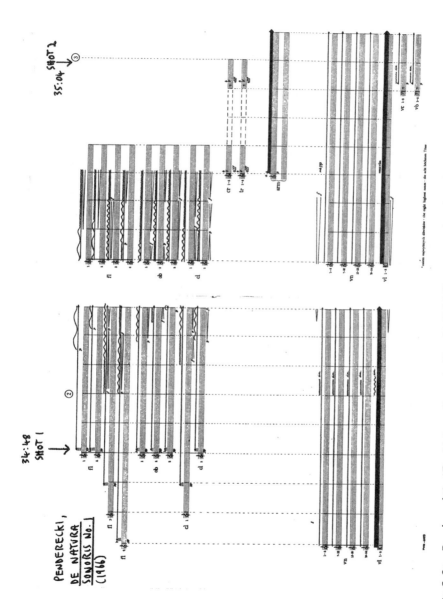

Appendix 9.2a Penderecki's 'De Natura Sonoris No. 1' (1966) annotated with Kubrick's shots in Danny's encounter with the Grady sisters

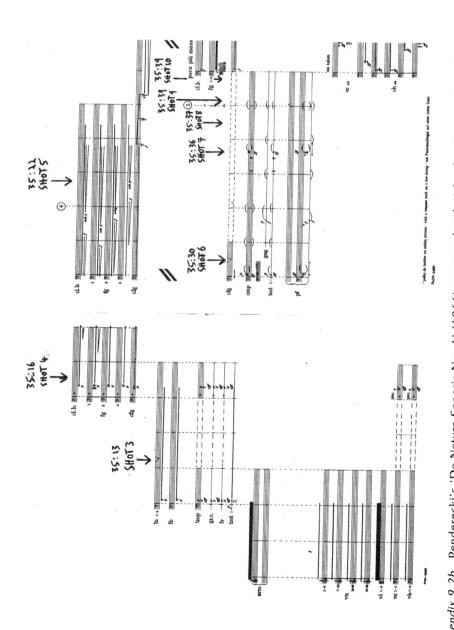

Appendix 9.2b Penderecki's 'De Natura Sonoris No. 1' (1966) annotated with Kubrick's shots in Danny's encounter with the Grady sisters

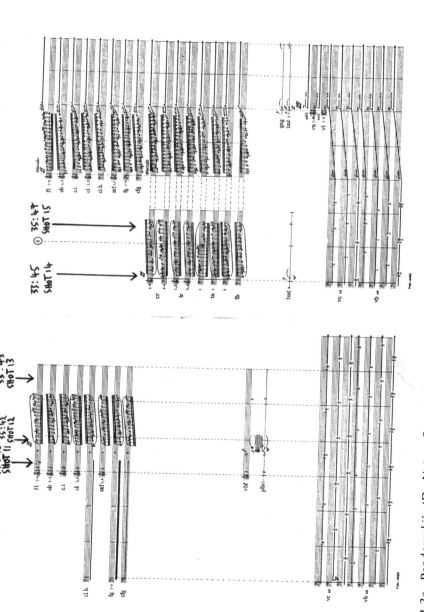

Appendix 9.2c Penderecki's 'De Natura Sonoris No. 1' (1966) annotated with Kubrick's shots in Danny's encounter with the Grady sisters

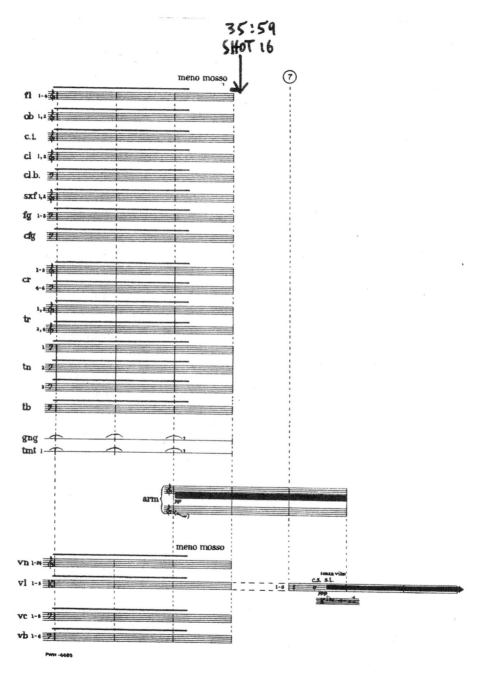

Appendix 9.2d Penderecki's 'De Natura Sonoris No. I' (1966) annotated with Kubrick's shots in Danny's encounter with the Grady sisters

10 Music of the Night
Scoring the Vampire in Contemporary Film

Janet K. Halfyard

The vampire is a familiar presence in the cinema. He first appears in Friedrich Wilhelm Murnau's 1922 *Nosferatu*, an unauthorized but clearly discernible adaptation of Bram Stoker's 1897 novel, *Dracula*. This was followed by Hollywood's first venture into vampire territory with Tod Browning's 1931 version of the novel starring Bela Lugosi. By the mid-1990s, around 3000 films had been made about vampires (Gelder, 1994: 86). The symbolism of the vampire as a predator, where the act of either killing or 'turning' the victim mimics the act of kissing, offers a powerful cinematic image that has kept both the industry and audiences consistently interested for decades. Dracula, however, presents a disturbing sexual metaphor: predatory, as likely to infect his victims with the contagion of vampirism as he is to kill them; bestial, feeding on human blood and, in many versions, capable of transforming into a bat or a wolf; and evil, a demon in human form who is, at the same time, thrillingly seductive. Although there is a strong homoerotic subtext to the construction of the nineteenth-century vampires, Lord Ruthven (in Lady Caroline Lamb's *Glenarvon* of 1816) and Carmilla (in the short story of the same name by Sheridan Le Fanu, of 1872), in Stoker's novel Dracula bites Lucy and Mina, while Jonathan Harker is bitten by Dracula's three wives, so casting an aura of predatory heterosexuality over the attacks. Similarly, both Hollywood and Hammer's male vampires have tended to have female victims (although Hammer introduced lesbian and bisexual female vampires in the 1970s), the bite being symbolic of the kiss, the vampire's teeth penetrating the victim, who then swoons – whether through blood loss or passion, it is sometimes hard to tell.

The vampire himself – because the memorable cinematic vampires tend to be male (in fact, they tend to be Dracula) – has generally been presented as a character simultaneously dangerous, terrifying and yet also exotic. He is a model of the colonial Other in Western culture, the foreign and demonic savage who seduces and destroys respectable white women, a threat to patriarchal dominance and to Western culture itself.[1]

However, since the early 1980s there has been a shift in the construction of cinematic vampires that arguably goes hand in hand with the increased recognition by

western culture of the danger of othering groups and individuals. Dracula has traditionally been enigmatically alien: his seductions have been a ruse, the means to achieving
his true goal, namely, drinking the blood of his victims. The modern vampire is often
cast as a victim himself, an altogether more sympathetic figure; and the way in which
this shift in our perceptions of what a vampire is has been articulated, in part, through
music. This chapter examines how the music written for cinematic vampire narratives has
changed since the days of Hammer (discussed by Michael Hannan in this volume), and
how these changes therefore affect how we read the vampire.

'Bela Lugosi's Dead': the vampire in the 1980s

The position of the vampire starts to change in the 1980s with several films, in
particular, Tony Scott's *The Hunger* (1983), Joel Schumacher's *The Lost Boys* (1987)
and Kathryn Bigelow's *Near Dark* (1987), all of which are set in modern America rather
than nineteenth-century England and Transylvania. *The Hunger* automatically distances
itself from the vampire's cinematic past: the opening scene is in a nightclub and the first
music we hear is Bauhaus performing 'Bela Lugosi's Dead', both referencing and reject-
ing Hollywood's first Dracula. Thereafter, the soundtrack is made up of two main types
of music: classical music, which is played diegetically by the vampires themselves; and
the underscore, which is a synthesizer-based score that broadly conforms to the
atonality of Hammer scores, now expanded to include non-instrumental, noise-based
sounds and tending towards ambient rather than dramatic affect. This music is mainly
used to create an aura of mystery and uncertainty, and is used as much in association
with the human characters and their reactions as it is to represent the vampires and their
activities. The classical music, meanwhile, is much more strongly and exclusively associated with the vampires, and has two functions. First, it is a covert signal: as I have
discussed elsewhere (Halfyard, 2006), one should never trust anyone in a Hollywood
film who is a performer of classical music, as this tends to be elided with European
identity and then positioned as being fundamentally threatening – morally or physically
– to American characters and their values. In *The Hunger*, both the classical music-
playing vampires are constructed as European (played by Catherine Deneuve and David
Bowie) and the music they play often alludes to elements of their vampiric lives. Miriam
(Deneuve) plays Ravel's piano piece, *Gaspard de la Nuit*, referencing the vampire's
traditional nocturnal environment, while the piece of music that frames the film, heard
immediately after the nightclub sequence and again at the very end, is the second
movement of Schubert's Piano Trio in E flat. One suspects that, ideally, they would have
used Schubert's string quartet 'Death and the Maiden', which would have served as an
apt metaphor for the fate of the teenage violinist Alice, who is being 'groomed' by the
vampires, and also for the way in which Sarah (Susan Sarandon) is pursued by Miriam.
In the context of the film, a trio was needed, not a quartet, but the Schubert trio that
they play bears a distinct resemblance to the more famous quartet, especially to the

introduction and piano accompaniment of Schubert's song, 'Death and the Maiden', on which part of his later Quartet was based.

The potential allusion to 'Death and the Maiden' is there mainly for the musicians and classical music lovers in the audience. However, the second function, which everyone will understand, is that this is a very sombre piece of music. It has a funereal air and a deep sadness about it, and this ties in with the characters of John and Miriam, who are not, as a rule, portrayed as bloodsucking fiends but as Quiet and contained, sad and lonely people, more so because John has started to age and Miriam realizes that she will lose him. We know they kill — we see this in the first scene of the film — but after that, the business of killing people and drinking their blood is largely pushed into the background, and the main thrust of the film's narrative is the tragedy of John's demise and of Miriam's search for a companion who will never fade. The vampires, particularly John, are made much more human in their emotions and desires, and we are asked to sympathize with them in a way not required by Hammer. However, the use of classical music is a double-edged sword: on the one hand, it constructs the vampires as possessed of a European, Old-World, highly cultured sophistication, the generally soft and soothing music softening the characters themselves; on the other, it alludes to their Otherness, their lack of American-ness, their very different system of values. At the same time that it makes them more human and less obviously threatening than a stridently atonal underscore might, it does little to make them less Other.

Near Dark and *The Lost Boys* go further in their de-Othering of the vampire. *The Lost Boys* is a black comedy that is all too aware of cinema's vampiric past. There are three interconnected plotlines, one for each member of the central family, a mother and her two sons, Michael and Sam. The mother's story alludes most self-consciously to the traditional cinematic vampire as she plays the unsuspecting woman who believes she is being gently seduced by a nice man, only for him to turn out to be an evil, probably ancient, Dracula-like vampire. The fact that his name is Max (as in Schrek, the actor who played the original vampire of *Nosferatu*) should probably have alerted the audience to his true nature early on. Set against this is the principal storyline of her elder son, Michael, who falls in with a coven of young male vampires and their not yet fully converted girl 'groupie', Star. Michael unwittingly drinks blood and starts to become a vampire, and his younger brother's plotline is essential to his redemption. Aided by the Frog brothers — whose names, Edgar and Alan, provide another horror reference, this time to Edgar Allan Poe — Sam uses their knowledge of vampires gleaned from comic books to both diagnose the threats posed to Michael and his mother and to save them. Here, the soundtrack is dominated by rock and pop songs, shifting the music even further from the orchestral sound of Hammer's vampire music, and relocating it in an even more contemporary-sounding musical environment than the synthesizers of *The Hunger*. The songs used here perform a double function. On the one hand they establish the centrality of American popular culture within the vampire world: the characters with whom the rock music is most associated are the gang of young male vampires led by David and Michael himself, who – as played by Jason Patric – bears an obvious resemblance to Jim Morrison of the Doors. The vampire gang even have a poster of Morrison in their cave, affirming that they identify themselves with popular music as much as with the infamous nihilism of Morrison's lifestyle.

The second level at which the music most obviously functions is as a commentary on various events in the film. The fear that Michael is turning into a vampire is alluded to in the lyrics of 'Don't Let The Sun Go Down On Me', while the Otherness of the vampires themselves is alluded to in the Jim Morrison song, 'People Are Strange'. This narrative level persists in a song written specifically for the film, 'Cry, Little Sister' by Gerard McMann. Embedded in the rock song is a choir of boys' voices, singing the words 'Thou shalt not fall/ Thou shalt not die/ Thou shalt not bleed/ Thou shalt not kill.' The first three lines of this clearly describe the vampire condition of the Lost Boys themselves, in particular the fact that these vampires can fly and so cannot fall in a physical sense; and the boys' voices seem both to embody and envoice *The Lost Boys* and also to juxtapose the apparent innocence of children's voices with the gleeful nihilism of David and his gang. The last line, however, counters the apparently idyllic, immortal state of the vampire with the impossibility of adhering to conventional morality: a vampire cannot keep all four of these commandments and, if he does, there is no saving him. In the end, the only reason Michael and Star can be saved is because neither of them has yet killed.

Near Dark has a curiously similar story line to *The Lost Boys*, with a teenage boy, Caleb, meeting a girl who turns out to be a vampire and who causes him to start to change. This is a conflicted love story that juggles ideas of family, loyalty, patriarchy and love. Caleb is torn between his true family and the vampire family to which Mae belongs. Like Michael and Star, Caleb and Mae are both saved at the end, turned back into humans; and again, we have a synthesizer score provided by Tangerine Dream alongside several popular music tracks.

However, *Near Dark* is not a comedy, and does not share the self-conscious knowingness about vampires that characterizes *The Lost Boys*. There is nothing noticeably camp or parodist about this group of redneck vampires, and whereas *The Lost Boys* were a nihilistic group of disaffected young men, their mentor classically evil and Star fundamentally innocent, the lines are drawn less clearly in *Near Dark*. Mae in particular is a fundamentally more ambivalent character than Star. For instance, she has no compunctions about killing.

The music of *Near Dark* is a significant departure from the conventions of horror scoring, and not only because it also abandons conventional orchestration. As other chapters in this volume have noted, horror scores before the 1980s tend to lead the audience into specific interpretations of what it is seeing. Although it is done somewhat unconventionally in terms of genre and idiom, music in *The Hunger* and *The Lost Boys* still mainly performs these tasks. However, in *Near Dark*, music largely ceases to function in this manner. The ambient music of the synthesizer underscore sometimes serves to create a sense of pace – for example, in the scene at the motel where the vampire family have to shoot their way out of their bungalow to escape the police – but often only adds an air of mystery to what we see. When Mae first bites Caleb, for example, classic Hollywood scoring might accompany this with searing strings to suggest the horror and tragedy of the fate that is befalling him, or dramatic, atonal music to suggest Mae's power over her victim. The music we have instead suggests almost nothing at all except that what is happening to him is mysterious and perhaps not entirely good. It is understated and ambivalent, creating an atmosphere but not one sufficiently specific as to allow us to reach an interpretation of what we see on screen; in the same way that Caleb does not properly understand what has happened to him.

Other scenes omit underscore entirely, as in one of the most famous episodes in the film, where the vampires descend on a roadhouse and proceed to murder the handful of people they find there in a protracted and wantonly sadistic fashion. The only music in this scene is the songs that play, fairly quietly, on the jukebox in the background, songs actually chosen by the ill-fated clientele of the bar, which jar with the events that then unfold. Bigelow refrains from using music to tell us what we should think of these vampires, refrains from using the underscore to demonize them and make us fear them. Arguably, in this particularly violent scene they need no music to appear demonic, but the lack of underscore and the presence of the various, slightly banal and inappropriately relaxed songs emphasizes the extent to which the vampires are, in fact, quite ordinary despite their abhorrent behaviour. They are remarkably nasty people indulging in a grotesque form of fun, but do not appear supernaturally evil in the way that a different musical strategy could have promoted. While the vampire family is not particularly likeable, its members are not entirely unsympathetic. At the end of the film, the slow, calm music used to accompany the death of Jesse and Diamondback as they burst into flames serves to move the viewer rather than suggest a sense of the evildoers getting their just reward; and to underline the emotional ambiguity of events the same music is playing a few minutes later when Mae wakes in the daylight to find herself cured of her vampirism, so eliding the import of these two events. We should be moved by Mae being saved just as we should be moved by the devotion of Jesse and Diamondback, who hold hands as they meet their doom.

The synthesizers used in the underscore reiterate the more contemporary setting of these vampires, but the popular music used in all three of these films asserts a new American identity for them. In *The Hunger*, the music most associated with two clearly European vampires is European classical music; in the other films, the music most closely associated with American vampires is popular music, particularly rock.[2] As cinematic vampires cease to be European and become American, so their music is required to change if that American identity is to be asserted. And if they are being identified as American, then rock music ensures that the primarily American audience is more encouraged to view vampires as being 'like us' rather than as Other.

By the end of the 1980s, therefore, a significantly new model for scoring vampire films had emerged, one that combined synthesizer scoring with rock music. However, the 1980s had one other significant musical development to offer, from a film that ostensibly has nothing to do with vampires at all, Tim Burton's *Batman* (1989). *Batman* is a superhero action-adventure. The same decade that had produced rock and synthesizer scores for vampires had been producing large orchestral scores for action-adventure films, typified by John Williams's scores for the *Star Wars* trilogy (George Lucas, 1977–83), the Christopher Reeve *Superman* quartet (Richard Donner, 1978; Richard Lester, 1980 and 1983; Sidney J. Furie, 1987) and the *Indiana Jones* films (Steven Spielberg, 1981-84). Like their heroes, these scores were punchy and militaristic, their main titles characterized by stable harmonies, regular rhythms and brightly optimistic, fanfare-like melodies delivered by the brass section. *Batman* marked a departure both in the nature of the hero and in the tone of the film and its score. Burton's film is literally very dark – there is no sunlight in any scene in the film, and most of its scenes take place at night. Unlike both the 1960s TV version, with Batman played by Adam West, and the heroic and superheroic characters of 1980s action-adventures, Burton's Batman is as dark as his environment, and a variety of elements in the film intentionally position him as a vampire-like creature. Part of this is in the nature of the comic-book creation itself: his affinity for and quasi-transformation into a bat mimics Dracula's own transformations, and his black cape visually echoes the flowing cape Dracula wears in both the Lugosi and Hammer versions. With his nocturnal environment, his wealth, his gothic mansion and the closely guarded secret of his identity, the idea that Batman might actually be some kind of Dracula figure lurks close below the surface of the original comic-book character, and Burton brings this out overtly in the opening section of the film with five references in quick succession to the idea that Batman may be a blood-drinking vampire.[3]

As I have discussed elsewhere (Halfyard, 2004), the film's music serves to support this positioning, with a score that takes the same militaristic brass and percussion textures of other 1980s action-adventure scores and then reflects them back through a darkened glass. The bright major keys and straightforward rhythms and harmonies of Williams's scores are transformed by composer Danny Elfman into a score that uses minor keys, rhythmic shifts and complex rhythms, and which is harmonically very 'slippery', the music constantly shifting from one key to another in a way that suggests the complexity and instability of Batman himself. Burton's Batman is a deeply conflicted hero, a tragic–heroic character who stands on the cusp between good and evil and who could potentially move either way. A particular theme of the film is the sense of duality between Batman and his adversary, the Joker, the most obvious level of this being that not only were they both abnormal personae created through a terrible trauma, but each was responsible for the traumatic event that created the other.

What Burton and Elfman bring to mainstream cinema with *Batman*, therefore, is the conflicted tragic hero who could easily cross the line and become a villain, who wants a normal life but is too damaged and too different — too Other — to be able to achieve it. One important aspect of his dysfunctional nature is his inability, at the start of the narrative, to have close personal relationships. Vicki Vale's socializing presence is essential to his integration as a good citizen operating with the sanction of the law: the monster is redeemed, in part, through love.

The narrative and musical traces of *Batman*, the covert vampire, can be found in the vampire films of the 1990s, particularly in the rather startling development of films which, rather than simply constructing the vampire as less evil and more sympathetic, now reposition vampires as potential superheroes, warriors fighting for the good of humanity.

Lovers and heroes: the vampire in the 1990s

In the 1990s, the two 1980s scoring models — the darkly orchestral score of the romantic–vampiric hero and the rock score of the 1980s American vampire film — traced largely divergent paths at first, with *Bram Stoker's Dracula* (Francis Ford Coppola, 1992) and *Interview with the Vampire* (Neil Jordan, 1994; hereafter, *Interview*) as the two most high-profile representatives of the orchestral group, and *The Crow* (Alex Proyas, 1994) and *From Dusk Till Dawn* (Robert Rodriguez, 1996) typical of the tendency to use popular music as the obvious successors to *The Lost Boys and Near Dark*.[4]

The 1980s gave us several new constructions of vampires as younger, more American and somewhat more sympathetic characters than the classical vampire of earlier Hollywood and Hammer offerings. Coppola's *Dracula* mediates between the old and new positions. The first half of the film is very much in the mould of vampire-as-monster movies, with specific visual allusions to *Nosferatu* and a score that emphasizes the dissonant and chromatic, with something of the same stridency that James Bernard brought to *Dracula* in the 1950s. However, the second half of the film takes a highly unusual route, especially given that the film purports to be an accurate representation of the novel. In Stoker's novel, Mina is Dracula's victim, attacked by him in her own bedroom with her husband unable to defend her, and forced to drink the Count's blood against her will. In the film, she meets the Count apparently by chance on the street while Jonathan is still missing in Transylvania, and they begin a series of secret liaisons. When the time comes, she willingly drinks his blood, as they both believe her to be the reincarnation of his dead wife, Elisabetta. The second half of the film then becomes a love story, and Dracula takes on the mantle of conflicted vampire-hero, torn between his centuries-old desire to drink blood and wreak havoc in revenge for Elisabetta's death and his genuine love for Mina. Whereas the book ends with the menfolk slaying Dracula in his coffin, the film ends with Mina killing Dracula as an act of love and final, holy release for him, and as redemption for herself.

This transformation of Dracula from *Nosferatu* monster to romantic hero is achieved musically by taking his chromatic theme from the first part of the film and turning it into a yearning love theme. Dracula's first sight of Mina coincides with the first aural

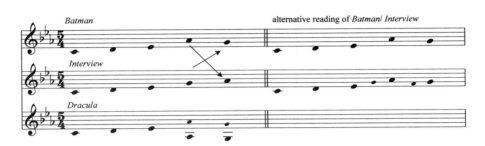

Figure 10.1 Melodic outlines of *Batman* theme, *Interview with the Vampire* 'Lux aeterna' and *Dracula* 'hunting' theme

appearance of this theme: Mina and the music share the function of rehabilitating the dysfunctional Dracula. Like Batman, who moves from a position of serious moral ambivalence in the early part of Burton's film to being successfully integrated into the legal and social structures of Gotham, thanks largely to the redeeming influence of Vicki, Gary Oldman's Dracula likewise becomes gradually less monstrous and more a tortured, conflicted hero who stands on the cusp between good and evil, but who may be redeemed by love.

Musically, the clearest indication that Dracula's characterization as a tragic–romantic hero may owe something to the Batman-as-vampire narrative of Burton's film comes in the 'hunting' theme that recurs throughout the film and is heard most clearly at the start of the end credits. It is a theme so similar to the *Batman* main title with its aggressively quasi-militaristic rhythm that *Batman* could plausibly have provided the temp track (see Figure 10.1).[5] Likewise, there is a strong melodic similarity to the theme set to the words 'Lux aeterna dona eis' in the main title of *Interview*. This was a replacement score written at short notice by Elliot Goldenthal at the same time that he was preparing to write the music for *Batman Forever* (Joel Schumacher, 1995) and is therefore also plausibly influenced by Elfman's *Batman* score, reinforcing the musical connection between *Batman* and subsequent vampire films.

If *Bram Stoker's Dracula* mediates between the old monster and the new romantic vampire, *Interview* goes the whole way and removes the Otherness from the vampire narrative entirely by eliminating all the humans. Horror movies traditionally play on the way a vampire is seen through human eyes; however, there are very few human characters in *Interview*, certainly none that remain both human and alive for more than one scene. This is a film about vampires from the vampires' own point of view, a study of what it is to be a vampire and the havoc they are capable of wreaking on their own lives rather than the havoc they can wreak on human existence. We are required to identify with them: there are simply no human characters in the film who are around long enough to perform this function for us. Sandra Tomc points out that the casting of Tom Cruise as Lestat was an important part of this process:

The vampire's transformation [from monster to yuppie] *had its corollary in a process of domestication, a process that seemed to be cemented with the casting of Tom Cruise, a squeaky-clean icon of normative masculinity, in the role of the amoral, sexually ambiguous Lestat... With Cruise playing Lestat... the vampire had ceased to be unrecognizable. Once a menace to the conclaves of average America, he was now an honorary resident.* (1997: 96)

Like *The Hunger* and other vampire films from the 1980s, *Interview* tells the story of a vampire family, but whereas the narratives of previous films about American vampires have been, like *Dracula*, almost exclusively heterosexual, *Interview* attempts to avoid any overt ideas of sexuality, for reasons that become clear in the context of Hollywood's conservative attitudes. There is a clear lesbian storyline to *The Hunger* but the sexual subtexts of *Interview* are left much more opaque, certainly in the film. The primary couple are two male vampires, Lestat (Cruise) and Louis (Brad Pitt), and their adopted vampire daughter, Claudia (Kirsten Dunst), who spends a century looking like a twelve-year-old. Thus, the film finds itself tiptoeing around issues of both homosexuality and paedophilia. Lestat is the alleged villain of the piece, who seduces Louis into agreeing to become a vampire and who appears to enjoy tormenting him and his rather finely honed senses of morality and guilt. Like the vampires of *The Hunger*, Lestat is a musician, a keyboard player of eighteenth-century European origin, and he uses his musical talents as part of his hunting tactics in the early nineteenth century as he 'educates' Claudia, once again demonstrating that European musicians are simply not to be trusted. In keeping with his history, his underscore music is almost exclusively played on the harpsichord.

The harpsichord has a long-standing association with vampires – Dracula plays the harpsichord in Stoker's novel, and we see this in some of the Hammer films – but it is also associated with a particular kind of villain in the cinema. This goes back to both Christopher Leigh's harpsichord-playing Dracula and John Addison's use of the harpsichord for the Laurence Olivier character in *Sleuth* (Joseph L. Mankiewicz, 1972). Something in the sound and the nature of the harpsichord's action seems to lend itself to a particular kind of calculated evil in films. The fact that the strings are plucked and not struck means that the player cannot expressively influence the sound of an individual note. Unlike the piano, when you strike a note on the harpsichord it simply sounds or does not; there are no nuances of dynamic available through the way the key is pressed. There is, by extension, something inhuman in the nature of the instrument: it resists mediation by human agency in a way that a piano does not.

Lestat is cast in the mould of the old, bad vampire, although he is not unsympathetic. Louis, however, is the most human vampire to have graced the screen in cinematic history, and his music captures this quality, and his inner conflict. The theme heard in the cue 'Born to Darkness' (which is associated with his voice-overs from the interview he is giving) is intensely lyrical, full of a sense of loss and longing. There is nothing conventionally vampiric about this theme, which associates him with the cello, not a traditional vampire instrument although, interestingly, it is the one played by John, the most 'human' vampire in *The Hunger*. Musically, *Interview* completes the project started by *Bram Stoker's Dracula*, with a historical vampire narrative that abandons the atonal, threatening music of Hammer scores for its representation of the central vampire characters. Louis, the title character, is described as the vampire with a human soul, and the lyricism and yearning of his music is an important aspect of this humanization.

The final piece of music in the film is the Rolling Stones song, 'Sympathy For The Devil', sung by Guns N' Roses, which takes the film into the credits. Lestat, having attacked Louis's interviewer in a moving car, takes over the steering wheel and switches on the radio, where he finds the rock song. Symbolically, he switches off his own eighteenth-century-coded harpsichord which is playing in the underscore at this point and appropriates not just his victim's car but also his century and his century's music, moving away from an archaic, baroque sound to embrace the new and modern world of pop and rock. Lestat's ability to embrace and use contemporaneous music, seen earlier in the film as part of his hunting tactics, appears to have remained intact. Although throughout the film we have been encouraged to identify primarily with Louis, at the end Lestat firmly asserts himself as the more vibrant character and the one most like us through his appropriation of 'our' music.

This appropriation is continued in *The Queen of the Damned* (Michael Rymer, 2002), the rather weaker sequel that — true to Anne Rice's novels — follows Lestat as he becomes a rock star. Eric Draven in *The Crow* was also a rock musician before his death and both films, therefore, use rock music not simply as underscore but as a central aspect of the diegesis, an idea hinted at, although not fully realized, in the association between Michael and Jim Morrison in *The Lost Boys*.

In terms of mainstream horror films, rock and popular music has continued to be significant in the creation of the musical sound of the film. Films such as *The Faculty* (Robert Rodriguez, 1998) and *Resident Evil* (Paul W. S. Anderson, 2002), which are specifically aimed at a teenage/twenties audience, are more likely to use soundtracks compiled from rock tracks familiar to their target audience, the difference here being that it is not the monsters that are being identified by and with the music but the human protagonists. It seems to be a particular property of the vampire narratives that vampires can be, and are regularly positioned as, less Other than most monsters in post-1980s films, and that this positioning is supported by music, whether it is the romantic scoring of Dracula and Mina, the lush strings and pathos of Louis's music or the ironically life-affirming appropriation of rock by Lestat.

The late 1990s and early twenty-first century brought several new vampire narratives, which exhibit distinct and sometimes quite novel musical strategies that reflect the continuing shift in how the figure of the vampire is constructed. The vampire has traditionally stood as a metaphor for our sexual anxieties (syphilis in the 1890s and AIDS in the 1980s), where the narratives of *Near Dark* and *The Lost Boys* offer reassuringly happy endings to young heterosexual men who accidentally stumble into vampirism, only for them and their vampire girlfriends to be cured by the final credits.[6] In the 1990s, three narrative themes come to the fore and indicate that the metaphor has shifted. First, the focus of vampiric evil moves to a corporate arena, rather than sex. Vampires increasingly become a community, a nation, and their ability to organize themselves along corporate lines is a potential threat to our security, bringing a whole new meaning to the idea of a 'blood bank'. Second, demonstrating the latent legacy of the vampire contagion as a metaphor for HIV, the new, potentially heroic vampire is a creature such as Louis, who strives for abstinence, a vampiric celibacy, neither biting nor seducing. Third, the heroic vampire is no longer always a pure vampire, but tends to be compromised in some way, and it is this diluting of their vampiric nature that allows them to be heroic rather than simply powerful. These constructions are seen in two manifestations of vampires in the late 1990s and early twenty-first century: the *Blade* trilogy (Stephen Norrington, 1998; Guillermo del Toro, 2002; David S. Goyer, 2004) and the *Underworld* series (Les Wiseman, 2003; 2006).[7]

In the first two films of the *Blade* trilogy (1998 and 2002)[8] there are two main types of music: orchestral scores written by Mark Isham (for *Blade*) and Marco Beltrami (for *Blade II*) that evoke the darkly sonorous sound world of *Batman* and *Interview with the Vampire*; and a number of popular music tracks – mainly techno in *Blade* and techno and rap in *Blade II* – some of which are diegetic in both films. Logically, one might expect one type of music to represent Blade and the other to represent his adversaries, but things are slightly less clear-cut, partly because he teams up with the vampire nation in *Blade II* in order to defeat a new and even more dangerous type of vampire. Blade himself is largely associated with the orchestral underscore, while the diegetic techno music of both films belongs unequivocally to his enemies: vampire clubs in both films play this music, Deacon Frost plays it on his personal stereo and at his party in *Blade*, and Scud, Blade's duplicitous assistant, also chooses to listen to it in *Blade II*. However, to upset this otherwise finally balanced plan are two divergent uses. First, Blade does not own the orchestral underscore in the same way that Batman, for example, owns the orchestral underscore of his eponymous film. In *Blade*, Deacon Frost effectively appropriates the underscore, thus positioning himself as the main narrative agent in the final act when it looks as if Blade will be defeated. Not dissimilarly, in *Blade II*, the orchestral underscore is as much the score of the vampires he is working with, who turn on him and again weaken him in the final act. Second, the vampires do not have an exclusive association with the popular music of the score. While all the diegetic popular music belongs to the vampires (or their familiars), Blade himself appears to 'use' it non-diegetically at exactly the same point in both films, namely, when he reverses his apparently failing fortunes in the last act and comes back fighting. When this occurs, the vampires have been associated with the orchestral music for some time; as Blade reasserts his authority over both the narrative and the sonic space, a popular music track (techno in the first film, rap in the second) is introduced into the underscore.

These uses of music, while not as tidy as the clear association of classical music with European vampires in *The Hunger*, nonetheless position Blade within his narratives in a way that reflects the complexity of his overall position in his diegetic world. He is a (comic-book) superhero, and orchestral music is typically the music of such figures in Hollywood scores. He is also black, and as writers such as Anahid Kassabian (2001) have observed, when central characters in Hollywood films are not the typical white, male heroes (e.g. women, black, Asian, lesbian or gay characters), they are more likely to be supported by popular music, which allows a greater range of identifications (e.g., of a non-white male character as heroic) than the default idiom of Hollywood's orchestral scoring. Finally, Blade is a hybrid, neither entirely human nor vampire, and having two distinct types of music operating in his sonic background is an aspect of this duality. Popular music, which has generally been identified with the vampire clubs where vampires dance, becomes the accompaniment to his highly choreographed battle-dance.

Perhaps the most remarkable thing about the two *Underworld* films is the difference in the musical strategies they display. Given that the overarching narrative concerns the hybridization of vampire and werewolf, the first film (in 2003) has an appropriately hybridized score that combines grittily industrial rock drumbeats, electronica, vocal samples from popular music and some more conventional orchestration, combined in a 'score' that largely defies categorization. It fits more into the realms of pop scores and the ambient synthesizer scores of *Near Dark* and *The Hunger* than the other 1990s vampire scores discussed here: its closest relative is *Blade*, but its textures are much more diverse. While there are moments in *Blade* when it is unclear whether a sound is non-diegetic electronica coming from the underscore or a diegetic sound, the diegetic/non-diegetic boundaries of *Underworld* are frequently very blurred indeed. This quite intentional sonic confusion is part of how the soundworld of this film reflects and supports our narrative interpretations of what we see: in that scores conventionally identify and give identity to their characters, this soundtrack fails to identify any specific character as more central than another. The classic strategies for doing this, such as giving a character a specific theme that helps define him or her and emphasize the importance of their actions, are absent.

There are two main candidates for this representation in both films: the vampire Selene and the human who ends up as a vampire–werewolf hybrid by the end, Michael. Michael is the obvious candidate for hero, and certainly seems to be the central character with whom we are most likely to identify. He starts out human and then undergoes a classic traumatic transformation event (bitten by first a werewolf, later a vampire) that results in him becoming supernaturally fast and strong. However, at no point is he able to act heroically, and he spends most of the film scared, helpless and generally disempowered, with Selene repeatedly rescuing him. He manages to save her life on one occasion (assuming that vampires can, in fact, drown) but even in the denouement of the film, it is Selene who comes to the rescue as Michael is on the brink of being defeated by her mentor, Viktor, and she who finally kills him. In terms of action, then, Selene is clearly the hero of the film, but both a reluctant one and a compromised one: she is part of an elite hit-squad of werewolf killers, and has been ruthlessly murdering them for centuries. Whereas Blade's representation with both orchestral and popular music formed a basically coherent image of him as man and vampire, hero and warrior, Selene is a warrior but, other than the opening sequence of the film, there is no obvious attempt by the music to position her as the heroic narrative agent of the film, despite the fact that she clearly is.

Underworld: Evolution (2006), on the other hand, has a completely different strategy, a big orchestral score cast from the *Batman* mould, again by Marco Beltrami. The rock drumbeats of the first film are not entirely missing from the second but their identity as rock has been effectively suppressed, subsumed into the orchestral textures of the score, appearing as timpani and snare drum in place of drum kit and drum samples. These drum sounds reflect the same militaristic topic that is referenced in *Batman's* superheroic music, and this in turn reflects the differences between the positioning of characters in the two films. In *Underworld*, we have a human central character, Michael, and various other members of the human world, such as his colleague, Adam. The industrial, rock-influenced score has a very urban feel to it, and the film takes place almost entirely within an unnamed city. In the second film, not only is the city absent, with the film largely taking place in unnamed mountains, but there are no named human characters, and Michael (like Selene) is non-human from the start. The second film is very much Selene's film: she continues to be the primary narrative agent (Michael is apparently dead for part of the film) and has left her old life behind to pursue her new mission, exposing the truth of the vampire nation's past. This, combined with the absence of humans, would explain the orchestral score: there is now no Otherness to be dealt with and Selene has, rather unusually, taken on the role of a true (as opposed to a female) superhero with a classically Hollywood superhero score.[9]

Both films use the same music at the end, an orchestral string arrangement that suggests resolution, hope and a sense of a destiny still to be discovered, but the differences in their overall strategies point to two different scoring practices in relation to two different types of narrative. The first of these might be termed the 'mediated' vampire film, in which the vampire interacts with humans and is no longer automatically evil, musically represented by a combination of different musics that may include rock, electronica and orchestral scoring (*Near Dark, The Hunger, Lost Boys, Blade*); the second is the 'fully identified' vampire film, in which there are few or no human characters with which the audience can identify, requiring us therefore to identify with the vampires themselves (e.g. *Interview*), where a classically orchestral score is used.

Nina Auerbach has observed that "every age embraces the vampire it needs" (1995: 145), and traces the way in which the potent metaphor offered by the vampire shifts and adapts to changing historical eras and their incumbent values and anxieties, particularly regarding sex and sexuality. The evil vampire still exists, but now so thoroughly assimilated into modern culture that the true evil is no longer sex but materialism, with the corporate vampire as the new threat. The metaphor of vampirism has taken on board the sexual anxieties of the age, presenting us with vampires who resist the desire to bite – in *Underworld* and the TV series, *Angel*, non-evil vampires appear more inclined to drink blood out of hermetically sealed plastic pouches than straight from the jugular – and their choice not to be killers creates the potential for the vampire, possessed of preternatural strength and immortality, to be someone who can therefore choose to do good instead, to become heroic. What can be observed since the early 1980s is a profound change in the way that vampires are constructed in terms of both narrative and the musics they have appropriated. In particular, they have appropriated popular music, romantic music and superheroic music, as they have gradually become less Other, more sympathetic and as likely to save us as kill us, while at the same time remaining rooted in the horror genre.

Notes

1. The vampire as a metaphor for cultural Others is a theme running throughout the essays in Gordon and Hollinger (1997).
2. Despite its setting, only one of the songs heard in *Near Dark* can be classified as country, George Strait's 'The Cowboy Rides Away' (1985).
3. In the sequel, *Batman Returns* (1992), the villain's name is Max Schrek, as if to remind us again that vampires lurk in the subtext of the narrative.
4. This is discussed in Iddon (2005). Although *The Crow* is technically not a vampire film, Iddon argues that Eric Draven is a form of anti-vampire in that "feeding on his victims, rather than prolonging his undead life, is intended to bring him a restful death". He cites both of these films as examples. (My thanks to Martin Iddon for sending me a copy of his paper.)
5. Films are generally not edited in silence and a temp (temporary) track is the collection of music assembled by the director and/or music editor to which a film is edited while the film's score is being composed. The purpose of the temp track is to provide the same kind of emotional and interpretative meanings that the final score is being asked to create for the scene in question, and it is not unusual for directors to ask composers to write music which resembles the temp track.
6. Nixon (1987: 118) points out that it is dangerous to conclude "that *The Hunger* is, in fact, an extended AIDS allegory", given that the film was released in 1983, at a point where there was little public awareness of the impending epidemic. In fact, the unequivocal connection between HIV and blood as the source of transference was only scientifically established in December 1982. The novel was published in 1981, and was therefore written before the first papers noting clusters of specific types of pneumonia and Kaposi's sarcoma among gay men were published in the summer of 1981. The film was released in April 1983, and the ease with which the film reads as an AIDS allegory is coincidental.
7. The observations made about these films can also be traced in the TV series *Angel*, a spin-off from *Buffy the Vampire Slayer*, in which the evil vampires run a law firm and Angel is the superhero vampire with a soul who fights against them

for the good of humankind. For more on the music and connections with cinematic narratives, see Halfyard (2005).

8. The third film, *Blade: Trinity* (2004), has a similar musical strategy but, in terms of plot, is the weakest of the three and is not discussed here.

9. Innes (1999) discusses at length the problem of pseudo-tough female heroes who need to be helped out by male counterparts. The idea of the true female superhero on screen found currency initially in television, with series such as *Xena: Warrior Princess*, *Buffy the Vampire Slayer* and *Alias*, with these new constructions of the female superhero feeding back into cinema.

References

Auerbach, N. (1995), *Our Vampires, Ourselves*, Chicago: University of Chicago Press.

Gelder, K. (1994), *Reading the Vampire*, London: Routledge.

Gordon, J., and Hollinger, V. (eds) (1997), *Blood Read: The Vampire as Metaphor in Contemporary Culture*, Philadelphia: University of Pennsylvania Press.

Halfyard, J. K. (2004), *Danny Elfman's Batman: A Film Score Guide*, Lanham, MD: Scarecrow Press.

Halfyard, J. K. (2005), 'The Dark Avenger: *Angel* and the Cinematic Superhero', in S. Abbott (ed.), *Reading Angel: The TV Spin-off with a Soul*, London/New York: IB Tauris, pp. 149–62.

Halfyard, J. K. (2006), 'Screen Playing: Cinematic Representations of Classical Music Performance and European Identity', in M. Mera and D. Burnand (eds), *European Film Music*, Aldershot: Ashgate, pp. 73–85.

Iddon, M. (2005), 'Sex, Blood and Rock'n'Roll: Diegetic Dark Rock and the Validation of the Gothic' (unpublished paper presented at the Bradford Film Festival Film and Music Conference).

Innes, S. A. (1999), *Tough Girls: Women Warriors and Wonder Women in Popular Culture*, Philadelphia: University of Pennsylvania Press.

Kassabian, A. (2001), *Hearing Film: Tracking Identifications in Contemporary Hollywood Film Music*, New York/London: Routledge.

Nixon, N. (1997), 'When Hollywood Sucks, or Hungry Girls, Lost Boys, and Vampirism in the Age of Reagan', in J. Gordon and V. Hollinger (eds), *Blood Read: The Vampire as Metaphor in Contemporary Culture*, Philadelphia: University of Pennsylvania Press, pp. 115–28.

Tomc, S. (1997), 'Dieting and Damnation: Anne Rice's *Interview with the Vampire*', in J. Gordon and V. Hollinger (eds), *Blood Read: The Vampire as Metaphor in Contemporary Culture*, Philadelphia: University of Pennsylvania Press, pp. 95–113.

11 Scary Movies, Scary Music
Uses and Unities of Heavy Metal in the Contemporary Horror Film

Lee Barron and Ian Inglis

One of the most profound developments in strategies of scoring films since the introduction of sound to cinema emerged in the 1970s, when the perennial reliance on the creation of a new, freshly composed, 'classical' film score began to be challenged by a preference for utilizing already existing (popular) musical sources. The first mainstream movie to emphatically demonstrate this change of trajectory was *The Big Chill* (Lawrence Kasdan, 1983); its success was rapidly followed by a string of other (often period-set) Hollywood films, including *Good Morning Vietnam* (Barry Levinson, 1987) and *Dirty Dancing* (Emile Ardolino, 1987), whose makers were quick to recognize popular music's capacity to "accompany, counterpoint, boost or ironically comment upon their visual work in a unique and sometimes spine-tingling manner" (Kermode, 1995: 11). Equally attractive, of course, was its capacity to provide a powerful commercial presence that was beneficial for both film admissions and soundtrack album sales.

The practice did not signal the end of the traditionally scored soundtrack. Composers like John Williams, Jerry Goldsmith, Hans Zimmer, Howard Shore and Thomas Newman have successfully continued the earlier examples and achievements of Dimitri Tiomkin, Henry Mancini, Bernard Herrmann, John Barry, Maurice Jarre, Elmer Bernstein, Alfred Newman *et al.* Nevertheless, as the practice became commonplace, a conventional aesthetic was established which served to effectively and routinely link contemporary popular musical genres with contemporary cinematic genres; furthermore, these associations are mutually, and broadly, recognized by producers and consumers alike. The urban gangster film may be built around a (typically non-diegetic) soundtrack of hip-hop and soul; the road movie is likely to rely on country and folk-rock; the love story is accompanied by pop and soft rock. However, one of the more striking and successful marriages of popular music and movies can be seen in the presence of heavy metal within the contemporary horror film. Through an examination of the justifications behind their combination, the characteristics of the associations that exist between the two forms, and the related demographic and artistic patterns that surround them, it becomes clear that there are historical, cultural and commercial explanations for the relationship.

Whatever its genre or origin, film music performs a number of functions. For Brown:

> [It acts] *as a wallpaper soporific to allay fears of darkness or silence, as an aesthetic counterbalance to the iconic/representational nature of cinematic signs,* [and] *as a co-generator of narrative affect that skews the viewer/ listener towards a culturally determined reading of the characters and situations.* (1994: 32)

Cohen describes its functions more succinctly: "music interprets and adds meaning, it aids memory, it suspends disbelief" (2000: 361). However they are presented, within the horror film the means through which these objectives are achieved may include rising levels of noise, reduced levels of noise, tonal distortion, accelerated or decelerated rhythms, turbulence and disorder, irregular lyrical contours, heightened pitch, and the juxtaposition of calm and chaos. What unites these components is that they are all, in one way or another, 'unsettling'. Indeed, a jarring musical soundtrack has been perceived as one of the crucial ways in which the horror film achieves its psychological impact (Urbano, 1998).

Moreover, this sense of disruption has been deliberately, and knowingly, pursued by both film and music audiences for whom emotional flights into fright, anxiety, horror and shock may be legitimate pleasures:

> [Movies became] *escape outlets that enabled people to forget, at least for a short time, the very conditions that fomented their discontent... and contemporary rock music, which sings, screams and shouts its defiance, creates its own world of fantasy.* (Bazelon, 1975: 75–6)

There is less agreement, however, about the precise manner in which music and film are able to provide pleasure to their consumers; different disciplines offer different theories, ranging across aesthetic, psychological, physiological and psychoanalytic explanations (Gorbman, 1987: 60–3). As sociologists, we would maintain a cultural explanation: responses (pleasurable or otherwise) are learned forms of behaviour, crucially dependent upon a complex set of contextual factors, including history, geography, socio-economic status, gender, education, age and location. It is therefore important to consider the contexts and conditions in which the contemporary horror film achieved, and has maintained, its position within commercial cinema and those in which heavy metal has become one of the principal genres of contemporary popular music, and, at the same time, to track the points of intersection and correspondence that unite the two.

After its somewhat uneven first fifty years, the remarkable reinvigoration of the horror movie in the early 1970s saw the boundaries of violence and sexuality extended far beyond those of previous decades. Significant titles included *The Last House on the Left* (Wes Craven, 1972); *The Exorcist* (William Friedkin, 1973); *The Texas Chain Saw Massacre* (Tobe Hooper, 1973); *Carrie* (Brian de Palma, 1976); *The Omen* (Richard Donner, 1976); *Dawn of the Dead* (George A. Romero, 1978); *Halloween* (John

Carpenter, 1978); and *The Amityville Horror* (Stuart Rosenberg, 1979). The rapid reinvention of a genre widely seen as dated and formulaic led, in turn, to the proliferation of a number of distinct subgenres, including: the slasher movie – *Friday the 13th* (Sean Cunningham, 1980), *Scream* (Wes Craven, 1996); the occult/supernatural thriller – *Angel Heart* (Alan Parker, 1987), *The Blair Witch Project* (Daniel Myrick and Eduardo Sanchez, 1999); the predatory alien – *Alien* (Ridley Scott, 1979), *Inseminoid* (Norman J. Warren, 1981); the zombie movie – *Zombie Flesh Eaters/Zombi 2* (Lucio Fulci, 1979), *Resident Evil* (Paul W. S. Anderson, 2002); the serial killer – *Henry: Portrait of a Serial Killer* (John McNaughton, 1986), *The Silence of the Lambs* (Jonathan Demme, 1991); and the horror-spoof – *Scary Movie* (Keenan Ivory Wayans, 2000), *Shaun of the Dead* (Edgar Wright, 2004).

As the horror movie was being reintroduced to the cinema, a development of equal impact was taking place within popular music. Inspired by the aggressive and flamboyant forms of rock musicianship, the cult of the guitar hero, and the cohesive momentum of lead guitar, bass guitar, drums and vocals that had distinguished Cream and the Jimi Hendrix Experience in the mid- to late 1960s, groups like Deep Purple and Led Zeppelin (in the UK) and Steppenwolf, Blue Cheer, Iron Butterfly and Vanilla Fudge (in the USA) were among the first to present a form of rock'n'roll that was notably harder, louder and more disturbing than other forms of contemporary popular music. Distancing itself from the 'acid-rock' of its antecedents, heavy metal – the origin of the term has been variously traced to scientific, science-fiction, musical and literary sources (Weinstein, 2000: 18–21) – chose to discard the implicit psychedelic overtones of the 1960s and to explicitly emphasize the abrasive power of rock.

Largely defined by the early recordings of Led Zeppelin, the genre quickly expanded in the 1970s through bands such as Black Sabbath, AC/DC, Kiss, Judas Priest, Motörhead, Saxon, Scorpions and Iron Maiden; and it continued its expansion through the 1980s via Twisted Sister, Mötley Crüe, Tesla, Def Leppard, W.A.S.P. and Guns N'Roses. A synthesis of ideology and technology distinguished many of its performers from their contemporaries within popular music:

> If most other bands were doing sex, love, peace, brotherhood, and so on, one way to be original was to turn that formula on its head and do alienation, menace, destruction, and nihilism. The creative possibilities of the new musical technologies almost invited this development... that pounding bass guitar could be used to create a sense of chaos and doom, that electric guitar – and the new effects gadgets being developed for it, such as fuzz boxes that could increase the distortion of the sound – could be made to screech and wail. (Arnett, 1996: 43)

Significantly, this change of emphasis was not only musical, but lyrical as well. Although heavy metal shared with rock music an anti-authoritarian stance, the emphasis on love was missing. In its place was a fascination with evil, with the dark side of the human heart and of human experience (*ibid.*).

Weinstein has noted that the musical outcomes of these tendencies were characterized by themes of chaos and nihilism, marked out by an:

> absence or destruction of relationships... from confusion, through various
> forms of anomaly, conflict, and violence, to death. Respectable society tries
> to repress chaos... heavy metal brings its images to the forefront, empower-
> ing them with its vitalizing sound. (2000: 38)

And just as the horror movie gave birth to a number of subgenres, so too heavy metal
fractured and splintered into a cluster of specialized variations, including thrash metal,
black metal, death metal, speed metal, power metal and glam-metal.

Not surprisingly, the explorations of violence, destruction and death contained within
the horror film and heavy metal have ensured that both have been implicated in sen-
sational and tragic events. Media claims that movies as diverse as the multi-Academy
Award-winning *The Exorcist* and the low-budget *Child's Play 3* (Jack Bender, 1991)
were directly responsible for a number of well-publicized suicides, attacks and murders
(Stanley, 2002: 190–2; Kermode, 2003) are uncannily similar to the arguments made
in court alleging that songs by AC/DC, Ozzy Osbourne and Judas Priest led their
listeners to take their own lives (Walser, 1993: 145–51; Weinstein, 2000: 250–7).
Whether these inducements to violence are on screen or on record, a number of writers
(Barker, 1984; Binder, 1993; Wright, 2000) have so clearly noted the presence of
persistent patterns of exaggeration and distortion, symbolization, and prediction that it
is legitimate to refer to the (social) actors involved as 'folk devils' and to the contro-
versies that surround them as 'moral panics' (Cohen, 1972: 27–48).

It was within the overlapping subgenres of speed metal and thrash metal that the
"violence and aggression, rapine and carnage" (Bangs, 1992: 459) attributed to heavy
metal as a whole were initially recognized. Appropriately, even the names adopted by
many of the performers – Metallica, Megadeth, Exodus, Vio-Lence, Suicidal Tendencies,
Anthrax, Nuclear Assault, Kreator, Testament – indicated their aggressive sound and
relentlessly pessimistic/angry lyrics. They were followed by the aptly named death metal
(after its lyrical obsession with songs of violence and death), performed by bands such
as Deicide, Obituary, Immolation, Cannibal Corpse, Death and Mortician.

> [Their] *lyrics describe bizarre creatures or events of violence, they give the*
> *songs the quality of an auditory horror story or horror movie. Like heavy*
> *metal songs, horror stories and horror movies from Edgar Allan Poe to*
> *Stephen King often involve violence and portray a grim, dark, brutal world.*
> (Arnett, 1996: 67)

A case in point is Slayer, the US thrash/death metal band whose musical output
exemplifies the musical articulation of the horror story. Its songs fall into distinctive and
familiar themes, including the supernatural – 'Haunting The Chapel', 'At Dawn They
Sleep', 'Crypts Of Eternity', 'Altar Of Sacrifice', 'Ghosts Of War', 'Born Of Fire',
'Bloodline'; the satanic – 'The Anti-Christ', 'Hell Awaits', 'Jesus Saves', 'Reborn',

'Black Magic', 'Spill The Blood', 'South Of Heaven', 'Raining Blood'; death and murder – 'Kill Again', 'Necrophiliac', 'Praise Of Death', 'Hardening Of The Arteries', 'Angel Of Death', 'Piece By Piece', 'Criminally Insane', 'Postmortem', 'Dead Skin Mask', '213', 'Sex Murder Art'.

That each of these song titles would function equally effectively as a film title says much about the degree of common territory between music and movies. Moreover, it may be significant that the most sustained descriptions of torture and death are to be found in Slayer's 'biographical' songs about the activities of serial killers such as Ed Gein and Jeffrey Dahmer, individuals who were also the inspirations for several well-known horror movies (see below). 'Dead Skin Mask' depicts the world of 1950s American murderer and grave-robber Gein and encourages the listener to share in the dark fantasies, the delight and arousal experienced by the murderer himself:

> Graze the skin with my fingertips
> The brush of dead cold flesh pacifies the means
> Provocative images delicate features so smooth
> A pleasant fragrance in the light of the moon.

Films based on Gein's story have included *Psycho* (Alfred Hitchcock, 1960), *Deranged* (Jeff Gillen and Alan Ormsby, 1974), *The Texas Chain Saw Massacre*, *The Silence of the Lambs* and *Ed Gein* (Chuck Parello, 2000). In much the same vein, '213' recreates the activities of Jeffrey Dahmer (the title derives from Apartment 213 Oxford Buildings, where he lived and carried out many of the seventeen murders to which he later confessed) and includes accounts of the necrophilia, dissection and cannibalism perpetrated on his victims.

In addition, Slayer's obsession with horrific themes extends to the design of its album covers. Not only do the albums' titles continue the band's emphasis on cruelty and evil – *Show No Mercy* (1983), *Hell Awaits* (1985), *Reign In Blood* (1986), *Seasons In The Abyss* (1990), *Divine Intervention* (1994), *Diabolus In Musica* (1998), *God Hates Us All* (2001) and *Christ Illusion* (2006) – but "the hideous images that decorated their album sleeves were unashamedly dark fantasies... an attempt to translate the hellish paintings of Hieronymus Bosch to vinyl" (Baddeley, 1999: 168). The wider significance of this tendency has been considered by Weinstein:

> Whereas the code for pop and country albums mandates photographs of the faces of the performers, the fronts of heavy metal albums are not graced with close-ups of band members. The heavy metal code specifies that what is depicted must be somewhat ominous, threatening, and unsettling, suggesting chaos and bordering on the grotesque. This metatheme was expressed in many ways until the late 1970s, when the code narrowed to include the iconography of horror movies, gothic horror tales, and heroic fantasies. (2000: 29)

A similar equation of the imagery of heavy metal and the iconography of horror has been consistently practised by Iron Maiden (a band whose name is taken from the medieval instrument of torture). At every concert, on every T-shirt, on every album cover is the band's 'mascot', Eddie, who accompanies the band in the form of an 'animated corpse'.

Indeed, even a cursory exploration of the heavy metal environment reveals a bewildering multiplicity of references to, and from, the horror movie. The band Send More Paramedics took its name from a line spoken by a brain-hungry zombie within the film *The Return of the Living Dead* (Dan O'Bannon, 1985), and the figure of the zombie is a recurrent theme within its music. Necrophagia's admiration of Italian horror-director Lucio Fulci pervades much of its work: the *Holocausto De La Morte* (1998) album cover combines painted images taken from several of his films, including *Zombie Flesh Eaters/Zombi 2* (1979) and *City of the Living Dead/Paura nella Citta dei Morti Viventi* (1980), and the *Black Blood Vomitorium* (2000) EP not only celebrates Fulci in song, but includes inner-sleeve photographs from his film *The Beyond* (1981). Finally, black metal band Venom's comparison of itself to rivals Black Sabbath concluded with the observation that "we are the Evil Dead to their Hammer Horror" (Herman, 2002: 202).

Given the strength of these correspondences, it was perhaps inevitable that a dynamic and deliberate synthesis between the media – which went far beyond a mere recognition of thematic similarities – should evolve. The first evidence of a film-maker's conscious selection and employment of heavy metal music within a horror movie soundtrack was in *Phenomena* (Dario Argento, 1985). Argento had previously recruited the rock group Goblin to provide bombastic, driving scores for *Profondo Rosso* (1975), *Suspiria* (1977) and *Tenebre* (1982). For *Phenomena*, he augmented the synthesizer-led score of Goblin members Claudio Simonetti and Fabio Pignatelli with existing songs from established heavy metal bands – Motörhead's 'Locomotive' and Iron Maiden's 'Flash Of The Blade'. The Iron Maiden track is heard at two key moments of the film: first, when the teenage Jennifer (Jennifer Connelly) witnesses a murder, and secondly, when she attempts to escape from the murderer's lair. Although it has been argued that the film's combination of differing soundtracks gives it an uneven, even "schizophrenic" quality (McDonagh, 1994: 189), the driving, guitar-led 'Flash Of The Blade' is, in fact, perfectly in keeping with the nature of a film characterized by impaling, decapitation and mutant-murderers. And, in fact, the policy was repeated in the Argento-produced *Demons* (Lamberto Bava, 1985), which brought together newly composed music by Claudio Simonetti and previous tracks by heavy metal bands such as Accept, Mötley Crüe and Saxon.

As the 1980s progressed, the alliance between the horror film and heavy metal intensified and shifted as a result of two key examples of a much more explicit fusion. Rather than duplicate Argento's use of pre-existing songs, *Friday the 13th Part VI: Jason Lives* (Tom McLaughlin, 1986) and *A Nightmare on Elm Street 3: Dream Warriors* (Chuck Russell, 1987) commissioned new heavy metal tracks to serve as the films' theme songs. In *Jason Lives*, Alice Cooper wrote and performed 'He's Back', which described the murderous activities of the series' central killer, Jason Voorhees, and contributed two other songs — 'Hard Rock Summer' and 'Teenage Frankenstein' — to the soundtrack. The theme song for *Dream Warriors*, the third movie in the series about phantom child-murderer Freddy Krueger — also titled 'Dream Warriors' — was written and performed by Dokken, and released as a single whose accompanying video interspersed footage of the band with footage from the film. And when the two series were united in *Freddy vs Jason* (Ronny Yu, 2003) the physical confrontation between the two protagonists was to the music of a number of heavy metal bands, including Ill Nino, Spineshank and Killswitch Engage.

The pattern continued through the 1990s, often with interesting variations. Motörhead contributed the song 'Hell On Earth' to *Hellraiser III* (Anthony Hickox, 1992) and, for its music video, combined scenes from the film with original sequences in which the band's lead singer, Lemmy, confronted the film's sadistic, interdimensional villain, Pinhead (Doug Bradley). In an increasingly common — almost obligatory — practice, *The Blair Witch Project* was accompanied by the simultaneous release of a soundtrack album. However, *The Blair Witch Project: Josh's Blair Witch Mix* was unique, in that it was the musical soundtrack to a film that had, in fact, no musical soundtrack. The justification was to build the album into the mythos of the film (and the legend of the Blair Witch) by characterizing the 'soundtrack' as a reproduction of the tape found in the dead Josh's car (Barron, 2003). As many of the songs were drawn from heavy metal, or goth-metal, by performers such as Type O Negative and Laibach, the album served therefore as a 'virtual soundtrack' that functioned effectively within the context of a film about the supernatural.

This search for synergy recurred in a number of subsequent films aligning contemporary heavy metal bands with horror film product in various ways. *Resident Evil*, based on the popular '*Capcom*' videogame series, presents Alice (Milla Jovovich) and assorted government task-force officers in a struggle to escape from an underground research facility infested by zombies and other deadly mutant creatures. The soundtrack combined a freshly composed score by Marilyn Manson — "perhaps the sickest artist ever promoted by a mainstream record company" (Wright, 2000: 375) — and pre-existing tracks from a range of bands such as Coal Chamber, Rammstein, Slipknot, Fear Factory, Static-X, Mudvayne and Saliva. Manson's input, fluctuating between conventional score and an aggressive, guitar-based, hard rock heard on albums like *Antichrist Superstar*, *Holy Wood* and *Mechanical Animals*, creates an 'industrial soundscape' whose music operates in strict accordance with the conventions of the horror score, cueing scares and building suspense through moody, atmospheric keyboard/synthesizer combinations. In contrast, the contributions from the other performers are limited to a montage that plays over the film's closing credits, thus allowing for their inclusion on the soundtrack, but in a way which clearly acknowledges Manson's greater commercial presence.

Just as heavy metal was incorporated into the creation of movies, so too were elements of movies invited into the creation of music. Some of the strategies adopted by the black metal band Cradle Of Filth provide telling examples:

> Horror movie legend Ingrid Pitt was... employed to provide voiceovers on Cruelty and the Beast, their concept album inspired by the life and crimes of the sixteenth-century Transylvanian countess, Erzebet Bathori. Their 2000 album Midian, its title track inspired by Clive Barker's novel Cabal... utilised the vocal talents of actor Doug Bradley, who attained cult status in Barker's series of Hellraiser movies as Pinhead, leader of the sadomasochistic Cenobites. (Baddeley, 2002: 269)

In addition, vocalist Dani Filth starred in the British-made, low-budget *Cradle of Fear* (Alex Chandon, 2002), which also featured cameos from the other band members. Key moments within the film depict the band members (and their music) in stylistically excessive 'gore-moments' which perfectly reflect their stage/album personae and recall their music videos; the video for 'From The Cradle To Enslave' (also directed by Chandon) casts the band as undead/vampiric entities playing within a church presided over by Satan himself. The video's narrative reveals how each member of the band met his or her fate and includes, within its familiar horror-movie ingredients, images of nudity, throat-slashing, wrist-cutting and hearts plucked from chests. Many other heavy metal bands have opted for similar, if less extreme, videos, mainly in order to protect mainstream television broadcasting opportunities: Iron Maiden's videos for 'The Number Of The Beast' and 'Bring Your Daughter To The Slaughter' combined performance shots of the band with clips from *How to Make a Monster* (Herbert L. Strock, 1958) and *The City of the Dead* (John Llewellyn Moxy, 1960). Other notable transitions from metal to horror included the acting appearances of Alice Cooper in *Monster Dog* (Claudio Fragasso, 1984), *Prince of Darkness* (John Carpenter, 1987) and *Freddy's Dead: The Final Nightmare* (Rachel Talalay, 1991), and Motörhead's Lemmy in *Hardware* (Richard Stanley, 1990).

Perhaps the union of music and film is best exemplified in the career of Rob Zombie. Originally the lead singer with White Zombie, a name derived from the movie starring Bela Lugosi – *White Zombie* (Victor Halperin, 1932) – he went on to make the solo albums *Hellbilly Deluxe* (1998) and *The Sinister Urge* (2001). Many of the albums' songs were saturated with references to, and influences from, B-grade movies – 'Superbeast', 'Demonoid Phenomenon', 'Living Dead Girl', 'Meet The Creeper', 'Dead Girl Superstar', and 'How To Make A Monster'. Zombie was subsequently invited by Universal Studios to write and direct *House of a Thousand Corpses* (2003). Although the movie, constructed as a homage to the rebirth of horror in the 1970s, alarmed the studio by a "visceral tone and intensity that we did not imagine from the printed page" (Baddeley, 2002: 271), it nevertheless signalled a pivotal moment in the marriage of heavy metal and horror, by allowing a musical performer not merely to contribute to a film's soundtrack, but to take effective control of the film-making process itself.

In trying to comprehend the repercussions of this fusion, it is important to remember that while the heavy metal/horror axis is subject to some specific – even unique – conditions, it is part of a wider historical convergence of film and popular music that began to be exploited in the late 1960s in movies such as *The Graduate* (Mike Nichols, 1967) and *Easy Rider* (Dennis Hopper, 1969). The practice of 'quotation', defined as "the importing of a song or musical text, in part or in whole, into a film's score" (Kassabian, 2001: 49) has impacted not only on the construction of movies (the technical skills of editing, sound engineering, music supervision and direction) but also on the consumption of movies (the perception, reception and retention of the text by audiences). In particular, much has been made of the potential that pre-existing music has to threaten two of the primary functions embedded in the traditional score, that of supplying a match between narrative action and musical accompaniment and that of concentrating rather than diverting viewers' attention to plot. It has to be noted, however, that despite those, and other, elements which:

> frequently brought it into conflict with some of the basic principles of the classical model... few would claim that the pop score fulfilled the dire prophecy initially attached to it. (Kalinak, 1992: 187)

Following on from that, Gorbman has posed a series of (semi-rhetorical) questions about the changed ways in which we watch and listen to a story on film, which help to explain popular music's place in contemporary cinema:

> Is the use of popular music in eighties films really different in kind from its use in the traditional Hollywood musical, where it is a matter of convention for the flow and space of the narrative to be disrupted by a musical number? Have listening habits and responses changed in response to commercial interests? Has it become 'normal' to listen to a rock song with lyrics at the same time we follow a story? (1987: 162–3)

Full answers to these questions can only be attempted if we situate their investigation within their appropriate socio-historical context. The concurrence of the birth of heavy metal and the rebirth of the horror film in the last three decades of the twentieth century has already been noted. Yet there are other, global, factors surrounding and shaping these years: sustained military conflicts, the growth of terrorism, corrupt and discredited political leaderships, economic crises, radically altered technologies, escalating patterns of drug use, environmental concerns, transformations in employment and industry, and legal interventions into gender, ethnic and sexual inequalities. For Walser, these are not random, unrelated occurrences:

> Both heavy metal and the horror film address the insecurities of this tumultuous era. Both provide ways of producing meaning in an irrational society; both explore explanations for seemingly incomprehensible phenomena. (1993: 161)

That the two thus coincided – and did so at a time when the cinema was beginning to recognize the commercial and creative advantages of popular music – allowed for their common interests and objectives to become formalized, industrially and culturally. Crucially, those common interests – themes of violence, chaos, death, the supernatural – enabled a fusion of new cultures within traditional structures:

> *Horror film music illustrates the modes of film music more generally... Horror film music functions as a central 'effect' in horror films, and thus as a principal player rather than simply 'window-dressing' accompaniment for scary visuals... Rather than merely providing an accompaniment to screen horror, film music is also able to embody horror, providing a demonic presence in itself.* (Donnelly, 2005: 106)

It is, conclusively, heavy metal's ability to provide "a demonic presence" that has made it such a suitable partner for the horror movie.

An examination of current directions in music and movies reveals that the early years of the new millennium have seen significant developments in both genres. A new category of heavy metal, nu-metal, has achieved considerable exposure and popularity via bands like Korn, Limp Bizkit, Staind, Adema, P.O.D., Linkin Park, Mudvayne, Disturbed, Papa Roach and Slipknot. And the most notable trend in the horror film has been the increased number of remakes: seminal 1970s movies have been remade for contemporary audiences – *The Texas Chainsaw Massacre* (Marcus Nispel, 2003), *Dawn of the Dead* (Zack Snyder, 2004), *The Amityville Horror* (Andrew Douglas, 2005); and contemporary Japanese horror movies have been remade for western audiences – *The Ring* (Gore Verbinski, 2002), *The Grudge* (Takashi Shimizu, 2004), *The Ring Two* (Hideo Nakata, 2005) and *Dark Water* (Walter Salles, 2005). While these two generic trajectories have occurred independently of each other, the established connection between the horror movie and heavy metal has nonetheless continued. Slipknot, DevilDriver and Cradle Of Filth were featured on the soundtrack of *Resident Evil: Apocalypse* (Alexander Witt, 2004); the remade *Dawn of the Dead* included songs by Stereophonics and Disturbed; and Rob Zombie wrote and directed *The Devil's Rejects* (2005), his ultraviolent sequel to *House of a Thousand Corpses*.

The history of a genre is commonly described as "an evolution from growth to maturity to decay, or a development from the experimental to the classical to the elaborated to the self-referential" (Maltby, 1995: 116). The continuing significance commonly attributed to the 'founding fathers' of heavy metal in the 1970s and their persistent popularity today, and the self-consciously intertextual references within the topography of the contemporary horror film might support each of those analyses. Whether the fusion of horror and metal ultimately indicates the creation of a new, lasting (sub)genre or merely a temporary artistic liaison born through convenience remains to be seen.

References

Arnett, J. J. (1996), *Metalheads: Heavy Metal Music and Adolescent Alienation*, Boulder, CO: Westview.

Baddeley, G. (1999), *Lucifer Rising: Sin, Devil Worship and Rock'n'Roll*, London: Plexus.

Baddeley, G. (2002), *Goth Chic: A Connoisseur's Guide to Dark Culture*, London: Plexus.

Bangs, L. (1992), 'Heavy Metal', in A. de Curtis and J. Henke (eds), *The Rolling Stone Illustrated History of Rock & Roll*, New York: Random House, pp. 459–64.

Barker, M. (1984) (ed.), *The Video Nasties: Freedom and Censorship in the Media*, London: Pluto.

Barron, L. (2003), 'Music from and Inspired by the Motion Picture: The Curious Case of the Disappearing Soundtrack', in I. Inglis (ed.), *Popular Music and Film*, London: Wallflower Press, pp. 148–61.

Bazelon, I. (1975), *Knowing the Score: Notes on Film Music*, New York: Van Nostrand Reinhold.

Binder, A. (1993), 'Constructing Racial Rhetoric: Media Depictions of Harm in Heavy Metal and Rap Music', *American Sociological Review*, 58(6), 753–7.

Brown, R. S. (1994), *Overtones and Undertones: Reading Film Music*, Berkeley: University of California Press.

Cohen, A. J. (2000), 'Film Music: Perspectives from Cognitive Psychology', in J. Buhler, C. Flinn and D. Neumeyer (eds), *Music and Cinema*, Hanover, NH: Wesleyan University Press, pp. 360–77.

Cohen, S. (1972), *Folk Devils and Moral Panics*, London: MacGibbon & Kee.

Donnelly, K. J. (2005), *The Spectre of Sound: Music in Film and Television*, London: BFI.

Gorbman, C. (1987), *Unheard Melodies: Narrative Film Music*, Bloomington: Indiana University Press.

Herman, G. (2002), *Rock'n'Roll Babylon*, London: Plexus.

Kalinak, K. (1992), *Settling the Score: Music and the Classical Hollywood Film*, Madison: University of Wisconsin Press.

Kassabian, A. (2001), *Hearing Film: Tracking Identifications in Contemporary Hollywood Film Music*, New York: Routledge.

Kermode, M. (1995), 'Twisting the Knife', in J. Romney and A. Wootton (eds), *Celluloid Jukebox*, London: BFI, pp. 9–19.

Kermode, M. (2003), *The Exorcist*, revised edition, London: BFI.

Maltby, R. (1995), *Hollywood Cinema*, Oxford: Blackwell.

McDonagh, M. (1994), *Broken Mirrors/Broken Minds: The Dark Dreams of Dario Argento*, London: Sun Tavern Fields.

Stanley, R. (2002), 'Dying Light: An Obituary for the Great British Horror Movie', in S. Chibnall and J. Petley (eds), *British Horror Cinema*, London: Routledge, pp. 183–95.

Urbano, C. (1998), 'Projections, Suspense and Anxiety: The Modern Horror Film and Its Effects', *Psychoanalytic Review*, 85(6), 909–30.

Walser, R. (1993), *Running with the Devil: Power, Gender and Madness in Heavy Metal Music*, Hanover, NH: Wesleyan University Press.

Weinstein, D. (2000), *Heavy Metal: The Music and Its Culture*, New York: Da Capo Press.

Wright, R. (2000), 'I'd Sell You Suicide: Pop Music and Moral Panic in the Age of Marilyn Manson', *Popular Music*, 19(3), 365–85.

12 "Like Razors through Flesh"
Hellraiser's *Sound Design and Music*

Karen Collins

"There is a secret song at the centre of the world, and its sound is like razors through flesh." (*Hellraiser III: Hell on Earth*)

Sound design in recent decades has developed beyond the creation of 'real' sounds in film, to a whole aesthetic in itself, in part through the use of sound as metaphor. Particularly in science-fiction and horror films, sound design – and how it functions with the underscore – has become a crucial aspect in the creation of fear and horror in cinema. To illustrate this idea, this chapter will explore the sound design and music of the *Hellraiser* films: *Hellraiser* (Clive Barker, 1987), *Hellbound: Hellraiser II* (Tony Randel, 1988), *Hellraiser III: Hell on Earth* (Anthony Hickox, 1992), *Hellraiser IV: Bloodline* (Kevin Yagher, 1996), *Hellraiser V: Inferno* (Scott Derrickson, 2000), *Hellraiser VI: Hellseeker* (Rick Bota, 2002), *Hellraiser VII: Deader* (Rick Bota, 2005) and *Hellraiser VIII: Hellworld* (Rick Bota, 2005).[1] The eight films in the series, originally based on a story by Clive Barker called *The Hellbound Heart* (first published in 1986), have led to a strong cult following and to a franchise of associated merchandising including comics, video games and action figures. The films lie somewhere between science fiction and horror in style: they share horror's interest in the grotesque and macabre, and have no small amount of gore, yet they also contain science fiction's blue-filter screens and cyborg-like demons. Both science fiction and horror, of course, deal with the unknown, and are inextricably linked in many types of crossover films: *Alien* (Ridley Scott, 1979), *The Fly* (David Cronenberg, 1986) and *Resident Evil* (Paul W. S. Anderson, 2002), for example. Most relevant to our discussion here, the *Hellraiser* films are sonically as close to popular science-fiction films as they are to those of the horror genre.

The *Hellraiser* movies are modern-day 'descent motif' stories, otherwise known as 'Harrowing of Hell' narratives, that is, the story of a visit to hell by mortals. Rather than the traditional routes to hell – the bridges of judgement, ladders of salvation or the dark wood cave – the doors to hell in *Hellraiser* are opened by an occult puzzle box, called LeMarchand's box. Unlike most descent narratives, hell in the majority of the films (*Hellraiser II: Hellbound* is a notable exception) is not so much a distinct place as a blurring of distinctions between reality and another world, and its presence is often signalled only by the presence of the demons, or 'cenobites', as they are known in the films. The demons are summoned by using the correct configuration of the puzzle box. The story, then, is an old tale: a combination of descent narrative with the idea of playing an intellectual puzzle game with death. The lead cenobite, called Pinhead, takes the place of Death, and LeMarchand's puzzle box substitutes for the more traditional chessboard.[2]

Although this plotline is the basic premise for each *Hellraiser* movie, the eight films made to date have been widely disparate. Each film has different characters and plots, and even different settings in time and place, ranging from eighteenth-century France to a space station in the twenty-second century in *Hellraiser IV: Bloodline*, although the majority of the films are set in the present day in Europe or North America. One film in particular, *Hellraiser V: Inferno*, sticks out as not belonging to the others with its film noir style detective story, complete with voice-over narrative. Nevertheless, the films all maintain the common descent motif, contain the box which opens the world of the cenobite demons, and all feature a dreamworld–reality gameplay in the narrative. Although the music can be quite inconsistent between the films (see below), one of the threads holding the series together is the sound design. It is worth exploring this in some detail, as each film shares a similar use of sound in creating a sense of reality in dreamworlds and to create a horrific, hellish aesthetic in general.

Hearing is believing: the dreamworld/reality dichotomy and sound design

Each of the *Hellraiser* films plays with a dream-state/reality confusion, in similar fashion to many others in the horror genre, such as *Final Destination* (James Wong, 2000), *A Nightmare on Elm Street* (Wes Craven, 1984) or *Friday the 13th* (Sean S. Cunningham, 1980), which commonly use the idea to add additional tension to a film. Rarely are we told where the line between dreamworld and reality lies, for that would spoil the surprise element. In effect, creating the illusion of reality-inside-a-dream allows the film to kill off a character in the dreamworld (with its subsequent audience reaction), and yet keep him or her alive to kill again. In this way, the audience gets to witness plenty of gore and death, without the confusion of having to meet too many characters. It also serves to play with the audience's emotions, in much the same way as the common 'false-alarm' killers, such as the hat and coat hanging on the door that resembles a stalker. Frequently, the music and sound design play a major role in getting the audience on the edge of their seats in these scenes. Unlike some of the above-mentioned films, however, in *Hellraiser* we do not see the characters fall asleep: we do not *know* in which scenes they are awake and in which they are dreaming. And, as is suggested in the dialogue of some of the *Hellraiser* films, the real world becomes a fantasy, and the dreamworld or hellworld becomes the reality.

Although present in all of the *Hellraiser* films, the dream-state/reality game is most prominent in the final three films of the series. In *Hellraiser VI: Hellseeker* the main character, Trevor, suffers delusions about his wife, whom he is accused of murdering. He frequently experiences daydreams and lapses of time, and we experience many dreams-within-dreams where the character is perpetually waking up from a dream-state of which we were unaware. Towards the end of the film we discover that the entire movie was shot from the same beginning point in time (his wife's death), but that in fact Trevor was the one who had died and was experiencing everything we have seen in his afterlife, adding yet another layer to the 'realities' presented. In *Hellraiser VII: Deader* the confusion between reality and fantasy worlds is equally blurred. After the protagonist Amy finds the box, she opens the gate to hell, and gets skewered by the flailing hooks and chains. She has several flashback memories, and then awakens without any evidence of the event. Similarly, she sees a man jump in front of a train, but when she calls the local police to the scene, there is nobody there. In addition to dreams, there are also frequent uses of flashback scenes in many of the films, and therefore many layers and types of dream-within-dream to confuse the audience. In fact, it could be said that psychologically disturbing the audience through the multiple layers of 'reality' in the films is one of the series' primary carriers of fear and horror. In *Hellraiser VIII: Hellworld*, for example, there is a constant back-and-forth between dream-states and reality. Near the end of the film, we are told that the entire film up to that point has been a dream-state, and that the characters were in fact not at a party, but underground in coffins, with mobile phones offering subliminal messages that placed them in the world we witnessed. When the cenobites come to take the teens' captor ('The Host', played by Lance Henriksen), he cries, "This is not happening" and the demons reply, "Seeing is believing". What we have *seen* in the films has been illusion, however, an illusion equally confused by the sound design.

Except when we are informed in a few special cases, the sound design gives us no clues as to where we are located in the reality/dreamworld. The dreamworlds are sonically presented to us as just an alternative reality. Unlike many films outside the horror genre, such as *The Matrix* (Wachowski brothers, 1999), which provide various clues in the sound design that help the viewer to distinguish the realms of reality and dream-state (see Evans, 2004), the absolute normality of the sound design in *Hellraiser*'s dream sequences helps to confuse the audience further, and thus heighten the tension. In other words, there is no 'bending' of sounds, no extra reverberation or other tricks to destroy the illusion of the dream-state. We as audiences, perhaps, have become accustomed in most non-horror genre cinema to changes in sound which indicate the fact that we are watching a dream sequence or flashback. Even in some horror films, we are still 'clued in' by sound or visual effects – such as in *28 Days Later* (Danny Boyle, 2002), in which a dream sequence is accompanied by considerable reverb.[3] By not changing from that which we experience throughout the rest of the film, the sound is, in effect, playing with the audience. The sound, then, has a critical role in the construction of reality and of our expectations as an audience of the horror film.

There are, of course, exceptions to this rule in the *Hellraiser* films, noted perhaps only by the perceptive audience. In *Hellraiser VI: Hellseeker,* despite the fact that most of Trevor's dream sequences come unaccompanied by digital signal-processing effects, in several sequences with his wife (a dream-within-a-dream-within-a-dream), there is some additional reverberation added. These additional multi-layered states, then, are identified for the audience as merely the dream within 'reality', rather than taking on the extra level of dreaming. Similarly, in *Hellraiser VII: Deader,* when Amy opens the box (opening the gate to hell), we hear what sounds like an unthreatening musical box, but as the box is opened and the demons come through, the box's music becomes dissonant, indicating a change in state. In another dream sequence, Amy is being held down on a bed while the 'deaders' (those who have been killed and yet still walk the earth) perform rituals to kill her: the voices are heavily choroused with a very unnatural reverb and other effects at this point, and she awakens shortly thereafter in a bathtub. In *Hellraiser V*, the protagonist in a dream sequence—flashback asks if he is dreaming, and, almost like a response, we hear soft tones like a musical box again, or wind chimes, in minor thirds alternating back and forth behind a quiet ethereal choir that drops from major to minor. The box's tinkling minor thirds are similar in timbre to those used in other horror films, such as Goblin's scores for Dario Argento's *Suspiria* (1977) and *Profondo Rosso* [Deep Red] (1975), or Mike Oldfield's *Tubular Bells* (1973), used in *The Exorcist* (William Friedkin, 1973) (see Donnelly, 2005: 102). By calling on what would be familiar references for most horror fans, the sound design signals to the knowing audience what will happen next.

Perhaps the most obvious sonic signifier of the dream-state/reality divide occurs in *Hellraiser VIII* at the very end of the film. Two survivors from the party, Jake and Chelsea, are in a car and we hear some country-rock music as they drive down an open road. When Chelsea looks in the rearview mirror to see the host, the country music stops and cuts abruptly to frightening orchestral music: when he disappears, the country music returns. It appears, in other words, that the sound and music are used in *most* places in the film to reinforce the reality of the event and to confuse the audience into believing it is 'real' (within the narrative of the film) – that 'hearing' is believing – but, in just enough places in the film to confuse us and to keep us guessing about the reality/ dream divide, the distinction between the real and the dreamworld is made evident to us. Even the experienced horror fan, then, is tested by the music and sound design's trickery.

Sonic motifs in *Hellraiser*

Aside from the dream/reality divide trickery, the sound design of the *Hellraiser* films – as much as, or even more than, the music – is critical to the movie's frightening atmosphere, and reflects a mixture of machinery and open cavernous spaces. Violent sound effects are always at the forefront of the mix in the films. At the very start of the original *Hellraiser* script, for instance, the sound design is presented in the script, clearly indicating its importance:[4]

> In darkness, a blood-curdling cacophony: the squeal of unoiled winches, the rasp of hooks and razors being sharpened; and worse, the howl of tormented souls. Above this din one particular victim yells for mercy – a mixture of tears and roars of rage. By degrees his incoherent pleas are drowned out by the surrounding tumult, until without warning his voice pierces the confusion afresh – this time reduced to naked scream.

The scripts for the other *Hellraiser* films in the series are comparable, calling for a combination of the sounds of industrial machinery with cacophonous noise. *Bloodline*'s script is full of sounds of "beating", "rattling chains", "banging", and describes:

> ... a low hellish rumbling on the very edge of perception – like a distant echo of unimaginable machines, indescribably vast and inexpressibly malicious... Horrible low sounds fill the air, like the laboured breathing of some vast asthmatic creature... Incredibly distant, but disturbing, sounds echo up the shaft. Sounds of flame, machinery, and agony.[5]

To have so much description of the sounds written directly into the script indicates their importance to the films, particularly in terms of foreshadowing, mood induction,[6] the creation of the sonic space, and metaphor.

As we have already seen with the musical-box elements described above, the main sound design motifs help to hold all of the *Hellraiser* films together. Other notable recurrent sounds include tolling bells, particularly since they appear right at the start of a few of the films (*Hellraiser I* and *II*, for instance). Of course, tolling bells are associated with death (as used, for instance, in Berlioz's 'March to the Scaffold' from his *Symphonie fantastique*). The tolling bells are used as foreshadowing in most of the sequences in which they appear. In the final *Hellraiser* movie, the opening sequence features a group of teens at a friend's funeral. One says, "I wish I could see him one last time", followed by a heavy tolling bell and organ accompaniment. The audience knows, of course, that she will, indeed, meet with him again.

Similar in its foreshadowing effect is the sound of a heartbeat, first obviously heard under the floorboards in the original *Hellraiser* as the dead Frank is coming back to life. In this case, however, the 'tell-tale heart' is non-diegetic: the character is unaware of the sound, but senses a presence in the room. At other points in both the first and second films in particular, the beating heart returns, and the character appears to be more aware of it, indicating a growing awareness that something is 'not right' with the environment. It is perhaps significant that the cenobite demons also seem to be particularly fond of hearts, either ripping them out of people, or massaging them sexually (*Hellraiser VI*). In one film (*Hellraiser VII*), the heartbeat becomes a piston-like machine sound as the protagonist kills her father. In the same sequence we hear a child screaming, but the sound resembles a pig squeal, having been treated with various digital effects to make it sound mechanical. The mechanization of the human is a recurring element in the films; the cenobites (previously humans), for instance, are accompanied by metal piston sounds in some of the films.

The presence of the cenobites is marked by the same sounds and effects: wind, reverb, low bass strings, tinkly-scrapes, and electricity. The box is always signified by heavy electrostatic sounds, which is significant because we are told it was built in the eighteenth century, by an expert toymaker, of wood. As Paul Théberge in his discussion of Cronenberg's films indicates, a similar merging of organic and mechanical is part of "the privileged conveyor of the power invested in technology... one finds various uses of electricity in the key moments of transformation depicted in the many films associated with the Frankenstein myth" (2003: 138). It could be that Barker (and later directors) intended LeMarchand's box to signify a kind of Pandora's Box of evil, and that by electrifying it – thus suggesting it is a modern technology – he is drawing connections to the Prometheus myth and intimating that the evil in the world is, at least in part, brought about by technology. This point is further suggested in the second film, in which hell is not only full of electricity, but contains what appear to be electricity pylons.

Of course, *Hellraiser* was not the first to create this aesthetic. It is, rather, a far older idea which is worth exploring, particularly since other more recent depictions of hell in films have used similar sonic motifs. *Constantine* (Francis Lawrence, 2005) and *What Dreams May Come?* (Vincent Ward, 1998) offer a more traditional view of hell than that of *Hellraiser*, but use a similar sound design of wind, echoes, deep, heavy rumbling, crashing thunderous sounds, the sound of winches turning, high-pitched squealing, screaming souls, metal clashing and slashing, and ethereal gothic choirs. We can trace this aesthetic back much further, to early literary depictions of hell, to find what we might expect from a hellish world: Virgil's *Aeneid* describes, "From here are to be heard sighs, and savage blows resound: Then the scrape of iron, and dragged chains" (Book VI, lines 557–8, in Steggle, 2001). Dante describes hell as loud and booming: "Such became these foul visages of the demon Cerberus, who so thunders at the souls that they would fain be deaf" (*Inferno*, Canto VI: 32–33). Similar descriptions are found in Milton (see Collins, 2003).

The most well-known sound of hell is probably the "wailing and gnashing of teeth" described in the gospel of Matthew (13:50), the Apocalypse vision of St John, and St Patrick's *Purgatory* (the 1153 vision of the Knight Owen), which is more specific in explaining that the teeth were made of iron (see Gardiner, 1989: 140) – setting a clear precedent for the metallic scraping noises heard throughout the *Hellraiser* films. The Irish monk Tundale's vision of 1149 likewise had a beast made of iron, gnashing teeth, howling souls, the sound of hammering and "singing the song of death" on a forge where "twenty or thirty or a hundred souls were reduced into one mass" (*ibid.*: 173–6). Perhaps the idea of the gnashing of teeth led to the image of the giant

Hellmouth, the cavelike great jaws which would serve as the gate to hell. In the English mystery plays:

> The wide jaws were often hinged and operated with winches and cables so that they could open and close. Smoke, flames, bad smells, and plenty of noise would emerge from within. (Turner, 1993: 116)

The twelfth-century *Mystère d'Adam* specifies chains, clouds of smoke, and the clatter of cauldrons and kettledrums. "Later productions added fireworks, gunpowder, flaming sulphur, cannons, mechanical serpents and toads" (*ibid.*: 114–15). Metallic percussion was clearly omnipresent, as kitchenware (banging on pots and pans) was once used to signify hell in many plays (see Rastall, 1992: 112).

A description of the theatrical panorama 'Satan Arraying His Troops on the Banks of the Fiery Lake, with the Palace of Pandemonium: From Milton', created by Philippe Jacques de Loutherbourg in London in 1782, called the *Eidophusikon*, illustrates the sounds once made to accompany hellish scenes:

> The sounds which accompanied the wondrous picture struck the astonished ear of the spectator as no less than preternatural, for to add a more awful character to peals of thunder and the accompaniments of all the hollow machinery that hurled balls and stones with indescribable rumbling and noise, an expert assistant swept his thumb over the surface of the tambourine which produced a variety of groans that struck the imagination as issuing from infernal spirits. (Turner, 1993: 188)

Clearly important to the sonic conception of hell – and obviously intended to frighten us – is the use of echo, low-pitched rumbling, groaning and wailing, banging metal and other percussion, and the sound of machines. Perhaps the most obvious threatening element is the use of low bass-register sounds, ever-present in horror film. It is likely there are biological, as well as environmental, factors in why we hear low bass associated with threat, terror, fear and doom (Collins, 2003). In nature it is typically the loud thunderous sounds of earthquakes and volcanic eruptions that represent threat. Traditionally, hell has been associated with volcanic areas, which would include the rumble of a tremor, steam from a geyser, unnatural warmth and subterranean life (Hughes, 1968: 159). The early Roman and Greek gods of volcanoes, thunder and fire such as Vulcan/Hephaestos were also associated with smithying, armoury and metalwork – generally, the accoutrements of war. Hephaestos even made his own mechanical helpers to assist him. Significantly, hell's underground location creates sonic associations that would enhance sounds through reverberation and echo (common effects used in the hell scenes of *Hellraiser*), creating large bass-heavy sounds. The hell in *Hellraiser II: Hellbound* is set in an enormously cavernous space of stone, one which also contains chains, pipes, steam, and even electricity pylons.

It seems clear, then, that there is a very long and quite imaginative history of the acoustic environment of hell, and that this sonic conception was a crucial element in descriptions of hell, used to frighten believers. The cacophonous hell-worlds of the past all had very obvious similarities: wailing souls, gnashing iron teeth, kettledrums or cauldrons, metallic percussion, explosions, thunder and rumbling, hissing. These sounds are clearly those most often associated with death and violence, and therefore fitting for hell-worlds. *Hellraiser* continues with this tradition in order to terrify viewers.

Raising hell (in the mix): the division between sound and music

An interesting point of note in the films is the disintegration of the distinction between sound effects and music, particularly in *Hellraiser II* and *V*. Kassabian (2003) discusses a similar case of score/sound design disintegration in *The Cell* (Tarsem Singh, 2000), *The Matrix* and *Tomb Raider* (Simon West, 2001), and links this effect primarily to the impact of videogames. There is indeed a prominence of a similar 'soundclash' in videogames. In games, there is not yet the technology for real-time mixing, and often music, dialogue and sound effects must compete with each other for the middle-range frequencies (Collins, 2007). With nobody at the mixing desk to prioritize the sound events, the result can sometimes be chaotic.

The opportunities opened up by affordable sampling technology and how it relates to changing sound-design aesthetics also come into play in the disintegration of the music/sound divide, as Donnelly argues:

> Technological and aesthetic developments have resulted in the 'musicalising' of sound more generally. Sound designers use musical instruments (synthe- sizers, samplers) and equipment, and now rethink sound design less in terms of a 'realistic' sound mimesis, and more as an aesthetic possibility. (2005: 2)

Of course, a long tradition in the avant-garde's association with science fiction is an equally likely culprit: non-musical sound as part of the score to science-fiction and horror cinema goes back to at least the 1950s. Goldsmith's score for the original *Planet of the Apes* (Franklin J. Schaffner, 1968) immediately comes to mind, as does the BBC Radiophonic Workshop's work on radio plays and television. Interestingly, early slasher films like the original *Texas Chain Saw Massacre* (Tobe Hooper, 1974) similarly adopt a mechanical metaphor in score and sound design. The score, by Tobe Hooper and Wayne Bell, makes the film all the more disturbing, consisting as it does of recurring motifs of strange drones with reverb, scraping, and half-human half-animal groans, closely resembling early work by industrial bands like Throbbing Gristle or Laibach. Electro- static, clanking metal and all of the other recurrent sound motifs discussed above hint at the mechanization process behind the mental instability of the murderous family.

A clear example of this disintegration between sound design and music in *Hellraiser* is the 'Leviathan' scene from *Hellbound* (Figure 12.1), in which metal percussion and scrapes, distorted metal, and bass drums mix. The characters are in the labyrinthine stone structure of hell and the main character, Dr Channard, is just about to realize he has been double-crossed by his lover, Maria. In a cue that is a cross between industrial-noise act Einstürzende Neubauten's cut-up experiment 'Hirnlego' and the sound of an oncoming train,[7] the percussion comes in as a signal to viewers that the head demon is arriving to take Dr Channard's soul. We are told in the script that the roaring thunderous sound is the sound of "Leviathan's breath". Similar trainlike percussive sections are also found in *Hellraiser VII: Deader*. There are several places where the music takes on a militant percussiveness and dissolves the boundary with sound effects, but most clearly when the protagonist kills the father-figure in a dream sequence, and we hear a piston-like train sound accompanied by what could be described as a stylized train whistle.

Sound effects in the films (most especially the last three) are mixed extremely loudly, particularly the sound for the box itself. This is undoubtedly to heighten the tension in the scenes where the box (and thus, hell) appears. To include loud percussive sounds in the music underscore as well as in the sound design, then, is most likely to expand on this effect, to take it to its extremes in shocking or frightening the audience. It is no coincidence that such a blurring of the distinction between music and sound design most commonly occurs in science fiction and horror, rather than other genres of film, as its purpose is clearly to induce fear. As Ribrant argues:

> Sound effects are important for the narration and for creating feelings of tension and horror... All the peak situations in films, scenes with great sentiment, tension or horror utilise effect sounds of various kinds to convey those emotions. The sound score is the emotional score. (1999: 2)

It is particularly percussive sounds that are often central to this impact during suspense and horror scenes: "fast attack sounds loud. Loud sounds are more frightening than soft sounds, and sudden loud sounds are the most frightening of all" (Kelleghan, 1996: np).

Figure 12.1 The 'train sound' in the 'Leviathan' cue from *Hellbound*

Music in hell

The music in the *Hellraiser* films is equally as disparate as the films themselves, ranging from symphonic scores to rock to synthesizer-based metal–techno fusion and trip-hop. Generally, the *Hellraiser* franchise has surprisingly avoided the 'Original Soundtrack' format, with the exception of the one *Hellraiser* soundtrack released as a collection of popular songs, *Hellraiser III: Hell on Earth*. The use of traditional underscore was probably one of the major factors in the popularity of the films, as it helped to keep them more firmly planted in a 'serious' horror genre rather than 'camp', a line which the films threaten to cross at times, particularly, for example, in the musical motif of the Western 'gun-slinger guitar' in *Hellraiser V*, which we hear with the arrival of the sheriff.

Because of the disparate nature of the films and their scores, this section will focus on the orchestral scores of the best-known *Hellraiser* films – the first two – which were both scored by Christopher Young. Young is renowned for his dark music, having scored *Nightmare on Elm Street 2: Freddy's Revenge* (Jack Sholder, 1985), *Species* (Roger Donaldson, 1995), *The Exorcism of Emily Rose* (Scott Derrickson, 2005), and more. Director Tony Randel instructed Young to make the music for *Hellbound* a "celebration of horror".[8] Young hired the Graunke Symphony Orchestra (now known as the Munich Symphony Orchestra), which would later work with Young on *Hider in the House* (1990). Young clearly had some enjoyment composing the music for the *Hellraiser* films, contributing the dissonance and tritones that we would expect from a hellish world, but also interjecting little tricks into the music. In his cue for 'Leviathan' in *Hellbound*, there is a low-pitched chanting sound, using Morse code to spell out 'G-O-D'.

Christopher Young's scores for the first two films are, arguably, the most interesting of the *Hellraiser* scores. In particular, Young makes expert use of silence. There are long periods without music in the films. In fact, the first real blast of music is not until 13 minutes into the first film, when we are introduced to Frank's reincarnated corpse. Incorporated after long periods of silence, the score becomes all the more shocking and contributes to heightening the tension and terror of the film.

Young establishes several motifs and a distinct style for the first two films which would be used on and off in other films of the series, even after he had abdicated his role as composer to those who would score the rest of the series (the lesser-known composers Randy Miller, Daniel Licht, Walter Werzowa, Steve Edwards, Henning Lohner and Lars Anderson). The recurrent motif of the *Hellraiser* cenobite theme (E♭-F, E♭-G♭-F), typically appearing whenever the cenobites arrive, serves the movies well, using a tension created with either low-pitched brass, eerie strings, or ethereal gothic chorus, depending on its location in the films. Young also creates the 'Devil's Horn' motif (Figure 12.2), a heavy, low-brass tolling which recurs throughout the hell scenes as a warning that the demons are about to appear and which resembles the drone of a foghorn. Similar uses of such foghorn-like groaning appear in other films at times of threat, such as *Terminator 2: Judgment Day* (James Cameron, 1991).[9] Likewise, Young

Figure 12.2 The 'Devil's Horn' motif in *Hellbound*

makes clever use of gothic choral aspects reminiscent of requiems, which are also intermittently used in the other film.

Much of the other scores for the *Hellraiser* films are standard horror fare and make reference to other popular horror movies. Of course, a horror film would not be complete without heavy low bass on strings or brass, and high string stabs, resembling those of Bernard Hermann's score for *Psycho* (1960), which are most prominent in *Hellraiser III*, when the lead cenobite Pinhead says, "I'll enjoy making you bleed, and I'll enjoy making you enjoy it." Although now cliché in horror (see *Carrie* [Brian de Palma, 1976], *Halloween* [John Carpenter, 1978], *Poltergeist* [Tobe Hooper, 1982]), such stabbing strings have clear precursors besides *Psycho* (Alfred Hitchcock, 1960). Berlioz's 'Dream of a Witches' Sabbath', for example, has low bass under (albeit more subtle) stabbing strings (approximately 60 seconds in). The ending of Grieg's 'In the Hall of the Mountain King' has similar dramatic stabs, and has also been used in much horror and suspense from *Soylent Green* (Richard Fleischer, 1973), Argento's *Dèmoni* [*Demons*] (1985), to *Needful Things* (Fraser Clarke, 1993). Megatrax, a library music production company for film and television, has one sample they name 'Psychotic Strings', described as "string stabs to sustaining tension", which they categorize as "dramatic", "horror", "intense" and "suspenseful".[10] Philip Tagg likens the use of similar piercing stabs to "unpredictable action and agitation" (2002: 181–2). A more unusual twist – certainly less clichéd – is the interesting use of minor ninth leaps in string stabs in *Hellraiser III*. While straight octave leaps are certainly disturbing in such contexts, having the leap to a minor ninth adds a new dimension of eeriness and dissonance.

Licensed songs and the use of *Hellraiser* in popular music

In addition to underscore, *Hellraiser* also makes use of some pre-recorded music in many of the films. As mentioned, *Hellraiser*'s only non-underscore soundtrack album was released with *Hellraiser III: On Earth*. The album featured mostly late 1980s and early 1990s rock and heavy metal, including tracks by the Soup Dragons, Material Issue, Electric Love Hogs, KMFDM, Triumph, Tin Machine and Chainsaw Kittens. The movie also featured a club scene in which the mid-1980s metal band Armoured Saint played a live set; this spawned a hit song and music video, Motörhead's 'Hellraiser', written by and later re-recorded with Ozzy Osbourne. Motörhead's several tracks in the film (not on the released soundtrack) were released on their *March Or Die* (1994) album. Author Clive Barker even directed the music video for Motörhead's title track, 'Hellraiser'. The mythologies behind the series are made even more explicit in the video, as described by Barker:

> We open on Motorhead's [sic] performance, set [in] a large, cavernous space. Dante-esque, dimly lit with pools of light on the band members and their instruments. As the camera moves around the space, various creatures are revealed, oily bodies shining through their ragged bits of clothing, prosthetic pieces (a claw, a beak etc.) and bandages, stylized make-up all showing that they are THE DAMNED... We cut to a scene of Lemmy and Pinhead in two chairs at a gaming table. Intercutting with performance footage and Hellraiser III footage, we see Lemmy and Pinhead playing cards, drinking.[11]

Other released soundtracks have included at most one or two popular tracks, such as that for *Hellworld*, featuring two songs by industrial-rock act Celldweller, a band whose music also ended up on the soundtracks to similarly dark films like *Doom* (Andrzej Bartkowiak, 2005), *Constantine*, and *The Punisher* (Jonathan Hensleigh, 2004), though most of the *Hellraiser* movies have only been released as symphonic scores.

It probably comes as no surprise that a movie thematically dealing with hell and death would choose heavy metal as its spokesperson, considering metal's long history of using hellish imagery.[12] And the industrial music songs – while characteristically containing less hellish imagery – are certainly related in their expression of anger and lyrical fondness for science-fiction worlds. As previously mentioned, the industrial band Coil was originally contracted to score the first *Hellraiser* movie. It was allegedly felt that the score was not appealing enough (or too scary) for a mainstream audience, and it was abandoned.[13] It has been suggested that Coil themselves inspired Barker to pen the *Hellraiser* stories, which would certainly explain the mechanical motifs in the films.

Industrial musicians have always had a fondness for the films, as is evidenced by the now clichéd use of samples from the movies. Front Line Assembly, for instance, used a few samples from *Hellraiser III: Hell on Earth* on their song 'Surface Patterns' (from the album *Reclamation*), as well as on the song 'Comatose' (from *Flavour Of The Weak*), and also sampled *Hellraiser VI* on 'Predator' (*ibid.*). Another industrial artist, Suicide Commando, sampled the first *Hellraiser* film's famous last line, on 'Jesus Wept' and 'Raise Your God' on the album *Mindstrip* (2000), and again on 'See You In Hell' (from their *Anthology*). The film was further sampled by Velvet Acid Christ, Project-X and many others before the overuse of sampling the film became too common for a genre that prides itself on ingenuity. Why the movies became a cliché in the industrial scene is probably related to a number of factors, including the fashion stylistic links between the leather-and-metal-clad cenobites and the thematic narrative elements of death and 'hell on Earth' presented in the films, as well as the dystopian sentiment common to industrial rock (see Collins, 2002), or simply the fact that Coil — an icon in the scene — was Barker's vision of what he would have preferred for the music. This would seem to fit with the mechanical motifs that did get included in many of the *Hellraiser* scores.

Conclusion

The use of sound and music in the *Hellraiser* films illustrates the changing attitudes towards sound design in film in general. Sound design is no longer just for 'real sounds', or the creation of a realistic world, but is becoming more of a creative aspect of film-making. As with the musical functions in film, the sound serves to heighten our fear and psychologically disturb us. In particular, the very physical aspect of sound in the films is influential in disturbing the viewer. As Donnelly argues:

> Music in horror films often attempts a direct engagement with the physical: for example, through the use of the very high (like the stabbing strings in the shower scene of Psycho) or the low (deep stingers or drones). These are not merely extremes of pitch, but are also tied to the intrinsic sounds of the human body. (2005: 105)

The same could be said for sound: the low thunderous rumbling, the metallic percussion, the flutter of wings, the beating of hearts, etc., all help to create a whole aesthetic which impacts upon the listener/viewer physically.

Not only do the sound and music impact upon us physically, but, as has been shown, the sound also affects us psychologically and perhaps intellectually through the use of metaphor. The mechanical metaphor gives us suggestions of cause (technology) and effect (hell) in the film. While such metaphors may work on a subconscious level for most viewers, perhaps after repeated viewings of similar movies (or all eight of the *Hellraiser* films) some will make connections between the sound and what it implies. The score and the sound, then, are in a sense carriers of an unannounced narrative, one which works not on a conscious level, but on a subconscious one — the level most disturbed by horror. Perhaps in itself, being unable to distinguish acoustically between the two also carries a particularly disturbing effect. The music takes on some of the roles of the sound design, and vice versa, and both, then, should be thought of perhaps not as distinct entities, but as partners in the creation of a particular sonic aesthetic.

Notes

1. Composer credits for the films are as follows: *Hellraiser* (Christopher Young); *Hellbound: Hellraiser II* (Christopher Young); *Hellraiser III: Hell on Earth* (Randy Miller); *Hellraiser IV: Bloodline* (Daniel Licht); *Hellraiser V: Inferno* (Walter Werzowa); *Hellraiser VI: Hellseeker* (Steve Edwards); *Hellraiser VII: Deader* (Henning Lohner); *Hellraiser VIII: Hellworld* (Lars Anderson). UK artists Coil were asked to produce a soundtrack for one movie, but the songs were never included.

2. The chess-game idea, made famous in Ingmar Bergman's film *Det sjunde inseglet* [The Seventh Seal] (1957), has been a theme throughout many centuries. Bergman himself was said to have been inspired by a fifteenth-century fresco in Stockholm.

3. However, in this case there is no attack sequence on the character, only a sense of abandonment, and so the tension created by the dream-state confusion is less important.

4. The film's script is available online (http://www.cenobite.com/library/, accessed 3 January 2006).

5. The film's script is available online (http://www.cenobite.com/library/, accessed 3 January 2006).

6. I borrow the term "mood induction" from Cohen (2001: 15), who cites Rosar in explaining the difference between emotional functions of film scores: "Mood induction changes how one is feeling, while communication of meaning simply conveys information. One may receive information depicting sadness without him or herself feeling sad."

7. Available on the CD *Haus Der Lüge* (1989), Rough Trade Deutschland.

8. See http://www.moviemusicuk.us/hellr2cd.htm, accessed 5 January 2006.

9. For more on this motif, see Collins (2003).

10. Online at http://www.megatrax.com/download/megatraxcatalog.pdf, accessed 5 May 2006.

11. Online at http://www.clivebarker.dial.pipex.com/hellmotorhead.html, accessed 6 January 2006.

12. See Walser (1993) or Halfyard (Chapter 10, this volume).

13. See online (http://www.brainwashed.com/common/htdocs/discog/coil1.html, accessed 1 May 2006).

References

Attali, J. (1996), *Noise: The Political Economy of Music*, Minneapolis: Minnesota University Press.

Cohen, A. J. (2001), 'Music as a Source of Emotion in Film', in P. N. Juslin and J. A. Sloboda (eds), *Music and Emotion: Theory and Research*, Oxford: Oxford University Press, pp. 249–79.

Collins, K. (2002), 'The Future Is Happening Already: Industrial Music and the Aesthetic of the Machine', PhD thesis, University of Liverpool.

Collins, K. (2003), 'I'll Be Back: Recurrent Sonic Motifs in the *Terminator* Films', in P. Hayward (ed.), *Off the Planet: Music, Sound and Science Fiction Cinema*, Eastleigh, Hampshire: John Libbey Publishing, pp. 165–75.

Collins, K. (2007), 'An Introduction to the Participatory and Non-linear Aspects of Video Games Audio', in S. Hawkins and J. Richardson (eds), *Essays on Sound and Vision*, Helsinki: Helsinki University Press, pp. 263–98.

Dante (2002), *Inferno*, trans. M. Musa, Harmondsworth: Penguin Classics.

Donnelly, K. J. (2005), *The Spectre of Sound: Music in Film and Television*, London: BFI Publishing.

Evans, M. (2004), 'Mapping *The Matrix*: Virtual Spatiality and the Realm of the Perceptual', in P. Hayward (ed.), *Off the Planet: Music, Sound and Science Fiction Cinema*, Eastleigh, Hampshire: John Libbey Publishing, pp. 188–98.

Gardiner, E. (1989), *Visions of Heaven and Hell Before Dante*, New York: Italica Press.

Gracyk, T. (1996), *Rhythm and Noise: An Aesthetics of Rock*, Durham, NC: Duke University Press.

Hughes, R. (1968), *Heaven and Hell in Western Art*, London: Weidenfeld and Nicolson.

Kassabian, A. (2003), 'The Sound of a New Film Form', in I. Inglis (ed.), *Popular Music and Film*, London: Wallflower, pp. 91–101.

Kelleghan, F. (1996), 'Sound Effects in Sci-Fi and Horror Films', Presentation given at the International Conference on the Fantastic in the Arts (online at http://www.filmsound.org).

Milton, J. (1989), *Paradise Lost*, Harmondsworth: Penguin Classics.

Rastall, R. (1992), 'The Sounds of Hell', in C. Davidson and T. H. Seiler (eds), *The Iconography of Hell*, Ann Arbor: Western Michigan University Press, pp. 102–31.

Ribrant, G. (1999), *Style Parameters in Film Sound*, Stockholm: Universitet Filmvetenskapliga Institutionen (available online at http://www.filmsound.studienet.org/bibliography/stylepara.pdf; accessed 10 October 2001).

Rosar, W. H. (2001), 'The *Dies Irae* in *Citizen Kane*: Musical Hermeneutics Applied to Film Music', in K. J. Donnelly (ed.), *Film Music: Critical Approaches*, Edinburgh: Edinburgh University Press, 103–16.

Sonnenschein, D. (2001), *Sound Design: The Expressive Power of Music, Voice and Sound Effects in Cinema*, Studio City, CA: Michael Wiese Productions.

Steggle, M. (2001), 'Paradise Lost and the Acoustics of Hell', in *Early Modern Literary Studies*, 7(1), 1–17 (online at http://www.shu.ac.uk/emls/07-1/stegmil2.htm, accessed 12 April 2006).

Tagg, P. (2002), *Kojak: 50 Seconds of Television Music: Toward the Analysis of Affect in Popular Music*, New York: Mass Media Music Scholars' Press.

Théberge, P. (2003), '"These are my nightmares": Music and Sound in the Films of David Cronenberg', in P. Hayward (ed.), *Off the Planet: Music, Sound and Science Fiction Cinema*, Eastleigh, Hampshire: John Libbey Publishing, pp. 129–48.

Turner, A. K. (1993), *The History of Hell*, New York: Harcourt Brace & Co.

Walser, R. (1993), *Running with the Devil: Power, Gender, and Madness in Heavy Metal Music*, Hanover, NH: Wesleyan University Press.

13 Spooked by Sound
The Blair Witch Project

Rebecca Coyle

> *"It was like there were two separate noises coming from two layers of space over here, and one of them was kinda like... an owl but the other one was like a cackling."* (Joshua Leonard, in *The Blair Witch Project*)

> *The sound is the most crucial part* [of *The Blair Witch Project*]. *We hardly show anything on the video. The actors aren't even on screen most of the time we hear them talk. BW is like a radio drama, really.*[1]

The Blair Witch Project (hereafter *BWP*) is a noisy film despite the near-absence of music or standard suddenly shocking horror sounds. This low-budget film, directed by Daniel Myrick and Eduardo Sànchez (1999), draws on dialogue, foley and location sound for its effect. Indeed, it is through its approach to and connections with the 'horror' elements that the film builds its affective impact. This chapter investigates how sound and music are tied into the narrative in *BWP*. I will analyse a selection of key scenes and their sonic elements to discuss the ways by which sound is used to situate, identify and enhance horrifying events that are not necessarily represented on-screen.

All horror movies use suspense techniques to create tension and/or excitement and play with the device of building up through suggestion, then delivering acts, images and sounds of graphic fright or horror. Some films are explicit in their horrific elements, and rely on frequent and/or prolonged use of shock scenes. Other films are more suggestive, relying primarily on the imagined rather than the evident and/or the continual deferral of the explicit. *BWP* is one of the latter and is significant for building its horror effect through an audio-visual text that (all but) eschews the use of non-diegetic music, relying instead on image and sound apparently recorded together *in situ* and on other elements of the audio track.[2]

My broader aim in this investigation is to explore the power of the soundtrack despite the lack of reference to sound and music in the majority of critical writings about the film.[3] *BWP* features sounds operating as signposts for unseen elements, thereby leaving the action open to an imagined event, unspecified places and an emotional response. Corbett argues that, by its very nature, sound can be exploited for this capacity:

> The way we in the West have learned to view ourselves and the world is through the lens of objectivity aided and abetted by a cultural hermeneutic steeped in the visual traditions of linear geometry and perspective... Vision guarantees knowability because seeing bestows permanence. Sound and hearing can offer no such certainty because we are immersed in it. (2003: 272–3)

Nevertheless, despite Sànchez's retrospective claim for the significance of the sound (quoted in the epigraph to this chapter), this was not originally an entirely conscious strategy on the part of the directors:

> We knew that the sound was going to be a major element of the film, but we never imagined that so much of the action would take place there. We just knew it was going to be very minimal and completely realistic.

In this chapter I will argue that it is the uncertainty generated by the sound that creates suspense and the impression of lack of control in *BWP*, thereby marking key elements as 'spooky' to the point of horrifying. My use of the term 'spooky' is deliberate; indeed, my discussion of the term serves to re-emphasize its historic usage rather than the more superficially scary sense in which it has been used more recently. *BWP* is spooky in two senses of the term, presenting the object of horror both as a 'spook' (an invisible spectre or ghost) and as one that 'spooks' the characters (causing nervous anxiety and extreme behavioural responses). The film – and, more importantly, its box-office success – illustrates the manner by which sound can convey and create narrative tension and dread (that is, without music) and, as such, it offers a significant case study of such an approach.

Narrative outline

The *BWP* storyline can be told in one sentence. In 1994, three student film-makers become lost, never to return from the woods of Burkittsville, Maryland, while making a documentary about witchcraft rituals and the Blair Witch folk-story.[4] While that may be the central storyline of the film, it is the conceit of the film as a 'pseudo-documentary' that provides the core of its impact. The film and video footage supposedly shot by the students is discovered one year later under a dilapidated house in the woods, and a production company (Haxan Films[5]) edits it into a documentary that tells the story of their encounters in the woods and the mysterious disappearance of Josh, the trio's cameraman. The film is structured around eight days and eight nights. The footage abruptly ends when the remaining two characters, seeking answers to the strange sounds and events they have experienced, enter the woodland house and are attacked by an unseen assailant.

The tension of *BWP*'s narrative development is led by anticipation of the students' disappearance, announced at the film's outset. The film's momentum is aided by set-up interviews and preparations, as the trio record leaving their homes, gathering film gear (a 16-mm film camera, Hi-8 video camera and DAT sound recorder), purchasing supplies for three days of camping, arriving at Burkittsville and conducting vox-pop interviews with townsfolk. This sequence of daytime 'normality' is represented in reasonably straightforward to-camera reports and street interviews (shot in colour with sharp lighting and focus) that hint at weirdness through accounts of strange occurrences. Interviewees relate the stories of Elly Kedward, who was accused of witchcraft and banished from the Blair village in the late 1700s, after which village children mysteriously disappeared, and of Rustin Parr, who lived in the woods and, supposedly under the influence of witchcraft, killed children from Burkittsville in the 1940s. The film-makers also visit 'crazy' Mary Brown at her trailer home, who relates her childhood encounter with the witch in the woods.

We do not see anything 'scary' in these sequences (and there are tongue-in-cheek references to the sanitized supernatural in the Halloween ghost cut-outs pasted on the window of the village shop). Rather, the spookiness is suggested by verbal story alone, a point registered by one interviewee's child who tries to hush her mother as she tells of strange happenings in the woods. Eventually the student film-makers drive to the woods to track down evidence of historical events, such as an unmarked graveyard. They leave their car on the road, collect camping gear and film a couple of scenes near their entry point. As they move further into the woods, "things immediately start to unravel", as Taylor (1999) outlines:

> The map Heather relies on leads the three in circles, and her insistence on filming everything, including the trio's arguments, exacerbates the tension. Soon they're awoken in the middle of the night by the sounds of children screaming. Strange piles of rocks and stick figures made out of branches are left outside their tent. Shortly after Josh finds his belongings strewn over their campsite, he disappears. A few days later, Heather finds a bundle made of torn strips of Josh's shirt with an unidentified piece of bloody viscera inside. With food and hope gone, Heather and Mike stumble on a house in the woods. (1999: np)

The Blair Witch Project as horror film

BWP has achieved both major profits and cult status. Reputedly made on a budget of just $US35,000, the film earned nearly $US30 million on its first weekend of general release and, after two months, became the highest-grossing independent film (to that time), earning more than $US140 million worldwide (Harris, 2001: 75). While the film was certainly produced on a relatively small budget, its initial box-office success was due in large part to a highly contrived marketing and promotion campaign that reputedly cost around $US15 million and was conducted by Haxan Films and the distributor Artisan Entertainment (*ibid.*: 97). According to Harris, within hours of the original film screening at the Sundance Film Festival in January 1999, Artisan purchased the distribution rights. The deal with the distributor included a remix of the soundtrack and an ambitious marketing package. Two elements that drove the marketing and critical debate around *BWP* were the film's pseudo-documentary approach and its particular address to the horror-film genre.

Prior to its screenings at the 1999 Sundance, Cannes and other film festivals, samples of the film had been aired and discussed on television (*Split Screen* in 1997) and a 'special' interrogating the Blair Witch legend was aired on the Sci-Fi Channel cable network a few days before the film's initial limited release (*ibid.*: 79). In addition, a crucial contributor to the marketing in the lead up to and follow-on from the film's release was its internet site (www.blairwitch.com). Official websites for feature films have become standard in promotional campaigns since the early 1990s but the internetworking "word of mouse" (Wells, 2001: 110)[6] exploited for the marketing of *BWP* made a considerable impact on such strategies into the 2000s.[7] Artisan collaborated with the directors to include more fictional items such as police reports, interviews with the students' parents, fake historical documentation and other material supporting the back-story of the film. This material was also used in an eponymous book by D. A. Stern published by Boxtree/Macmillan in 1999. Paul Wells notes that these elements enhanced "the credentials of the film" and authenticated the idea that "the viewer is within a world, not observing one, and that this kind of horror is about a personal dread rather than a shared knowledge of motifs and generic norms" (2000: 110).

The most significant storyline element exploited by Artisan was the 'truth claim' of the film. This is suggested from the outset, as, instead of a fiction film-styled opening credit sequence, Artisan suggested to the film-makers that the film commence with an on-screen statement ('crawl') claiming the subsequent footage to be compiled from original student material. The end credits do not debunk this impression, merely crediting the writing, directing and editing to Myrick and Sànchez. Artisan and Haxan persisted with the promotion of the film as documentary, as Harris meticulously details (2001: 78–9).[8] Many critics appear to have bought the hype and negatively dissected it in terms of whether the 'real' events depicted were frightening and how such effect was achieved.[9]

These elements came together to create what Harris (after William Warner) has called a "media event", that is, a media production generating interest that "feeds upon itself", triggering "repetitions and simulations" as well as critical commentary and interpretation (2001: 76).[10] One factor contributing to the media event was the soundtrack CD, *The Blair Witch Project: Josh's Blair Witch Mix*, released in July 1999 and promoted as the mix tape devised as road music for the trio's trip that was found in Josh's car.[11] The CD includes well-known tracks by Lydia Lunch, Public Image Ltd, the Creatures and others[12] but also shows a self-reflexive reference by including the original music track (entitled 'The Cellar') by Antonio Cora (detailed below) used in the final scene of the film. In lyrical content, the tracks support the film's witchcraft theme but the inclusion of several tracks that employ an experimental approach to instrumentation, sound and voice supports the sound-design approach in the film. In addition, the CD's songs segue into extracts of dialogue from significant film scenes, thereby creating, according to Barron, "a 'virtual' soundtrack independent of the original film" (2003: 160).

One of BWP's distinct aspects is that it deviates from prior horror-film genre conventions by aligning with the victims in cinematography and sound and eschewing on-screen violence. The affective sonic and musical textures in BWP are reminiscent of some of the industrial and electronically manipulated sounds composed by Wayne Bell and Tobe Hooper for the house scenes in The Texas Chain Saw Massacre (Tobe Hooper, 1973).[13] Yet the avoidance of overt body mash scenes sets BWP apart from the visceral 'splatter' emphasis of the earlier film, and many films influenced by it. BWP's scenes oscillate between monochrome and muted colours, with dim camera lighting emphasizing grainy, barely distinguishable (and therefore highly suggestive) objects.[14]

The major part of the film moves through a limited range of locations, including the woods by day and by night, the overgrown and informal cemetery, alongside a stream, inside the tent and around the campfire. A visible, on-screen 'monster' as identified in Cosimo Urbano's model of representational strategies used in the modern horror film is not provided (Urbano, 1998). Indeed, there is some confusion as to whether the monster the trio seeks is the so-called Blair Witch or a ghostly Rustin Parr. We hear from the vox-pops about the 'monster', imagined or real, and we rely on this spoken characterization to create an image in the mind's eye. The absence of a configured monstrous suggests that, despite their documentary pretence, the film-makers wanted to avoid a considered address to broader themes, such as, in Lindemann's terms:

> the nature of terror and the terror of nature... the powerful allure of witch stories and the cultural compulsion to label certain types of (usually female) deviant behavior as witchery, a threat to social order, to bodily integrity, and to life itself. (2000: 758)

Rather, as Wells argues:

> [BWP] essentially [recovers] 'suggestion' and 'allusion' in the horror film, and with them the idea that the most persuasive horror is the one suggested in the mind of the viewer, rather than that which is explicitly expressed on the screen. (2000: 108–9)

Psychologically spooked

BWP has been marketed as a horror film: the film's DVD sleeve includes a claim from Entertainment Weekly that it is "one of the creepiest films since The Exorcist". However, BWP is primarily a study of student team dynamics and a psychological test of character under pressure, "an exploration of how casual alliances and untested self-confidence can collapse under stress".[15] This is indicated by the lack of a visible 'monster' but also in terms of the perspective adopted in the sound mix. The recorded sound frequently privileges the character closest to the camera, consistent with the sound priority of directional hand-held or camcorder microphones. Added to this, the heightened aggravation and breakdown of team dynamics is heard in changes in conversational tone, reflecting the increasingly stressful situation and the characters' developing panic.

The anticipation and suspense is enhanced by the fact that those images designed to scare us are not overly horrific: piles of rocks and stick figures in trees. Rather these are used cumulatively to establish a spooky context. The dim lighting, black-and-white footage and scenes featuring intermittent and lengthy moments of black screen or almost total darkness all rely on sound and sonic reaction to create an effect. Furthermore, in fact we do not actually hear the 'sound' of the witch: we are merely told about the cackling Josh claims to hear (as quoted at the start of this chapter). Rather than the witch having her own sound profile, we hear those affected by 'her', for example, children crying and Josh calling. Applying Andrew Crisell's terms for radio sounds, the *BWP* sounds are indexical, that is, "a form of signification which exists 'out there' in the real world" (1986: 47). Yet the sounds in *BWP* are not matched to 'real' images. We believe that there is something 'out there' because sound is being created. As Crisell notes, while sound on radio – and indeed on film audio-track – is iconic insofar as it is a reproduction or contrived interpretation of the 'original' sound, it is most often used to "manifest the presence of something else" (*ibid.*). Without matching images, rather than diluting the impact of the spooky scenes, the sound offers its own layer of horror. In his work on war and cinema, Paul Virilio (1989) contends that technologies that enable sight can remove us from the action. In *BWP*, we are shown the effects of the invisible but sonically marked antagonist, such as Josh's body part wrapped in a scrap of his checked shirt – possibly the most conventionally 'horror' element in the film. However, the monstrous form overall is left to our imagination, rendered by sound stimulation.

Sound elements are therefore essential in enhancing the psychological spooking. *BWP* features few generically scary scenes. Indeed, the unseen is as important as the on-screen images. For night-time scenes in the tent, we expect to see horror but we don't. Rather, low-resolution, dark scenes picture the inside of the tent (as Heather obsessively documents their film-making process). Without screen images, we strain to create images in our heads via other means: we experience the film through sound. Sequences of "impenetrable darkness" (Pomerance, 2004: 8) are too long for our eye to make the leap between one image and the next, and it is left to the ear to make that connection. In this scenario, gaps in sound are palpable – not silence as such, but in the sense Balázs notes: "we feel silence when we can hear the most distant sound or the slightest rustle near us" (1985: 118). Crisell argues that in radio, noises and silence "use time, not space, as their major structuring agent" (1986: 45). Silence (or the absence of obvious sound) is used as a framing mechanism and also, beyond a certain duration, to convey dysfunction, 'dead air' (*ibid.*: 56). This is not the case for film sound that uses the placement of sound in space as importantly to locate the characters and the viewer in the action. Corbett notes that "sound offers ambiguity and the possibility of space travel (from inside to outside and back again)" (2003: 273). Audiences perceive visuals and sound differently, not as competing but working together. The highly regarded Hollywood sound designer/editor Walter Murch is cited by Fiona Kelleghan as arguing that, in film, "The eyes are the front door, and the ears are the back door" (1996: np). However, it is sound that drives the narrative for much of the action in *BWP*.

Sound production

Stylistically, the majority of the sound relates to the handheld camera work and the impression that it is all location sound. Insofar as the film purports to be filmed without contrived sets, special effects and complex camera work, it has been aligned with the Dogme 95 manifesto.[16] Devised by a collective of film-makers in Copenhagen in 1995, and generally associated with the films of Lars von Trier, the manifesto claims to challenge conventional film language by drawing on 'authentic' or uncontrived sound, lighting, *mise-en-scène*, make-up and sets. For *BWP* the student film-makers are played by actors using their own names – Heather Donahue (director), Joshua Leonard (camera) and Michael Williams (sound). The actual film-makers adopted a version of what might be called method film-making. Provided with film, video and DAT recorders plus provisions for a week, the actors were required to shoot the footage themselves based on daily instructions that outlined general events but required them to improvise the action and ad-lib the dialogue.[17] As a way of maintaining emotional intensity, Taylor reports that the directors induced fear in the actors by 'spooking' them at night: playing tapes of children screaming; leaving unexpected objects outside their tents; and for the climactic scene, "having camouflaged crew members leap out of the darkness to grab Heather" (Taylor, 1999: 1).[18]

The actors were given instructions on how to use the various recorders just prior to entering the woods and Sànchez argues that this assisted in realizing 'student-like' audio and visual footage. Consequently, as Goldman notes, "many of the film scenes are grainy and poorly lit, many of the video scenes shake wildly and are hard to follow, and audio quality varies from scene to scene".[19] The footage was shot in just eight days but editing took six months, as 20 hours of film and video footage were edited to 87 minutes of final film release.

For the Artisan remix, the audio track was highly manipulated at the Wilshire Stages in Los Angeles. Indeed, despite Myrick's statements that all the audio came from the camcorder's microphone or a DAT recorder used by the actors, additional sounds were provided, for example, in the foley mix (later credited to foley artist Shawn Kennelly[20]). Myrick reports:

The mixing people cleaned up a lot of very raw audio and really took the film to a new level... We told them to go ahead and add things, but it had to be in keeping with the sensibility of the film. They really understood what we were going for, and so they were able to add background ambient noise like crickets, cracking sticks, wind, and other things that really help the film. (quoted in Goldman, see note 18)

These sounds added a significantly rich layer of contextual sound to the location recordings. The Dogme 95 'vow of chastity' included a prohibition on extra-diegetic music: "The sound must never be produced apart from the images or vice versa. (Music must not be used unless it occurs where the scene is being shot.)"[21] Nevertheless, soundtrack processing/design seems to have fallen outside the prohibition, perhaps illustrating how rarely soundtrack is consciously perceived and/or perceived as manipulated.[22]

Spooky sounds

Discussing sound design for horror film, Kelleghan argues that:

Though horror films can feature supernatural creatures and events, ironically enough what they need is an uncomplicated sound that will disturb the audience viscerally rather than interest them intellectually. You might think I'm talking about sound effect libraries [using specialist sounds]... soundtracks do use these. But they also use much more mundane sounds. (1996)

The establishing scenes that open the film (and are rarely mentioned in reviews) draw on relatively standard contextualizing sounds behind the dialogue: music in the car and in a café, church bells and traffic noise, chirpy birdsong as the trio first approach the woods (and muted as they move further in). The camping scenes rely on reaction sounds made by the characters (and foley), for example, heavy breathing, sharp intakes of breath, exclamations, frantic rustling. Dialogue also serves several functions, for example, it draws our attention to exterior sound and remarks on the protagonists' experiences of it and how they feel about it: "it's all around us", "on all sides of us", "Jesus Christ, what the fuck is that?", "but it sounds like footsteps", "whatever that was last night sounds like the same fuckin' thing". Significantly though (and unlike radio), the dialogue does not explain or signpost the sounds but in fact enhances its scary component by remarking on its unknown/unseen source.

The focus on the student protagonists adopted by location sound is overlaid by 'external' sounds strategically placed around them. Theo van Leeuwen argues that "sound is dynamic: it can move us towards or away from a certain position, it can change our relation to what we hear" (1999: 18). Van Leeuwen suggests a model for describing how perspective is used to divide simultaneous sounds into groups, and place these groups at different distances from the listener "so as to make the listener relate to them in different ways" (*ibid.*). Following Walter Murch, and adopting Murray

Table 13.1

Layers of sound	Figure	Ground	Field
BWP Woods Sounds	Breathing, voices, foley, tent zipper	Spooky cries, calls, cracking sticks	Wind, birds, crickets

Schafer's terms, van Leeuwen identifies three layers of sound, namely, figure, ground and field. Figure is "the most important sound… which the listener must identify with, and/or react to and/or act upon"; the ground layer provides those sounds in the listener's social world, familiar sounds that are provided as "context we take for granted" (*ibid.*);[23] and field sounds are those in the listener's broader physical world, the background.

Applied to *BWP*, the breathing, close-miked voices and foley sounds tell us about characters' responses to the situation and operate at the figure layer (see Table 13.1). Ground sounds occur in the external environment, where the protagonists respond to specific 'spooky' cries and calls that intervene in the narrative and force them to strain to hear and identify what they signify. The external physically contextualizing sounds, like the street sounds in the opening sequence and the wind, water and birds in the woods,[24] offer the field layer that we, along with the characters, take for granted. In horror films, generic sonic signifiers are commonly used, such as high-pitched music to build fear, fast attack sounds to cause a jump-out-of-seat impact, and synthesized effects for otherworldly sounds that have no real-world equivalent. If these are the standard techniques used to generate fear, then how does *BWP* operate? Human fear is indicated by rapid breathing, exclamations, effects like the tent zipper sound and foley audio-like scratching on the tent interior. This is particularly evident in the third night-camping scene.

At this point, the students agree not to burn a fire or show any lights, arguing that the creepy events of the last two nights may be linked to evidence of their woodland presence. In the dark, Heather is woken by distant voices; there is noisy breathing and scrabbling amongst whispers to "get the DAT ready". The tent is rocked around by an exterior force; the students shout and cry out, then leave the tent in panic. Interspersed with lengthy stretches of black, we catch glimpses of their figures, lit by the camera lights, fleeing the scene, as well as shots of grass and woods. All frantically hyperventilating, they hold a whispered conversation in which they agree to wait for daylight before returning to the campsite. There they find their belongings scattered, Josh's pack is missing and his gear covered in slime. Mike loses his temper as Heather continues to film their reactions, the camera is dislodged and we learn from the vocal exclamations that Heather bites him as he tries to grab the camera. The sequence concludes with shaky camerawork as Mike straps up his wrist. As in other scenes, but particularly here, sound is employed as narrative continuity, leading our comprehension of the fractured and discontinuous image flow.

Apart from the choice of sounds, placement of them in the sound space is critical. We hear the detail of the sounds in the context of sound design, from perspectives on the horizontal plane (near and far), and drawing on frequency range (whispering in the high-frequency figure layer with low-pitched wind as background) to provide a sonically 'full' and rich environment. In addition, Corbett notes: "We do not just hear sounds, we make them as well" (2003: 273). When Josh discovers his scattered belongings, he becomes agitated and frets about how he will cope with a further night of frightening events. Heather tries to reassure him by arguing that the "monster" will not follow them, that "this is America… and it's not possible – we've destroyed most of our natural resources", denying a connection between the witch or the spooky events and the natural environment. Josh responds by singing the line "America! America! God shed his grace on thee" from 'America the Beautiful' (a patriotic song written in 1893 by Katharine Lee Bates, who was inspired by the idea of the American landscape as rural idyll). Mike and Josh proceed on their trek through the woods singing lines from the US national anthem 'The Star-spangled Banner', using sound to reassure themselves that a higher power (the USA nation-state, perhaps?) will overcome unnamed terrors in the wild.

Sonic resolution

Added to the sounds discussed above, vocal tone and intensity (as in conversations and reactions to events) are affective audio elements. The harshness in their addresses to each other is amplified as the protagonists become more terrified and this builds to vocal hysteria that takes the form of screaming in the final sequence. Corbett observes that:

> We Moderns demand to know where a sound comes from – to see it with our own theoretically disembodied eye. With the assurance of sight, sound is rendered visible and effectively silenced. (2003: 33)

In BWP's closing sequence, sound (song) draws the viewer and the actors into the action, but the visible is never actually provided for us and the film closes with an unresolved jolt. Without clearly resolved images, the sound retains a principal and prominent narrative function.

The final scene is preceded and set up by a to-camera monologue in which Heather admits responsibility for the disastrous fallout from the student film shoot. The impact of Heather's apology is in her self-doubt that heightens audience engagement with the personality breakdown occurring on-screen. Heather's admission of management error has been foreshadowed sonically: several scenes earlier, Josh taunted her by singing a snatch of the Gilligan's Island television series theme song (written by George Wyle and Sherwood Schwartz). Heather responds with assurance that, "This ship has a good captain", referring to Josh, while ironically analogizing herself with the often-bumbling crewman Gilligan (although, as director, she is actually team leader).

In her later monologue, Heather directly addresses the camera. With lighting from below and awkward framing to reveal only one-quarter of her pale and red-nosed face, she speaks with tears forming and nose running. Vocally, she whispers close to the microphone so we hear all the detail of the bodily performance as she cries and sniffs her halting confession:

> I just want to apologize to Josh's mom, and Mike's mom, and my mom – I am so sorry! Because it was my fault. I was the one who brought them here. I was the one that said, 'keep going south'. I was the one who said that we were not lost. It was my fault, because it was my project. I am so scared! I don't know what's out there. We are going to die out here! I am so scared!

The impact of the scene derives from its marking the situation as now out of control. The character that seems to be set up, in Clover's horror-film formulation, as the 'final girl' hero with whom we have aligned ourselves as a non-victim, is reduced to a feminized anti-hero (1992: 35). This provides a suitable narrative context for the film climax. Despite its foreshadowing at the film's outset, the final scene is still a surprise. It occurs very suddenly, highlighted by the slow build-up leading to the abrupt conclusion that suggests the 'monster' is still present (and the possibility of a sequel). Furthermore, the final scene does not end well for either of the characters, thereby avoiding the emotional comfort connected with an identified survivor.

After Heather records her farewell, Mike and Heather emerge from the tent with two cameras as they hear calls from outside. It is dark and images shot by the characters are randomly lit by their camera lights as they move towards the sound, their movement indicated by camera shake and by sounds of footsteps scrunching twigs and swishing through grass. As they discover the dilapidated house, the calls from Josh identify them by name, although his location is indeterminate. Heather follows Mike through the house, calling to him not to go too fast. The cameras show only flashes of the characters as the student film-makers swing them around the house detritus, and the edited footage is alternately in colour and monochrome. They find a staircase and move upwards, only to be 'called' down. Mike runs downstairs calling that he is coming, Heather panics that she can't see Mike and screams hysterically as she pursues him down to the cellar. Finally, we hear a thump and Mike's camera falls to the floor. Heather descends to the cellar, frantically calling and crying, and discovers Mike standing with his face in the corner.[25] There is another thump and we are left with a blurry picture after the camera is dropped on the floor.

Tony Cora's music emerges from the hissy clicking sound of the camera that continues to roll. We hear what sounds like rocks or stones being piled together in a highly reverberant musical concoction. Rumbling strings fade up and a deep bass drone increases in volume, then combines with metal pipe clangs and a highly resonating tapping sound like that produced inside a silo. Sànchez recalls that he and Myrick instructed Cora to produce a sound cue that would not "betray" the film that preceded it: "We wanted it to be dark and fucked up, with no recognizable instruments in the mix. We said something like the soundtrack of a journey into hell. Organic. Nasty."[26] Continuing over the end credits, this music and its highly reverberant quality suggest a mechanized soundscape of events that occur beyond the control of the protagonists and at a supernatural level.

Conclusion

In his discussion of horror-film effects, Urbano argues that:

> ... although music and sound are absolutely necessary to [horror] films' effect, they clearly are not connected only with the monster, and this is perhaps why their role is so often overlooked by these theorists. We, however, in trying to account for that very effect which, helped by music and sound, the films want to produce, must try to reset the balance in the soundtrack's favour. (1998: 3)

This chapter has attempted just such an account, bringing the sound (and music) in *BWP* 'up in the mix', so to speak. Rather than an absence of sound, *BWP* employs a carefully pared-back but nonetheless concentrated approach to sound and music. This supports the narrative as well as the 'truth claim' of the film. The film-makers have avoided the temptation to overemphasize the most obvious generic sonic markers of horror cinema; rather than working against the film affect, this understated approach has assisted its appreciation.

The sound in *BWP*, operating often without clearly resolved corresponding synchronized images or action, perhaps represents the unnamed and unseen horrors within our social psyche. We experience the darker side of ourselves in current human rights abuses, attitudes to environmental concerns or designations of 'others'. With its emphasis on the unseen, *BWP* suggests that today's horror resides within us, our imaginations and obsessions, and our disorganized and self-motivated social interactions. It centres on psychological horror – unnamed, unidentified, like the anonymous suicide bomber – and, as such, is about terror itself, that is, the ability to cause terror (a term that goes back to the Romans). The horror is generated by the protagonists' terror and their responses to it. In this manner, *BWP* relates to our obsession with terror itself. In this scenario, the sound plays a major role. In general, sound in isolation is unseen. Where linked to screen images, sound is tagged to an action, object, subject or event. Where no evidence of what the sound means or indicates is provided on-screen, the sound itself becomes the object of terror. In this case, *BWP* spooks us with sound and generates an audio reaction. For *BWP*, sound is the central narrative and the affective force that enables its generic designation as horror film.

Acknowledgement

Thanks to Eduardo Sànchez for emailed interview responses, Philip Hayward for critical and research assistance on early drafts and Andrew Jones for preliminary research assistance.

Notes

1. Eduardo Sànchez (email to the author, 2 January 2007). Unless stated otherwise, all references to Sànchez are to this correspondence.
2. In contrast to *The Blair Witch Project*, *Blair Witch 2: Book of Shadows* (produced on a budget upped from the original US$38 million to US$60 million), includes many well-known popular music tracks used diegetically, non-diegetically and extra-diegetically, as well as an original score by Carter Burwell. Jancovich (2002) discusses the connection between Top 40 hits used in horror films and reactions to this by horror-film fans who deem such films to be 'inauthentic'. See also Cooper (1997).
3. Although critics marginalized or ignored sound or made pejorative comments, interestingly, viewers registered the impact of it as a critical element, for example: "I loved the creepy noises in the woods as it made the film extremely effective and spine chilling" and "The directing is terrific by both Daniel Myrick & Eduardo Sanchez especially with the scenes where the students hear the noises but don't see anything which makes it scarier" (unattributed reviewers online, http://racksandrazors.com/blair.html, accessed 27 January 2006). In addition, Heather's pseudo-diary written for the supporting eponymous book includes her observation of the significance of sound: "How do I document what is happening so people know. How many shots of trees in the dark can one person have? So much of it is sounds" (Stern, 1999: 166).
4. According to the story devised, the outpost of Blair, named after the founding family of Nathan and Virginia Blair, was established around 1630. The Burkittsville town was later developed next to the original outpost site in the Black Hills Forest.
5. *Haxan* is also the name of a 'pseudo-documentary' made by the Danish director Benjamin Christensen in 1922 about the history of witches in Western culture.
6. As part of its distribution deal, Artisan took over management of the film's website that had been launched by the directors in June 1998. According to Harris (2001), the website was the most accessed site in 1999.
7. The internet effect has continued to be important for fanning the cult movie status of the film, as evidenced by the sheer volume of websites, satires, copies, etc. available online. These additional media products have also been used for what have become other media 'events' that have picked up and considerably enhanced an existing area of interest, such as the supernatural in the *Harry Potter* novels and films, or the rise of self-aware documentaries such as those produced by Michael Moore.

8. See also J. Roscoe (2000), 'The Blair Witch Project: Mock-Documentary Goes Mainstream', *Jump Cut*, 43: 3–9.
9. R. Gonsalves, 'The Blair Witch Project review' (http://www.angelfire.com/movies/oc/blairwitch.html, accessed 27 January 2006). In another online review, Luke Buckmaster argues, "It takes discipline to rob audiences of the 'money shots' commonly associated with the horror genre: those quick 'RRAAA' moments, when we might jump in surprise" (http://www.infilm.com.au/reviews/blairwitch.htm, accessed 27 January 2006).
10. Warner's definition focuses on a film-marketing interpretation, although Dayan and Katz (1992) define 'media event' in terms of television broadcasting as primarily a ceremonial event broadcast live, interrupting regular programming and preplanned, as distinct from a news event.
11. While he is the cameraman in the film narrative, Josh is characterized as musically oriented, as he is depicted singing a couple of songs to express his reactions to various situations.
12. Track listing:
   'Gloomy Sunday', Lydia Lunch
   'The Order Of Death', Public Image Ltd
   'Draining Faces', Skinny Puppy
   'Kingdom's Coming', Bauhaus
   'Don't Go To Sleep Without Me', The Creatures
   'God Is God', Laibach
   'Beware', Afghan Wings
   'Laughing Paid', Front Line Assembly
   'Haunted' – Type O Negative
   'She's Unreal', Meat Beat Manifesto
   'Movement Of Fear', Tones on Tail
   'The Cellar', Antonio Cora
13. Sànchez acknowledges that this film was discussed by the directors, although not in terms of its music. Where *BWP* is markedly different from *The Texas Chain Saw Massacre* and other films incorporating many pre-recorded songs is in its minimal use of music. Indeed, the limited use of music is more analogous to Alfred Hitchcock's *Rear Window* (1954) insofar as, apart from the Cora track, the music is built into the diegesis, thereby highlighting the 'authenticity' of the sound and narrative. Similarly to Hooper and Bell on *The Texas Chain Saw Massacre*, Cora devised his own instruments to create the music. The recordings were made in a studio he set up in the back of the Haxan offices.
14. There is a curious reference to 'body horror' genre in a scene in which Heather films and comments on Mike's chest hair. Other aspects of bodily functions are referred to in a scene in which the two males film Heather urinating, and elsewhere Heather comments on Mike farting inside the tent. Harris (2001: 89) argues that the lack of on-screen violence reflects an industry response to a call to temper depictions of violence made by the then US President Bill Clinton after a spate of school shootings. Harris observes that the lack of on-screen violence and non-

sexual content in *BWP* is as much to do with the directors' wish to differentiate the film from what had become generically predictable.

15. A. Bernstein, online review of *BWP* (http://www.audiorevolution.com/movies/ blairwitchproject/, accessed 16 July 2005).

16. R. Scheib (1999), 'The Blair Witch Project: online review (http://www.moria.co.nz/ horror/blairwitch.htm). Sànchez argues that he had no knowledge of Dogme prior to Sundance and that the directorial approach "was dictated by our need to get the most realistic-looking footage we could get" (email to the author).

17. The actors were provided with a global positioning satellite system to navigate through the woods. They were required to collect film-making supplies and drop off footage from the previous day at specific checkpoints. (See M. Goldman, 'Behind the Blair Witch Project', posted 1 August 1999; http://millimeter.com/ mag/video_behind_blair_witch, accessed 16 July 2005.)

18. It is curious that this method of film-making exploits the 'truth claim' marketing approach. Sound was used to provoke reaction in the production: Sànchez is quoted by Goldman (see note 17) as saying that the directors "yelled in the woods late at night and played various sounds through boom boxes".

19. See Goldman (cited in note 17). According to Sànchez (email to the author), Mike had no training in audio, and composer and (then) "sound guy" Cora instructed him in the use of the DAT recorder. Mike recorded audio for all the 16-mm footage, as well as additional material.

20. Other members of the sound team include: Final mixers: Wilshire Stages, Gerry Lentz, Rich Weingart, Harry Cohen; Audio: Jack Sherdei and the entire staff at Digitec; Music assistant: Dan Barrio; songs are credited as performed by Digginlilies [Rigors]. The sound mix for the Sundance version of the film was created on a deferred-payment basis by Dana Meeks but, according to Sànchez, none of this was used in the Artisan remixes for the theatrical or DVD releases.

21. Online at http://www.dogme95.dk/menu/menuset.htm.

22. Apart from attention-drawing created noises such as those popular in science-fiction film – see the Introduction and various contributors to Hayward (2004) – or deployed to produce such dramatic elements as the dinosaur voices of the *Jurassic Park* series (Steven Spielberg, 1993, 1997) or creatures in fantasies such as *Lord of the Rings* (Peter Jackson, 2001).

23. See also R. M. Schafer (1977), *The Tuning of the World*, Toronto: McClelland & Stewart.

24. Greg Gerlich and Mike Wetherwax of Visiontrax discuss the background sounds from *BWP* that they adapted for use on a 21-minute promo for the sequel in R. Street and F. Lewis (2000), 'Final cut – Blair Witch 2' (http://www. audiomedia.com/archive/features/, accessed 16 July 2005).

25. This refers to the story of Rustin Parr, who slew the village children after requiring them to face into the corner.

26. Sànchez's cousin, Cora, had composed music for Sànchez's student feature, *Gabriel's Dream* (1991) and, at the time of the *BWP* production, was attending the Full Sail School of Film, Art, Design, Music and Media Production in Orlando, Florida.

References

Balázs, B. (1985), 'Theory of the Film: Sound', in E. Weis and J. Belton (eds), *Film Sound, Theory and Practice*, New York: Columbia University Press, pp. 116–25.

Barron, L. (2003), '"Music Inspired By… ": The Curious Case of the Missing Soundtrack', in I. Inglis (ed.), *Popular Music and Film*, London: Wallflower, pp. 148–61.

Clover, C. J. (1992), *Men, Women and Chain Saws: Gender in the Modern Horror Film*, Princeton, NJ: Princeton University Press.

Corbett, J. M. (2003), 'Sound Organisation: A Brief History of Psychosomic Management', *Ephemera*, 3(4), 265–76.

Cooper, B. L. (1997), 'Terror Translated into Comedy: The Popular Music Metamorphosis of Film and Television Horror, 1956–1991', *Journal of American Culture*, 20(3), 31–4.

Crisell, A. (1986), *Understanding Radio*, London: Methuen.

Dayan, D., and Katz, E. (1992), *Media Events: The Live Broadcasting of History*, Cambridge: Harvard University Press.

Harris, M. (2001), 'The "Witchcraft" of Media Manipulation: *Pamela* and *The Blair Witch Project'*, *Journal of Popular Culture*, 34(4), 75–107.

Hayward, P. (ed.) (2004), *Off the Planet: Music, Sound and Science Fiction Cinema*, Eastleigh, Hampshire: John Libbey Publishing.

Kelleghan, F. (1996), 'Sound Effects in Sci-Fi and Horror Films', presentation given at the International Conference on the Fantastic in the Arts, Fort Lauderdale, Florida, 21 March 1996 (http://www.filmsound.org, accessed 27 January 2006).

Jancovich, M. (2002), 'A Real Shocker: Authenticity, Genre and the Struggle for Distinction', in G. Turner (ed.), *The Film Cultures Reader*, London/New York: Routledge, pp. 469–80.

Lindemann, M. (2000), 'Who's Afraid of the Big Bad Witch? Queer Studies in American Literature', *American Literary History*, 12(4), 757–70.

Pomerance, M. (ed.) (2004), *Bad: Infamy, Darkness, Evil and Slime on Screen*, New York: State University of New York Press.

Stern, D. A. (1999), *The Blair Witch Project*, London: Boxtree Macmillan.

Taylor, C. (1999), Review of *The Blair Witch Project*, *Sight & Sound*, November 1999 (http://www.bfi.org.uk/sightandsound/review/232).

Urbano, C. (1998), 'Projections, Suspense, and Anxiety: The Modern Horror Film and Its Effects', *Psychoanalytic Review*, 85(6), 909–30.

van Leeuwen, T. (1999), *Speech, Music, Sound*, London: Macmillan.

Virilio, P. (1989), *War and Cinema: The Logistics of Perception*, trans. P. Camiller, London/New York: Verso.

Wells, P. (2000), *The Horror Genre: From Beelzebub to Blair Witch*, London: Wallflower.

14 Popular Songs and Ordinary Violence

Exposing Basic Human Brutality in the Films of Rob Zombie

Laura Wiebe Taylor

In a review of the horror film *House of 1000 Corpses* (Rob Zombie, 2003), *Sight & Sound*'s Kim Newman notes that director/writer Rob Zombie has "a musician's ear for the right 'wrong' sound", referring to the way scenes like the slow-motion shoot-up played out to Slim Whitman's 'I Remember You' situate "horrors in unusual context[s]" (2003: 36). Zombie's next venture into feature film-making, *The Devil's Rejects* (2005), embraces this use of "the right 'wrong' sound" wholeheartedly, its graphic violence jarring and mating persistently with its primarily country and Southern rock soundtrack.

The merging of iconic American music with scenes of horrific torture and violence in *House of 1000 Corpses* and *The Devil's Rejects* embeds the villains' brutality within US history and reality, and makes it difficult to see these vicious killers – the Fireflys – as entirely 'other'. The Fireflys' love of popular music and the films' juxtaposition of familiar hit songs and horror establish a sense of shared cultural history and taste between villain and viewer, supporting the idea that these villains, while sadistic and violent, are not entirely unlike the rest of American society. Combined with the films' ambivalent attitude towards their brutal but basically human psychopaths, this blending of music and horror depicts extreme violence, not as an aberration in American society, but as an integral, though ugly, part of it.

Rob Zombie (who started life with the more mundane name Rob Cummings) first ventured into the world of on-screen entertainment as a production assistant for the mid-1980s US cult TV series *Pee-wee's Playhouse* (Christe, 2003: 224), but he is much better known as a musician. After several years as front man and mastermind of White Zombie, a group of individuals "drawn together by a mutual love of Black Sabbath-style metal and schlocky horror B-movies" (Berelian, 2005: 402), Zombie launched a successful solo career and designed two attractions for Universal's annual haunted house (*ibid.*: 350), the second of which was based on his then upcoming feature film directorial debut *House of 1000 Corpses*. He also directed several music videos for White Zombie's and his own records, jamming them full of B-grade movie and classic horror-film references, and working with several actors he would later use in his films.

The Devil's Rejects displays obvious connections to outlaw road movies and revisionist Westerns (Koresky, 2005: 75; Newman, 2005: 54), with its brutality, notions of vigilante justice, and its focus on characters running from the law who face their end with determined fierceness and independence. Yet both of Zombie's movies, particularly *House of 1000 Corpses*, allude to *The Texas Chain Saw Massacre* (Tobe Hooper, 1974) as well (Kerr, 2003: 45; Newman, 2003: 36), in part through their shared premise of 'true horror' and a Texas setting. Using the American Southwest as a battleground, these movies take advantage of the region's associations with rugged landscapes and hard people, and play on the notion that backwoods pockets of rural America represent and shelter the last vestiges of savagery that have, as yet, resisted the spreading veneer of civilization. These films also complicate the viewers' relationship with that savagery and, rather than depicting completely inhuman monsters, they suggest that the capacity for brutality is something all humans still share. Zombie's killers are less abject and more charismatic than Hooper's, and Zombie's films use popular music as a means of further emphasizing the links between villain and viewer.

Like *The Texas Chain Saw Massacre*, *House of 1000 Corpses* features a group of young people who, while on a road trip, meet up with a monstrous family, in this case, the Fireflys. After stopping at a gas station/museum of horrors/fried-chicken stand, the two young couples pick up a female hitchhiker (Baby), and when her brother (Rufus, or R.J.) shoots out their tyre, they end up at the Firefly home for an evening of weirdness that turns to horror. The Fireflys (the household includes Mother Firefly, Otis Driftwood and two other Fireflys) torment and eventually kill the young people, and also shoot two policemen (Lieutenant Wydell and his deputy) and a father who come looking for the missing youths. One girl manages to escape, but the first car to find her belongs to the gas station owner (Captain Spaulding), who is an extended member of the Firefly clan. One of the last shots of the film shows Otis rising up from the back seat with a knife in his hand.

The Devil's Rejects, a sequel of sorts, opens with the police descending on the Firefly home while the family is asleep. Rufus dies during the ensuing shoot-out, and Mother is captured and later killed, but Baby and Otis escape and meet up with Spaulding (identified here as Baby's father), now on the run as well. After demonstrating their persistent capacity for sadism and violence, the three remaining Fireflys find temporary sanctuary at the 'Frontier Fun Town' (a flashy Old West whorehouse owned by Spaulding's 'brother' Charlie), until vigilante justice catches up with them. Sheriff John Quincy Wydell, a lawman seeking vengeance for the murder of his brother (Lieutenant Wydell), tortures and tries to kill the family but meets his own end in the process. Baby, Otis and Spaulding make one last futile attempt to get away, only to go down in a final exchange of gunfire when a police barricade brings them to the end of their road.

Despite the disgust which the Fireflys' sadistic and horrific violence inspires, it is impossible to entirely detach oneself from the characters. Zombie's films, like *The Texas Chain Saw Massacre*, challenge the distance between their horror and 'ordinary' society, particularly through the ambivalence with which they portray their villains. Robin Wood argues that *The Texas Chain Saw Massacre* demonstrates ambivalence in its depiction of the monstrous family precisely because they are a family, and therefore, "we cannot cleanly dissociate ourselves from them" (1984: 190). The fact that these characters also "manifest a degraded but impressive creativity" (*ibid.*) further complicates notions of their 'otherness' by highlighting their basic underlying humanity.

Similarly, *House of 1000 Corpses* and *The Devil's Rejects* make it clear that the Fireflys, however despicable, are indeed a family, bickering like any 'ordinary' family and even demonstrating affection now and then. Baby and Mama, for example, exchange declarations of love in both films, and when it comes time to act – whether dealing out torture and death or confronting a threat – the Fireflys act together. *The Devil's Rejects* further emphasizes the satirical relationship between the Fireflys and the 'ideal' family through a series of home movie clips cut into the final scene of the film, contrasting close-ups of the bruised and bloody faces of Baby, Otis and Spaulding with glowingly lit images of the three characters together, laughing and well.[1] In these 'ideal' shots, the Fireflys look like an ordinary, happy family rather than a horde of violent psychopaths, yet the camera repeatedly returns to the battered outlaws in the car, reminding us of what they are 'really' like, in effect suggesting that a similar brutal 'reality' may lie beneath the glowing surface of every 'ideal' American family.

Another characteristic the Fireflys share with a large segment of the American viewing audience is a love of popular music. The Fireflys' enthusiasm for music is only one facet of the "aesthetic sense" they have in common with the monstrous family of *The Texas Chain Saw Massacre*, a quality Wood identifies as "characteristically human… however perverted in its form" (1984: 190). In Zombie's films, the Fireflys demonstrate their artistic sensibilities in several ways, including their performance of an amateur vaudeville act and Otis's corpse-sculpting, but popular music is particularly Baby's and Otis's domain. Baby lip-syncs, sings along, or dances to familiar tunes in both movies; in *House of 1000 Corpses* she gets excited when a song she likes comes on the car radio and also plays music on a portable stereo while Otis tortures one of their victims. In *The Devil's Rejects* Otis shows his interest in music through an exchange with country musician/victim Roy Sullivan, accusing Sullivan of being a top-forty-loving "city faggot with a cowboy hat" who is merely posing as a "true blue balls Ernest Tubb country fucker". Baby and Otis are nearly perfect (and gendered) stereotypes of 'ordinary' music fandom – the girl who likes everything and the male popular music snob.

Several academics have pointed out an increase in the use of popular music on film soundtracks since the mid-1970s, attributing the rise to factors such as technological developments, the tight relationship between the film and recording industries, and marketing strategies.[2] The music and movie industries' quest for 'synergy' – the "cross-promotion" of music and film (Jeff Smith, quoted in Coyle, 2004: 121) – could hardly have found a better outlet than Rob Zombie: he wrote and directed both films and contributed roughly half of the soundtrack to *House of 1000 Corpses*, and thanks to his horror-infused music career he had a ready-made audience. Yet, as Donnelly remarks, choosing a movie soundtrack is not all commerce (2003: 135). According to Rick Altman (2001), popular song in film is often used to set a specific mood or historical time period, and this is one of the functions of music in Zombie's films. Both movies are set in the late 1970s, a fact apparent in characters' clothing styles, car and television set models, and in the case of *The Devil's Rejects*, an introduction that specifies 1978 as the year in which these events took place. The films' music supports this 1970s setting; aside from Zombie's own songs and the score, the soundtracks comprise popular songs from 1977 and earlier, most of them American-made.

The *House of 1000 Corpses* soundtrack features two hit songs that help situate the action in the late 1970s – the Commodores' 'Brick House' (1977) and the Ramones' 'Now I Wanna Sniff Some Glue'(1976) – while its country selections are slightly more 'historical' – Slim Whitman's 'I Remember You' (1972) and Buck Owens's 'Who's Gonna Mow Your Grass?' (1969). The only other non-Zombie song is a Helen Kane performance of the 1928 Broadway tune 'I Wanna Be Loved By You', which provides Baby's lip-syncing material and extends the Fireflys' taste beyond the American South-west and the recent past. All of these songs, or the albums they appeared on, experienced fairly widespread popularity, most of them making it onto one or more of *Billboard*'s music charts.[3]

The songs used in *The Devil's Rejects*, mostly Southern rock, country and blues, put more emphasis on the film's southwestern setting, but almost all these tracks experienced widespread popularity as well. The country numbers include another Buck Owens song ('Satan's Gotta Get Along Without Me' [1966]) and Kitty Wells's 'It Wasn't God Who Made Honky Tonk Angels' (1952), but the film also features country blues by Blind Willie Johnson and Muddy Waters, the Chicago blues of Otis Rush, and rock by bands like Steely Dan, the James Gang, Joe Walsh, the Allman Brothers and Lynyrd Skynyrd. The more recent songs reinforce the film's 1970s setting, while the older selections situate the film, and its violence, within a broader cultural history and tradition. Additionally, the popularity of most of these songs lends the movie (both movies, in fact) a sense of 'ordinariness' that first seems an awkward and uncomfortable accompaniment for the brutal violence on screen. Yet the continued pairing up of horror and popular song serves to undermine the 'extraordinariness' of the violence.

Discussing the use of popular music in Quentin Tarantino's *Reservoir Dogs* (1992), *Pulp Fiction* (1994) and *Jackie Brown* (1997), Garner suggests that the films' emphasis on the "switching on and off" of music demonstrates an explicit celebration of musical selection as an indication of character but little regard for the musical choices themselves (2001: 189). In Zombie's films, what the characters choose to listen to is important for its mundane quality. They like the same music that the rest of America likes (or liked at some time) and the songs provide the soundtrack for both their fun and their brutality, which are often one and the same. Many of these songs have a clear place in the diegesis and, therefore, demonstrate the characters' musical preferences. For example, Baby turns on and dances to 'Brick House' while Otis takes a razor blade and an axe to one of their victims in *House of 1000 Corpses*. In *The Devil's Rejects*, the song 'Rocky Mountain Way' (1973), which initially appears as non-diegetic, dominating the soundtrack during scenes of revelry at the Frontier Fun Town, fades out enough so one can faintly hear Baby as she sings along. It becomes clear that this is the Fireflys' party music. The blues, country and rock on the soundtrack is exactly what these characters willingly and actively listen to – as did a large part of the American and international popular music audience. Viewers are linked to the violence on screen by the nostalgia the songs evoke and by the musical history and taste the audience and killers share.

Robb Wright, discussing a scene in *Apocalypse Now* (Francis Ford Coppola, 1979), argues that non-diegetic popular songs on a film's soundtrack can create a "disturbing" sense of "calmness," the "ironic juxtaposition" of the Doors' music, in this case, and "the napalm torching of a jungle village" underlining the movie's horror (2003: 15–16). Tarantino has similarly commented on his own use of popular music to increase the "disturbing" nature of a "torture scene" (Garner, 2001: 193). *House of 1000 Corpses* also uses popular songs to emphasize the horror of its violence, in the 'Brick House' scene but also during the shooting of the police officers and father. Whitman's 'I Remember You' begins just after the deputy and father open the door to a shed of horrors, and the song continues while, in slow motion, Mother Firefly shoots Lieutenant Wydell through the head and Otis fires several shots into the father's back. The music does not end until Otis stands with his gun to the deputy's head, ready to fire. *The Devil's Rejects* uses this kind of "ironic juxtaposition" as well; Otis and Baby carry out their first act of brutal violence in the film (a vicious stabbing) to the accompaniment of the Allman Brothers' 'Midnight Rider' (1970), for example.

But it is not just the Fireflys' violence that gets a popular music soundtrack in *The Devil's Rejects*, which further complicates any casting of backwoods villains as the only repository of horror in American society. While the Fireflys relax at the Frontier Fun House, a soft and melancholy song by British blues/folk rocker Terry Reid begins as the background accompaniment to Spaulding and Charlie's friendly chat. Soon the music rises up and drowns out all ambient noise and dialogue, and the camera shows the rest of the family enjoying themselves – Baby in a bubble bath drinking and laughing with one of the whores, Otis in bed with another. While the song continues to play, enjoyment abruptly turns to violence on the screen as Baby's friend gets her throat slashed, a laughing thug shoots the other whore before tossing Otis out of the window, and the throat-slasher yells at Baby (his mouth moves but still the music prevails) and puts a gun to her head. The music finally fades away as a close-up of Spaulding smoking a joint cuts to a medium shot of Sheriff Wydell, the origin of this violent attack, walking into the room, and the sound of violence erupts as Wydell shoots Spaulding. At first the music and the brutality seem poorly matched, but before the sequence ends the combination of violence and song suggests that the same culture holds responsibility for both.

The Devil's Rejects further emphasizes the relationship between popular music and horror by using familiar tunes as a prelude to violence, implying meaning by montage-like association rather than accompaniment. Wright suggests that when popular songs with lyrics are not introduced to a soundtrack through the action they may serve as a "distraction", potentially "undermin[ing] the dramatic thrust of the scene" (2003: 14). But when the focus, at least momentarily, is meant to be *on* the song (whether diegetic or not), this "distraction" can be beneficial. In *The Devil's Rejects* Zombie often focuses the viewer's attention on non-diegetic popular songs before providing a diegetic source for music. By making the viewer blatantly aware of the songs before justifying their presence as part of the action, the film reinforces the relationship between the more 'ordinary' world of popular music consumption and the 'extraordinary' horror within the movie. For example, Elvin Bishop's popular 'Fooled Around And Fell In Love' (1976) – the song that inspires Otis to call Sullivan a fake – introduces a scene that ends in sadistic violence, its melody dominating the soundtrack for a few shots before the camera takes the viewer inside a moving van to reveal that the music is playing on the van radio. This segment leads to a scene where Otis psychologically torments his captives ('inauthentic' country musicians Banjo and Sullivan), then stabs, shoots and beats them. When Otis moves in to slice off Banjo's face (one of his favourite pastimes), Banjo's cry seamlessly blends into the "I" beginning Otis Rush's 'I Can't Quit You Baby' (1956), which almost immediately appears on a motel-room television. The cut from Southern brutality to a blues musician is a subtle reminder of the region's history of racial violence, and the sadistic potential latent even in avid popular music fans is further underlined by Baby's mental and physical torture of her female captives in the remainder of the motel-room scene – she forces one woman to hit the other in order to be allowed to go to the bathroom, for example. The movement between music and sadistic violence in both these scenes makes it difficult to extricate the two and, by the use of familiar hit songs, implicates the viewer in both.

Wright suggests that specific combinations of music and image have become cinematic conventions, a "universally familiar part of cinematic language" (2003: 13). One example Wright offers is "the motorcycling scene of *Easy Rider* [Dennis Hopper, 1969]" – whose accompanying song, Steppenwolf's 'Born To Be Wild' (1968) – "quickly became an anthem for defiant individualism" (*ibid.*). Wright argues that such sequences suggest a sense of "illicit escape" into the rural landscape, the sound of amplified instruments evoking the power of the motorcycle's engine (*ibid.*). Donnelly argues that using "music to drive the action" in this way can result in "musical time" replacing "film time," to the effect that popular song's "repetitive beat" implies "forward movement is inevitable" (2003: 141). *The Devil's Rejects* has several such scenes, pairing road trips and popular music, but it is the Fireflys' final bid for freedom to the accompaniment of Lynyrd Skynyrd's 'Free Bird' (1973) that most thoroughly and effectively combines the concepts of defiance and inevitability.

This getaway scene resists the notion of forward movement or progress with a sense of circularity that emphasizes the futility of both the attempt to escape and the final showdown. The opening organ chords of 'Free Bird' begin as a helicopter shot swoops down onto the landscape, giving us a glimpse first of the highway and then of the getaway car, small, distant, and un-empowered. As the song continues, the camera closes in on the convertible from several angles, then intercuts extreme close-ups of the damaged faces of the remaining Fireflys with the 'ideal family' home-movie footage mentioned earlier and long shots of the car as it moves down the highway. The car moves toward the right in one shot, left in the next, negating any sense of actual forward movement until the camera eventually shows the wheels roll to a stop, all while the song continues to play. From an extreme close-up of Otis looking bothered the scene finally cuts to what he sees – a police barricade. Just before 'Free Bird' shifts from its softer opening to the faster-paced hard rock conclusion a close-up shows Baby's mouth shouting, "mother fucker!" The tyres begin to roll again as Lynyrd Skynyrd's vocalist draws out the word, "cha-a-a-a-a-ange," but the repeating syllable implies circular motion rather than forward momentum. The shoot-out extends just beyond the end of the song, which is cut short by a loud whooping noise before a faint heartbeat and, finally, the actual sound of gunfire accompany freeze-frame close-ups of each dying Firefly. Both song and last stand come to a harsh, truncated, and futile conclusion, and the scene fades from those final stills into black, suggesting that only death can free these characters from the cycle of human violence.

'Free Bird' is popular culture history. It is an iconic Southern rock song, a classic rock radio staple, and a beloved favourite for many people. It clearly evokes American culture of the 1970s as well as all the glory and sorrow of the American South. It imbues the Fireflys' last stand with these qualities. But the blood on their faces is a reminder of the torture they committed, as well as that which they endured, and their final gesture is clearly useless – they are badly outnumbered, wounded, and Otis made it clear while killing Banjo that he has no respect for heroics. This scene closely associates a classic American song with these villains and their violent, defiant natures, suggesting that the brutality they demonstrate is as much an underlying part of American society as is this music.

Citing Andrew Britton, Robin Wood finds in *The Texas Chain Saw Massacre* the message that "annihilation is inevitable", and suggests that the film shows a nightmarish world where "escape" only leads to recapture (1984: 187). Yet Wood also argues that the "apocalyptic horror film", in its negation, can be viewed as progressive rather than reactionary because it is not recuperable into the dominant ideology (*ibid.*: 192). Zombie's films are equally negative; all violence, whether the Fireflys' or the vigilante sheriff's, leads to more violence and ends in the perpetrator's death, and *House of 1000 Corpses* and *The Devil's Rejects*, sharing the ambivalence of Hooper's movie, similarly resist recuperation. Despite the films' emphasis on the Fireflys as a family, this is one seriously dysfunctional unit, only removed from 'ordinary' society by the degree of their taste for horror, not by kind – even 'ordinary people' in Zombie's films demonstrate a fascination with horror, reading about it, watching it on television, and seeking it out on back roads. The Fireflys' family 'bonding' does not save them from ultimate destruction, and attempts to rout them out demonstrate the cyclical nature of violence, as the sheriff becomes as sadistic as they.

Zombie's use of popular music in his horror films produces not so much a counter-narrative as an alternative reading that resists conservatism rather than affirming it. By relentlessly pairing extreme brutality with popular – often beloved – tunes from the (primarily) American past, Zombie exposes the violence that lies embedded in American history and society. The music prevents the horror the films reveal from being 'othered'; just as the music belongs to society, so does the violence. And while the movies are decidedly American in their setting and references, Zombie's use of British rockers on *The Devil's Rejects* soundtrack and allusions to Australian outlaw/hero Ned Kelly in the Fireflys' homemade armour suggest that violence is not strictly an American trait. Tania Modleski reads films like *The Texas Chain Saw Massacre* as focusing an "undifferentiated lust for destruction" that lies under the surface of our "collective consciousness" (2004: 771). Similarly, in his analysis of extreme violence in films from the 1970s, 1980s and early 1990s, Michael Eric Stein argues that many extremely violent movies express the belief that society itself is "inherently vicious and unforgiving" (1995: np) – violence is human nature. Zombie's films express a similar view of humanity and the societies we construct. Humanity in *The Devil's Rejects and House of 1000 Corpses* is brutal, and it is popular music that most audibly exposes the relationship between human nature and horrific brutality.

Notes

1. Thanks to Fred Meissner for bringing the satire to my attention.
2. See Altman (2001); Anderson (2003); Coyle (2004); Donnelly (2003); Gorbman (1987); and Wright (2003).
3. See All Music Guide (http://allmusic.com, accessed 7 February 2006 and 18 April 2006).

References

Altman, R. (2001), 'Cinema and Popular Song: The Lost Tradition', in P. R. Wojcik and A. Knight (eds), *Soundtrack Available: Essays on Film and Popular Music*, Durham, NC: Duke University Press, pp. 19–30.

Anderson, L. (2003), 'Case Study 1: *Sliding Doors* and *Topless Women Talk about Their Lives*', in I. Inglis (ed.), *Popular Music and Film*, London: Wallflower, pp. 102–16.

Berelian, E. (2005), *The Rough Guide to Heavy Metal*, London: Rough Guides.

Christe, I. (2003), *Sound of the Beast: The Complete Headbanging History of Heavy Metal*, New York: Harper Entertainment.

Coyle, R. (2004), 'Sound and Music in the *Mad Max* Trilogy', in P. Hayward (ed.), *Off the Planet: Music, Sounds and Science Fiction Cinema*, Eastleigh, Hampshire: John Libbey Publishing, pp. 109–28.

Donnelly, K. J. (2003), 'Constructing the Future through Music of the Past: The Software in *Hardware*', in I. Inglis (ed.), *Popular Music and Film*, London: Wallflower, pp. 131–47.

Garner, K. (2001), '"Would You Like to Hear Some Music?" Music In-and-out-of-Control in the Films of Quentin Tarantino', in K. J. Donnelly (ed.), *Film Music: Critical Approaches*, New York: Continuum, pp. 188–205.

Gorbman, C. (1987), *Unheard Melodies: Narrative Film Music*, Bloomington: Indiana University Press.

Kerr, P. (2003), 'Murder Most Foul', *New Statesman*, 6 October, p. 45.

Koresky, M. (2005), 'The Devil's Rejects', *Film Comment*, 41(4), 74–5.

Modleski, T. (2004), 'Terror of Pleasure: The Contemporary Horror Film and Postmodern Theory', in L. Braudy and M. Cohen (eds), *Film Theory and Criticism: Introductory Readings*, New York and Oxford: Oxford University Press, pp. 764–73.

Newman, K. (2003), 'House of 1000 Corpses', *Sight & Sound*, 13(12), 36.

Newman, K. (2005), 'The Devil's Rejects', *Sight & Sound*, 15(8), 54.

Sharrett, C. (1984), 'The Idea of Apocalypse in *The Texas Chainsaw Massacre*', in B. K. Grant (ed.), *Planks of Reason: Essays on the Horror Film*, Metuchen, NJ: Scarecrow, pp. 255–76.

Stein, M. E. (1995), 'The New Violence or Twenty Years of Violence in Films: An Appreciation (Part I)', *Films in Review*, 46 (January/February). Available online at http://0-search.epnet.com.catalogue.library.brocku.ca (accessed 23 January 2006).

Wood, R. (1984), 'An Introduction to the American Horror Film', in B. K. Grant (ed.), *Planks of Reason: Essays on the Horror Film*, Metuchen, NJ: Scarecrow, pp. 164–200.

Wright, R. (2003), 'Score vs. Song: Art, Commerce, and the H Factor in Film and Television Music', in I. Inglis (ed.), *Popular Music and Film*, London: Wallflower, pp. 8–21.

15 Terror in the Outback
Wolf Creek *and Australian Horror Cinema*

Philip Hayward and Harry Minassian

> *I have always loved the stories I grew up with about weird lights in the sky, UFOs and people who simply 'disappeared' while in the Outback. Australia is a magical country with amazing and yet terrifying qualities, and I really wanted to put a face to the nameless fear of what lurks 'out there' on those long lonely highways* (Greg McLean, director of *Wolf Creek*).[1]

Introduction

Since its revival in the 1970s, Australian cinema has chiefly been known for its period pieces (the 'art cinema' of films such as *My Brilliant Career* [Gillian Armstrong, 1979] and *Newsfront* [Philip Noyce, 1978]) and, more latterly, quirky and irreverent comedies (such as *Young Einstein* [Yahoo Serious, 1989] and *Muriel's Wedding* [P. J. Hogan, 1994]). A minor, disparate and often overlooked group of films has also reflected on life, death and the mysteries of Australia's huge and sparsely populated outback. This group has included arthouse successes such as *Picnic at Hanging Rock* (Peter Weir, 1974), quirky micro-budget films such as *The Cars That Ate Paris* (Peter Weir, 1974), the original *Mad Max* (George Miller, 1979), the one-off, MTV-influenced extravaganza of *Razorback* (Russell Mulcahy, 1984) and, most recently, stylish genre pieces such as the zombie/alien abduction movie *The Undead* (Michael and Peter Spierig, 2003) and the hard-edged horror film *Wolf Creek* (Greg McLean, 2005). The critical and box-office success of the latter in Australia and the USA[2] is all the more notable since horror had a low profile in Australian cinema – and, indeed, Australian popular culture in general – during most of the twentieth century. Reflecting this, Hood has argued that there is no "tradition" of Australian horror cinema (unlike US, British or Italian cinema):

> *Though Australians have made horror and horror-related films... they tend to be a bit isolated, with little specific on-going influence. The very best ones, which are more essentially 'Australian' in approach, often minimise narrative movement and hence don't fit snugly into the form of the essentially narrative-driven horror genre.* (Hood, 1994)

As Hood identifies, while there have been directors who have produced a number of low-budget horrors (such as Terry Bourke[3]) and, more latterly, mavericks such as Philip Brophy (who directed the inventive 'splatter' feature *Body Melt* [1993]), the limited circulation and minimal attention afforded to the genre has rendered it a pale presence in Australian cinema history. One of *Wolf Creek*'s many significances is that it has broken through to the mainstream and managed to produce a local inflection of the genre with international appeal. This chapter examines the authorial intentions behind the film's design, direction and soundtrack composition and the manner in which the final film text combines, develops – and/or deviates from – these.

Production aesthetics

McLean has stated, "It was my intention to make Wolf Creek an unforgettable, shocking and genuinely scary movie that is also distinctly Australian".[4] In attempting to develop the idea of a distinctly Australian horror film, McLean set out to create a dark inversion of one of the most popular stereotypes of Australian 'outback' life, the rugged, inventive and droll 'bushman' popularized internationally in the *Crocodile Dundee* films (John Connell, 1986, 1988) and Steve Irwin's TV series *The Crocodile Hunter* (late 1990s to early 2000s). Reimagining such a character as an intense and resourceful psychopath lurking in the Australian bush, McLean was attempting to create "a uniquely Australian 'Bogeyman'".[5] During the project's inception, a number of young travellers were murdered while holidaying in Australia. The perpetrators of the crimes, Ivan Milat and Bradley Murdoch, attracted national attention and darkened Australia's reputation as a safe destination for backpacker tourists. These real-life events informed McLean's development of plot, narrative and imagination:

> [Milat and Murdoch] *committed crimes characterised by unparalleled violence, brutality and chilling, cold-blooded planning. Australia, once the world's favourite beach, suddenly became a place where lonely, deranged men with murder on their minds stalked empty highways looking for vulnerable tourists a long way from home. And while* Wolf Creek *is not based on any one story or case, Mick Taylor is the bastard child of all of these men and their hideous crimes.*[6]

Reflecting this, the film's narrative is centred on three characters – Australian Ben Mitchell (Nathan Phillips) and English tourists Liz Hunter (Cassandra Magrath) and Kristy Earl (Kestie Morassi) – who set out on a road trip from Broome (in Australia's northwest) across to Cairns, on the opposite coast. One of their first stops is at a gigantic meteor crater at Wolf Creek,[7] where unexplained mechanical failures occur: first their watches stop, then their car fails to start. At this point the narrative heads straight into the heart of horror as resourceful outback dweller Mick Taylor (John Jarratt) passes by and offers help. Mick promises to fix their car but informs them that he will have to tow them back to his base to do so. Some hours later, after the group arrive at his camp and Mick starts to work on the car, they fall asleep. Later, Liz wakes bound and gagged; she manages to free herself only to discover the unspeakable nightmare which she, Kristy and Ben have stumbled into. From this point on the narrative pitches its travellers into a scenario that recalls the climax of Tobe Hooper's *Texas Chain Saw Massacre* (1974) and a host of similar violent shockers.

Wolf Creek was made on a budget of AU$1.3 million (US$1 million) and was shot on digital video. McLean has said that:

> [Its style] *was always intended to be ultra-realistic, semi-documentary. We designed the film to appear to be little more than a 'recreation' of an actual criminal case. The reason for adopting this storytelling technique is that when there's an element of 'truth' to a horror film the audience is more readily able to become complicit. Fact-based stories mean it is easier for an audience to suspend their disbelief, thus creating a much more intense reaction. Examples are* The Exorcist, The Amityville Horror, The Texas Chainsaw Massacre *and* The Blair Witch Project. *All play with the idea that they are based on or are 'true stories'. All went to great lengths stylistically to convince the audience of the 'reality' of their environment, characters and events. The object being with this kind of movie to generate audience reaction. And have lots of fun doing it – as finally that's what horror movies are for! As Stephen King said, "Without first belief, there can be no fear." This maxim by the master of horror is one we adhered closely to in the preparation, design and construction of* Wolf Creek.[8]

While acknowledging his affection for classic Hammer horror films, McLean has also explicitly identified that his approach was inspired by the Dogme95 group, founded in the 1990s and led by Danish film-maker Lars von Trier. The Dogme film-makers developed a highly personal and compact approach to production based around digital shooting and editing, predominantly using locations rather than studios – "focussing all their energy into telling great stories innovatively with compelling performances".[9] McLean has stated that:

> *I truly admired their original and daring cinema... And even though many of their original ideas were cast aside as they became more successful, the original concepts served to prove that shooting in this way re-focuses a film on its essential elements, and re-asks the question; what do you need to make a good movie? Their answer was – a great idea, excellent actors and a digital camera... So this formed the basis of my approach to making* Wolf Creek. *I was influenced by certain elements of Dogme95* [economy, focus on script and performance for cinematic effects] *and my favourite elements of the classic horror movies* [strong central storyline, few characters, an isolated setting, a unique and unforgettable monster] *and decided* [probably subconsciously] *to mesh them together to create* Wolf Creek.[10]

While the above quotations indicate McLean's conscious genre influences in the visual, narrative and thematic design of *Wolf Creek*, they offer no insight into the film's approach to audio and/or music. Indeed, the director's specification of his influence by "certain aspects" of Dogme95 points to an obvious difference in that Dogme specified that music should only be present when it occurs in the diegesis of the film (i.e., as heard in the place of film action from material sources).[11] *Wolf Creek* offers several examples of this, such as the background music audible when the lead characters are throwing a goodbye party in Broome, or the music playing in the Emu Creek roadhouse, where the travellers stop to refuel their car. But, as an extensively scored film, *Wolf Creek* consistently departs from Dogme95. But, despite this, it deviates in a manner that suggests a broad agreement with von Trier's original aesthetic principle.

The first notable violation (featuring source music) occurs so promptly after the title sequence as to suggest it as a (scene-setting) continuance of this (rather than an element of the film proper). Accompanying footage of the start of the film's central road trip, the soundtrack features a vintage Australian pop-rock song, Daddy Cool's 'Eagle Rock' (1972). Composer François Tétaz has identified the choice of this track as a collaborative act, made in careful discussion with the director, due to its crucial role in establishing an association that could be echoed later in the film:

> It is a quintessential Australian song that was a hit in its day and has some international currency. It is closely associated with Australia and is somewhat timeless (for a young audience). It makes the audience feel very comfortable at the beginning of the film and sets a false sense of security.[12]

Despite his stress on the track's familiar datedness for a young Australian audience McLean has also elaborated that:

> ...we tried forty-five different songs for that sequence. We tried contemporary stuff, we tried some classical... a few weird selections. But I definitely wanted a rock 'n' roll track. Something from Mick's era. I wanted it to be something he might listen to and there's something very creepy about having a happy song like that to be in this kind of movie. I think on some level you hear that song and you think it's some kind of a trick. It's too good to be true to listen to a pop sequence like that. You know something is going to get fucked up. (quoted in Turek, 2005)

As the following sections discuss, music and sound composition play a crucial role in *Wolf Creek* and, in the early parts of the film, at least, operate within what we might understand as an 'expanded' Dogme95 aesthetic, where underscore is paramount and the tonalities and musical features are designed to work in a manner that blurs with and arises out of aural ambiences.

The sound of horror

Wolf Creek's musical score was created by François Tétaz, a Melbourne-based composer, performer, engineer and producer with a prolific history in experimental music production. Tétaz began scoring for films with *Angst* (Daniel Nettheim, 2000) and went on to receive nominations for an ARIA (Australian Recording Industry Award) best film score for the crime thriller *The Hard Word* (Scott Roberts, 2003) and a similar nomination in the 2004 Australian Film Institute awards for the comedy *Thunderstruck* (Darren Ashton, 2004).[13]

In discussion with McLean, Tétaz developed a concept for the film's music whereby "the role of the score was to take the film out of specific genre tradition and make it complete with its own aural language" and was concerned that this musical vision was also integrated with the overall sound design:

> *I think it is important that the whole sound department,[14] music included, talk to each other about what they are attempting to achieve to create a cohesive result. It avoids the mix becoming a collision of ideas.*

Appropriately enough, the sound of nature, such as birds chirping, flies buzzing and wind noise, is used throughout the film. This is not just to create atmosphere, but also to comment on the narrative and underscore viewers' emotional responses. In this regard, the film's pre-credit scenes set up a significant point of departure. Before the characters are introduced, we see images of waves breaking on the sand in the half-light of dawn and hear wave sounds and seagull cries. These sounds reoccur as the main female protagonists lie on the beach after breakfast, soaking up the sun, then again the morning after their farewell revels, as they wake on the sand and as Liz takes a final swim. In this regard, the sounds work as an audio memoire of the 'safe coast' they depart from in order to cross the unforgiving interior and are never heard again after the title sequence.

The dialogue is strongly naturalistic throughout the film and, along with atmosphere, initially dominates the soundtrack. In sequences such as Ben and Kristy's conversation outside the roadhouse, their dialogue appears semi-improvised, with Kristy's lines moving between confident banter and faltering phraseology (retained, unedited). Such dialogue – and scenes such as when Liz and Ben share a first, awkward kiss at the meteor crater – serves to establish an emotional affinity and rapport with the characters prior to the intense drama of the film's second half. In order to achieve this, (perceptible) music is deliberately kept to a minimum. Tétaz offers the following explanation for this strategy:

> *For an audience to actually be affected by the film, we had to forget some film conventions. I believe score and sound design is a chance to add qualities to the images that aren't present, or to focus the elements that are. The idea behind the score is that it would not pre-empt the emotion on screen, and therefore leave the audience to read a moment. The lack of emotional support early in the film adds to the idea that this is a*

documentary – 'it is happening'. The transition slowly to the emotive metaphysical score is very late in the film. I tried very hard not to flag the film with 'here comes the music' or 'oh I'm meant to feel this now'. Its absence adds to the sense of being lost in the middle of nowhere. It's like the filmmaker's emotionally abandoning the audience.

As the film progresses, the mood slowly changes and the tension and suspense begin to build. As Tétaz elaborates:

The overall structure of the film starts with documentary style realism, travels through the horrific central crossroads into a metaphysical conclusion. The score's aim was to support and enhance this arc. It was important that the score was somewhat obtuse and existed below the film, staining the images rather than painting them.

While the composer may have been aiming at such subliminal underscoring at particular points in the film, other aspects of the soundtrack wrench away the primacy of the images at key narrative points. The first of these, that staple of horror cinema, screams – and, in particular, young women's screams – provides a startlingly intense coloration to the narrative around its central 'hinge', when the film moves into full-blown horror.

Female screams, and the sobs, shouts and pleas that routinely accompany them in horror cinema, are ably performed, crisply recorded and prominently mixed in *Wolf Creek*. They first enter the narrative as Liz escapes her initial confinement and attempts to explore the camp as quietly as possible, in the still of the night (to a faint, ambiguous musical accompaniment). Hearing a woman's screams and sobs from a point in the middle distance, she moves over to a shed, peers through a window and sees Kristy, chained and bloody, begging hysterically for her life. Mick's demeanour is all the more unsettling. Clearly amused, he aims a rifle at Kristy's head but, instead of shooting, yells "Bang!" and cackles, only to raise the gun again and pull the trigger to a resounding actual bang, leaving Kristy shrieking as she realizes that he has deliberately aimed to miss. Shushing her, with his finger to his lips, he announces his intention to rape her and moves slowly towards her. Outside, Liz is initially shown stunned, still and silent, but recovers sufficiently to cause a diversion that deflects Mick's attack on her friend. Sprinkling petrol inside a car, she throws a match in and backs away. The explosive roar of the flames draws Mick from his shed, allowing Liz to slip in and mount a rescue attempt. One of the most striking aspects of this scene is Mick's mocking, self-amused vocal banter, in contrast to the whole range of human communicative sound being used by Kristy to vocalize her terror and to articulate the question she expressly asks of her captor, "Why are you doing this?" (The unspoken answer appearing to be simply "because I can".) While there is nothing generically unique about the combination of sounds and sonic interactions in this scene, the sound mix and progression (with minimal use of emphatic horror music 'signals' of the type discussed below) make the human soundscore all the more effective and complement Tétaz's restraint.

Music types

Kassabian has identified two types of musical operation in horror films. The first she terms a "commentary function" whereby consciously recognizable musical techniques and conventions are understood by audiences to signify (or play with signification of) threat or danger. The most obvious of these are marked crescendos and/or dissonances at climactic points (2001: 59). The other is a form of orthodox underscoring that she refers to as the "mood function" that produces an "unconscious increase in tension (leading to terror)" (*ibid*.). McLean and Tétaz's stated desires to avoid standard musical clichés of the genre principally apply to use of Kassabian's "commentary function" in all but the final, blood-soaked denouement. The composer characterizes this in an unusual, visually allusive manner, referring to his attempts to subtly "stain" the images with music. But even with this intention, Tétaz had to work within commercial-generic constraints:

> *It is a mainstream movie. There has to be some acknowledgment of style and a reference to something a mainstream audience can feel comfortable with. To alienate the audience is pointless for this film. It's about universal fears and engaging people to put themselves in the actors' shoes. That's the most powerful aspect of the film.*

This mediation of intent and vision is reflected in the film's progression, as the movie 'changes gear' halfway through and becomes a more vivid and intense narrative experience. As Tétaz has described:

> *The music at the beginning of the film is subtle and hard to define. The middle section is unusual and uncomfortable and the last third is quite emotive, verging on cliché.*

In seeking to create an unsettling and eerie musical coloration to the narrative that nestled into the film's sonic ambience, Tétaz turned to the work of an Australian composer who has worked on the borders of sound art and music, Alan Lamb. Lamb attracted attention in the 1980s through a series of projects which utilized metallic wires and wind vibration to produce source recordings. Describing these as his 'Aeolian works', his online artist's biography characterizes them as using:

> *long wires (up to a kilometer) supported in spans (50 to 300 meters) between massive rigid supports. The wires are preferably of high tensile steel 2.5 to 3.2 mm in diameter. Tensions are kept high (approx 200 kilograms) but well within the elastic limits of the steel to allow for unex-pected forces and impacts. These dimensions appear to produce the optimal ranges and complexities of sounds which are effectively infinite over time. Big open spaces are needed where the winds can flow without obstruction or turbulence.*[15]

The mechanical and electronic modifications of these wire instruments are:

> designed to respond chaotically to a variety of chance and deliberate actions mediated by all sorts of sensors to whatever seems appropriate... The aim is to produce unpredictable sound complexes which cannot be repeated.[16]

He emphasizes his intended purpose as:

> An exploration of sound structures, neither musically "designed" nor of random occurrence. Such structures... possess the properties of beauty, complexity and evocation of the emotional, the spiritual and the imaginary.[17]

Tétaz used Lamb's recordings due to the ambiguous nature of their sound sources (music or ambience? composed or environmental? etc.), their subtle textures and in allusion to previous local soundtrack work:

> I started with Alan Lamb's recordings of abandoned telegraph wires. They are hard to define. No one is quite sure what the sound source is and they are texturally quite complex and emotive. That illusive quality seemed to set up the titles and the landscapes very well. Subtle and hard to define. They have been used before in Australian films, The Boys [Rohan Woods, 1997] and Kiss or Kill [Bill Bennett, 1997], so they have a bit of heritage. I wanted to make them feel very musical rather than textural, so I re-pitched and manipulated them heavily to make them concise musical works.

According to a passage in the soundtrack CD cover booklet:

> The wires, resonated by the wind, generate a vast range of sounds: from low pitched drones to subtle metallic twangs to huge, buzzing walls of sound.

In the latter part of the film, this sonic-musical palette is deployed for more conventional "communicative" functions, the low bass drone being used to signify danger in scenes such as that in which a wide shot reveals the area where Mick lives, or in another key scene when Mick attacks Liz, when we hear a very dark, bottom-end drone.

Along with his use of ambiguous musical tonalities derived from the wire recordings, Tétaz also produces highly processed sounds from conventional musical instruments (in a manner familiar to post-Cagean avant-gardist musicians). The piano is particularly prominent in this regard, where he used:

> the guts of a piano, without the keys. Strings, frame and soundboard. The frame was prepared with screws, bolts, coins and gaffer tape. It was struck with hands, mallets, forks, coins, super balls on bamboo skewers and bowed with a double bass bow. Through these methods, pitch and partials were manipulated. This again was attempting to find new musical sources for the torture scenes. The sounds are metallic and interact well with the metal of the shed and the mine. These were augmented by Dave Brown's laptop guitar. A semi-acoustic guitar with alligator clips on the strings, flicked and hit.

But while the shrill, scraping sounds perform a function similar to that of Herrmann's dramatic violins in films such as *Psycho* (Alfred Hitchcock, 1960), Tétaz also employs more conventional string-dominated instrumental passages. As Kalinak has identified, this musical usage has distinct connotations in that:

> The string family, because of its proximity in range and tone to the human voice, is thought to be the most expressive group of instruments in the orchestra. In particular, the violin is characterised by its ability to 'sing' because its timbre or tonal quality is close to that of the human voice (2003: 20).

In classic Hollywood soundtrack mode, *Wolf Creek* features a string-quartet motif that is repeated with variations to signal progression of narrative theme and circumstance. The motif is first introduced to the audience in the scene where Mick tows the travellers' car. This motif is more melodic and somewhat emotive than the other string sections, in which there are single bowed notes that sound more jarring. As Tétaz describes it:

> that's the closest you get to a lead motif... It carries the undertow/weight and was designed to give just enough to carry you through without feeling 'this is too much'. I think of it as being like a requiem theme. Much like 'March to the Scaffold' (Berlioz) was used in the opening of The Shining by Wendy Carlos/ Stanley Kubrick.

Towards the end of the film, when Ben frees himself, the motif is further developed, and from here on starts to sound even more melodic and more emotive, particularly in the scenes when Ben is rescued by foreign tourists and when he is flown away by the Royal Flying Doctor Service, when we hear a fuller string section, encouraging an emotional response from the audience.

Providing an overarching characterization of the film's score, Tétaz identifies that the score "starts somewhat tonal, then abandons tonality, and ends up very modal". Atonality and dissonance are, of course, widely used in horror movies, their lack of apparent musical 'direction' and/or resolution creating a continually unsettling effect. The modality of the final sections of the film is compounded by the irregular rhythmic patterns of the music, which Tétaz identifies as "based on the cuts of the film", exemplifying Kalinak's observation that:

> Irregular or unpredictable rhythms attract our attention by confounding our expectations and, depending on the violence of the deviation, can unsettle us physiologically through increased stimulation of the nervous system (2003: 18).

Together with rhythm and dissonance, the film also employs a conventional approach to volume, as Tétaz describes, the music is "very subtle in the beginning, loud in the middle section and ever-present in the conclusion". In this manner, the film's musical score and overall sound levels mirror its development of narrative intensity and of horrific affect in a classic cinematic genre pattern.

Conclusion

In the characterization that opens this chapter, McLean described his inspiration for *Wolf Creek* as the "nameless fear" of what "lurks" unseen on the "long lonely highways" that traverse Australia's vast interior. This colourful description, rich in ambiguous threat and unease, has distinct parallels with a group of previous Australian 'outback' films that imbue the landscape with a local–national version of the European tradition of the brooding romantic/gothic landscape. Imported to Australia, this sensibility permeates a locale where it is not so much dramatic ruins, statuesque buildings and Western histories and folklores that engender it, rather than the spaces and absences perceived by a Western settler society still uncertain of its relationship to the continent's scarcely populated interior. The use of Lamb's environmental sound sources is singularly appropriate here – the long, humming wires offering an acoustic mirror to the long highways and aural ambiences of the outback. *Wolf Creek* combines these delicate ambiences with uses of standard Hollywood techniques. The latter propel the film from its opening scenes into a hardcore horror climax that was effective enough to secure major US distribution and to succeed with a mainstream audience. Mixing mainstream, Dogme 95 and Australian genre traditions, *Wolf Creek* illustrates the potential of contemporary genre cinema to retain diversity and local address without sacrificing box-office potential. Returning to the quotation that prefaces this chapter, along with putting "a face to the nameless fear of what lurks 'out there' on those long lonely highways", Tétaz and McLean have also established enduring sound signs of lost and alienated urban travellers untuned to the country they traverse and isolated in the face of adversity.

Acknowledgement

This chapter originated from Australia Research Council Discovery Research Grant DP 0770026, 'Music Production and Technology in Australian Film: Enabling Australian Film to Embrace Innovation'.

Notes

1. *Wolf Creek*, 'Production Notes', available online (http://www.eofftv.com/notes/w/wol/wolf_creek_2005_notes.htm, accessed November 2005).
2. The film grossed AU$5.6 million for Australian cinema attendances in 2005 and took US$5.9 million on its opening weekend in the USA in December 2005 (showing at 1749 screens nationwide). See Ziffer (2005: 3).
3. Director of *Night of Fear* (1973), *Inn of the Damned* (1975) and *Lady Stay Dead* (1982).
4. *Wolf Creek*, 'Production Notes' (see note 1).

5. *Ibid.*
6. *Ibid.*
7. Wolfe Creek (with the final 'e') is an actual location in th. Kimberley region of Western Australia.
8. *Wolf Creek*, 'Production Notes'.
9. See Dogme95's 10-point 'Vow of Chastity', available online (http://www.martweiss.com/film/dogma95-thevow.shtml).
10. *Wolf Creek*, 'Production Notes'.
11. 'Vow of Chastity'.
12. Unless otherwise attributed, all comments by composer François Tétaz in this chapter are taken from an interview with Harry Minassian in October 2005.
13. For *Wolf Creek*, Tétaz won the 2006 APRA–AGSC Screen Music Award for 'Feature Film Score of the Year'.
14. Comprising Pete Best (supervising sound editor), Tom Heuzenroeder (sound effects editor), Adrian Medhurst (foley artist) and Peter D. Smith (sound mixer and sound re-recording mixer).
15. (Unattributed) (nd) 'Alan Lamb – bibliographical entry', on Australian Sound Design website (http://www.sounddesign.unimelb.edu.au/web/biogs/P000277b.htm).
16. *Ibid.*
17. *Ibid.*

References

Buhler, J., and Neumeyer, D. (2001), 'Analytical and Interpretive Approaches to Film Music (I): Analysing the Music', in K. Donnelly (ed.), *Film Music: Critical Approaches*, New York: Continuum, pp. 16–38.

Hood, R. (1994), 'Killer Koalas: Australian (and New Zealand) Horror Films – a History' (parts 1 and 2), reproduced online (http://www.tabula-rasa.info/AusHorror/OzHorrorFilms1.html).

Hubinette, J. (2005), 'Music and sound effects in horror films', online at (http://www.eng.umu.se/monster/john/sound_music.htm).

Kalinak, K. (2003), 'The Language of Music: A Brief Analysis of *Vertigo*', in K. Dickinson (ed.), *Movie Music: The Film Reader*, London: Routledge, pp. 15–23.

Kassabian, A. (2001), *Hearing Film: Tracking Identifications in Contemporary Hollywood Film Music*, New York: Routledge.

Stevens, B. (2000), *Fear Codex*, Melbourne: Jacobyte Books.

Turek, R. (2005), 'Interview with *Wolf Creek* director Greg McLean', online at (www.esplatter.com/main/wolfcreekinterview.htm).

Ziffer, D. (2005), 'Violent *Wolf Creek* a Hit in America', *The Age* (Melbourne), 28 December, p. 3.

16 The Ghostly Noise of J-Horror
Roots and Ramifications

James Wierzbicki

Near the end of Hideo Nakata's 1998 *Ringu* the character Ryuji is in his apartment, busily working on the notes he has made during his harrowing recovery, with his ex-wife, Asakawa, of the corpse of a long-ago murdered girl named Sadako.[1] Startled by a faint noise behind him, he turns and finds that his television set has somehow turned itself on. On the screen, he sees the final shot of the mysterious videotape that spurred his and Asakawa's investigation: the grainy image of the well that held Sadako's body. Then the screen shows something that was not on the videotape. Sadako emerges from the well and crawls toward what, were this normal footage, would be the camera. To Ryuji's surprise and eventual shock, the battered and filthy Sadako – "still in her grimy white dress, face hidden beneath long, oily strands of hair"[2] – crawls out of the television set and, now corporeal, advances toward him until he is literally frightened to death. According to the stage directions in Hiroshi Takashi's screenplay, when Ryuji first looks at the television set, "the sound from before comes louder now, more insistent, a metallic screeching that both repulses and beckons him closer".[3]

In his authoritative study of Japanese music and musical instruments, ethnomusicologist William P. Malm describes an episode in a 1956 production of the kabuki play *Momiji Gari* [The Leaf-viewing Party]. Despite its bucolic title, *Momiji Gari* is an action-packed thriller that climaxes in an encounter between the hero, Koremochi, and the ghost-demon Kijo. According to Malm's report, in the second act:

> There is a flash of lightning and the villain [Kijo] comes flying on stage, his face hidden by a veil and hotly pursued by Koremochi. An added effect to the lightning is the grating of a bronze hand gong over the rough surface of a much larger, thinner gong (the soban). This gives a real lightning 'ripping' sound. It is also used when the villain reveals himself in all his horror and begins to twirl his long hair about by violently swinging his head. (1959: 231–2)[4]

These two scenes – one from the 1998 film that arguably sparked the current western interest in so-called J-horror, the other from a production of a traditional kabuki play[5] – have in common not just the supernatural characters' coiffures. They also share a sonority – a "metallic screeching" in the case of *Ringu*, a "grating" or "ripping" sound in the case of *Momiji Gari* – that announces the presence of ghosts. Lest this seem merely coincidental, comparable sounds are associated with ghostly activity in at least two other recent examples of J-horror, namely, Nakata's *Honogurai mizu no soko kara* (2002) and Takashi Shimuzu's *Ju-on* (2003). As different as are their plots, the films' consistent linkage between a high-pitched raspy noise and the manifestation of ghosts clearly suggests a convention. When the J-horror films were remade in Hollywood, much was changed, but, remarkably, this sonic convention seems not to have been lost in translation.

In 2002, Gore Verbinski remade Nakata's *Ringu* as *The Ring* (set not in Japan but in the Pacific Northwest region of the United States). The next year Shimuzu himself, in co-operation with Hollywood horror mogul Sam Raimi, converted *Ju-on* into *The Grudge* (the film retains the original Tokyo locale and even some of the original cast members, but the much-simplified plot focuses on American sojourners). In 2005, Walter Salles remade *Honogurai mizu* as *Dark Water* (set in New York City). The music for the Japanese films is by diverse hands: Kenji Kawai scored *Ringu* and, in collaboration with Shikako Suga, *Honogurai mizu*, and the score for *Ju-on* is by Shiro Sato. Likewise, the music for the Hollywood films comes from different sources: the composers are Hans Zimmer (*The Ring*), Christopher Young (*The Grudge*) and Angelo Badalamenti (*Dark Water*). Stylistically unique as all these composers are, they nevertheless share, at least vis-à-vis the limning of ghostly characters in the films just mentioned, an affinity for certain sonic colorations.

Except for *The Grudge*'s title sequence and, obviously, its Tokyo setting, none of the remakes seems especially 'Japanese' in terms of visual design, narrative flow, or even, philosophically speaking, content. Yet the scores of the Hollywood films, at least in their peak moments, bear a striking resemblance to their Japanese counterparts, and in this they seem to reflect not just the influence of modern J-horror but also, albeit perhaps second-hand, the influence of traditional Japanese theatre.

In his introduction to a recent anthology on Japanese horror films, Jay McRoy (2005: 2–9) notes that the range of subject matter is as wide as is to be found anywhere in the world. Since the screen debut in 1954 of *Godzilla*,[6] Japanese audiences have had a special taste for *daikaiju eiga*, that is, films that have plots built around giant monsters. However, the Japanese film industry, like most of its western counterparts, has also produced plenty of examples of what McRoy calls "the torture film", "the techno/body-horror film", "the apocalyptic film", and more or less realistic films that focus on serial killers and people who engage in "dove style violence".[7] In addition, there has long been cultivated a genre that is arguably unique to Japan: the *kaidan* ('ghost story'), the agent of which is the spectre of a human being, usually female, who in life was somehow grievously wronged and who in death is determined to find revenge.

As a distinct genre, the ghost story that centres on a vengeful female spirit came into prominence during the Tokugawa shogunate, which lasted from 1603 until the start of the Meiji restoration in 1868 (Keene, 1984: 379). There might be political reasons for this. The Tokugawa regime was notoriously authoritarian, and some scholars argue that the fanciful conditions of *kaidan* in general allowed for the symbolic expression of sentiments otherwise unspeakable (Pounds, 1990: 168; Reider, 2000: 260) and that stories involving vengeful female ghosts in particular represented "an extreme reaction to the repressed position of women in society" (Jordan, 1985: 22–3).

One of the first uses of the word '*kaidan*' – made up of the shorter '*kai*' ('strange or mysterious apparition') and '*dan*' ('narrative') – indeed dates from early in the seventeenth century. This is in *Kaidan zensho*, a five-volume collection of stories translated from Chinese around 1627 or 1628 by the physician–scholar Razan Hayashi (Reider, 2000: 266). However, the idea of *kaidan* dates to well before the Tokugawa period. Indeed, as Leon Zolbrod notes in the introduction to his translation of stories by the eighteenth-century author Akinari Ueda:

> In China, despite Confucian exhortation that the spiritual world is not a proper topic for human inquiry, tales and anecdotes about supernatural beings are as old as recorded literature. (1977: 54)

There is a Japanese belief that body and spirit are two separate entities, and this is important to an understanding of *Ringu* and J-horror films in which ghosts loom large. It stems both from Japan's indigenous Shinto religion and from the Buddhism that was imported from China *c.* 550 A.D. According to Zvika Serper:

> One of the expressions of this belief is the erection of two separate graves: one for the impure body and another for the soul. After death, the soul (*tamashii*) wanders for several years until it is purified and becomes a quasi-god (*kami*) that resides in another world, beyond the sea or sky. It is there that the dead spirits become the ancestral souls. At the time of death, the soul of a person can become either an angered or a peaceful spirit, according to the psychological status of the person at the moment of death. Emotions such as jealous love or hatred will engender a very dangerous spirit. (2002: 346)

Generally, this dangerous spirit is known as an *onryō or goryō*, and its particular female manifestation is called a *yûrei*. Folklorist Klaus Antoni notes that:

> The 'vengeful spirits of the dead' are a specimen of deities whose cult flourished especially in the Heian period [794–1185] of Japanese history. The first incident of a goryō-e, a ceremony for the pacification of such vengeful spirits which were regarded as a great danger for the community of the living, is reported from the year Jōgan 5, that is, A.D. 863. (1988: 127)

Antoni notes further that some time around 1219, the monk Jien, in a treatise titled *Gukanshō*, wrote in detail about the problems presented by the *onryō* and its kin:

> *The main point about a vengeful soul* [according to Jien] *is that it bears a deep grudge and makes those who caused the grudge objects of its revenge even while the resentful person is still alive. When the vengeful soul is seeking to destroy the objects of its resentments... the state is thrown into disorder by the slanders and lies it generates. The destruction of the people is brought about in exactly the same way. And if the vengeful soul is unable to obtain its revenge while in this visible world, it will do so from the realm of the invisible.* (1988: 127–8)

Pre-Tokugawa compilations of stories that somehow stepped into 'the realm of the invisible' include the ninth-century *Nihon ryōiki* and the twelfth-century *Konjaku monogatari*. Given their general popularity, it is hardly surprising that such stories figured importantly in the several thousand *noh* plays that began to be written in the fourteenth century but whose origins probably date back to the Kamakura (1192–1333) and Heian periods.[8]

The *noh* plays, of which only about two hundred survive, dealt with the topics of "filial piety, love, jealousy, revenge, and [the] samurai spirit" (Daiji and Tatsuo, 1969: 98). Usually the plays were presented in five-part cycles, the components of which fell into the strictly delineated categories of brief "celebratory plays" (*waki-noh*) or "god plays" (*kami-mono*); "ghost plays" (*shura-mono*); "woman plays" (*onna-mono*) or "wig plays" (*katsura-mono*); "mad woman plays" (*kyojo-mono*) or "frenzy plays" (*kurui-mono*); and "concluding plays" (*kirino-mono*) (Hand, 2005: 20).[9] In contrast to the antagonists of the J-horror films considered here, the central character (*shite*) of a *noh* 'ghost play' is usually the spirit of a slain warrior, who recounts his deeds on earth, describes his current existence in the netherworld, and ultimately begs a priest (*waki*) to pray for his soul. On the other hand, revenge usually drives the central character of a 'mad woman play' or 'frenzy play'; in some cases, the revenge (*shunen*) can only be realized after the character has died.

Religious in content and ritualistic in presentation, the finite *noh* repertoire was created in the fourteenth and fifteenth centuries. The secular and much looser type of theatre known as *kabuki* – whose repertoire continues to grow – began late in the sixteenth century, supposedly with a somewhat lascivious festival dance performed by a woman on a *noh*-style stage near Kyoto. Following this model, the first professional *kabuki* companies were made up of women who likely supplemented their thespian earnings by working as prostitutes. Attempting to crack down on vice, in 1629 the Tokugawa government declared that only males could perform in what was rapidly becoming a very popular form of theatre, and in 1642 it declared further that kabuki casts should consist only of adults.

Essential differences between *noh* and *kabuki* can be gleaned from the words themselves. As remains the case today, *noh* was always geared to highly educated audiences who could appreciate not only the refinement of the texts but also the highly developed skills of the performers; indeed, the word '*noh*' means 'ability'. *Kabuki*, on the other hand, has been, from the start, a genre whose appeal easily crossed social boundaries. In the seventeenth century, the word 'kabuki' was an adjective that meant 'unusual' or 'unconventional', but the modern Japanese ideogram consists of three characters that mean 'music', 'dance' and 'acting.' The *noh* theatre, of course, involves all three of these performance modes, and participants in *kabuki* certainly exhibit impressive amounts of ability. However, the emphases are as the words suggest. Whereas *noh* fairly demands to be esteemed as a lofty form of art, *kabuki* seems to want no more than to be regarded as entertainment.

Despite its lack of pedigree, *kabuki* in its early years borrowed heavily from the plots of *noh* plays. In particular, it looked to *noh*'s 'woman plays' for material that eventually would typify *kabuki*'s *wagoto* ('gentle') style and to the 'frenzy plays' for material for its *aragoto* ('rough') style (Hand, 2005: 21). And it was largely within the environment of the 'rough' style — characterized by colourful costumes, garish make-up, acrobatic acting, and spectacular stage effects — that *kabuki*'s ghost stories were first conjured up.

The Japanese *kaidan* has deep historical roots. But the progenitors of the modern theatrical ghost story — that is, the direct ancestors of the films under discussion here — were likely *kabuki* plays written by Nanboku Tsuruya (1755–1829). In a recent review of a four-volume anthology of *kabuki* plays, Goff writes:

> [Tsuruya's] *taste for themes of sex, violence, and death reached a new level in his most famous ghost story, Tōkaidō Yotsuya kaidan ('The Ghost Stories at Yotsuya on the Tōkaidō'), [whose] eerie atmosphere... is heightened in performance by grotesque stage effects.* (2005: 429)[10]

Special stage effects, generally known as *keren*, were endemic to *kabuki* from the start, and their designers flourished as the fashion for ghost plays escalated during the Tokugawa period. *Yûrei*, who in drawings and paintings were usually depicted as legless, in *kabuki* were made to swing from wires or make their entrances on small carts hidden beneath the actors' long robes; amputations and decapitations were regularly enacted on stage; spurts of blood, either liquid or represented by the unfurling of scarlet ribbons, were common. But bloodshed in the Tokugawa-period *kabuki* theatre was hardly limited to plays involving vengeful female ghosts; indeed, graphic violence figured in almost everything except romances and comedies solidly in *kabuki*'s 'gentle' style, and it formed the basis of what *kabuki* scholars term *zankoko no bi* (the 'aesthetics of cruelty').[11]

Notwithstanding Baroque opera's tradition of *deus ex machina* finales and Restoration England's famously gory productions of Shakespeare, the western theatre, generally speaking, has not gone in much for this sort of thing. Nor, in western literature, does one often find ghosts of the particular type that flit on a regular basis through Japanese *kaidan*.

Western literature, to be sure, has had ghosts aplenty. Their appearances range from Shakespeare's *Hamlet* and *Macbeth* to Horace Walpole's 1764 novel, *The Castle of*

Otranto; from the Victorian-era short stories of Henry James and their operatic trans-formations (in Benjamin Britten's *The Turn of the Screw* [1954] and *Owen Wingrave* [1970]), to such diverse films as Robert Wise's *The Haunting* (1963), Stuart Rosenberg's *The Amityville Horror* (1979), Stanley Kubrick's *The Shining* (1980), M. Night Shyamalan's *The Sixth Sense* (1999), and Alejandro Amenábar's *The Others* (2001). While some western ghosts, especially as manifest on screen, have been decidedly comic (one thinks, for example, of the *Caspar the Friendly Ghost* cartoons that Isador Sparber made for Paramount beginning in 1948, or Jules Dassin's *The Canterville Ghost* [1944] and Ivan Reitman's *Ghostbusters* [1984]), most of them have been adequately scary. Few of them, however, have been even half as mean-spirited as the Japanese *goryō-shinkō* ('vengeful souls').

Numerous scholars have attempted to account for the prominence that female *goryō-shinkō* have held in Japanese culture at least since the late eighteenth century. Already noted was Jordan's idea that the popularity of malicious *yûrei* during the Tokugawa period was "an extreme reaction to the repressed position of women in society" (1985: 22–3). Leiter supports this assessment when he writes of the Tokugawa-period *kabuki* plays:

> One of the ways in which women who have been trampled on become empowered is to turn into vengeful spirits after they have died. The entire world of selfish, unfaithful husbands and lovers must take cover when one of these women comes back from the other world to seek revenge on those who have wronged her. (2002: 225)

These views are generously feminist, and perhaps anachronistic, considering that without exception the Tokugawa-period *kabuki* plays were not only performed but written by men. More realistic and more apropos of the enduring popularity of *goryō-shinkō* stories, it would seem, is the opinion of Wilson, who in a review of a 1996 book on 'the fantastic' in modern Japanese literature takes the female author to task for eschewing:

> the obvious opportunity to address gender issues in postwar Japan. She does not discuss, for example, why the woman as Other is a medium of sadistic male fantasy. The omission is reinforced by the inclusion of Donald Richie's observation that 'the Japanese ghost (almost always female and demonic) is constructed by males for males'. (1998: 326)[12]

The author lambasted here is Susan Napier, who in subsequent writings has indeed made contributions to the gender debate. In his introduction to *Japanese Horror Cinema*, McRoy writes:

> As Susan Napier and Ann Allison posit, in a transforming national and international landscape informed by increasingly reimagined gender roles, Japanese men have 'apparently suffered their own form of identity crisis,' resulting in a panicked cultural reassessment in which contemporary mani-

festations of the 'avenging spirit' motif can be understood as symptomatic. (2005: 4)

The *yûrei*'s sexual politics are clearly of interest. Yet however one casts her in terms of contemporary gender debate, it seems an incontrovertible fact that the vengeful female ghost remains as prominent in modern J-horror films as she was in the *kaidan mono* of the Tokugawa shogunate. It seems fact, too, that the *yûrei* – especially in her lack of discrimination as to her victims and her imperviousness to human intervention – is foreign to western culture.

In the western literary–cinematic tradition, people come to bad ends either because they somehow deserve it or because – in the case of minor characters – they make stupid choices; in the tradition of Japanese *kaidan*, people as often as not meet horrible fates simply because they happen to be in the wrong place at the wrong time. Since its inception, musical accompaniment to western cinema has responded primarily to what many directors call 'motivation'; in other words, the music illustrates not just what is happening on screen but, importantly, why it is happening. In Japanese ghost stories, typically there is no good reason why anything is happening other than the fact that someone has stumbled across the path of a *yûrei* who is really, really angry. Compared to long-established western norms, there is little in the horrific events of Japanese *kaidan* that might be considered rational. Perhaps this is why western composers, in scoring Hollywood remakes of J-horror films whose plots are in essence irrational, have abandoned familiar modes of operation in favour of Japanese models.

On the influence that *noh* and *kabuki* have had on Japanese cinema, Richie, a prolific commentator on all things Japanese, has stated flatly: "The truth is that the traditional theater in Japan has given almost nothing to the film" (Richie and Anderson, 1958: 2). He points to Akira Kurosawa's 1957 *Kumonosu-Jo* ('The Castle of the Spider's Web', generally known in the West as *Throne of Blood*), which indeed features traditional visual and sonic elements, but he emphasizes that these elements were "consciously and experimentally included" (*ibid.*: 8). Even in costume dramas and historical epics, Richie writes, acting and music has most often followed western models. This is because, he argues:

> No matter how exotic the style and action of the period film appears to foreign audiences, to the Japanese this film style is a part of the realist tradition, adopted from the West and therefore without connection to the classical Japanese drama. Because so much Japanese classical music exists only in relation to the classic drama, the use of this music in films must present a severe stylistic clash. (*ibid.*: 9)

But Richie came to that conclusion almost a half-century ago, and since then scholars have had plenty of time to develop differing opinions. Burch, for example, in 1976 offered a summary that directly contradicts Richie's. He writes:

> *The overwhelming majority of films from [the] early period drew their sub-
> stance from the kabuki repertoire, or from the repertoires of its derivatives
> shimpa and shin-kabuki... In this early period, there can be absolutely no
> doubt that pertinent visual traits of kabuki appear constantly on the screen...
> They helped to guarantee the Japanese cinema against the ideology of
> 'realism' which was then taking over Western cinema.* (Burch, 1976: 38–9)[13]

Along with traditional costumes and acting styles, Kurosawa's *Kumonosu-Jo* ('Throne
of Blood') uses music by Masaru Satô that draws directly from *kabuki*. The film is an
adaptation of Shakespeare's *Macbeth*, and among its most stunning moments are the
scenes during which fully human characters in one way or another confront the supernatural. These scenes are scored primarily for the small transverse flute called the *nohkan*
(narrow in bore, about half the length of the western concert flute) and a large
stick-struck drum called the *ô-daiko* (approximately the size of a trap set's free-standing
tom-tom).[14] At the core of these scenes is a musical signifier that is long associated
in *kabuki* with ghosts. It features wobbly flute tones called *netori* set over a drum pattern
in which a series of sharp accents is surrounded by single-stroke rolls that rise and then
fall in volume level. The combined flute-and-drum gesture is known as *dorodoro* (see
Figure 16.1).

Dorodoro is one of hundreds of stock gestures that, during a *kabuki* performance,
would be realized by an off-stage group of musicians collectively known as *geza* (the
word means 'lower place', which describes the musicians' location relative to the main
stage). Traditionally, *kabuki*'s *geza-ongaku* ('off-stage music') involved flutes (not just
the *nohkan* but also the end-blown *shakuhachi*), stringed instruments (*koto, shamisen*
and the bowed lute called the *kokyû*), and a wide variety of percussion instruments
(drums, clappers, gongs, bells, cymbals, rattles, etc.). Traditionally, too, members of the
geza ensemble would animate the on-stage activity with figures that, like the *dorodoro*,
are not so much musical compositions as simply motifs or, in some cases, onomatopoetic
sound effects.

The repertoire of *geza* music is huge. Along with aural accompaniments for ghost
scenes, it includes sounds appropriate for water, mountains, wind and rain, for suicides,

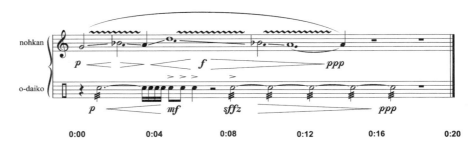

Figure 16.1 Kabuki theatre's *dorodoro* gesture[15]

conversations between samurai knights, and the capturing of thieves, for priests, beautiful women, and drunkards. As Malm observes:

> It should be obvious by now that a large part of the appreciation of geza music depends on previous knowledge of the music and the patterns used. In this respect it is similar to the leitmotif technique of the Wagnerian operas. (1959: 224)

It is also similar, at least in concept, to the music that in the West accompanied silent film.

As dependent as it is on tradition, *kabuki's geza* music has ample room in which to grow. Unlike *noh* accompanists, who perform music that typically was composed by the same people who wrote the text, the creators of sound effects in the *kabuki* theatre have always been free both to experiment artfully and to pander to whatever they might perceive as current taste. Even when it strays boldly from tradition, however, *geza-ongaku* tends to maintain an affiliation with two important elements of classical Japanese music.

One of these involves an aural spacing of sonic events that Japanese composer Jōji Yuasa describes as "substantial silence" (1989: 183) and which Japanese musicians have long identified as *ma*. The other involves an aspect of sound colour. Dean writes:

> 'Noise' may seem an overly harsh term, although this is the word (sō-on, 'noisy sound, noise') that modern Japanese musicologists tend to use. Japanese performing musicians themselves, of course, do not view the phenomenon as noise: to them it is simply part of the music. There is in fact no word in the traditional Japanese musical lexicon for this general phenomenon; there are only technical words for this or that particular effect. (1985: 153)

Among the "obviously noisy" particular effects, Dean explains:

> are the [koto] techniques of suritsumi, literally, 'the scraping pick', and soetsumi, 'the inserted pick'. In the former, the player rapidly slides the edges of the picks attached to the first and second fingers lengthwise across two adjacent strings left to right, then back to the starting position. The textured strings, made of woven strands of silk and pulled very tight, produce a dramatic scraping sound... In the soetsumi technique... the player inserts the left index fingernail under a designated string making light contact with that string, and plucks as usual with the right-hand pick. A high buzzing noise results, simultaneous with the pitched sound of the string. [And for players of the shakuhachi], purposeful overblowing... produces a hissing noise. (ibid.: 154–5)

Whether hissing, scraping or buzzing, the 'noise' inherent in traditional Japanese music compellingly enlivens what western ears might mistake for single sustained sonorities. In western music, one tends to notice differences between more or less 'pure' tone colours, but in Japanese music, as Yuasa explains:

> *The most important characteristic of timbre is timbral transformation. In Japanese traditional music there is no clear distinction between pitched sound and noise. There is an interpenetration between sound and noise... A single sound has a complex component, and a compound sonority may often be heard as just one sound.* (Yuasa, 1989: 192)

The J-horror films *Ringu, Ju-on* and *Honogurai mizu* do not feature in their soundtracks anything that even remotely resembles the wobbly flute tones of *kabuki*'s *dorodoro* figure. When ghosts enter the foregrounds of their narratives, however, these films are extraordinarily rich in noise-filled raspy sounds that, like the scraped-gong effect in the *kabuki* scene described early in this chapter, have a frightful 'ripping' quality about them. And these sounds, apparently sustained but in fact ever-shifting, apparently simple but in fact acoustically complex, are made all the more potent by being framed, far more often than not, by the 'substantial silence' of *ma*.

Generally, the scenarios of the remakes are only similar to those of the J-horror originals. There are instances, however, where direct match-ups can be made, and in these cases it will generally be found that the Japanese soundtracks – in terms of their use of animate noise and substantive silence – are more extreme than their Hollywood counterparts. Two examples can serve to illustrate the point.

The first pair of directly comparable scenes consists of the episodes from early in *Ju-on* and *The Grudge* during which the character of a nurse (named Rika in the Japanese film and Karen in the Hollywood remake), upon her first visit to a haunted house, tries to find the cause of a noise she hears coming from an upstairs room. As analysed here, both scenes begin at the moment the nurse, involved in housecleaning, begins to ascend the stairs to the second floor (the *Ju-on* scene starts at 0:08:06 mins and the scene in *The Grudge* starts at 0:16:48 mins); the scenes end precisely as the nurse is shown speaking on the telephone to make a report on the young boy she has found hiding in a taped-up attic room (the *Ju-on* scene ends at 0:11:18 mins, the scene in *The Grudge* at 0:18:35 mins). The scenes differ considerably in length – 3 minutes and 12 seconds in the case of *Ju-on*, 1 minute and 47 seconds in the case of *The Grudge* – but their action is in essence the same, and so is their dramatic import: the boy, it will eventually be revealed, is the ghostly son of the horrible *yûrei* who inhabits the house and seeks to destroy all who enter it.

Figure 16.2 offers a timeline on which are mapped the scenes' key events. As noted above, the scenes begin (at 0:00 on the timeline) as the nurses – upset that the house is filthy but not otherwise given reason to be frightened – start to climb the stairs. It takes them about 6 seconds to get to the second floor, whereupon they set down their vacuum cleaners and, accompanied only by natural sound, assess the upstairs situation. Karen hears the strange noise a mere 9 seconds into the scene; in contrast, Rika does not hear the noise until the scene has played for 32 seconds.

Marked on the timeline are the points at which the nurses open the door of the largely empty storage room that is apparently the source of the noise. In *Ju-on*, music

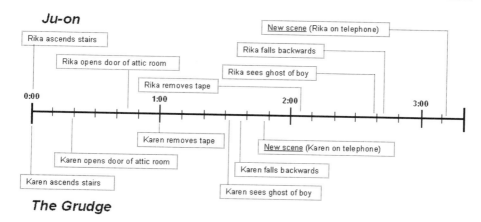

Ju-on

New scene (Rika on telephone)

Rika ascends stairs

Rika falls backwards

Rika opens door of attic room

Rika sees ghost of boy

Rika removes tape

0:00   1:00   2:00   3:00

Karen removes tape

New scene (Karen on telephone)

Karen opens door of attic room

Karen falls backwards

Karen ascends stairs

Karen sees ghost of boy

The Grudge

Figure 16.2 Comparison of 'ghost boy' scene in *Ju-on* and *The Grudge*

starts 6 seconds before Rika arrives at the room: electronic 'whisper' sounds, so quiet that they seem to emerge from the ambient noise, accompany Rika's tentative walk down a corridor. As she stands in the doorway, her wariness is indicated by what sounds like a prolonged stroke of a violin bow across the edge of a large cymbal, and after several seconds a second bowed-cymbal stroke is heard as Rika looks about the room. As she starts to leave she is startled by a loud creak, and a sustained upper-register violin tone sounds as her eyes settle on a taped-up closet door. A mixture of electronic sounds and dense string harmonies accompanies her arrival at and visual examination of the taped door. Rika is startled by a loud cat noise and clasps her hands to her ears (indicating, perhaps, that the ghostly sound is somehow diegetic), and the sustained sonorities are punctuated by quick plucks from a harp. The sound builds in intensity as Rika tears the tape from the door; it stops – abruptly, leaving only a sustained electronic resonance – as she spots in the closet an innocent-looking cat perched on some bedding, and as she reaches gently to pet the cat, the electronic sonority morphs into low string sonorities. As the camera pans past the cat to reveal the boy, the sound intensifies rapidly into an orchestral/electronic shriek; as the boy looks up at Rika, the sound coalesces into a sustained single but very loud high-pitched violin tone. It is at this moment of maximum musical intensity that Rika, in shock, falls backwards. This same string sonority, still intense in timbre but now playing a slow melody that descends by minor thirds and half-steps, continues as Rika rushes downstairs to question the old woman who has been living in the house. The string sonority spreads into warm harmonies as Rika examines a torn photograph that shows a man, a woman and a boy who resembles the one she has just seen. The music fades as Rika is shown engaged in her urgent telephone conversation.

In *The Grudge*, the music does not start until 13 seconds after Karen has entered the storage room: it takes the form of quiet, sustained, high-pitched dissonances played by orchestral strings, and its onset coincides with Karen's first sight of the taped-up closet door. She backs away from the door and is startled by a loud noise from, apparently, a distressed cat; after a few seconds of hesitation and some more cat noise, she starts to remove the tape. Upon looking into the closet Karen sees not a cat but a scrapbook, and with this the music relaxes – as it does for Rika – into low-register single string tones. As Karen picks up the scrapbook she is startled, much more than before, by a cat's angry screech; appropriately, the orchestral music turns 'growly', and then it relentlessly builds until the moment when the boy's eyes meet Karen's. Instead of being marked, like Rika's, by a forceful single violin tone, Karen's shock is illustrated by a full orchestral chord embellished with electronic sounds and heavy percussion. Following the chord's sharp cut-off there is a sustained resonance that ends 3 seconds after Karen is shown speaking on the telephone.

Although the narrative content in these scenes is in essence the same, the durations in the scene from the Hollywood film are much compressed when compared with their counterparts in the Japanese film. The films feature similar time spans between the removal of the tape and the nurses' first sight of the 'ghost boy', but whereas in *The Grudge* the tape ripping begins just 1 minute into the entire scene, in *Ju-on* the same action does not take place until more than twice that amount of time has passed. In both films the music, once it starts, is continuous. Nevertheless the *Ju-on* music, although it lasts longer, contains fewer sonic events. Once articulated, the various sounds in the *Ju-on* score are given much more opportunity to shift their timbres before they decay, and often they are surrounded by silences that have the effect not of pauses but simply of 'breathing spaces'. Significantly, most of the *ma* moments in the *Ju-on* score happen in the tension-filled portion of the scene that leads up to the opening of the closet door.

A second pair of scenes that provides opportunity for comparison comes from *Ringu* and *The Ring*. In this case, the examples come from late in the films and represent not a character's tentative initial meeting with a *yûrei* but, rather, a psychologically violent final encounter (described in the first paragraph of this chapter). Figure 16.3 shows a timeline for the activity in both films during the scene in which the vengeful ghost of a murdered girl emerges corporeally from a television monitor and frightens a man to death.

Simply from looking at the timeline it is apparent that the parallel scenes are almost the same length. As delimited for the purpose of this analysis, the scenes begin with the moment the camera shows the man (Ryuji in *Ringu*, Noah in *The Ring*) at his desk; they end with what in essence is a new scene in which the main character is the female co-investigator (ex-wife Reiko Asakawa in *Ringu*, estranged former lover Rachel in *The Ring*). In *Ringu* the scene begins at 1:25:26 mins and ends, with a cut to Reiko at her father's house, at 1:28:08 mins; in *The Ring*, the scene begins at 1:39:23 mins and ends – still in the same locale, with Rachel entering Noah's apartment – at 1:42:31 mins. In the case of *Ringu* the scene's total duration is 2 minutes and 42 seconds, and in the case of *The Ring* the duration is just 10 seconds more than that.

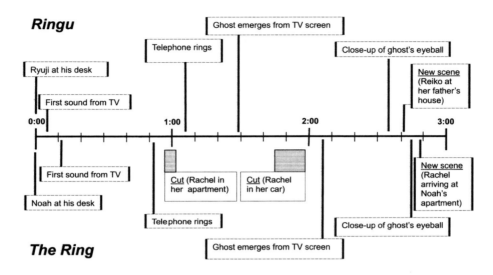

Figure 16.3 Comparison of 'television' scene in *Ringu* and *The Ring*

The 'television' sequences of *Ringu* and *The Ring* begin in more or less the same way. Ryuji/Noah is busy working when his concentration is broken by a quiet noise that emanates from a television set that presumably had been turned off (in *Ringu*, the noise is a series of metallic scrapes separated by silences; in *The Ring* the noise is sustained static). Although the noise does not get appreciably louder, the fear exhibited by Ryuji/ Noah intensifies as he realizes what is contained in the video images, and it fairly explodes when the telephone suddenly rings. After this, in both films, the volume level of the noise increases until the ghost emerges from the screen, at which point the soundtrack is taken over by more or less conventional orchestral music that builds until the horrific close-up of the *yūrei*'s staring eyeball. In *Ringu*, the musical climax features a sustained orchestral shriek that devolves, after Ryuji falls dead from fright, into a swirly electronic cluster that sinks rapidly in pitch; in *The Ring*, the close-up of the eyeball is marked by a high-pitched 'scrape' sound that, upon Noah's fall, shifts abruptly to a loud hiss.

At least in their sibilant qualities, the preliminary sounds in these two scenes (metallic scraping in *Ringu*, television static in *The Ring*) are similar, and there are similarities as well in the sounds' dynamic patterns. But at two points in the Hollywood film the scene is interrupted by cut-away shots that sever not just the action but also the sonic flow. The brief shot that shows Rachel, in her own apartment, trying to reach Noah by telephone has no music and is dominated by her shouting "Pick up the phone, Noah. Come on, pick up!" The longer shot that shows Rachel frantically driving to Noah's apartment likewise has no music, and it is filled to capacity with the noise of honking automobile horns, squealing tires, and screeching brakes. After both interruptions *The Ring*'s crescendo of static picks up where it left off, but in both cases momentum has been lost. In striking contrast, in *Ringu* the sound of metallic scraping moves inexorably towards the scene's climax.

The potency of the uninterrupted sequence in *Ringu* is apparent when the soundtrack is regarded not as accompaniment to filmic imagery but as music in its own right. Figure 16.4 is a transcription of the scene's sonic elements. Like the segment in *Ju-on* that precedes the loud ripping of the tape from the closet door, the opening segment of *Ringu*'s 'television' scene is noteworthy both for its slow pace and its tension-fraught silences. Heard simply as music, the introductory 'passage' lasts long enough to establish a sonic norm, and after more than a minute that norm is violated by the simple ringing of a telephone.

The loud ring of the telephone is in itself musically startling, and in the context of the filmic drama it is surely frightening. Just as frightening, but, perhaps ironically, providing a calming musical resolution to all that has transpired, is the quiet recapitulation of the metallic scrapes after the climax of the orchestral interlude (represented in Figure 16.4 as a mix of three distinct motifs over a steady rhythmic figure). In Ryuji's apartment the telephone receiver is still off the hook, and over the line a perplexed Reiko hears the same noise that Ryuji heard. Quite apart from what they signify in terms of the film's narrative, the metallic scrapes form the principal motif of what might be heard as a musical composition comprising all the elements – not just music in the conventional sense, but also dialogue and diegetic noise – of a multiplane soundtrack. The motif's recurrence at the end gives the 'composition' a well-defined musical

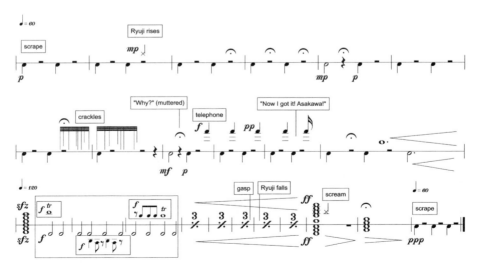

Figure 16.4 Transcription of sonic elements in the 'television' scene of *Ringu*

structure, and it seems significant, in light of the aesthetics of traditional Japanese music, that a large portion of the motif consists of nothing but silence.

Like the *geza-ongaku* of the *kabuki* theatre, the underscores in the above-described scenes from *Ringu* and *Ju-on* are rich both in subtly shifting sound colours and in the purposeful absence of sound. Doubtless because they were intended for western audiences, the accompaniments of the Hollywood remakes tend not to luxuriate – as do their Japanese models – in *ma*. Nevertheless, the sonic palettes of the Hollywood films, insofar as their tone colours relate specifically to supernatural characters, closely resemble those of the J-horror films. Indeed, if one were exposed only to the remakes, one might easily get the impression that Hollywood's currently fashionable signifier for 'ghost' is a single sonority – sharply articulated, then diminishing in volume over a period of several seconds, somehow fluid and 'swishy' in its complex of overtones – that in one way or another suggests hissing, scraping or buzzing.

Along with this characteristic sonority, the Hollywood remakes to a large extent share with their J-horror models the dramatic function of 'ghostly noise' within the filmic narratives. Neither in the Japanese films nor in the remakes is the ear-catching hiss/scrape/buzz noise ubiquitous throughout the soundtrack. In all of these films, there are plenty of moments when characters have reason to be anxious, or at least to suspect that something in their environments is not quite as it should be. For these creepy moments that do not directly involve the supernatural, the Hollywood composers as well as their Japanese counterparts tend to rely on familiar horror-film clichés involving rhythm, melody and harmony. The ghostly noise they hold in reserve, to be used only when human characters actually come face to face with a *yûrei* or, more subtly, when human characters feel the chill of the *yûrei*'s invisible presence.

The ghosts in these films all qualify as *yûrei*, but their personalities are hardly the same. In *Ringu/The Ring*, the cursed videotape offered to the entire world is the product of a psychically empowered girl who even in life seemed to enjoy causing trouble. In *Ju-on/The Grudge*, nastiness is effected by a murdered wife whose spirit bothers only those who enter the house in which the bloody crime of passion took place. In *Honogurai mizu/Dark Water* the ghost is that of a child who drowned accidentally (albeit as the result of parental neglect) and who in death seeks not so much revenge as simply a mother. By and large the films' music – its ghostly noise as well as its more conventional underscore – reflects these differences. *Ringu/The Ring* and *Ju-on/The Grudge* are open-ended stories, and even through the final credits the music hints that in terms of horror there might well be more to come; moments of *Honogurai mizu/Dark Water* are scary as hell, yet ultimately the music leaves the filmgoer with an almost 'warm' feeling as the female protagonist yields to her maternal instincts.

Kenji Kawai (*Ringu, Honogurai mizu*) and Shiro Sato (*Ju-on*) have their roots in pop music. In their biographies as posted on various websites, there is no evidence that either of them formally studied the music of *noh* theatre or the traditional courtly Japanese music called *ongaku*. This is hardly surprising; current ethnographic reports on music in Japan have it that *noh* and *ongaku* remain rarefied art forms, in essence unfamiliar to the general population that in recent decades has leaned increasingly in the direction of western-style music. Nevertheless, the mere fact of Kawai's and Sato's being born and raised in Japan suggests at the very least an awareness of the musical norms exhibited by the still popular, and highly plebeian, *kabuki* theatre.

Whatever the composers' actual influences, it seems indisputable that their recent film music is characterized both by 'timbral transformation' and by 'substantial silence', and insofar as it relates to on-screen *yûrei* it seems strongly redolent of *kabuki* convention. For theatrical presentations of Japanese ghost stories, the combination of subtly shifting sound colours and purposeful *ma* has done the trick for centuries. Knowingly or not, Kawai and Sato with their scores for J-horror films have tapped into longstanding Japanese tradition. Perhaps instinctively, but more likely because they realized they were dealing with subject matter far removed from western culture, the composers assigned to the Hollywood remakes have gravitated towards a time-tested Japanese model.

Acknowledgement

This essay could not have taken shape without encouragement from University of Michigan ethnomusicologists Judith Becker, Joseph S. C. Lam and (emeritus) William P. Malm. For their moral support and invaluable comments, the author is most grateful.

Notes

1. In this chapter, Japanese names are presented in western style, with given name first and surname second. In *Ringu*, Ryuji is identified only by his given name and his ex-wife – whose given name is Reiko – is usually identified only by her surname. Similarly, in the 1991 novel by Koji Suzuki on which the film is based Ryuji is identified by given name and Asakawa by surname. In the novel, however, the character in the scene described here is Ryuji Takayama, and his fellow investigator is not his ex-wife but a male friend – like the film's Reiko, a journalist – named Kazuyuki Asakawa.

2. The translation of the screenplay by J. Lopez is available at http://www.theringworld.com/RingText.txt.

3. The novel by Suzuki on which Nakata's film is based offers details only about the videotape's visual content and its more or less natural sounds. Nevertheless, in the section that corresponds with the climactic film scene summarized here, Suzuki writes:

   > [Ryuji] *placed both hands on the desk and tried to figure out what was behind him. His apartment was in a quiet place just off a main street, and all sorts of indistinct sounds came in from the street. Occasionally the revving of an engine or the squeal of tires would stand out, but other than that the sounds from outside were just a dull, solid mass stretching out behind him to the*

left and right. Pricking up his ears, he could figure out what was making some of the noises. Among them were the voices of insects. This mixed-up herd of sounds now started to float and flutter like a ghost. (2004: 262)

4. Malm uses the masculine pronoun to refer to Kijo, presumably because he is describing the performer, not the character. In the 1950s the role surely would have been played by a male actor, but synopses of *Momiji Gari* invariably describe Kijo as an ogress or she-devil.

5. *Momiji Gari* was written in 1887 by Mokuami Kawatake. It is based, however, on a *noh* drama by Nobumitsu Kojirô (1435–1516). Kawatake's play was filmed in its entirety in 1899 and is historically important as one of Japan's earliest feature-length silent films.

6. The name 'Godzilla', doubtless familiar around the world, is a western corruption of the original 'Gojira'.

7. Quoting from Thomas and Yuko Mihara Weisser's (1998) *Japanese Cinema Encyclopedia: Horror, Fantasy, Science Fiction*, McRoy writes:

   The term 'dove-style violence' stems directly from [the] *expression of detached cruelty and refers to the practice of 'certain species of bird; when a flock member is different or weaker, the others peck at it dispassionately until it's dead'.* (2005: 8)

8. In his entry on *noh* theatre in the 1980 *Grove Dictionary of Music and Musicians*, Shigeo Kishibe attributes the founding of *noh* to Kiyotsugu Kannami (1333–84) and his son Motokiyo Zeami (1363–1443). The roots of *noh*, Kishibe writes, can be traced to such early performance forms as dengaku, sarugaku, soga, ennenmai and kusemai (vol. 9: 515).

9. For more on the classifications of *noh* plays, see Arthur Waley, *The Nô Plays of Japan* (London: Allen and Unwin, 1921), and P. G. O'Neill, *A Guide to Nô* (Tokyo: Hinoki Shoten, 1953).

10. The reference is to the 1748 *Kanadehon Chûshingura* ('The Treasury of Loyal Retainers,' also known as 'The Forty-Seven Loyal Ronin') by Isumo Takeda, Shôraku Miyoshi and Senryû Namiki; originally a puppet play, *Kanadehon Chûshingura* was quickly adapted for the *kabuki* theatre.

11. Richard J. Hand, appropriately, uses the term 'aesthetics of cruelty' in the title of his contribution to *Japanese Horror Cinema*. In his essay he quotes Samuel L. Leiter, who defines *zankoku no bi* as "a highly aestheticized, even fantastical world where the inherent sadism is muted by artistic techniques" (Leiter, 2002: 221).

12. Wilson gives a page number (100) for the Richie quote, but not the source.

13. Other scholars have noted the influence of traditional theatre on early Japanese film. Jeffrey A. Dym (2000), for example, has examined the important role that the *benshi* —the narrator whose running commentary, or *setsumei*, was from the Tokugawa period on a hallmark of *kabuki* theatre – played in Japanese silent film. In a recent essay that deals specifically with horror films, Richard J. Hand concludes that the influence of traditional Japanese theatre might well extend beyond the Japanese cinema:

> *Although much is made of Greek or Elizabethan–Jacobean theatre as pre-*
> *cursors to modern horror, it is clear that classical Japanese theatre boasts the*
> *most developed template for contemporary horror cinema. Time and again*
> *in Noh and Kabuki theatre we see the iconography of demonic women and*
> *other horrors in worlds that oscillate between the real and the supernatural*
> *in a manipulated structure of suspense.* (2005: 27)

14. The pairing of *nohkan* and *ô-daiko* can also be heard in Kurosawa's 1990 *Yume* ('Dreams,' music by Shinichirô Ikebe), especially in the scenes involving super-natural foxes in the episode titled 'Sunshine Through the Rain'. With comparable effect composer Tôru Takemitsu in his score for Masaki Kobayashi's aptly titled 1964 *Kwaidan* uses another type of Japanese flute, the end-blown *shakuhachi*, to illustrate a character's awareness of ghostly presence.

15. The pitch-to-pitch 'slides' in the notated example are effected by finger movement; the 'wobble' between a notated pitch and its lower neighbour is effected by exaggerated breath vibrato.

References

Antoni, K. (1988), 'Yasukuni-Jinja and Folk Religion: The Problem of Vengeful Spirits', *Asian Folklore Studies*, 47(1), 123–36.

Burch, N. (1976), 'To the Distant Observer: Towards a Theory of Japanese Film', *October* 1 (Spring), 32–46.

Daiji, M., and Tatsuo, Y. (1969), *Noh*, Osaka: Hoikusha.

Dean, B. (1985), 'That "Howling" Music: Japanese *Hôgaku* in Contrast to Western Art Music', *Monumenta Nipponica*, 40(2), 147–62.

Dym, J. A. (2000), '*Benshi* and the Introduction of Motion Pictures to Japan', *Monumenta Nipponica*, 58(4), 509–36.

Goff, J. (2005), Review of *Kabuki Plays on Stage*, ed. by James R. Brandon and Samuel L. Leiter, *Monumenta Nipponica*, 60(3), 425–34.

Hand, R. (2005), 'Aesthetics of Cruelty: Traditional Japanese Theatre and the Horror Film', in J. McRoy (ed.), *Japanese Horror Cinema*, Edinburgh: Edinburgh University Press, pp. 18–28.

Jones, S. (1976), 'Hamlet on the Japanese Puppet Stage', *Journal of the Association of Teachers of Japanese*, 11(1), 15–36.

Jordan, B. (1985), 'Yûrei: Tales of Female Ghosts', in S. Addiss (ed.), *Japanese Ghosts and Demons: Art of the Supernatural*, New York: George Braziller, pp. 25–33.

Keene, D. (1984), *Dawn to the West*, New York: Holt, Rinehart, and Winston.

Kishibe, S. (1980), *Grove Dictionary of Music and Musicians*, s.v. 'Japan: Noh', London: Macmillan.

Leiter, S. L. (2002), 'From Gay to *Gei*: The *Onnagata* and the Creation of *Kabuki*'s Female Characters', in S. L. Leiter (ed.), *A Kabuki Reader: History and Performance*, New York: Sharpe, pp. 211–29.

Malm, W. (1959), *Japanese Music and Musical Instruments*, Rutland, VT, and Tokyo: Tuttle.

Malm, W. (1980), *Grove Dictionary of Music and Musicians*, s.v. 'Japan: Kabuki', London: Macmillan.

McRoy, J. (ed.) (2005), *Japanese Horror Cinema*, Edinburgh: Edinburgh University Press.

Pounds, W. (1990), 'Enchi Fumiko and the Hidden Energy of the Supernatural', *Journal of the Association of Teachers of Japanese*, 24(2), 167–83.

Reider, N. (2000), 'The Appeal of *Kaidan*: Tales of the Strange', *Asian Folklore Studies*, 59(2), 265–83.

Richie, D., and Anderson, J. (1958), 'Traditional Theater and the Film in Japan', *Film Quarterly*, 12(1), 2–9.

Serper, Z. (2002), '"Between Two Worlds": The Dybbuk and the Japanese Noh and Kabuki Ghost Plays', *Comparative Drama*, 35(3/4), 345–76.

Suzuki, K. (2004), *Ring*, trans. by Robert Rohmer and Glynne Walley, New York: Vertical (first published in Japanese as *Ringu*, Tokyo: Kodokawa Shoten, 1991).

Wilson, M. N. (1998), Review of *The Fantastic in Modern Japanese Literature: The Subversion of Modernity*, by S. J. Napier, *Harvard Journal of Asiatic Studies*, 58(1), 324–7.

Yuasa, J. (1989), 'Music as a Reflection of a Composer's Cosmology', *Perspectives of New Music*, 27(2), 176–97.

Zolbrod, L. (ed. and trans.) (1977), *Ugetsu Monogatari: Tales of Moonlight and Rain*, Tokyo: Tuttle.

Index

Note: Film titles are in italics, with date in parentheses; album titles are italic, with 'album' in parentheses; song titles are in quotation marks; book titles are italic; musical works are either in italics or quotation marks, with composer's name in parentheses

2001: A Space Odyssey (1968)   137
'213'   190
28 Days Later (2002)   200
5,000 Spirits (album)   103

AC/DC   188, 189
Academy Award for Sound Mixing   6
Accept   191
Addison, John   39, 179
Adema   195
Adler, Harold   57
Adorno, Theodor   137, 141, 156
Aeneid   203
Afghan Wings   226
Akiyama, Kuniharu   76, 80, 86
Alias (TV series)   185
Alien (1979)   188, 198
Alien films   8
Allman Brothers   232, 233
'Altar of Sacrifice'   189
Altman, Rick   142, 232, 236
Amenábar, Alejandro   159, 254
'America the Beautiful'   222
Amityville Horror, The (1979)   188, 254
Amityville Horror, The (2005)   195
Anatomy of a Murder (1959)   52, 53, 54
Anderson, J.   255
Anderson, L.   236
Anderson, Lars   207
Anderson, P.   139
Anderson, Paul W. S.   180, 188
Andi Sex Gang   97

Angel (TV series)   184
Angel Heart (1987)   188
'Angel Of Death'   190
Angst (2000)   242
Ansatsu [The Assassin] (1964)   80
Anthology (album)   209
Anthrax   189
'Anti-Christ, The'   189
Antichrist Superstar (album)   192
Antoni, Klaus   251
Apocalypse (Bible)   203
Apocalypse Now (1979)   233
Applause (1929)   8
Arbogast, Milton   18, 23
Ardolino, Emile   186
Argento, Dario   9, 88–99, 191, 201, 208
Arliss, Leslie   60
Armoured Saint   209
Armstrong, Gillian   238
Arnett, J. J.   188, 189
Arnold, Malcolm   61
Artemiev, Eduard   138
Artisan Entertainment   215
Ashton, Darren   242
Astley, Edwin   61
'At Dawn They Sleep'   189
Auerbach, Nina   183
Auger, Brian   91, 98

Bach, Johann Sebastian   138
Bacon, Francis   138
Bad Lord Byron (1948)   60
Badalamenti, Angelo   250

Baddeley, G. 190, 193
Baird, R. 39
Baker, Roy Ward 61, 62
Balázs, Béla 156, 218
Balsam, Martin 18
Bangs, L. 189
Banks, Don 61
Barham, Jeremy 10, 142
Barker, Clive 189, 193, 198–211, 209
Barker, E. 115
Barrio, Dan 227
Barron, Bebe 138
Barron, Lee 11, 192, 217
Barron, Louis 138
Barry, John 64, 186
Bartkowiak, Andrzej 209
Bartlett, Roger, and Friends 132, 135
Bartók, Béla 57, 137, 139, 140, 143, 145, 149, 152, 154–5, 156, 158, 159
Bass, Saul 18, 47
Bates, Katharine Lee 222
Bates, Norman 15, 23
Bathori, Erzebet 193
Batman (1989) 176, 177, 178, 181, 183
Batman Forever (1995) 178
Batman Returns (1992) 184
Bauhaus 226
Baumgarten, M. 134
Bava, Lamberto 191
Bava, Mario 96
Baxter, J. 142
Bazelon, Irwin 16, 121, 187
Beethoven, Ludwig van 57
Bell, Wayne 205, 217
Bellour, R. 35, 36, 38, 41
Beltrami, Marco 181, 183
Bender, Jack 189
Bender, John 89–90, 91
Bennett, Bill 245
Bennett, Richard Rodney 61, 89
Berelian, E. 229

Berg, Alban 43
Bergman, Ingmar 211
Berlin Conservatorium 7
Berlioz, Hector 5, 143, 202, 208, 246
Bernard, James 61, 62, 64–5
Bernstein, A. 227
Bernstein, Elmer 39, 47, 186
Bertolucci, Bernardo 90
Best, Pete 248
'Beware' 226
Beyond, The (1981) 191
Big Chill, The (1983) 186
Bigelow, Kathryn 172
Binder, A. 189
Bingham, D. 142
Birds, The (1963) 35, 38, 63
Bishop, Elvin 234
Bixio, Carlo 98
Black, Stanley 61
Black Blood Vomitorium (EP) 191
'Black Magic' 190
Black Sabbath 188, 191, 229
Blade trilogy (1998, 2002, 2004) 181, 182, 183, 185
Blair, Linda 120
Blair Witch 2: Book of Shadows 225
Blair Witch Project, The (1999) 9, 10, 188, 192, 213–27
Blair Witch Project, The: Josh's Blair Witch Mix (CD) 192, 216
Blatty, William Peter 116
blaue Engel, Der (1930) 7
Bloch, R. 42
'Bloodline' 189
Blue, Arkey 135
Blue Cheer 188
Blue Oyster Cult 2
Body Melt (1993) 239
Body Snatcher, The (1945) 7
Boeddeker, Steve 122
Bordwell, D. 38
'Born Of Fire' 189
'Born To Be Wild' 234

Bosavi 112, 122
Bosch, Hieronymus 190
Bota, Rick 198–211
Bour, Ernest 143
Bourke, Terry 239
Bowie, David 172
Bowles, Stephen 114, 116, 118, 123
Bowlly, Al 144
Boyle, Danny 200
Boys, The (1997) 245
Brahms, Johannes 63
Bram Stoker's Dracula (1992) 177, 178, 180
Brave New World (album) 103
Brewis, Peter 104
'Brick House' 232, 233
Bride of Frankenstein (1935) 6
Bride Wore Black, The (1968) 36
Brides of Dracula (1960) 61
Brief Encounter (1945) 60
'Bring Your Daughter To The Slaughter' 193
Britten, Benjamin 254
Britton, Andrew 235
Bronson, Charles 90
Brontë, Emily 34
Brooks, Mel 17
Brophy, Philip 8, 12, 13, 84, 90, 93, 120, 121, 123, 239
Brown, Royal S. 15, 24, 27, 36, 39, 42, 48, 49, 50, 51, 54–5, 56, 94, 103, 187
Browning, Tod 171
Bruce, Graham 16, 23, 27, 39, 43, 55, 57
Buckmaster, Luke 226
Buffy the Vampire Slayer (TV series) 184, 185, 190
Buhler, J. 65
Burch, N. 255–6
Burns, Robert 104
Burnt Offering – the Cult of the Wicker Man (TV documentary) 109
Burr, Jeff 125–36

Burt, George 16, 20
Burt, Peter 84
Burton, Tim 12, 176
Burwell, Carter 225

Cacavas, John 62
Caddy, Eileen 105, 110
Caddy, Peter 105, 110
Cage, John 80, 84, 85
Cahiers du Cinéma 38
Callard, P. 117
Cameron, Evan 19, 20, 28, 40, 48
Cameron, James 58, 207
Carmilla 4
Cannibal Corpse 189
Cannibal Holocaust (1980) 134
Canterville Ghost, The (1944) 254
Cantori Moderni di Alessandrini 89
Carlos, Wendy 143, 145, 159, 246
Carpenter, Brian 13
Carpenter, Gary 104, 108, 110
Carpenter, John 1, 2, 99, 187–8, 193, 208
Carrie (1976) 187, 208
Carroll, N. 38
Cars That Ate Paris, The (1974) 238
Cary, Tristram 61
Casino Royale (2006) 58
Caspar the Friendly Ghost (1948 onwards) 254
Castle of Otranto, The 3, 253–4
Castle of the Spider's Web, The [Kumonosu-Jo] (1957) 255
Cat People (1942) 7
Catholic News 117
Cell, The (2000) 205
'Cellar, The' (music track) 216, 226
Celldweller 209
Chainsaw Kittens 208
Chandon, Alex 193
Cherry Ripe 98
Child's Play 3 (1991) 189
Chion, M. 41
Chopin, Frédéric 64

Christ Illusion (album) 190
Christe, L. 229
Christensen, Benjamin 225
Ciment, M. 141
Cinefantastique 95
Cinema Journal 15
Citizen Kane (1941) 34, 40
City of the Dead, The (1960) 193
City of the Living Dead [Paura nella Citta dei Morti Viventi] (1980) 191
Clarke, Fraser 208
Clouzot, Georges 39
Clover, C. J. 1, 38, 223
Coal Chamber 192
Cohen, A. J. 187, 211
Cohen, Harry 227
Cohen, S. 189
Cohn, R. 58
Coil 209, 210
Cole, Michael 104
Collins, K. 204, 205, 210, 211
'Comatose' 209
Combs, R. 139, 140
Commodores 232
Connell, John 239
Constantine (2005) 203, 209
Conversation, The (1974) 120
Cooper, Alice 191, 193
Cooper, B. L. 225
Cooper, David 53, 57
Cooper, Kyle 58
Cooper, Merian 7
Coppola, Francis Ford 120, 177, 233
Cora, Antonia 216, 226
Cora, Tony 223
Corbett, J. M. 213–14, 219, 222
'Cowboy Rides Away, The' 184
Coyle, R. 232, 236
Cradle of Fear (2002) 193
Cradle Of Filth 193, 195
Crane, Lila 23
Crash (1996) 78
Craven, Wes 17, 187, 188, 199
Crazed Fruit (1956) 76

Crazy Baldheads 89
Cream 188
Creatures 216, 226
Creepers [*Phenomena*] (1984) 97
Crime and Dissonance (CD) 88
'Criminally Insane' 190
Crisell, Andrew 218
Crocodile Dundee films (1986, 1988) 239
Crocodile Hunter, The (TV series) 239
Cronenberg, David 78, 85, 198
Crow, The (1994) 177, 180, 184
Crowther, Bosley 14, 37
Cruelty and the Beast (album) 193
Cruise, Tom 178, 179
'Cry, Little Sister' 174
'Crypts Of Eternity' 189
Cummings, Rob 229
Cunningham, Sean 188, 199
Curci, L. 99
Curse of Frankenstein, The (1955) 61
Cutler, Ian 104, 110

Daddy Cool 241
Dahlhaus, Carl 139
Dahmer, Jeffrey 190
Daiji, M. 252
Damiani, Damiano 89
Dante Alighieri 203
Dante, Joe 17
Dark Water (2005) 195, 250, 263
Dassin, Jules 254
Davies, Russell 95
Davis, M. 39
Dawn of the Dead (1978) 97, 134, 187
Dawn of the Dead (2004) 195
Dayan, D. 226
de Bont, Jan 58
de Ferranti, Hugh 85
de Loutherbourg, Philippe Jacques 204
De Martini, Alberto 89
de Palma, Brian 19, 187, 208
'Dead Girl Superstar' 193

'Dead Skin Mask' 190
Dean, B. 257
Death 189
'Death and the Maiden' (Schubert) 173
Debussy, Claude 43
Deep Purple 91, 188
Def Leppard 188
Deicide 189
del Toro, Guillermo 181
Delightful Rogue, The (1929) 7
Dell'orso, Edda 89
Demme, Jonathan 188
Dèmoni [Demons] (1985) 208
'Demonoid Phenomenon' 193
Demons (1985) 191
Deneuve, Catherine 172
'Der Erlkonig' (Schubert) 3
Deranged (1974) 190
Derrickson, Scott 198–211
Det sjunde inseglet [*The Seventh Seal*] (1957) 211
Deutsch, Didier C. 89, 91
Devil Girl from Mars (1954) 60
Devil's Rejects, The (2005) 195, 229–37
DevilDriver 195
Diaboliques, Les (1955) 39
Diabolus In Musica (album) 190
Digginlilies 227
Dirty Dancing (1987) 186
Disturbed 195
Divine Intervention (album) 190
Dokken 192
Donaggio, Pino 97
Donahue, Heather 219
Donaldson, Roger 207
Donnelly, Kevin 142, 157, 159, 195, 201, 205, 210, 232, 234–5, 236
Donner, Richard 150, 176, 187
'Don't Fear The Reaper' 2
'Don't Go To Sleep Without Me' 226
'Don't Let The Sun Go Down On Me' 174
Don't Look Now (1973) 134

Doom (2005) 209
Doors 174
Douchet, Jean 38
Douglas, Andrew 195
Dr Jekyll and Mr Hyde (1931) 8
Dracula (Bram Stoker novel) 4, 60, 171
Dracula (1931) 171
Dracula (1958) 61
'Draining Faces' 226
Drakula Halála (1921) 5
Draven, Eric 180
'Dream of a Witches' Sabbath' (Berlioz) 208
Dreams [*Yume*] (1990) 266
Dresden Music Academy 7
Drunken Angel (1948) 76
Duchess of Malfi, The 73
Duke Bluebeard's Castle (Bartók opera) 156
Dunst, Kirsten 179
Durgnat, Raymond 15, 16, 33, 38, 40, 48, 52
Dvořák, Antonin 5
Dym, Jeffrey A. 265

'Eagle Rock' 241
Easy Rider (1969) 194, 234
Eclipse (1966) 75
Ed Gein (2000) 190
Edgar, R. 58
Edison, Thomas 5
Edwards, Steve 207
Eidophusikon 204
Einstürzende Neubauten 206
Eisler, Hanns 137, 141, 156
Ekland, Britt 103
Electric Love Hogs 208
Elfman, Danny 176
Elkind, Carlos 143, 159
Elkind, Rachel 143, 159
Emerson, Keith 97, 98
Emerson, Lake and Palmer 88
Entertainment Weekly 217

Erdmann, Hans 5
'Erlkönig, Der' [The Elf King] 3
Escape from New York (1981) 99
Esquire 14
Evangelisti, Franco 89
Evans, M. 11
Ex-S: The Wicker Man (TV
   documentary) 109
Exodus 189
Exorcism of Emily Rose, The (2005)
   207
Exorcist, The (1973) 1, 2, 88, 112–24,
   137, 138, 187, 189, 201

Faculty, The (1998) 180
Fahrenheit 451 (1966) 40, 43
Falsetto, M. 142
Fantastic Voyage Of Mark The Beetle,
   The [*Il fantastico viaggio del
   'bagarozzo' Mark*] (1978, rock
   opera) 97
'Fantastich-Romantische Suite'
   (Erdmann) 5
*Fantastico viaggio del 'bagarozzo' Mark,
   Il* [The Fantastic Voyage Of Mark The
   Beetle] (rock opera) 97
Farrell, T. 116, 117
Fear Factory 192
Feld, Steven 112, 119
Fiancée de Dracula, La (2002) 13
Film Asylum, The 135
Filth, Dani 193
Final Destination (2000) 199
Fincher, David 58
Fisher, Terence 61
'Flash Of The Blade' 191
Flavour Of The Weak (album) 209
Fleischer, Richard 208
Flinn, Caryl 6
Fluorescences (1961) 150
Fly, The (1986) 198
Foley, Jack 12
'Fooled Around And Fell In Love' 234
Forbidden Planet (1956) 138

Fowles, John 109
Fragasso, Claudio 193
Franju, George 9
Frankenstein (Mary Shelley novel) 3, 60
Frankenstein (1910) 5
Frankenstein (1931) 7, 61
Frankenstein Meets the Wolf Man
   (1943) 7
Franklin, Richard 97
Frazer, James 102
Freddy vs Jason (2003) 192
Freddy's Dead: The Final Nightmare
   (1991) 193
'Free Bird' 235
Frentz, T. 116, 117
Freud, Sigmund 53
Friday the 13th (1980) 188, 199
Friday the 13th film series 125
Friday the 13th Part VI: Jason Lives
   (1986) 191
'*Friday the 13th*' (videogame) 11
Friedkin, William 1, 88, 112–24,
   137, 187, 201
From Dusk Till Dawn (1996) 177
'From The Cradle To Enslave' 193
Front Line Assembly 209, 226
Fukutomi, Yukihiro 89
Fulci, Lucio 89, 188, 191
Furie, Sidney J. 176
Fussible 89

Gabriel's Dream (1991) 227
García Mainar, L. 142
Gardiner, E. 203, 204
Garner, K. 232–3
Garris, Mick 95
Gaslini, Giorgio 98–9
Gaspard de la Nuit (Ravel) 172
Gassmann, Remi 39
Gavin, John 23
Gein, Edward 135, 190
Gelder, K. 171
Genesis 97, 98
'Gently Johnny' 106, 107

Gerlich, Greg 227
Ghezzi, E. 94
Ghost and Mrs. Muir, The (1947) 49, 57
Ghostbusters (1984) 254
'Ghosts Of War' 189
Gibson, Alan 61
Gillen, Jeff 190
Gilligan's Island (TV series) 222
Gilling, John 102
Gioia, Ted 112
Giovanni, Paul 103–4
Giusti, M. 94
Glenarvon 171
'Gloomy Sunday' 226
Gluck, Christoph Wilibald 43
Goblin 88–99, 191
God Hates Us All (album) 190
'God Is God' 226
Godzilla (name) 265 n.6
Godzilla (1954) 250
Goethe, Johann Wolfgang von 3
Goff, J. 253
Golden Bough, The (1958 edition) 102, 103, 108
Goldeneye (1995) 58
Goldenthal, Elliot 178
Goldfinger (1964) 64
Goldman, M. 219, 220, 227
Goldsmith, Jerry 138, 186, 205
Gollmar, R. 42
Gonsalves, R. 226
Good Morning Vietnam (1987) 186
Good, the Bad and the Ugly, The (1966) 90
Gorbman, C. 95, 184, 187, 194, 236
Gottlieb, Sidney 43
Goyer, David S. 181
Graduate, The (1967) 194
Graham, Billy 117
Grant, Michael 35
Gregory, David 135
Grieg, Edvard Hagerup 208
Grudge, The (2004) 195, 250, 258, 259, 260, 263

Guest, Val 61
Gukansho 251
Guns N' Roses 180, 188

Halfyard, J. 172, 176, 185, 211
Hall, Henry 144
Halloween (1978) 1, 99, 134, 187–8, 208
'Halloween' (videogame) 11
Halloween Online Magazine 125, 134
Halperin, Victor 193
Hamilton, Guy 64
Hamlet 253
Hammer films 60–73, 240
Hammer: The Studio That Dripped Blood (CD) 71
Hand, R. 252, 253, 265
Hangman's Beautiful Daughter, The (album) 103
Hannan, Michael 12
'Hard Rock Summer' 192
Hard Word, The (2003) 242
Harden, Tim 132
'Hardening Of The Arteries' 190
Hardware (1990) 193
Hardy, Françoise 89
Hardy, Robin 103
Harker, Dave 105
Harlin, Renny 122
Harris, M. 215, 225, 226
Harry Potter novels 225
'Haunted' 226
'Haunting The Chapel' 189
Haunting, The (1963) 254
Haus Der Lüge (CD) 211
Haxan (1922) 225
Haxan Films 214, 215
Hayasaka, Fumio 76
Hayashi, Razan 251
Hayward, Philip 8, 227
'He's Back' 191
Hearn, Lafcadio 78, 79
Heebel, N. 123
Hell Awaits (album) 190
'Hell Awaits' 189

'Hell On Earth' 192
Hellbilly Deluxe (album) 193
Hellbound Heart, The (1986) 198
Hellbound: Hellraiser II (1988) 198–211
Hellraiser (1987) 198–211
Hellraiser III: Hell on Earth (1992) 198–211
Hellraiser IV: Bloodline (1996) 198–211
Hellraiser V: Inferno (2000) 198–211
Hellraiser VI: Hellseeker (2002) 198–211
Hellraiser VII: Deader (2005) 198–211
Hellraiser VIII: Hellworld (2005) 198–211
Hellraiser movies 193
'Hellraiser' 209
Henkel, Kim 125–36
Henry: Portrait of a Serial Killer (1986) 188
Hensleigh, Jonathan 209
Herman, G. 191
Herrmann, Bernard 2, 9, 10, 14–44, 47–58, 93, 138, 186, 208, 246
Heuzenroeder, Tom 248
Hickox, Anthony 192, 198–211
Hider in the House (1990) 207
High Anxiety (1976) 17
'Highland Widow's Lament, The' 104, 105
Hill, Debra 1
Hill, R. 142
'Hirnlego' 206
Hitchcock, Alfred 1, 9, 14–44, 47–58, 93, 138, 190, 208, 226, 246
Hobson's Choice (1954) 60
Hocket 104
Hogan, D. 139
Hogan, P. J. 238
Hollinger, V. 184
Hollingsworth, John 62
Hollywood Chainsaw Hookers (1988) 134

Holocausto De La Morte (album) 191
Holy Wood (album) 192
Honô [The Flame; Takemitsu] 77
Honogurai mizu no soko kara (2002) 250, 258, 263
Hood, R. 238
Hooper, Tobe 125–36, 187, 205, 208, 217, 226, 230, 240
Hopper, Dennis 194, 234
Hosokawa, S. 85
Hosono, Haroumi 89
Hough, John 68
House of 1000 Corpses (2003) 193, 195, 229–37
How to Make a Monster (1958) 193
'How To Make A Monster' 193
Howard, J. 142
Howard, James Newton 158–9
Howarth, Allan 2
Huckvale, D. 68, 70
Hughes, R. 204
Hummel, C. 142
Hunger, The (1983) 172, 174, 175, 179, 180, 182, 183, 184
Hunter, I. Q. 73
Huntingdon, Tom 12
Hylton, Jack 144

'I Can't Quit You Baby' 234
'I Remember You' 229, 232, 233
'I Wanna Be Loved By You' 232
Iddon, M. 184
Ifukube, Akira 76, 85
Ikebe, Shinichirô 266
Ill Nino 192
Immolation 189
'In the Hall of the Mountain King' (Grieg) 208
Incredible String Band 103
Indiana Jones films (1981–84) 176
Inferno (Dante) 203
Inferno (1980) 97
Inglis, I. 11
Inn of the Damned (1975) 247

Innes, S. A. 185
Inseminoid (1981) 188
Interview with the Vampire (1994) 177, 178, 179, 180, 181
Iron Butterfly 188
Iron Maiden 97, 103, 191, 188, 193
Irwin, Steve 239
Isham, Mark 181
'It Wasn't God Who Made Honky Tonk Angels' 232

Jackie Brown (1997) 232
Jackson, Peter 227
James, Henry 254
James Gang, the 232
Jameson, R. T. 139
Jancovich, M. 8, 9, 225
Jansen, P. 159
Japanese Ghost Stories [Kwaidan] (1964) 75–86, 266
Jarre, Maurice 186
Je t'aime, je t'aime (1968) 138, 159
Jeffress, L. 139, 140
'Jesus Saves' 189
'Jesus Wept' 209
Jien 251
Jikken Kobo 85
Jikken Kôbô [The Experimental Workshop] 76, 85
Jimi Hendrix Experience 188
Johnson, Blind Willie 232
Jordan, B. 251, 254
Jordan, Neil 177
Ju-on (2003) 250, 258, 259, 260, 263
Judas Priest 188, 189
Jump Cut 226
Jurassic Park films (1993, 1997) 227

Kabinett des Doktor Caligari, Das (1919) 5
Kagan, N. 142, 157
Kaidan zensho (stories) 251
Kalinak, K. 194, 246

Kanadehon Chûshingura [The Treasury of Loyal Retainers] 265
Kane, Helen 232
Kannami, Kiyotsugu 265
Kapsis, Robert E. 14, 37
Kasdan, Lawrence 186
Kassabian, A. 182, 194, 205, 244
Katz, E. 226
Kaun, Bernhard 12
Kawai, Kenji 250, 263, 264
Kawatake, Mokuami 265
Keene, D. 250–1
Keil, C. 119
Kelleghan, F. 206, 219, 220
Kelly, Ned 236
Kennelly, Shawn 219
Kermode, Mark 112, 115, 116, 117, 118, 120, 123, 186, 189
Kerr, P. 230
Kierkegaard, Søren Aabye 158
'Kill Again' 190
Killswitch Engage 192
King, Stephen 159
King Crimson 98
King Kong (1933) 7, 8
'Kingdom's Coming' 226
Kishibe, Shigeo 265
Kiss 188
Kiss of the Vampire, The (1964) 61
Kiss or Kill (1997) 245
Kiyose, Yasuji 76
Kleinman, Daniel 58
KMFDM 208
Knowles, Bernard 60
Kobayashi, Masaki 9, 266
Kojirô, Nobumitsu 265
Kolker, Robert 15, 40, 48, 142
Koppl, R. 159
Koresky, M. 230
Korn 195
Kracauer, S. 138
Kreator 189
Kubrick, Stanley 10, 137–70, 246, 254

Kumonosu-Jo [The Castle of the Spider's Web] (1957) 255, 256
Kurosawa, Akira 76, 255, 266
Kwaidan [Japanese Ghost Stories] (1964) 9, 10, 75–86, 266

Lacan, Jacques 53, 58
Lady Stay Dead (1982) 247
Laibach 192, 205, 226
Lajthay, Károly 5
Lamb, Alan 245
Lamb, Lady Caroline 171
Lampe, J. Bodewalt 5
'Landlord's Daughter, The' 106
Lang, E. 5
Laplantine, Anne 103
Laplantine, Momus 103
Larson, R. D. 2, 61, 65–6
Last House on the Left, The (1972) 187
'Laughing Paid' 226
Lawnmower Man, The (1992) 11
Lawrence, Francis 203
Le Fanu, J. Sheridan 4, 171
Leaf-viewing Party, The [*Momiji Gari*] (1956) 249, 250, 265
Lean, David 60
Leatherface: Texas Chainsaw Massacre III (1990) 125–36
Led Zeppelin 188
Lee, Christopher 103
Lee, Roland 7
Lee, Y. 39
Legend of the 7 Golden Vampires (1974) 61
Leibowitz, E. 139, 140
Leigh, Christopher 179
Leiter, Samuel L. 265
Lemmy 193
Lentz, Gerry 227
Leonard, Brett 11
Leonard, Joshua 219
Leone, Sergio 90
Lester, Richard 176

Levinson, Barry 186
Lewis, F. 227
Lewton, Val 7
Leydon, R. 158
Licht, Daniel 207
Liebesman, Jonathan 125–36
Ligeti, Gyorgy 137, 138, 140, 143, 145, 158
Lim, B. C. 81
Limp Bizkit 195
Lindemann, M. 217
Lindsay, C. 108, 111
Linkin Park 195
Lionnet, L. 142, 157, 159
'Living Dead Girl' 193
Livingston, J. 115
LoBrutto, V. 142, 159
'Locomotive' 191
Lohner, Henning 207
Looney Tunes: Back in Action (2003) 17
Lopez, J. 264
Lord of the Rings (2001) 227
Los Angeles Free Press 44
Lost Boys, The (1987) 172, 173, 174, 180, 183
Lucas, George 138, 176
Lugosi, Bela 171
'Lullaby' (Brahms) 63–4
Lunch, Lydia 216, 226
Lutyens, Elizabeth 61, 89

Macbeth 253, 256
McCambridge, Mercedes 120
McDonagh, Maitland 88, 89, 90, 91, 93, 96–7, 191
Macdonald, David 60
MacGuffin, the 43
McLaughlin, Tom 191
Maclean, Dorothy 105
McLean, Greg 238–48
McMann, Gerard 174
McNaughton, John 188
MacPhail, Angus 39

McRoy, J. 78, 250, 254, 265
Macklin, A. F. 139, 140
Mad Max (1979) 238
Madulid, Jerome 114–15, 122
Magus, The (1968) 109
Mahler, Gustav 139
Malm, William P. 249, 257, 264
Malmus, Stephen 110
Maltby, R. 195
Mamoulian, Rouben 7, 8
Man Who Knew Too Much, The (1956) 38
Man with the Golden Arm, The (1955) 47
Mancini, Henry 186
Mankiewicz, Joseph L. 49, 179
Manoir du diable, Le (1896) 4
Manson, Marilyn 192
Marangolo, Agostino 95
March Or Die (album) 209
'March to the Scaffold' (Berlioz) 202, 246
Maria Marten, five film versions of 4
Markowski, Andrzej 143
Marnie (1964) 34, 38
Marriott, J. 119, 121
Martell, Philip 62
Martin, Shawn 159
Maslin, J. 139
Massenet, Jules 43
Material Issue 208
Matrix, The (1999) 11, 200, 205
Matthew, gospel of 203
Mayersberg, P. 139, 140, 141
Meat Beat Manifesto 226
Mechanical Animals (album) 192
Medhurst, Adrian 248
Meeks, Dana 227
'Meet The Creeper' 193
Megadeth 189
Meisel, M. 157
Meissner, Fred 236
Méliès, Georges 4
Merrick, James W. 39

Metallica 189
Midian (album) 193
'Midnight Rider' 233
Mihara, Yuko 265
Milat, Ivan 239
Miller, George 238
Miller, Randy 207
Miller, T. 118
Milton, John 203
Mindstrip (album) 209
Miyoshi, Shôraku 265
Moby Dick (Herrmann cantata) 42
Modleski, Tania 236
Mogg, Ken 43
Momiji Gari [*The Leaf-viewing Party*] (1956) 249, 250, 265
Monster Dog (1984) 193
Moore, Michael 225
Morante, Massimo 94, 97
Morricone, Ennio 88–99, 117
Morrison, Jim 174
Mortician 189
Mostro di Frankenstein, Il (1921) 5
Mötley Crüe 188, 191
Motörhead 97, 188, 191, 192, 193, 209
'Movement Of Fear' 226
Moxy, John Llewellyn 193
Mr. Bean (TV series) 17
Muddy Waters 232
Mudvayne 192, 195
Mulcahy, Russell 238
Mulvey, Laura 38
Murch, Walter 219, 220
Murdoch, Bradley 239
Muriel's Wedding (1994) 238
Murnau, Friedrich Wilhelm 5, 171
Murray, Bernard 104
Music for Strings, Percussion and Celeste (Bartók) 152, 156
Music for the Movies (documentary, 1994) 79
Music From Dario Argento's Horror Movies (album) 99

Music To A Film That Doesn't Exist (album) 97
Muti, Riccardo 89
My Brilliant Career (1979) 238
Myrick, Daniel 188, 213–27
Mystère d'Adam 204

Nagle, Ron 117, 119
Nakata, Hideo 195, 249, 250, 264
Namiki, Senryû 265
Napier, Susan 254
Naremore, J. 16, 40, 41
National Lampoon's Vacation (1983) 17
Near Dark (1987) 172, 173, 174, 180, 182, 183, 184
'Necrophiliac' 190
Needful Things (1993) 208
Needham, Gary 90, 91
Neill, Roy William 7
Nelson, T. 142
Nettheim, Daniel 242
Neumeyer, D. 65
New York Times 39
Newman, Alfred 186
Newman, Joseph 138
Newman, Kim 95, 96, 229, 230
Newman, Thomas 186
Newsfront (1978) 238
Newsweek 14
Nichols, Mike 194
Night of Fear (1973) 247
Nightmare on Elm Street, A (1984) 199
Nightmare on Elm Street 2: Freddy's Revenge (1985) 207
Nightmare on Elm Street 3: Dream Warriors (1987) 191
Nihon no Mon'yo [Japanese Crests] (1962) 80
Nispel, Marcus 125–36, 195
Nitzsche, Jack 117
Nixon, N. 184
Noble, Ray 144
'Nocturne' (Chopin) 64

Nonhosonno [Sleepless] (2000) 97
Norrington, Stephen 181
North by Northwest (1959) 35, 38, 49
Nosferatu, eine Symphonie des Grauens (1922) 5, 171, 173, 177
November Steps (1967) 75
'Now I Wanna Sniff Some Glue' 232
Noyce, Philip 238
Nuclear Assault 189
Nuova Consonanza 89

O'Bannon, Dan 191
O'Brien, D. 9, 73
O'Neill, P. G. 265
Obituary 189
Observer (London) 37, 95
Obsession (1975) 19
Ohtake, Noriko 84
Okuyama, Jyunosuke 86
Oldfield, Mike 2, 96, 117, 121, 201
Oldman, Gary 178
Olivier, Laurence 179
Omen, The (1976) 150, 187
Once upon a Time in the West (1969) 90
'Order Of Death, The' 226
Orff, Carl 43
Ormsby, Alan 190
Osbourne, Ozzy 189, 209
Others, The (2001) 159, 254
Oto no Shiki [Symphonic Poem for Concrete Sound Objects and Music; Takemitsu] 77
Otoshiana [The Pitfall] (1962) 77
Owen Wingrave (Britten opera) 254
Owens, Buck 232

Palmer, Christopher 16, 42
Papa Roach 195
Parello, Chuck 190
Parker, Alan 188
Pasolini, Pier Paolo 89
Patrick, St 203
Patrick (1977) 97

Patton, Mike 88
Pearce, Leslie 7
Pee-wee's Playhouse (TV series) 229
Peel, John 110
Penderecki, Krzysztof 137, 138, 140,
   143, 144, 145, 149, 150, 151–2,
   158
'People Are Strange' 174
People's Periodical 3
Perfect Woman, The (1949) 60
Phenomena [Creepers] (1985) 97, 191
Phillips, G. 142
Picnic at Hanging Rock (1974) 238
'Piece By Piece' 190
Pierce, Dale 95, 99
Pignatelli, Fabio 95, 98, 191
Pink Floyd 110
Pinner, David 102
Pitt, Brad 179
Pitt, Ingrid 103
Plague of Zombies, A (1966) 102
Planet of the Apes (1968) 138, 205
P.O.D. 195
Poe, Edgar Allan 173
Polidori, John 3
Poltergeist (1982) 208
Polymorphia (1961) 150
Pomerance, M. 218
'Postmortem' 190
Poulan chainsaw 127
Pounds, W. 251
'Praise Of Death' 190
Prawer, S. S. 158
'Predator' 209
Preminger, Otto 47, 52
Prendergast, Rob 16
*Presumption: or The Fate of
   Frankenstein* 3
Prince of Darkness (1987) 193
Profondo Rosso [Deep Red] (1975)
   92–100, 191, 201
Project-X 209
Proyas, Alex 177
Psycho (1960) 1, 2, 14–44, 47–58,
   93, 134, 138, 190, 208, 246

Psycho: A Narrative for Orchestra
   (Herrmann) 36, 37, 44
Psycho: Suite for Strings (Herrmann) 44
Public Image Ltd 216, 226
Publishers Weekly 123
Pulp Fiction (1994) 232
Punisher, The (2004) 209
Purgatory 203

Quatermass (TV series) 61
Quatermass II (1957) 61
Quatermass Xperiment (1955) 61
Queen of the Damned, The (2002)
   180

'Raining Blood' 190
'Raise Your God' 209
Ramis, Harold 17
Rammstein 192
Ramones 232
Randel, Tony 198–211
Rapée, E. 5
Rashomon (1950) 76
Rasmussen, R. 142
Rastall, R. 204
Ratcliffe, Michael 43
Ravel, Maurice 172
Ravna, Carl 66
Ray, Fred Olen 134
Razorback (1984) 238
Rear Window (1954) 38, 226
Rebello, S. 14, 18, 19, 34, 37, 39,
   40, 43, 48, 54, 57
'Reborn' 189
Reclamation (album) 209
Record of a Living Being (1992) 76
Reeve, Christopher 176
Reid, Terry 233
Reider, N. 251
Reiff, S. 122, 123
Reign In Blood (album) 190
Reitman, Ivan 254
Relief statique (Takemitsu) 85
*Remick Folio of Moving Picture
   Music* 5

Requiem for String Orchestra
(Takemitsu) 76
Reservoir Dogs (1992) 232
Resident Evil (2002) 180, 188, 198
Resident Evil: Apocalypse (2004) 195
'*Resident Evil*' (videogame) 11
'*Resident Evil 4*' (videogame) 126
Resnais, Alain 138, 159
Return of the Living Dead, The (1985)
191
Ribrant, G. 206
Rice, Anne 180
Richie, D. 255
Ring, The (2002) 195, 250, 260,
261, 262, 263
Ring Two, The (2005) 195
Ringu (1998) 249, 250, 258, 260,
261, 262, 263, 264
Rite of Spring, The (Stravinsky) 159
Ritual (1967) 102
Roberts, Scott 242
Robinson, Harry 61
Rocky Horror Picture Show, The
(1975) 8
'Rocky Mountain Way' 233
Rodriguez, Robert 177, 180
Roller (album) 97
Rollin, Jean 9
Rolling Stones 180
Romero, George 97, 187
Romper Stomper (1992) 118
Rosar, W. H. 211
Roscoe, J. 226
Rose, G. 44
Rosemary's Baby (1968) 134
Rosenberg, Stuart 188, 254
Rothman, W. 16
Rothstein, E. 43
Rush, Otis 232, 234
Russell, Chuck 191
Rymer, Michael 180

Sala, Oskar 39
Saliva 192

Salles, Walter 195, 250
Salò (1974) 89
Salter, Hans 7
Salzedo, Leonard 61
Sam Fox Moving Picture Music 5
Samuels, Robert 53–4, 58
San Francisco Chronicle 122
Sànchez, Eduardo 188, 213–27
Sarris, Andrew 15, 38
'Satan Arraying His Troops on the
Banks of the Fiery Lake, with the
Palace of Pandemonium: From
Milton' 204
'Satan's Gotta Get Along Without Me'
232
Satanic Rites of Dracula, The (1973)
61
Satô, Masaru 76, 256
Sato, Shiro 250, 263, 264
Saxon 188, 191
Scary Movie (2000) 188
Scary Movie films 8
Schaeffer, Pierre 77
Schafer, Murray 220–1, 227
Schaffner, Franklin 138, 205
Scheib, R. 135, 227
Schifrin, Lalo 117, 138
Schlieb, Richard 130
Schoedsack, Ernest 7
Schoenberg, Arnold 49, 57
Schreck, Max 5
Schubert, Franz 3, 172
Schuetz, J. 117
Schulte-Sasse, L. 93
Schumacher, Joel 172, 178
Schwartz, Sherwood 222
Schweiger, Daniel 96, 99
Scorpions 188
Scorsese, Martin 42
Scott, Ridley 188
Scott, Tony 172
Scream (1996) 17, 188
'Se Telefonando' 89
Se7en (1994) 58

Seasons In The Abyss (album) 190
'See You In Hell' 209
Selig, William 4
Send More Paramedics 191
Seppuku [Harakiri] (1962) 80
Serious, Yahoo 238
Serper, Zvika 251
Seven Samurai (1954) 76
Seventh Seal, The [Det sjunde inseglet]
    (1957) 211
'Sex Murder Art' 190
Shaffer, Anthony 103
Shakespeare, William 253
Sharman, Jim 8
Sharp, Don 61
Shaun of the Dead (2004) 188
'She's Unreal' 226
Sheffield Telegraph 43
Shelley, Mary 3, 7, 60
Sherdei, Jack 227
Shimizu, Takashi 195, 250
Shin Sakkyokuka Kyokai [the New
    Academy of Composers] 76
Shining, The (1980) 10, 134,
    137–70, 246, 254
Shinoda, M. 80
Sholder, Jack 207
Shore, Howard 78, 186
Shores, Lyn 7
Show No Mercy (album) 190
Shyamalan, M. Night 158–9, 254
Sibelius, Jean 59
Sichtbare Mensch, Der [The Visible
    Man] (1924) 156
Side Street (1929) 7
Sight & Sound 229
Silence of the Lambs, The (1991)
    188, 190
Silent Hill (1999) 11
Simms, B. 57
Simonetti, Claudio 95, 97, 99, 191
Simpsons, The (TV series) 17
Sindroma di Stendhal, Il [The Stendhal
    Syndrome] (1995) 92

Singh, Tarsem 205
Sinister Urge, The (album) 193
Sisters (1972) 19
Sixth Sense, The (1999) 158–9, 254
Skinner, Frank 7
Skinny Puppy 226
Skynyrd, Lynyrd 232, 235
Slayer 189
Sleepless [Nonhosonno] (2000) 97
Sleuth (1972) 179
Slipknot 192, 195
Sloan, Jane 43
Smith, Jeff 232
Smith, Peter D. 248
Smith, Steven C. 19, 20, 33, 43
Smuts, Aaron 93, 98
Snell, Peter 103
Snow White and the Seven Dwarfs
    (1937) 96
Snyder, S. 157
Snyder, Zack 195
Solaris (1972) 138
Soldier's Tale, The (Stravinsky opera)
    98 n.4
Son of Frankenstein (1939) 7
Sondheim, Steven 12
Soup Dragons 208
'South of Heaven' 190
Souvenirs de voyage (Herrmann) 44
Soylent Green (1973) 208
Sparber, Isador 254
Species (1995) 207
Spielberg, Steven 176, 227
Spierig, Michael 238
Spierig, Peter 238
'Spill The Blood' 190
Spineshank 192
Spivak, Murray 8
Spoto, Donald 39
Springfield, Dusty 97
St Clair, Malcolm 7
Stack, P. 122
Stages, Wilshire 227
Staind 195

Stainforth, Gordon 137–70
Stanley, Richard 189, 193
Star Wars (1977–83) 176
'Star-spangled Banner, The' 222
Static-X 192
Steeleye Span 110
Steely Dan 232
Stefano, Joseph 18, 20, 34, 35, 43
Steggle, M. 203
Stein, Michael Eric 236
Steiner, Fred 16, 21, 23, 27, 39, 48, 56
Steiner, Max 7
Stendhal Syndrome, The [*Il sindroma di Stendhal*] (1995) 92
Steppenwolf 188, 234
Stereophonics 195
Stern, D. A. 216, 225
Stevenson, Robert Louis 4
Stihl, Andreas 126
Stivell, Alan 110
Stoker, Bram 4, 60, 171
Strait, George 184
Strange Case of Dr Jekyll and Mr Hyde, The 4
Strauss, Richard 6, 43
Stravinsky, Igor Fedorovich 98, 159
Street, R. 227
'String of Pearls, The' (short story) 3
Strock, Herbert L. 193
Suga, Shikako 250
Suicidal Tendencies 189
Suicide Commando 209
Sullivan, Jack 16, 20, 34, 39, 43
Summerisle (album) 103
Suna-no-onna [Woman in the Dunes] (1964) 77
'Superbeast' 193
Superman films (1978, 1980, 1983, 1987) 176
'Surface Patterns' 209
Suspiria (1976) 88–9, 93, 134, 191, 201
Suzuki, Koji 264
'Sympathy For The Devil' 180

Symphonie fantastique (Berlioz) 202

Tachibana, Takashi 76, 77, 86
Tagg, Philip 208
Takeda, Isumo 265
Takemitsu, Tôru 9, 75–6, 266
Takiguchi, Shuzo 85
Talalay, Rachel 193
Tarantino, Quentin 232
Tarkovski, Andrei 138
Tartini, Giuseppe 98
Tatsuo, Y. 252
Taxi Driver (1975) 42
Taylor, C. 215, 219
Tchaikovsky, Piotr Ilyich 139
'Teenage Frankenstein' 192
Tenebre (1982) 97, 191
Terminator 2: Judgment Day (1991) 207
Teshigawara, H. 77
Tesla 188
Testa, Eugenio 5
Testament 189
Tétaz, François 241–8
Texas Chain Saw Massacre, The (1973) 125, 187, 190, 205, 217, 226, 230, 231, 235, 236, 240
Texas Chain Saw Massacre – the Shocking Truth (documentary, 2001) 135 nn.16, 23
Texas Chainsaw Massacre Part 2, The (1986) 125–36
Texas Chainsaw Massacre, The (2003) 195
Texas Chainsaw Massacre: The Beginning (2006) 125–36
Texas Chainsaw Massacre: The Next Generation (1994) 125–36
That '70s Show (TV series) 17
'The Number Of The Beast' 193
Théberge, Paul 203
This Island Earth (1955) 138
Threnody for the Victims of Hiroshima (Penderecki) 150
Throbbing Gristle 205

Throne of Blood (1957)   255, 256
Thunderstruck (2004)   242
THX 1138 (1970)   138
Tieck, Johann   3
Time   14
Tin Machine   208
Tiomkin, Dimitri   186
Titterington, P. L.   139, 140
To Catch a Thief (1955)   34
Tobe Hooper's Original Uncut [Special
   Edition] *The Texas Chainsaw Massacre*
   (2000)   136 n.23
Todd, Sweeney   3
Tomb Raider (2001)   205
Tomc, Sandra   178–9
Tompkins, Andrew   104
Tones on Tail   226
Torn Curtain (1966)   39, 43
Total Film   134
Touch of Evil (1958)   38
Tourneur, Jacques   7
Trauma (1992)   97
Travers, P.   122, 123
Treasury of Loyal Retainers, The
   [*Kanadehon Chûshingura*]   265
Triumph   208
Trouble with Harry, The (1955)   38, 57
True Lies (1994)   58
Truffaut, François   14, 35, 36, 37, 43
Tsurura, Kinshi   80
Tsuruya, Nanboku   253
Tubular Bells (album)   2, 96, 117,
   121, 201
Tundale   203
Turn of the Screw, The (1954)   254
Turner, A. K.   204
Twins of Evil (1971)   68
Twisted Sister   188
Twister (1996)   58
Tynan, Kenneth   37–8
Type O Negative   192, 226

Ummagumma (album)   110
Undead, The (2003)   238

Underworld (2003, 2006)   181, 182,
   183, 184
Underworld: Evolution (2006)   183
Urbano, Cosimo   187, 217, 224

Valse triste (Sibelius)   159
'Value of the Supernatural in Fiction'
   (lecture by Lafcadio Hearn)   78–9
Vampire, The (play)   3
Vampire Lovers, The (1970)   62
Vampyre, The (Polidori novel)   3
van Leeuwen, Theo   220
Van Sant, Gus   40
Vanilla Fudge   188
Variety   37, 39
Velvet Acid Christ   209
Venom   191
Verbinski, Gore   195, 250
Vertigo (1958)   38, 49
Village Voice   15
Vio-Lence   189
Viol du vampire, Le (1968)   13
Virgil   203
Virilio, Paul   218
Visible Man, The [*Der sichtbare
   Mensch*] (1924)   156
Voci dal silenzio [Voices from the
   Silence] (2002)   89
von Karajan, Herbert   143
von Sternberg, Josef   7
von Trier, Lars   219, 240

W.A.S.P.   188
Wachowski Brothers   11, 200
Wagner, Richard   5, 6, 139
Wainwright, Loudon, III   135
Wake Not the Dead   3
Waley, Arthur   265
Walker, D.   39
Walpole, Horace   3, 253
Walser, R.   189, 194, 211
Walsh, Joe   232
War of the Worlds   131
Ward, Vincent   203

Warner, William 216
Warren, Norman J. 188
Wasserman, E. 35
Waxman, Franz 7
Wayans, Keenan Ivory 188
Webb, Roy 7
Webster, John 73
Wegener, Paul 5
Weingart, Rich 227
Weinstein, D. 188, 189, 190
Weir, Peter 238
Weis, Elisabeth 40
Weisser, Thomas 265
Welles, Orson 34, 38, 131
Wells, H. G. 131
Wells, J. 139
Wells, Kitty 232
Wells, P. 216, 217
Werzowa, Walter 207
West, Adam 176
West, G. 5
West, Simon 205
Wetherwax, Mike 227
Whale, James 6, 61
What Dreams May Come? (1998) 203
Wheeler, Hugh 12
White Zombie (1932) 193
White Zombie 193, 229, 230
Whitman, Slim 229, 232
'Who's Gonna Mow Your Grass?' 232
Wicked Lady, The (1945) 60
Wicker Man, The (1973) 101–11, 134
Wiene, Robert 5
Wierzbicki, James 12
Wilcox, Fred M. 138
Williams, John 176, 186
Williams, Michael 219
Williamson, Malcolm 61
Wilson, M. N. 254
Wise, Robert 7, 254
Wiseman, Les 181
Witt, Alexander 195

Wolf Creek (2005) 238–48
Wong, James 199
Wood, Robin 16, 38, 40, 41, 231, 235
Woods, Rohan 245
Woodward, Edward 103
Worman, Ray 110
Wright, Edgar 188
Wright, Geoffrey 118
Wright, R. 189, 192, 233, 234, 236
Wrobel, W. 57
Wrong Man, The (1956) 38
Wuthering Heights (Herrmann opera) 42, 57
Wuthering Heights (Emily Brontë novel) 34
Wyle, George 222
Wyman, Bill 97
Wyman, Dan 2

Xena: Warrior Princess (TV series) 185

Yablans, Irwin 1
Yagher, Kevin 198–211
Yes 88, 98, 110
Yeux sans visage, Les (1959) 9
Yokoyama, Katsuya 80
Young, Christopher 207, 250
Young Einstein (1989) 238
Yu, Ronny 192
Yuasa, Joji 257, 258
Yume [Dreams] (1990) 266

Zador, Leslie 44, 57
Zamecnik, J. S. 5
Zeami, Motokiyo 265
Ziffer, D. 247
Zimmer, Hans 186, 250
Zolbrod, Leon 251
Zombie, Rob 193, 195, 229–37
Zombie Flesh Eaters/Zombi 2 (1979) 188, 191
Zwerin, Charlotte 79